CINEMATIC MODERNISM

Susan McCabe juxtaposes the work of four American modernist poets with the techniques and themes of early twentieth-century avant-garde films. The historical experience of the First World War and its aftermath of broken and shocked bodies shaped a preoccupation with fragmentation in both film and literature. Film, montage, and camera work provided poets with a vocabulary through which to explore and refashion modern physical and metaphoric categories of the body, including the hysteric, automaton, bisexual, and femme fatale. This innovative study explores the impact of new cinematic modes of representation on the poetry of Gertrude Stein, William Carlos Williams, H. D., and Marianne Moore. *Cinematic Modernism* links the study of literary forms with film studies, visual culture, gender studies, and psychoanalysis to expand the usual parameters of literary modernism.

SUSAN MCCABE is Associate Professor of English at the University of Southern California. She is the author of *Elizabeth Bishop: Her Poetics of Loss* (1994) and a member of the Board of the Modernist Studies Association.

CINEMATIC MODERNISM

Modernist Poetry and Film

SUSAN McCABE
University of Southern California

CAMBRIDGE
UNIVERSITY PRESS

PUBLISHED BY THE PRESS SYNDICATE OF THE UNIVERSITY OF CAMBRIDGE
The Pitt Building, Trumpington Street, Cambridge, United Kingdom

CAMBRIDGE UNIVERSITY PRESS
The Edinburgh Building, Cambridge, CB2 2RU, UK
40 West 20th Street, New York, NY 10011–4211, USA
477 Williamstown Road, Port Melbourne, VIC 3207, Australia
Ruiz de Alarcón 13, 28014 Madrid, Spain
Dock House, The Waterfront, Cape Town 8001, South Africa

http://www.cambridge.org

First published 2005

Printed in the United Kingdom at the University Press, Cambridge

Typeface Adobe Garamond 11/12.5 pt.   *System* LATEX 2$_\varepsilon$ [TB]

A catalogue record for this book is available from the British Library

ISBN 0 521 84621 8 hardback

Contents

Illustrations

Acknowledgments

I owe my deepest gratitude to Cassandra Laity whose belief in this project made it possible. Without her urging, the book in its present form would not exist.

I thank the College of Letters, Arts and Science at the University of Southern California for funding some of this work through a Zumberge Research Grant. I thank the staff of the Beinecke Rare Book and Manuscript Library at Yale University for its archival materials as well as for its providing several stills. I am grateful as well to the Museum of Modern Art / Film Stills Archive for its assistance. Portions of this book have been published in other forms in journals: "The *Ballet Mécanique* of Marianne Moore's Cinematic Modernism" in *Mosaic: A Journal for the Interdisciplinary Study of Literature*, vol. 33 no. 2 (2000), "'Delight in Dislocation': The Cinematic Modernism of Stein, Chaplin, and Man Ray" in *Modernism / Modernity*, vol. 8 no. 3 (2001), and "Borderline Modernism: Paul Robeson and the Femme Fatale" in *Callaloo*, vol. 25 no. 2 (2002).

Among my colleagues in the English Department at USC, I would like to thank my dear friends, Joseph Allen Boone for his attentive scrutiny of the manuscript, Carla Kaplan for her unrelenting encouragement and support, and Tania Modleski, whose film scholarship and friendship served as guiding lights. I also thank Leo Braudy for his kind and tutelary words (they came at the right moment), David St. John, whose immediate and abiding excitement about my writing, kept me afloat throughout these labors. I appreciate as well Annalisa Zox-Weaver (my tireless Cesare) who proofread and helped edit the manuscript.

In addition, I owe much thanks to the anonymous readers for Cambridge University Press for their suggestions and observations, and to my editor, Ray Ryan.

Among the academic community at large, I thank Judith L. Sensibar whose friendship consistently provided me with searching and stimulating insights. Others who have helped this work in various ways include Steven

G. Axelrod, Sam Girgus, Cynthia Hogue, Laura Hinton, Cristanne Miller, Robin Schulze, and Marjorie Perloff.

My sister, Marilyn McCabe, gave an inexhaustible array of emotional and intellectual help, sharing her knowledge of psychoanalysis and reading the manuscript in its multiple incarnations. I could count on Brian Lizotte, an honorary family member, to accompany me to many silent screenings. His wise and quirky perceptions have certainly contributed to this book.

Finally and always, I am grateful to Kate M. Chandler beyond the power of words to express. She is the book's veritable midwife and muse, who shepherded, inspired, criticized, questioned, admired, and begot all phases of it. Without her, mind and body would not be together.

Abbreviations

SE	*Freud*, Standard Edition
CU	*Close Up*
CPP	*The Complete Poems and Plays of T. S. Eliot*
SA	*Spring and All*, William Carlos Williams
KH	*Kora in Hell*, William Carlos Williams
CP	*The Collected Poems of William Carlos Williams volume 1* (chap. 3)
CP	*Collected Poems 1912–1944*, H. D. (chap. 4)
CP	*Complete Poems*, Marianne Moore (chap. 5)

Introduction
Cinematic modernism

This book arose from a conflux of scholarship and serendipity. I had long been familiar with H. D.'s poetry when I discovered her passion for cinema through Anne Friedberg's essay on *Borderline*, a 1930 silent film that the poet both acted in and helped to edit.[1] In 1995, I rented the only circulating copy from the Museum of Modern Art to screen in my modernism course; about a year later, I chanced upon it airing on Turner Classic Movies as part of a Paul Robeson retrospective. I quickly rushed for a video tape, and by this stroke of luck was able to watch the film repeatedly.

The charge that *Borderline* gave me, I imagined, was akin to the thrill H. D. and other modernists must have felt in response to the emergence of film in its revolutionary ability to represent somatic movements and gestures as they had never been represented before. The body could be deliriously elsewhere, uncannily absent, yet viscerally present. *Borderline* dramatically recasts H. D.'s poetry as cinematic. She claimed that seeing Greta Garbo in *Joyless Street* in 1925 was her "first real revelation of the real art of the cinema."[2] Yet by setting the poems of *Sea Garden* (1916) in the context of early silent film and contemporary film theory, they appear precursors to the embodied "revelations" H. D. experienced. What intensified my excitement about *Borderline* was how its avant-garde montage deftly portrays the way sexual and racial fantasies are inscribed upon the body. In its seventy-five minute length, it exposes the projection and displacement of white desires upon the black body, disrupting the myths formulated by D. W. Griffith's 1915 *Birth of a Nation*, a film often credited with the invention of montage.

Along with her performance in several silent films, H. D. was one of the founders of *Close Up* (1927–33), the first film journal in English to treat cinema exclusively, and she contributed eleven reviews. Dorothy Richardson, Gertrude Stein, and Marianne Moore were among its other literary contributors.[3] Prominently, the journal translated Sergei Eisenstein, featured work by the psychoanalyst Hanns Sachs, and articulated a progressive politics that overlapped with its fostering of an avant-garde aesthetic.

H. D.'s explicit involvement with film catalyzed for me a number of questions about the relationship of other modernist poets to cinema. What impact did this medium have upon poets before *Close Up*? What films might they have seen and enjoyed? To what extent were poets intimidated by the upstart medium? What otherwise unexpressed desires were projected upon the screen? What techniques did they borrow, or conversely, what might their poetic styles have anticipated in the medium of film? Aside from the fairly well worn sense that modern poets juxtapose their images through a method akin to film montage, how could this notion be more fully elaborated? This book is the result of my investigation of these largely neglected questions.[4]

H. D. was clearly not the only film enthusiast among modern poets. Stein broadly and retrospectively announced in 1933: "I cannot repeat this too often any one is of one's period and this our period was undoubtedly the period of the cinema and series production."[5] Her intimate relationship to modern painting has eclipsed the cinematic dimension of her writing, yet Stein claimed the "period of cinema" and her place in it as extending back to 1903 when she wrote her epic *Making of Americans* cinematically without knowing it. Likewise, H. D.'s admiration for the medium did not become publicly manifest until 1927 when she began publishing her film reviews.

The period Stein designated, roughly between 1903 and 1933, coincided with the beginnings of "series production" (the ability to reproduce successive identical images), the burgeoning of technical and artistic experiment in early film, and finally the demise of film as a silent medium.[6] It was also during this era that a stunning number of historical shifts irrevocably altered human epistemology and variously rendered modernity as "an experience of crisis."[7] Among the array of scientific discoveries, cultural movements, and political upheavals Stein witnessed, she identified cinema as a foundational term for the syntax of modernism.

Miriam B. Hansen has argued that cinema constitutes "the single most expansive discursive horizon in which the effects of modernity were reflected, rejected or denied, transmuted or negotiated."[8] It is, as Hansen writes, "the critical fixation on hegemonic modernism" that unnecessarily separates artistic practices from "the political, economic, and social processes of modernity and modernization, including the development of mass and media culture."[9] As this book brings into relief, modernists could be profoundly cinematic even when not fully cognizant of it. Even for those modernist poets who were intensely ambivalent about the medium (as we shall see with Ezra Pound and T. S. Eliot), cinema's material presence asserted a tremendous impact upon them. As Michael Wood states, "the principle of montage" along with "the construction of imaginary space through the direction of the gaze" is "quintessentially modernist."[10] I consider the direct historical links between modern poetry and film where and when they can be established, but I also attend to more indirect connections, including those that challenge "the direction of the gaze."

In the spirit of montage, my project links texts and silent films not previously brought together, primarily connecting the American poets, Stein, William Carlos Williams, H. D., and Marianne Moore (hereafter referred to as "the four poets") with the period of silent cinema. The four poets shared an excitement for the vital flux of modernity. H. D., the one in this quartet most affiliated with the high modernist goal of excavating and resuscitating the past, nevertheless admired "the lean skyscraper beauty of ultra modernity."[11] Stein made a kinesthetic practice of refusing literary tradition; Williams sought to draw "the whole armamentarium of the modern age" into his poems;[12] and Moore zestfully absorbed popular culture, including baseball games, travel and fashion magazines, "'business documents and school-books.'"[13] Most important, all four are bound by their enthusiasm for film, expressed both in their critical writing and in their poetic techniques.

With some significant exceptions, the four poets were drawn to European avant-garde films, crossing continental and stylistic boundaries, including Soviet film, French Dada and Surrealism, and German Expressionism. As I will demonstrate, these films not only evoke the "peculiar atmosphere of a modern poem,"[14] but also raise questions about cohesive corporeality, emphasizing bodily rhythms and gestures rather than narrative continuity.

By pairing poetic texts and films, I clarify a central modernist paradox: a desire to include bodily experience and sensation along with an overpowering sense of the unavailability of such experience except as mediated through mechanical reproduction. Cinematic montage and camera work often exposed the body's malleability. Sped up or slowed down, the pacing and piecing of film could recreate the moving "lived" body, while these methods ruptured fantasies of physical self-presence or wholeness. Broadly speaking, film showed that the temporal present could be endlessly repeated; it was mechanical yet created a *felt* immediacy; and consequently, it subordinated the inherited conceit of the Cartesian mind to less aggregated kinesthetic processes. In sum, film crystallized a cultural debate in modernity over the unstable conjunctions between the mind and the sensate body.

The medium of film opened up a new vocabulary for modernist poets not only to challenge modes of mimetic representation, but also to explore and reconstruct cultural tropes of fragmented, dissociated corporeality, most notably the hysteric and mechanical body, newly fabricated in modernity. The larger argument of this book is that the four poets engaged in an ongoing dialogue that emerges on one axis through the concourse between modern poetry and film, and on another between versions of embodiment generated by the prominent discourses of psychoanalysis and experimental psychology.

Modernist poets were not only of "the period of the cinema," as Stein puts it, but also "of" the period of psychoanalysis; these domains, frequently configured as a twin birth, seem ineluctably part of modernity's production of forms of corporeality.[15] The problematic place in feminist theory of psychoanalysis in general and the figure of the hysteric in particular has been debated at length. My book shares to some extent contemporary film theory's preoccupations with the legacy of Freud. At the same time, I reveal how cinematic writing reshapes psychoanalytic notions of embodiment.

Modern phenomenology, as important to film theory as psychoanalysis, dovetailed with "the new psychology" in its goals of studying the "lived body," how it could be extended, trained, shaped, or mechanically reproduced. Derived from the laboratory studies of the German scientist Wilhelm Wundt in the 1860s and 1870s, experimental psychology privileged physiology, viewing the brain as an organ whose processes could be measured empirically. Vivian Sobchack differentiates phenomenology through its recognition of "the activity of embodied consciousness realizing itself in the world and with others as both visual and visible, as both sense-making and sensible."[16]

The Freudian model is most visible in H. D.'s work, whose therapy with Freud both allowed her to "name" her bisexuality as much as it pathologized her. Williams too borrowed from Freud's theories of masculine desire and amplified upon their fluidity. Stein and Moore, on the other hand, bypassed the psychoanalytic tropes of female hysteria, invoking an alternate but related tradition of experimental psychologists, including Charcot, William James, and Pavlov, who adumbrated bodies styled by conditioned and unconditioned reflexes.

The modern disease of hysteria, a phenomenon central to both psychoanalysis and experimental psychology, is of particular significance to the liaisons between poetry and film for multiple reasons. First of all, hysteria is a disease of the part, and in this sense, a disease exemplary of modernity. As such, it was linked to series production, Ford's assembly line, and the bodily shocks Walter Benjamin attributed to mechanical reproduction. In fact, from Benjamin's point of view, mechanical reproduction and the emergence of film threatened to render the lyric obsolete. Secondly, the simultaneous prominence and elusiveness of hysteria made it readily adaptable for modern poetry and film. For Louis Aragon, for instance, hysteria was among the "greatest poetic discoveries" and is "a supreme mode of expression" paralleled only by film.[17] It would appear that the hysteric performed her dis-ease, as if in a silent film, through somatic gestures and oblique images rather than through transparently denotative language. Conversely, film had the capacity to induce in the spectator the hysteric's physical symptoms of dislocation, amnesia, suggestibility, and even anesthesia.

Most significantly, modernist hysteria brought into the open the blurred ground between corporeality and consciousness, undermining absolutist categories of sexual difference. Rita Felski reminds us that the hysteric in this period was most often linked with the female body and conflated with that of the "new woman" and the modern feminist.[18] As this book elaborates, the hysteric became contiguous with other fragmented bodies, including the automaton, the bisexual, the femme fatale, the masochist, the fetishist and the effeminized male hysteric. Operating within a kind of hydraulic system, these idiosyncratic bodies, both literal and figurative, populated the modernist landscape, gaining visibility during a period when potentially liberating notions of bodily difference proliferated, and when heightened Aryan ideals of masculinity and whiteness began to be widely disseminated.

Finally, the body of the hysteric fascinated poets as a correlative for what Eliot refers to as "dissociation of sensibility," a concept I touch upon throughout. Literary and film representations of the hysteric confirmed a "compliance," if dissociated, between mind and body. The resulting bodily ego engendered an epidermal poetics that could be cut up and fashioned anew. I thus argue that the hysteric body was not simply a figure depicted *in* the modernist poem or film, but more provocatively, coincided with the fragmented and dissociated bodies created *as* montage.

Eisenstein specifically linked film to modern poetry, clarifying a key methodology for the enactment of hysteric bodies. He theorized a rhythmic dynamism produced through the "collision of independent shots," in which the "*irregularity of the part* exists in relation to the laws of the system as a whole."[19] If film is viewed as a material corpus, the disproportionate, fragmentary shot registers as an "irregular" body part. In principle then, montage fractures while it embodies. Moreover, a montage poetics represents a kinesis where the "irregularity of the part" and its explosive "impulses" reverberate in an economy of hysteria. As we will see, poetic and cinematic texts supply somatic maps of erotic displacements and investments in fragments.

In 1891, Thomas Hardy expressed a particularly modern phenomenology in *Tess of the D'urbervilles*, a novel that existed at the cusp of a number of cultural transformations. Four years after its publication, Breuer and Freud published *Studies in Hysteria*, and the Lumière brothers produced the first film documentaries, "Arrival of the Train" and "Workers Leaving the Lumière Factory." At one point in the novel, Tess tells Angel that "'[t]he trees have inquisitive eyes'"; he is surprised to discover that she "has feelings which might almost have been called those of the age, the ache of modernism."[20] Like the prototypic male poet/seer in Baudelaire's "Correspondences" who discovers his own sensibility encrypted in the "temple" of nature with its watching leaves, Tess self-consciously intuits herself as both seer and seen. Tess expresses and projects the "ache of modernism," Hardy implies, because her "corporeal blight had been her mental harvest."[21] That Tess's bodily predicament directly and unpredictably impinges upon her mind suggests the "compliance" as well as disconnection realized in the modern hysteric.

Moreover, Tess has a "double and reversible" perspective, which for Sobchack characterizes the phenomenology of film experience, its "communication based on bodily perception as a vehicle of conscious expression" (*Address of the Eye* 9). In effect, a desire for the "directly felt, sensuously available" translates in film as a displaced but "expressed perception of an anonymous, yet present, 'other.'" This "anonymous 'other'" – like the seeing trees in *Tess* – stirs a recognition that the "*I* is someone else," to quote the proto-modernist, Arthur Rimbaud.[22] Modernist cinematography externalized this literary legacy of the doppelganger and perceiving "other."

Film's ability to represent and mediate bodily "otherness" both created and exposed what I will develop as a phenomenology of fragmentation. In brief, poets could be captivated by early cinema's "*embodied existence*" (*Address of the Eye* 4) or "corporeal subjectivity."[23] At the same time, the very mechanics and constraints of the medium as well as the use of experimental film techniques exposed the disintegrative and indeterminate aspects of the body.

Film's role as a specifically embodied medium that has contributed to the revolution in modernist literary practices has been partly obscured because of the compelling intercourse between modern painters and poets.[24] However, the non-narrative underpinnings of early film corresponded as well to the abstract strategies of painting. Indeed, Malcolm Le Grice argues that the gradual divorce of cinema from the influence of painting and cinema's consequent alignment with narrative was an "historical mistake," leading us to lose sight of early film's brief but nonetheless significant period of radical experiment.[25]

The revolution in painting as in film pivoted upon the fracturing, cutting and reviving of the "lived body." Marcel Duchamp's "Nude Descending a Staircase" (1911), with its fragmentation of the body and attempt to sequence its motion within time, epitomized the closeness of modern painting to film. In fact, the series photography and motion studies of Eadweard Muybridge and Etienne-Jules Marey in the 1870s prefigured the dislocated body in Duchamp's painting. His painting signaled the paradigmatic transition from a static model of art to a cinematic one, subverting the expectations of a human body idealized, pinioned or framed by Cartesian perspective. Further, as Elizabeth Joyce suggests, the painting alluded to the "classical academic nude" while making it "impossible to objectify" or even to assign a fixed gender identification to the figure.[26] This "outrageous" work, like others featured in the Armory Show (1913), underscored modern art's capacity to blur, to enlarge, to cut away outlines, particularly those which fix or delimit gender morphology.

Enter cinema. It made visible a body never visible before – one that is at once whole and in pieces. Cinema's departure from prior representational mediums resided, as Gilles Deleuze proposes, in its turn away from an absolute "higher synthesis of movement," its "abandoning figures and poses" for "the any-instant-whatever."[27] The physical body became visible through parts in continual mutation and flux, displaced as the "film's body," Sobchack's phrase denoting both the materiality of the medium and the spectator's physical investment in it (*Address of the Eye* 23). The visceral yet preternatural mechanisms of film, distinct from painting, projected the body as a mass of moving "parts," and at the same time, enacted Merleau-Ponty's revelation that "[o]ur body is not in space like things; it inhabits or haunts space."[28] Cinematic bodies haunt, permeate, fragment and are fragmented by representation.

The crosshatching between avant-garde painters and filmmakers extended to their relationship to poets, most recognizably those of the French avant-garde. Apollinaire, who like Stein wrote scenarios, invoked a lyric phenomenology, and by 1917 urged poets to take part in the "new discoveries in thought and lyricism" and the physical "liberties" made possible by cinema.[29] Two years earlier, the American poet Vachel Lindsey had challenged poets to be as inventive as film.[30] In 1921, the French film critic Jean Epstein proposed what he called a "lyrosophy," an unconscious epistemology that structured both film art and modern poetry.[31] Epstein's epistemology was notably kinesthetic, realized through "photogénie," the power of the hypnotic close-up to usurp narrative by tracing the intricate motions of a physical "crisis": "Muscular preambles ripple beneath the skin. Shadows shift, tremble, hesitate. . . . The lip is laced with tics like a theatre curtain. Everything is movement, imbalance, crisis. Crack."[32]

The meshing of film and poetry into an embodied medium, begun in the early 1910s and throughout the First World War when melodramas and physical comedies were popular, continued into the late twenties. For instance, poets (including Apollinaire, Stein, and even Eliot) had already assimilated Chaplin into their lyric avant-garde. Hart Crane's "Chaplinesque" (1921) recreates the poet as clown whose "fine collapses are not lies / More than the pirouettes of any pliant cane."[33] Filmmakers, for their part, turned to poetry as an important resource. Thus, Griffith adapted poems by Tennyson and Browning in several films, and used a fragment from Whitman's "Out of the Cradle Endlessly Rocking" to punctuate *Intolerance* (1916). To offer another example, one of the first lesbian filmmakers, Germaine Dulac was indebted to nineteenth-century Symbolist and Decadent poets and emphasized embodied mental states, using close-ups and distorting shots to denote internal states almost seeping out of the body into the environment. *The Smiling Madame Beudet* (1923) shows her female protagonist, frustrated in her role as wife, plunged into intense depression after she reads lines from a book of Baudelaire. Even more directly, Dulac's experimental film, *L'Invitation Au Voyage* (1927) recreates the atmosphere and images from Baudelaire's poem of the same title.

Among the more literal collaborations, the surrealist poet Robert Desnos inspired, for instance, Man Ray's 1928 *L'Etoile de Mer*. The poet Philippe Soupault created multiple "cinematographic poems" filmed by Walter Ruttmann, works destroyed in the bombing of Berlin during the Second World War. Pound himself briefly collaborated with Fernand Léger on the 1924 experimental film *Ballet Mécanique*. And H. D. made several films with Kenneth Macpherson and Bryher (orignally Winnifred Ellerman), the poet's long-term lesbian partner. Film, it would appear, was ultimately sidetracked not only from painting (as Le Grice suggests) but from poetry as well. While the connections between American poets and filmmakers was never as manifest as it was within the French avant-garde, from the start film vernacular borrowed many of its tropes from poetics (including the rhythmic splicing of images) which in turn, found its "body" (its material, fleshly expression) in experimental cinema.

In contrast to painting's substance and self-presence, the phenomenology of film, its flammable materiality (literally cellulose nitrate), functioned as an evocative undercurrent in modernist poetic composition. Modernist poems, exposed to and coexistent with the emergent medium of film, likewise attempted to record kinesthetic processes and "lived experiences of time."[34] In its rudimentary form, cinema provoked the sensory experience of the viewer and appeared to cross the surface of the body, enter through the very pores, into the bones and nerves. This might explain why Sergei Eisenstein compared certain montage effects to the dizzying ride of a roller-coaster.[35] According to Siegfried Kracauer, film potentially offered the "redemption" of physical reality partly because "representations of movement do cause a stir in deep bodily layers."[36] In activating otherwise insensible "bodily layers," early film underscored the body's piecemeal, mutable existence.

The history of silent film has been discussed extensively elsewhere,[37] but it is important to stress that it was not until the emergence of sound in the late twenties and the eventual codifying of cinematic conventions that a more stark division between mainstream and avant-garde productions developed. While the "classical period" in Hollywood would perfect a "mechanism for producing an illusion of Renaissance space, flowing movements compatible with the human eye,"[38] early film experimentation conjured up bodies that were deliberately fractured. Griffith's methods, for instance, included the manipulation of parallel action as well as what Deleuze calls "deframing," the disconcerting method of not including the whole body in a frame (*Movement-Image* 17). Further, the silence of early film diverted attention away from denotative meaning and towards partial somatic gestures.

As Tom Gunning points out, "early cinema is not dominated by narrative" but rather partakes of the "sensual and psychological impact" of the fairground, suggestive of a kaleidoscopic sensory experience not circumscribed by Cartesian perspective.[39] Early cinema then was not a primitive phase in a teleological movement, but subverted aims of continuity and coherence for particular effects. Thus a poet such as Williams would see in the medium a match for his own anti-narrative impulse to break with "banality of sequence" and "the paralyzing vulgarity of logic."[40] This overthrowing of linear movement combined with the literary ambition to restore vitalism and the primacy of experience, directives of both Henri Bergson and William James.

Early film, in this context, appeared to subvert what Louis Menand calls the "mechanistic conclusions of traditional empiricist epistemology."[41] Moreover, silent film's status as a form of hieroglyphics promised that an Esperanto or universal language might be attained. At the same time, film increasingly signified a pronounced dualism: a potential for tactile immediacy and an insistence upon disjunctive mediation. Akin to Henry Head's experiments conducted after the First World War to regenerate severed nerves, film both dissected and restored sensibility.[42] In other words, even as mechanical reproduction ultimately erodes immediacy and wholeness, early film carved out new spaces for the dislocated body and revivified sensation.

The four poets had to negotiate not only revolutions in aesthetic representation, but were also intensely aware of the literal bodily disfigurements and psychological traumas caused by the First World War, including the deflation of the myth of an impermeable white masculinity. Shell-shocked bodies might find their experience echoed in the dislocating capacities of film. On the other hand, as Paul Virilio reminds, "the nitrocellulose that went into film stock was also used for the production of explosives," while the tactics of cinematic shooting have physiological effects parallel to those of warfare: "[w]eapons are tools not just of destruction but also of perception – that is to say, stimulants that make themselves felt through chemical, neurological processes in the sense organs and the central nervous system."[43] With such "weapons," filmmakers could hope to shock and restructure experience. For the modern poets studied here, fragmentation might be an aesthetic choice, but it could never be entirely divorced from an awareness of its physical manifestations.

Insofar as narrative can produce a "méconnaissance" of a unified bodily gestalt,[44] the screen (like Lacan's mirror stage) becomes, as Christian Metz famously argues, "a veritable psychical substitute, a prosthesis for our primally dislocated limbs."[45] However, instead of performing an exclusively orthopedic function, early films, especially but not exclusively those created by the avant-garde, could foreground their spectral materiality, shatter a comfortable or seamless verisimilitude, and return the spectator to her serialized, "dislocated limbs." In this way, film montage might expose the way "a unified bodily ego comes into existence only as the result of a laborious stitching together of disparate parts."[46] With dismemberment an aspect of its modus operandi, film often connected the lived body as fragile and ephemeral with "film's body." This is not to minimize the literal traumas and injuries of war but to emphasize that dislocation in multiple forms haunted modernist texts and films.

PROSE KINEMA: THE GENDER OF FILM

Peter Nicholls identifies the "triumph of form over 'bodily' content" as a prominent motif in literary modernism since Baudelaire.[47] This triumph, he contends, usually emerges through the ironic distance of a male spectator at the expense of an objectified female body. As I explore in chapter 1, such a dynamic helps account for Pound and Eliot's relative reticence about arguably the most revolutionary art form of their time. They made their general disdain for the "rough beast" of the present an almost ideological mantra. Even considering Pound's importation of the Chinese ideogram (model for the montage unit) into poetics, his "most positive comments on photography and film are filled with grudging qualifications," as Michael North observes.[48] The medium of film, in short, appears inconsistent with the high modernist's variously voiced attempts to transcend flimsiness, evanescence and what Garrett Stewart aptly calls the "attention surfeit disorder" of modern culture.[49]

By the twenties, the central figures of high modernism – Pound, Eliot, Joyce, Yeats – each called for a return to past literary traditions using what Eliot tagged the "mythical method" – "a way of controlling, of ordering, of giving a shape and a significance to the immense panorama of futility and anarchy which is contemporary history."[50] The "mythical method" is not far afield from the cinematic use of simultaneity and juxtaposition of different temporal periods. However, this method also allowed the high modernist, at least in principle, to remain "impersonal" and resist the fugacious present as well as the eroding boundary between art and life. If high modernism opposed mass culture, the avant-garde, on the other hand, called the institution of art itself into question and set out "to organize a new life praxis from a basis in art."[51] While the definitions of "modernism" and "avant-garde" cannot be in this context fully disentangled, avant-garde generally encompasses a set of radical artistic practices and movements, often concomitantly linked to social critique as well as to popular culture, that place the artist at the vanguard of the times. Modernist poets can be construed as avant-garde insofar as they seek out a "new life praxis" and "serve as the political and revolutionary cutting-edge of the broader movement of modernism."[52] Clearly the terms of "modernism" and "avant-garde" often overlap, especially in the 1910s when modern art (including Duchamp's "Nude") sought to displace the Victorian past and to undermine bourgeois culture through experimental practices.[53]

In fact, the four poets call into question the divisions between the categories of popular, modernist and avant-garde, traversing these categories through the embodied medium of film. They can be seen as part of a continuum extending from "high modernism" through popular culture. The dividing line between high modernists and the four poets is not clear-cut. Certainly, the four poets, while open to modernity's new technologies, did not write "popular" poetry, and more significantly, themselves maintained a polarity between the "art film" and the so-called "popular" movie.

Nevertheless, the four poets enjoy the resources of popular culture and appropriate it for avant-garde purposes. Even the most mundane of photoplays, as Robert Herring writes, possesses avant-garde features; it is not the characters or plots that make them "magical" but "the drama of movement and pattern. Images, if you like, in which it doesn't matter essentially whether it's a woman or a chair there. It's the space they occupy, the light they make manifest by being there."[54] Impelled by this sense of abstract phenomenology, Stein was an avid Chaplin fan and perceived him as an icon of the avant-garde. Williams hailed an age where "the phenomenal / growth of movie houses" had displaced the cathedrals for mass "entertainment"; yet he was quite tentative about embracing "the dynamic mob." H. D., apparently the most "elitist" in her development of a film aesthetic, idealized Garbo up to the time of her transplant from German film to Hollywood where the star's incandescence, in the poet's opinion, was "tarnished" by being dressed up as solely carnal ("Beauty" 26). Yet H. D. invoked melodramatic conventions in her cinema reviews. And Moore dismissed Eisenstein's *Potemkin* while she admired and enacted the filmmaker's theories; at the same time, she was a "movie" enthusiast, drawn to more "popular" animal documentaries, early Disney shorts and newsreels essentially for the way they employed avant-garde methods of dislocation and discontinuity. With these contradictory responses in mind, my aim is not to separate too strictly the high modernists from the more overtly cinematic poets of this study: they all wrestled with the effects of mechanical reproduction upon their poetry. As I will demonstrate, cinema provided a ground upon which divergent aesthetic theories as well as notions of embodiment could be staked out and debated.

During the late twenties, "art films" were progressively pitted against Hollywood narrative conventions. I suggest, however, that the model for the film that could capture the "atmosphere of the modern poem" necessarily linked to the movie made for popular appeal through the technology of mechanical reproduction. In fact, as Andreas Huyssen has argued, "mass culture" was "the repressed other of modernism, the family ghost rumbling in the cellar."[55] This mass culture was from the late nineteenth century on given "pejorative feminine characteristics" while "high culture, whether traditional or modern, clearly remains the privileged realm of male activities."[56] Film, whether popular or not, was generally excluded from this "privileged realm" because viewing it was an ephemeral event, a sensation or moment in time, a feature evidenced in the disappearance or unavailability of many early silent films. For good or for ill, cinema registered as "the transient, the fleeting, the contingent" in opposition to "the eternally subsisting portion as the soul of art."[57] As such, as Huyssen suggests, it was inextricably tied in the modernist imagination with the feminine.

Male poetic modernism can be seen as a reaction formation against hysteric effeminacy as well as the sensory saturation and excess of the Decadent aesthetics of the 1890s. Pound's own brand of ambivalence to film stemmed in part from a linkage between the ephemeral art form and the feminine. For instance, in "Hugh Selwyn Mauberley" when Pound refers to "a prose kinema" that is "made with no loss of time" to provide an image of modernity's "accelerated grimace," he aligns film with the less exalted genre as well as with mechanical reproduction.[58] In the same poem, he mourns the men who died in the First World War for an unworthy "civilization," construed as an "old bitch gone in the teeth."[59] Turn-of-the-century sexual politics, including the Wilde trial and its consequent naming of deviance, led to a "masculinity crisis" (hinted at in Pound's poem), further aggravated by the First World War. This crisis, as I will elaborate, expands into a wider consciousness of bodily dislocation afflicting both genders.

I argue that the medium of film, associated with the cellular, mutable and hystericized body, offered an important means for many modernists to picture, project, and reconstruct their fragmented bodies in a "drama of dismemberment and reintegration."[60] Ultimately, the cultural meanings attached to film impinge upon the work of Pound and Eliot who, to a large extent, considered the medium outside the scope of their poetics. Cinema's very materiality, often linked to female corporeality, energizes and haunts their poems. As we will see in chapter 1, these poets write cinematically, and at the same time, distance the cinematic bodies their fissured texts invoke.

THE BODY OF THE TEXT

Chapter 1 explores how Baudelaire's "disembodied spectator," further styled by Pound's proto-cinematic Imagism, simultaneously creates and distances the visceral, rhythmic body. Devoted to upsetting traditional forms, Imagism affiliated Pound with the avant-garde, and indeed even anticipated Eisenstein's montage theories. Eliot's poetic methods appeared strikingly akin to those of silent avant-garde film. *The Waste Land* (1922), his quintessential montage poem, figures forth the dissociated male hysteric or what I name the "Tiresias complex." The poem enacts with one hand the very cinematic phenomenology Eliot would reject with the other. Tautological as it sounds, the poet is hysterical about hysteria. Chapter 1 further considers Eliot's awareness and use of popular film conventions even as he associated them with a despised effeminacy.

I devote each of the next four chapters to Stein, Williams, H. D., and Moore respectively, charting their dialogue with modern tropes of the body. Chapter 2 examines Stein's 1896 debut in publishing, "Motor Automatism," which tellingly belonged to the emergent field of experimental psychology. This article initiated Stein's obsession with bodily movement in a cinematic "continuous present," unanchored from the burdens of teleological narrative and memory.

I develop Stein's montage and automaton poetics in counterpoint to Man Ray's avant-garde *Emak Bakia* (1927) and Chaplin's work in the late 1910s. His spasmodic body elucidates her comic and cinematic rendering of the automaton and the hysteric. Stein choreographed these figurative dislocated bodies against the backdrop of the physical ravages of war (she and Alice B. Toklas transported the wounded as volunteers for the American Fund for the French Wounded in 1916.) Rejecting the literary traditions of the past, she insisted upon a simultaneous willed forgetfulness along with an expansion of bodily, sensory pleasures. In fact, she rewrites hysteria, not as sexual anesthesia, but as a means of locating new erogenous zones.

Chapter 3 focuses upon Williams's development of a cinematic spectator whose gaze is malleable and shifting, embedded within the bodily discontinuities it observes. As a general practitioner who rendered obstetric care on an almost daily basis, his relationship to female patients positioned him as precariously "in charge" of the discourse of hysteria. Yet the poet's visual vocabularies (the camera, voyeuristic eye, the screen, the moving image) demand that his own body be implicated within a cinema of vivisection.

Repeating and revising tropes of the sexed body posited by contemporary psychological discourses, including Freud's model of oedipal development, Williams tracks, risks, and metaphorically cuts the desiring eye, accomplishing what Juan Gris recommends for the painter, that he "must be his own spectator." *Spring and All* (1923) anticipates the breach between spectator and unconscious fantasy prominent in surrealist film, particularly in Luis Buñuel's *Un Chien Andalou* (1928) and Dulac's *Seashell and the Clergyman* (1927). Further, such films, like his poetry, invoke shocking immediacy, "automatism" and "cinematic delirium" to subvert the institutions of literary, medical, and psychoanalytic knowledge.[61] More specifically, these poems propose a masochistic spectator disarrayed by his desires, a spectator continually putting his own ocular powers in crisis.

Unlike Williams, H. D. resists a masochist position. She complains about Carl Dreyer's *The Passion of Joan of Arc* (1927) because of its sadism towards the female spectator, deployed with the "remorseless rhythm of a scimitar."[62] As chapter 4 demonstrates, her poems, film reviews, and performance in *Borderline* attempt to dislocate cinema "constructed by men for a male spectator."[63] At the same time, H. D. derived her central tropes for the cinematic body from psychoanalysis. Her relationship to Freud began in 1909 when she and her first love Frances Gregg read and translated him, and culminated in her therapy with Freud in 1933. Her cinematic editing of poems delineate the Freudian bodily ego as "a projection of a surface" that can be cut into and recreated.

H. D. sustained a number of traumatic personal losses – a stillborn child, her husband's adultery, the nearly simultaneous deaths of her brother and father during the First World War. In contrast to Stein's deliberate creation of an amnesiac body, her poems use shock as a means of salvaging sensory experience. Her first poetry volume, *Sea Garden* (1916), employing film methods of cutting and splicing, displaces singular erotic identification and desire. It is as if her own poetry trains and prepares her for the cinematic theories she expresses in reviews in the late twenties, during what was for her a period of poetic silence. H. D.'s early poems, like the melodramatic and Expressionist films she later admires, accentuate embodiment as scriptable. In an effort to revise the forms of female embodiment available to her through psychoanalysis, she summons and connects a myriad of fragmented bodies, extending from her mythic precursors of Sappho, Helen, and Eurydice to the film icons Garbo, Asta Nielson, and Louise Brooks.

The chapter culminates in an analysis of the cultural displacement of the trope of the femme fatale (inherited from G. W. Pabst's *Pandora's Box*), upon the black male body in *Borderline*. The film underscores the way bodies are created through the stitching of the film itself, composed of sequences that feature "clatter montage," what H. D. described as the frenetic editing of "short shots" or multiple segments ("Borderline Pamphlet" 230).

Like Williams and H. D., Moore was fascinated by the tools of surgery ("Are they weapons or scalpels?" she will ask) with their capacity to make incursions and cuts in the skin. Chapter 5 aims to dispel the perception of Moore, praised by Pound for her disembodied "logopoesis," as a predominantly cerebral, asexual poet. She bridges (without entirely integrating) the often-divorced realms of mind and body through montage and camera work. Rather than invoking the hysteric body developed in previous chapters, I delineate Moore's fetishist embodiments in syllabic poems which catalogue, join, and eroticize a variety of fragments, including quotations from other texts, mechanics, and fabrics. Fernand Léger's *Ballet Mécanique* (1924) along with her film reviews of animal documentaries clarify her fascination with hybrid bodies that override cultural divisions between the abstract and the corporeal, the "natural" and the artificial. In her hands, montage enacts a collision between geometric artifice, the mechanical, and the corporeal.

Finally, Moore's idiosyncratic lyric forms are provocatively aligned with the "queer" bodies in two films she reviewed and admired, Leontine Sagan's 1931 *Maedchen in Uniform* and J. Sibley Watson's *Lot in Sodom* (1933). Faced with the lesbian erotics of Sagan's film, she questions why viewers find such "'loveing pictures'"(sic) unnatural.[64] Watson was an experimental psychologist, doctor, inventor of the early internal x-ray procedure as well as the owner of *The Dial* (the literary journal Moore edited for many years). His *Lot*, a purportedly "fiction" film, draws upon the filmmaker's knowledge of science and deploys "camera work, with a correlating of poetic influences" to reproduce unlikely sensations.[65] These films not only mark the end of the silent era (and are therefore suitable for my last chapter), but Moore's responses to them acutely manifest her fetishist poetics.

The four poets featured in this book explore an alternative erotic economy to the binary heterosexual/homosexual divide, identified by Eve Sedgwick as the stronghold of modern sexuality.[66] Moore camouflages herself as "virgin," disembodied modernist; in this way, male poets inevitably turn her into a kind of "phallic mother," transcendent of female materiality. Yet she herself takes on a fetishist disposition (a role usually reserved for men). Stein's erotics are Irigarayan as well as Pavlovian, and they disperse forgetfully. She discovers her autoerotic double in Chaplin's reflexive body. Williams would seem to be "the odd man out" in this study; yet his rendering of the masochistic male spectator identifies him with femininity and sexual inversion, forms of embodiment that Pound and Eliot, for instance, more evidently eschew. His erotics are rooted in the visual, but through surrealist forms of dismemberment, delineate the "unpleasurable pleasure" of scopophilia. And H. D. ultimately revises the psychoanalytic and literary figures of the hysteric and femme fatale by inhabiting them through what I call her "bisexual apparatus."

To date, there has been no book that specifically connects the four poets as affiliated through a somatic and avant-garde film aesthetic. P. Adams Sitney's *Modernist Montage*, an inspiration for this book, joins texts and films not usually read side by side, but his focus is upon the opacity of modern visual experience. Laurence Goldstein's *The American Poet at the Movies* examines the intersections between popular movies and poets, and like Sitney, he spans the entire century, beginning with Crane and Archibald MacLeish and culminating with Jorie Graham. My book is distinguished by its particular attention to the first third of the century, but more importantly, by its emphasis upon non-narrative films and their recreation of cultural tropes of embodiment. To this end, I uniquely draw upon the insights of film theory, phenomenology, and psychoanalysis, domains with roots in "the period of cinema" itself.

This book is admittedly ambitious, crossing between the discourses of modern poetry, film, and psychology. As such, it cannot present a comprehensive reading of any single poet or filmmaker's entire oeuvre but rather clarifies relations between the media by zooming in upon exemplary texts. My aim is to demonstrate how modern poets can be read in fresh ways by examining them in the context of the modernist period of cinema. Through the delicate balancing act required by interdisciplinary work, I hope to reorient literary studies by extensively drawing upon films that are often unavailable or difficult to locate except in archives.

The four poets that form the basis of my study are certainly not the only ones shaped by cinema, but taken together they represent a "tradition" of openness to cinematic possibilities for enacting new forms of embodiment. While the unresolved tension between the mind and body was a cornerstone of modernity, Stein, Williams, H. D., and Moore each made this dialectic the subject of intensive scrutiny. How they imagined corporeality, whether from a psychoanalytic or mechanistic point of view, became part of each poet's formal disfiguring of an impervious or universalized sensibility. By making somatic dislocations visible, film furnished another vehicle for addressing the gendered body/mind divide already dictating literary traditions. Rather than perceiving film as extraneous to their poetic styles, the four poets engaged the modern crisis of embodiment with an awareness of the medium's tangible synchronicity, multiplicity, and evanescence. The kinesthetic became kin-aesthetic.

CHAPTER I

Modernism, male hysteria, and montage

In 1915, Vachel Lindsey issued a call to arms to modern poets: "Why would you be imitators . . . when you might be creators in a new medium?"[1] This challenge marks a drive to join the disparate arts of poetry and film as well as a competitive anxiety over the emergence of film as dominant art form. Benjamin directs us towards a source of the poet's anxiety when he observes that the "age of mechanical reproduction" raises the question of "how lyric poetry can have as its basis an experience for which the shock experience has become the norm."[2] In other words, the lyric, historically a locus of contemplation and transcendence of the fragile body, was seemingly at odds with film, a medium calibrated to the "accelerated grimace" of mass entertainment. "Words are shocks," Stein writes in *Useful Knowledge*,[3] and as Benjamin implies, they *must* function as shocks in the age of cinema.

The body of the modernist poem gained new angles, line-breaks, asymmetries, and synapses, shifting within and through the very technologies that disoriented the relationship of the human body, no longer framed or harmonized by Cartesian perspective, to time and space. More particularly, film's ability to repeat a series of movements, separated within time, effectively displaced any illusion of wholeness as either an aesthetic or bodily principle.

A 1923 textbook in experimental psychology by William McDougall (a student of William James) dramatically gives voice to a similar crisis in epistemology: "All the categories of physical science, matter, energy, motion, momentum, mass, and Space and Time themselves, are in question; and no man can say whether any of them will emerge alive from the fermenting chaos of modern physical speculation."[4] This commentary is followed by a lengthy footnote about the "unknown content" of the physical world "which must surely be the stuff of our consciousness."[5] Modern behaviorism, McDougall tells us, derived from Descartes and his "reflex theory," which allows that "even when the brain is wholly out of action or destroyed and the individual remains unaware of the whole process," the body still

18

possesses the capacity for movement.[6] In the behaviorist's splitting of the body from the mind, "the nervous system has taken the place of the soul."[7] The fantasy that the rational mind could be detached from the merely mechanical body paradoxically opened the way for a universe where the out-of-control body gains prominence.

McDougall's panic over the evisceration of "all the categories of physical science" meshes with a pervasive sense that a breakdown in the unifying laws of Cartesian perspective, of mimetic transparency, and organic order, irreversibly altered the representational practices in modernist visual and literary arts. Even more striking, McDougall inadvertently echoes the language of Pound and Eliot in their efforts to solidify the artist's intellectual triumph over the "fermenting chaos" or unruly corporeal, often coded as the feminine. Pound explicitly configures creativity as "the phallus or spermatozoid charging head-on the female chaos."[8] To offer a less overt example, Eliot complains that Hamlet lacks an "objective correlative" and suffers from "the stuff that the writer could not drag to light."[9] This "stuff" is linked, as I later develop, to an anxiety over indeterminate sexuality.

These brief instances drawn from the two favorite sons of literary high modernism point towards a collapsing of "unknown content" with the fragmented, mutable, and feminized body. Based on the work of film and cultural theorists as well as the word "celluloid" (itself derived from the word for skin), cinema was associated with the body and the feminine. More specifically, the modern crisis in poetic and bodily representation escalated into a "masculinity crisis" or male hysteria, which the texts I discuss of Pound and Eliot will help to delineate.

The evolution of male hysteria into a pronounced and even commonplace condition was coincident with an array of historical and cultural shifts that changed the parameters of sexual and gender categories. The Wilde trial stands out as a point of departure in bringing homosexuality into public consciousness while simultaneously reinforcing its place in the closet. For modernists like Pound and Eliot, as Cassandra Laity makes clear, the sexual consciousness provoked by the trial fuelled their negation of the previous generation's Decadent and effeminized poets, including Pater and Swinburne.[10]

The most well documented event in undoing social, gender, and sexual categories was the mass destruction of the First World War. It leveled any tidy divisions that might have predated it. Further, as Gilbert and Gubar write, "the unmanning terrors of combat lead not just to a generalized sexual anxiety but also to an anger directed specifically against the female."[11] These "unmanning terrors" found correspondence in the flickering evanescence of film so that the war poet Siegfried Sassoon begins his "Picture-Show": "And still they come and go: and this is all I know– / That from the gloom I watch an endless picture-show."[12]

Symptoms of shell-shock and of the "war neurotic," as Freud articulates in *Beyond the Pleasure Principle*, overlap with those of the hysteric, typically constructed as female. The trauma men exhibited after months of being stuck in the trenches seemed to replicate the less easily definable traumas of domestic confinement. Yet, in Freud's view, the war neurotic did not primarily suffer, as does his female counterpart, from sexual anesthesia so much as from an overly feminine responsiveness to shock. Such "female" susceptibility to shock reeked havoc with strict gender divisions, raising the specter of sexual indeterminacy and increasing the visibility of a "third sex." Although Eliot and Pound did not participate directly in war, they were highly conscious of the male body's fragility and its potential resemblance to the female hysteric.

A primary "mechanism" of hysterics, Freud outlines, is their capacity for "identification": they can "express in their symptoms not only their own experiences but those of a large number of other people."[13] More crucially, however, hysteric identification, the taking on of another's symptomology, stems from "a *fear* of having the same kind of attack," which in itself generates "assimilation" of the resisted response.[14] Identification, of course, is a chief component of the film experience and is suggestive of the "hypnotism" cinema exerts over its viewers.

Freud elsewhere theorizes that the hysteric's capacity for "multiple identification" is related to bisexual fantasies where the subject plays both masculine and feminine roles.[15] His analysis points to the "complicating circumstance" and "double orientation" in the oedipal complex: "a boy also wants to take his *mother*'s place as love-object of his *father* – a fact which we describe as the feminine attitude."[16] In other words, "even boys" have difficulties distancing from maternal identification, thus paving the way for the male hysteric's "unconscious tendency to inversion."[17]

In addition to delineating the modern hysteric (particularly the male hysteric), this chapter adumbrates the cultural body of the automaton. The paradigmatic films, G. W. Pabst's *Secrets of the Soul* (1926) and Vsevolod Pudovkin's *The Mechanics of the Brain* (1926), respectively illustrate these bodies, newly defined through the intersecting discourses of psychoanalysis and experimental psychology. These films depict and enact attempts to control the involuntary reflexes and instabilities of somatic experience.

Eisenstein provides, as I suggested in the introduction, a methodology for the embodiment of the hysteric and mechanical bodies prominent in poetry and film. He insists that film is phenomenological – an "esthetic growth from the cinematographic eye to the image of an embodied viewpoint on phenomena."[18] This "embodied viewpoint" is not smooth, transparent or mimetic; "dynamism" emerges out of mechanically reproduced "tension," a "rhythm" produced through the "collision of independent shots" ("Dialectic Approach" 49). Metric measurement in itself, however, does not necessarily produce either montage or modern poetics.

The "whole charm of poetry," as Eisenstein writes, is no longer grounded in traditional lyric forms, but depends upon a "rhythm" that "arises as a conflict between the metric measure employed and the distribution of accents, over-riding their measure" ("Dialectic Approach" 48). The study of meter has been historically linked to the corporeal through its vocabulary of feet and rhythm, but both experimental film and modern poetry render this connection more apparent through their dismembering tactics. Like the "variable foot" of a newly conceived poetic line, the shot is not simply a montage "element" but a "cell" in its splintering and dynamic becoming: "shattering the quadrilateral cage of the shot and exploding its conflict into montage impulses between the montage pieces."[19] These "montage pieces" coincide with the jerks, tics, and flaying of hysteric and automaton bodies.

This chapter seeks to uncover the extent to which Pound and Eliot practice a montage poetics founded on these bodily tropes. I contend that they resist identification with the hysteric, feminized body specifically through their cinematic writing. After all, Pound's Imagism anticipates Eisenstein's highly somatized theories of montage, while he reinforces Baudelaire's model of the poet as disembodied spectator of the female body. I further argue that Eliot assimilates the male hysteric's "double orientation," or what I call the "Tiresias Complex," enacted by his quintessential montage poem, *The Waste Land*. Almost in spite of itself, the poem indulges in a fantasy of being both sexes.

Eliot's theory of "dissociation of sensibility" (1921) schematizes the "hysteric" disposition of *The Waste Land*, while it also reverberates as a dislocated generation's desire for sensate experience and simultaneous ambivalence towards the somatic.[20] According to Eliot, a "dissociation" or split between intellect and emotion, a "disparity between idea and image," reflects a "progressive deterioration of poetry since the thirteenth century."[21] In his famous essay praising the Metaphysical poets, he broods: "In the seventeenth century a dissociation of sensibility set in, from which we have never recovered."[22] Yet literary dissociation, transposed on the cultural body of the male hysteric, energizes innovation of the modern lyric. In fact, Eliot even hails the dissociated subject as the ideal poet: "the more perfect the artist, the more completely separate in him will be the man who suffers and the mind which creates."[23]

Modern dissociation culminates precisely as mechanical reproduction foregrounds the split between mind and sensate body, a split often couched in an inherited dialogue between masculine and feminine, between "hard" form and diffuse matter, between conscious and unconscious impulses.[24] H. D., as this chapter later illustrates, specifically turns to the cinematic "underground" in order both to sever from sensation and to vitalize embodiment. But for Eliot, the severing seems to move in reverse.[25] While he may fantasize about a "cooperation between acute sensation and acute thought," he stresses that intellect must gain the upper hand over "sensibility" or evidence of "bodily content," a desire that might be traced to his differentiation from the Decadent poetry of the previous generation.

Stellan Rye's 1914 Expressionist *The Student of Prague* is almost a parable of Eliot's characterization of dissociation. Conrad Veidt plays a character who sells his mirror-image to a magician, and is then, as H. D. puts it, controlled by "another master."[26] The disowned image gains ascendancy over the character's will. H. D. indicates that the power of *Student of Prague* lies in its exceeding "objective correlative": "There are things we can't say or paint at the sight of windows half-closed in moonlight. There is the spirit of the garden, the spirit of the water, the lake, the sea, the wind, the ghost itself of all our lives come visually before us."[27] By extending the body through projection and displacement into a spectral "other," *Student of Prague* performs the "dissociation of sensibility" which structures many modernist works. As we shall see, dissociation characterizes the male hysteric's paradoxical attraction to and disavowal of the corporeal image.

FILMING HYSTERIA: *SECRETS OF A SOUL / MECHANICS
OF THE BRAIN*

The categorical wherewithal to delineate the modern hysteric's body derived from Jean-Martin Charcot's "theater of living pathology" in the 1870s and 1880s at the Salpêtrière Hospital, where building upon his earlier studies in epilepsy, he catalogued the hysteric's contractions, paralysis and anesthesia.[28] Photographs of the exaggerated gestures of his patients, formalized by the publication of *Iconographie photographique* (1876–77), prefigured the cinematic reproduction of bodily dislocation. Hysteria necessitated the camera, as Sander L. Gilman argues, "[f]or hysteria must be 'seen' to have observable symptoms."²⁹ The photographic image also participated in hysteric responses, and in its very novelty, could elicit a "startle effect."³⁰ Indeed, Charcot to some extent induced "performances" by presenting the patient with images of the fit.

Building upon Charcot's theory of the disease's etiology as inherited, Pierre Janet's *Psychological Automatism* (1889) and *Mental State of Hysterics* (1892) emphasized the patient's "loss of memory," "restricted field of vision" and "suggestibility" due to "psychic weakness" and "mental disaggregation."³¹ The hysteric, according to Janet, was a victim of "dissociation of personality," or "unassimilated second self, independent of our known one."

By inducing the hypnoid state, a doctor might paradoxically glimpse an hysteric's "second self." Charcot's use of hypnosis and behavioral methods (including suspension therapy, vibrating helmets, electrical stimulation, and even photography) to recreate symptoms anticipated the techniques of modern experimental psychology. These kinds of methods also led to the production of suspect but powerful doctor figures, presented in such films as Robert Weine's *The Cabinet of Dr. Caligari* (1919) and Fritz Lang's *Dr. Mambuse* (1922). While Freud himself gravitated away from using hypnosis as an exclusive "mechanical" means of uncovering the sources of trauma, the cultural perception of hypnosis continued to evoke images of the "magical" powers ascribed to doctor, filmmaker, and poet alike.

"Hysterical theatre," Christopher Bollas writes, is "always something of a séance, as ghosts of the past are brought into some strange light and the hysteric feels himself or herself to be something of a medium for the transition of the absents into a type of materialisation."³² In this sense, the hysteric converges with the figures of the hypnotic and the automaton, "ghosted" and transmuted into plural forms, the sequelae of Charcot's shotgun approach; he was accused of seeing "hysteria everywhere" (*Charcot* 211).

The prototypical modern hysteric is a body neither fully under the control of consciousness nor entirely accountable by psychological discourses. Along with hysteria's most recognizable "stigmata" of amnesia, anesthesia, "double personality" or dissociation, its overriding feature lies in its very evasion of definitional boundaries. As J. A. Omerod concludes in a special issue of *Brain* (1910–11) devoted to the disease, hysteria remains "quietly smiling in her sleeve."³³

While psychoanalysis and experimental psychology clearly were not the only theoretical constructs created to visualize or pin down the indeterminate "hysteric" relationship between mind and body, they represent dominant versions pervading cinematic modernism. The psychoanalytic model posits that bodily consciousness succumbs to past traumas, resulting in shock and dissociation. Freud and Breuer trace a number of otherwise inexplicable symptoms to repressed experience: "the psychical trauma, or the memory of it, acts as a kind of foreign body constituting an effective agent in the present."[34] In "The Aetiology of Hysteria" (1896), Freud ties this "foreign body" of trauma to early sexual experiences. Most importantly, he later binds the hysteric to an "unconscious tendency to inversion."[35]

Within Freud's scheme of hysteria, repressed psychic processes convert into bodily symptoms, confirming the ego as a "projection of a surface," thereby linking it with the "cinematic apparatus."[36] The body as a projected surface both recalls Charcot's photography of hysteric poses and also points towards the dislocated movements in early film.[37] Indeed, Freud describes hysteria as a specifically gestural medium: "as I have heard Charcot say, hysteria is a malady with extravagant manifestations . . . The degree of distortion that can be produced by hysterical contractures is well known."[38] Bodily distortion and exaggeration belong as well to the parlance of melodrama and Expressionist silent film.

Along with the psychoanalytic model, the tradition of experimental psychology dating from Charcot and extending to Pavlov, emphasizes that physical behavior is governed by involuntary and conditioned mechanical reflexes. Pavlov's hysteric is construed as the victim of a "weak nervous system," whereby the cerebral cortex is susceptible to either over-stimulation (resulting in spasmodic movements) or to extreme "inhibition" (states of hypnosis or trance).[39] Under the behavioral model, the "normal" human subject, like the Pavlovian dog, excited or inhibited by external stimuli, can learn to respond or obey by conditioning. Theoretically, the body may transgress into the realm of the machine or automaton, akin to Eliot's "patient etherized upon a table."

Stein's experiments with automatism in the 1890s at Radcliffe (explored in the next chapter) belonged to the field opened up by William James and later represented in Pudovkin's *Mechanics of the Brain*. Eisenstein also incorporates Pavlov's model into his view of the "mechanics" of montage: "Human expression is a conflict between conditional and unconditional reflexes" ("Dialectic Approach" 47). In fact, he appends that "'[r]eason' and the 'soul' . . . correspond remotely with the ideas of conditioned and unconditioned reflexes," reinforcing the binary configuring of "dissociation." Eliot even portrays his admired predecessor Jules Laforgue as a behaviorist, who archly investigates "neuropaths" with their uncoordinated impulses and reflexes. Eliot's own poetic credos of "dissociation of sensibility," "objective correlative," and the "impersonal theory" of poetry are themselves indebted to a vocabulary of experimental science.[40] As if invoking the hallmark of automatism, he claims, for instance, that "[i]t is in depersonalization that art may be said to approach the condition of science" ("Tradition" 30).

Experimental psychology frames a number of questions relevant to cinematic modernists: how are our bodies geared to perform activities, including the act of attention required by writing and film viewing? To what extent are we hypnotized, depersonalized, and fragmented by external stimuli? And conversely, how can the body be rewired or differently eroticized through montage?

The process of film montage, its literal cutting and sewing, acts as a somatic map for libidinal attachment and/or mechanical joining, thus making visible a tension as well as a continuum between psychoanalytic and behaviorist figurations of corporeality. Benjamin accounts for these dual yet interdependent modes by paralleling the mechanics of camera work with the uncovering of concealed psychic materials: "The camera introduces us to unconscious optics as does psychoanalysis to unconscious impulses."[41] In this way, the unconscious postulated by psychoanalysis collaborates with the mechanical isolation of responses posed by experimental psychology.

Pabst's *Secrets of a Soul* and Pudovkin's *Mechanics of the Brain* stand as surrogates for each side of the dialogue between the psychoanalytic and experimental models of embodiment. These quasi-documentary films not only clarify how divergent psychological theories yoke fragmented corporeal experience with consciousness, but their methods operate like the very hysteric bodies they strive to delimit.

Created in consultation with psychoanalysts Hanns Sachs and Karl Abraham, *Secrets* opens with a shot of a famous photograph of Freud presiding on the wall above the film's doctor writing up a case.[42] Sachs summarizes the film's agenda:

The actor stands on an equality with inanimate things. Like them, he can embody the movement of the drama, but only so far as his embodiment is of such psychic events that are before or beyond speech; by this means, reflexes – and, above all, those small unnoticed ineptitudes of behavior described by Freud as symptomatic actions – become the centre of interest.[43]

Thus, film has the power to frame objects and gestures that "ordinarily escape our notice."[44] Moreover, the camera with its "unconscious optics" reproduces the mechanics of the body: its own "reflexes" become "symptomatic actions."

In the first sequence of the film, Martin (a chemist and hence a scientific figure) shaves hair from the back of his wife's neck; he accidentally cuts

1. G. W. Pabst's *Secrets of a Soul* (1926).

her when he hears men in an adjacent apartment discussing a murdered woman: "he did it with a razor." This sequence, with its inter-cutting of two scenes, reveals Martin's hysterical identification with the woman's murderer; hence, his "slip of the razor," like a Freudian "slip of the tongue," betrays his unconscious aggression towards his wife, who doubles with the unseen woman who was in fact murdered. Martin's ensuing nervous disorder, a form of male hysteria, necessarily depends upon and disavows the fantasy of a slain woman.

We learn that Martin's unconscious murderous instincts towards his wife have arisen out of the impending visit of a man (just returned from an exotic adventure) who he imagines is his sexual rival. From the initial scene onward, he becomes obsessed with phallic signifiers – letter opener, dinner knives, a sword, each inanimate object taking on an exaggerated, distorted life of its own (fig. 1). To allay his aggressive instincts, Martin enters into analysis.

Disjunctive montage, the cutting and piecing of disparate temporal and spatial elements, replicates psychoanalytic processes, including the repetition of trauma in dream analysis. Freud emphasizes that dreams are non-narrative: they "do not reproduce experiences" but rather "yield no more than fragments of reproductions."[45] Like the methods of montage, the

2. From *Secrets of a Soul.*

therapeutic methods elucidated by the film are by no means linear but operate by paralleling the hysteric's "tendency to transfers and equivalents."[46]
The film shows Martin wavering between evident psychological disturbance
and a repressive, blotting amnesia. An inter-title reads: "He dreamed . . .";
a "wipe" (an editing maneuver where the screen is blacked out from left
to right) follows to signal that upon awakening the patient has "forgotten"
everything.

By cutting between Martin's fantasies and his daily life, the film blurs the
division between them. The patient's gesticulatory reliving of his dreams
upon the couch (at one point he slashes at it as a stand-in for the female
body) allows him to have multiple identifications with other bodies, including that of his imagined rival. For instance, inter-cut within a psychoanalytic
session, we see the helmeted rival aiming a rifle from high in a tree, and
then Pabst reframes the image to include a phallic-shaped body shot and
suspended in mid-air (fig. 2). Both figures serve as the dreamer's hysterical
"parts": the out-of-proportion rival, costumed in male "uniform" but with
indeterminately sexed visage and presumably Martin's own body catapulted
into space.

By the end of the film, the analyst closes his casebook. Martin has apparently been "cured" through the recreation of his unconscious aggressive impulses towards his wife and his rival, but *Secrets* exposes, almost in spite of itself, the male hysteric's fear and erasure of women's sexuality and embodiment. The fantasy of psychoanalysis to master or pin down a "whole" body often fails to account for bodies outside a phallic economy; the self-conscious splicing together of film fragments underscores the gaps within this economy.

The film's unexcavated secret is the identity of the wife's surrogate, the real dead woman next door.[47] In the opening scene, the film cuts away from the murdered woman to stage Martin's "masculinity crisis." As Breuer and Freud theorize, *"hysterical patients suffer principally from reminiscences."*[48] Ostensibly, only when analysis reproduces his memory fragments can he "work through" their traumatic import. Yet what Pabst's experimental film confirms is the persistence of dissociated experience. The razor scene calls attention to Martin's threatened castration and murderous desires as well as to the use of this implement to make precise cuts in celluloid, which in *Secrets* doubles for female skin.

Pudovkin's *Mechanics of the Brain*, made in collaboration with Pavlov, clearly more of a documentary than *Secrets*, also proposes a theory to contain the modern splintered body. Like the "soul" emphasized in Pabst's title, the "brain" appears to be this film's primary metaphor. Both films expose how the kinesthetic, bound in the modernist imagination to the feminine, ultimately short-circuits intellectual mastery. The splicing between kinds of reflexive behavior in *Mechanics*, like the razor action in *Secrets*, represents the manipulation of the body's automatic responses. A key scene in *Mechanics*, for instance, recreates one of Pavlov's canine experiments, stimulating conditioned responses through the beating of a metronome (a word with the same root as poetic meter). Here the metronome, regulating whether or not the dog in the film will respond, reflects as well the viewer's timed or "hypnotized" reactions.

Along with shots of the "Pavlovian dog" conditioned to behave by triggers and cues, the film inter-cuts close-ups of a woman's face during the throes of childbirth. In her history of Soviet films, Bryher identifies the "greatest part of [*Mechanics*]" as this sequence: "These shots were more full of pain and terror and helplessness than anything ever written."[49] While the film's associative montage implies a disturbing connection between the Pavlovian dog and the woman in labor, it also divests motherhood of its romanticized associations with a transcendent Madonna figure.

Perhaps what Bryher observes as "terror and helplessness" are the result of the woman being monitored by a pair of white-robed doctors at a "control"

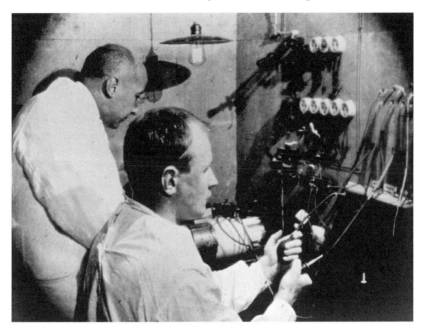

3. Vsevolod Pudovkin, *Mechanics of the Brain* (1926).

panel, significantly removed from the body they observe (fig. 3). The film erects a sharply defined division between the doctors and the woman in labor. Meticulous attention to the woman's facial agony, given to us in piecemeal images, bestows upon her a vulnerable, yet mechanized corporeality. Like Martin in *Secrets*, she has little control of her body. While Martin struggles to master his unconscious, this anonymous woman is "cut into" by involuntary processes and wired to an experimental control panel. Bryher captures the film's dualism with its startling physical portrait of labor along with its "investigation into the processes of the mind as cold, as full of possibility and check, as a page from da Vinci's notebook."[50] In spite of its "cold" restrained diagramming, the "film's body" asserts somatic experience, mechanically pulsed and spliced.

Experimental montage sequences in both *Secrets* and *Mechanics* expose a "failure" to master or produce a whole body. Each film manifests a tension between interior impulses and exterior control. Unlike Freud's model, the behavioral approach did not explicitly place sexuality at its center, and Pudovkin's film specifically addresses "normal" stimulus and response patterns. Nevertheless, the film's mechanized, conditioned body, passively responding with discrete reflexes and gestures, itself partakes of the feminine valences of hysteria.

As is well known, it is difficult to separate the notion of hysteria, given its etymology, from the female body. It still bears the stamp of Plato, who located this "extremity" in women's barrenness: "the animal within them is desirous of procreating children" and if frustrated in this project, the childless animal ends up "wandering in every direction."[51] Thus the juxtaposition in *Mechanics* between animal and woman in labor calls upon a long-entrenched concept of the uncontrolled female body, "wandering" out of rational purview. However, a "mechanistic" focus upon external stimulus and response, rather than upon the psychic interior, allowed both Stein and Moore, as we will later see, to map alternate erogenous zones upon a pliable somatic surface.

The cultural depiction of modern hysteria, whether configured as a form of Charcot's inherited psychic "lesion," as Janet's "behavioral" theory of "reflex insanity in women," or as evidence of Freud's claim that early sexual trauma was the "motive force of every separate symptom," provides ample justification for modernists like Pound and Eliot to distance themselves from the female body. While Freud iconoclastically asserted that men could also be hysterics, he ultimately collapsed femininity with the material body, particularly with the uterus.[52]

In *Dora* (1905), Freud's heightened need and inability to comprehend his patient's derelict "fluids" and her "fragment of an analysis" (as he subtitles the case study) transforms him into the very hysteric he depicts.[53] Freud reproduces what Irigaray has called the "old dream of symmetry" whereby female sexuality can only be understood as "self-same," dependent upon the schema that defines bodies according to whether or not they bear the phallus.[54] Within this framing, the female hysteric can double for the male invert, whose oedipal "complications" have identified him as having a "feminine attitude." Psychoanalysis, as Alice Jardine has argued, needs the female hysteric in its constitution of male subjectivity; at the same time, it allows for "a hallucinatory conceptual leap" in its definition of hysteria so that "'the hysteric is a woman who can also be a man.'"[55] In the context of Eliot's sexual poetics, as we will see, it is appropriate to invert this motto: "the hysteric is a man who can also be a woman."

The hysteric body in this period functioned not only as a reminder of corporeal fragmentation but of sexual fluidity. Spliced bodies of modernity, like the surrealist game of "exquisite corpse," or the body in René Clair's experimental film *Entr'acte* (1924) with its male head sutured on to a female ballerina's torso, exposed the way the body might be cut into and refashioned (fig. 4). At the same time, Clair's figure persists in claiming the "brain" as masculine. If the cultural trope of hysteria threatened myths of bodily

4. René Clair's *Entr'acte* (1924).

wholeness, the resulting "fragmented body" also presented a ground upon which poetic texts, like the sexes, could divide, converge and re-emerge in new configurations of subjectivity and sexuality alike.

Baudelaire conceived the poet as an incipient camera, "a kaleidoscope endowed with consciousness," thus connecting poetry with mechanical reproduction. At the same time, he polarized "the transient, the fleeting, the contingent" in a binary that subordinates the "variable element," associated with the female body, to "the eternally subsisting portion as the soul of art."[56] Baudelaire's dandy poet/spectator, "a prince enjoying his incognito," plunged into the metropolis as "into an enormous reservoir of electricity," while his ironic detachment allowed him to remain untouched and unseen. Akin to Baudelaire's poet figure, Pound's Imagist represented another version of the disembodied spectator. Much like other proclamations in the manifestos of male modernists, Imagist principles of direct treatment, succinctness, and non-metrical rhythm implicitly collapsed the excesses of romanticism with a despised, hysteric effeminacy.[57] Indeed, the ideal Imagist poem evoked a sleek, masculine body pulled out of the murky female chaos. Eliot's theory of the impersonal poet whose art is "not a turning loose of emotion, but an escape from it" as well as T. E. Hulme's notion of the "classical" modern poem as a "dry" and "hard" body complemented Pound's directives. "An Imagist film," as Lindsay further correlated, could correct "the overstrained emotion, the overloaded splendor" of "what are at present the finest photoplays."[58]

Pound derived Imagism from Ernest Fenollosa's 1901 draft manuscript on the Chinese Ideogram (which included a list of lantern slides Fenollosa planned to use to illustrate visual compression). As I have suggested, the renovation of the lyric coincided with the beginnings of experimental montage. Imagism with its ideographic roots anticipated Eisenstein's theory of montage as "copulation (perhaps we had better say, combination) of two hieroglyphs" ("Cinematographic" 29). Eisenstein, like Pound, turned to the lyric forms of haiku and tanka as "montage phrases" or as "shot forms."

The ultimate in quick "shot forms," Pound's prototypic Imagist poem, situated in London's underground, converts a "posthumous shock" ("Motifs" 175) into a snapshot, the result of the "copulation" of "two 'depictables'" ("Cinematographic" 29–30):

In a Station of the Metro

The apparition of these faces in the crowd;
Petals on a wet, black bough.   (*SP* 35)

Fundamental is the poem's compression (Pound cut it from thirty-six lines to three) which in itself rebukes the "softness of the nineties." Without verbs, except for the ghost of one in "apparition," the poem presents an image stopped in its moving tableau. Hinged by its semi-colon, "Metro" thrives upon what it leaves out or upon the "undepictable" (the result, according to Eisenstein, of joining "two depictables") in its visual metamorphosis. The underground metro shades into the realm of cinema where bodies double as phantoms.

This touchstone poem epitomizes a modernist ambivalence to "film's body." Pound engenders a cinematic space that amounts to the "filming" of commuters rushing through a station. Assuming the distanced camera eye, the poem replicates to some extent Baudelaire's position in his paradigmatic poem "To a Red-Haired Beggar Girl," which according to Nicholls, objectifies the female body so that the poet can attain "a contrasting disembodiment."[59] Baudelaire's poem presents a fractured blazon, stanza by stanza indulging the eye by "mentally undressing" the exoticized beggar. He substitutes her tatters for "some splendid robe of court" but then commands: "unveil / your breasts."[60] Similarly, Pound's poem approximates a long shot to clear a visual pathway for the sake of a brief close-up and then withdraws. Unlike "To a Red-Haired Beggar Girl," his poem is "in" the station but bears no first-person embodiment. In fact, there is no female body as such – only traces of one in the detached vision of stray "petals" in this tunnel as vulva.[61]

Along these lines, Marianne DeKoven reads "Metro" as "containment of an erotic response" with "the platonic maternal cave transmogrified into a hell of the degraded modern."[62] The "maternal cave" resonates as a disavowed corpus, and like Plato's womb-like "chora," it would be an inactive receptacle but for the poet's vision. Pound, following Baudelaire, crafts a spectator that is simultaneously a sexual agent (enacting the "copulation" of images) and a disembodied observer.

The modernist male spectator anticipates the viewer Laura Mulvey imagines when she argues that the "determining male gaze projects its phantasy on to the female figure which is styled accordingly"; as erotic spectacle, it reflects a "*to-be-looked-at-ness*" ("Visual Pleasure" 27). For Mulvey, Marlene Dietrich's body exemplifies the spectacle that interrupts "the development of story line, to freeze the flow of action in moments of erotic contemplation"

("Visual Pleasure" 30). Dietrich's body, like Baudelaire's beggar girl, is "frag-mented by close-ups" geared to fulfill a "fetishistic scopophilia." Simi-larly, Pound's Imagist credo, as represented in the still moment achieved in "Metro," eroticizes the chiseled fragmentary form of the poem itself.

"Hugh Selwyn Mauberley," Pound's portrait of an effete poet, insists upon the detachment that Imagism recommends. In succumbing entirely to the lure of the sensuous over the abstract, Mauberley has forsaken the poet's necessary ironic aloofness. Thus he "[d]rifted . . . drifted precipitate" and suffers "bewilderment" and "anesthesias"; only "maudlin confession" remains. He is all sensation, "washed in the cobalt of oblivions" (*SP* 76). Mauberly's consciousness, which might be likened to the flickerings of early film, is "but this overblotted / Series / Of intermittences" (*SP* 76). As with hysteric identification, there is no distance, only overexposed close-ups. An anxiety over close-ups makes sense in this poem, which after all, confronts the hell and waste of the First World War, vividly evoked by the compact image of misplaced laughter erupting "out of dead bellies."

Like Pound, Eliot ties female embodiment to mechanical reproduction, the latter represented in "The Love Song of J. Alfred Prufrock" as "a magic lantern [that] threw the nerves in patterns on a screen." This kaleidoscope gadget, precursor to the moving picture and projector, mediates Prufrock's somatic dissociation. By imagining his nerves projected on a screen, Eliot invokes a kind of neuromimesis, a process by which hysterical symptoms are both etched upon the body's surface and projected elsewhere.

Eliot's early poetry frequently portrays dissociated states. As Marjorie Perloff points out, the very sound structure and use of caesura in the first line of "Prufrock" – "Let us go then, you and I" – "creates a note of torpor, an inability to move," while the following two lines ("When the evening is spread out against the sky / Like a patient etherised upon a table") evokes a "dragging along in a catotonic manner."[63] Eliot's image of the drugged patient not only approximates an out-of-body experience, but the passive cinema spectator who, like the hysteric, is susceptible to suggestion.

Moreover, the alluring mermaids in the "chambers of the sea," like the romantic sirens of silent film "chambers," possess a sensuality that threatens to drown the poem's anti-hero. While Prufrock elegizes that he is cut off from these phantasmal mermaids ("they will not sing to me"), he has been alternately attracted to a montage of "arms, braceleted and white" and discombobulated by a close-up of them "downed with light brown hair."[64] Like the hysteric, his field of vision is severely foreshortened and in this instance, by the shock of a compulsive close-up of hair, a sign of carnal mutability. In staging what almost amounts to the primal scene of modern poetry, "Prufrock" makes tangible the male hysteric's fear of identification with the female body.[65]

Clearly cognizant that the hysteric is most often culturally construed as female, Eliot often represents mental illness as uterine: his "Mr. Apollinax" is "unbalanced," for instance, and "laughed like an irresponsible foetus" (*CPP* 18). He is also aware "that hysteria / Might easily be misunderstood" ("Sweeney Erect," *CPP* 26). "Hysteria," written during the First World War, even more precisely depicts the assimilation Freud describes as a signature of the disorder.

In this prose poem, a purposefully detached tone counterpoints with an anxiety of "catching" the female malady. The male speaker in "Hysteria" so entirely identifies with his female companion that he "is aware of becoming involved in her laughter and becoming part of it" (*CPP* 19). With each moment, the "close-ups" of his companion continue to engulf him "until her teeth were only accidental stars with a talent for squad-drill." As he struggles to regain composure, the speaker is more "drawn in" by the automatic rhythms of the woman's convulsive "short gasps." This hallucinatory close-up, a version of vagina dentata, culminates with the speaker "lost finally in the dark caverns of her throat."

The female body in "Hysteria" becomes an automaton whose parts can be isolated as if in a behaviorist experiment, such as those represented in Pudovkin's film. Scientific objectivity disintegrates in the "precise instant when a thing outward and objective transforms itself, or darts into a thing inward and subjective," to reiterate Pound's exacting formula for the Imagist poem. In "Hysteria," by contrast, there is no remove or standing apart from such a "precise instant." The teeth with their "talent for squad-drill," governed by a set of involuntary reflexes, *might be* controlled with the right amount of "concentration." Or so Eliot's persona implies while revealing this control as illusory: "I decided that if the shaking of her breasts could be stopped, some of the fragments of the afternoon might be collected, and I concentrated my attention with careful subtlety to this end." Fixation upon the woman's "shaking breasts," however, only accentuates an awareness of corporeal fragmentation.

The desired "concentration" that the speaker in "Hysteria" privileges has another set of associations in "Tradition and Individual Talent." Eliot's essay redefines Coleridge's oddly more "controlled" version of poetic creation ("emotion recollected in tranquility") as "a concentration, and a new thing resulting from the concentration which to the practical and active person would not seem to be experiences at all; it is a concentration *which does not happen consciously or of deliberation*" ("Tradition" 33; emphasis mine). In other words, the concentration achieved by zooming in upon an object (here the "shaking breasts") can itself express dissolving mastery or involuntary response.

If the divide between subject and object, viewer and viewed breaks down in the hysteric scenario depicted in Eliot's poem, how might the female or the "inverted" spectator fit into the visual dynamics of scopophilia and fetishism presented by Mulvey? As Mulvey herself has detailed, these dynamics do not adequately account for the female or non-heterosexually-identified spectator. Mary Ann Doane theorizes that women experience "an 'over-identification' with the image."[66] However, as Tania Modleski observes in her study on Hitchcock, "distantiation" has been an overrated feature of film viewing, and that "to overidentify with other women and with texts, is less a problem for women . . . than it is for patriarchy."[67] Eliot's "Hysteria" explicitly exposes how "over-identification" creates a crisis for the culturally constructed masculine subject.

Like Pound's "disembodied spectator," Eliot's poetic principles potentially mediate the sense of a protracted close-up. Hence, his theories appear symptomatic of hysteria, enacting with one hand the very dynamics they seem to refute with the other. As Eliot famously admits: "of course, only those who have personality and emotions know what it means to want to escape from these things" ("Tradition" 33). His acute sense of a pervasive cultural "dissociation of sensibility" allows him to reinvent the modern poem's "body" as well as to approximate the hysteric's somatic fragmentation visualized by cinema.

Like Eliot's concept of "dissociation of sensibility," his well-known requirement for an "objective correlative" in poetry corresponds to the displacement of psychical traumas into physical symptoms. Eliot defines "objective correlative" as "the only way of expressing emotion in the form of art," or as an "object, set of images, chain of events . . . that will be a formula for a particular emotion." He dismisses Swinburne for his "thrill" in words to the point where "the object has ceased to exist, because the meaning is merely the hallucination of meaning."[68] Eliot's craving for the "object" echoes Freud's strict requirement in "Aetiology" that the analyst determine a very precise originary traumatic "correlative" for hysteria.[69] Using the example of a patient with "hysterical vomiting," Freud claims that the inciting scene must have "justifiably produced a high amount of disgust" and must have "suitability as a determinant."[70]

For Freud, "[h]ysteria begins with the overwhelming of the ego" that then creates a repressive "defense." Repression operates through the "intensification of a boundary idea" which then splices "a motor manifestation," with one foot in the defending ego and the other in the triggering traumatic event.[71] The "boundary idea," Freud provocatively notes, is not "manifested in a replacement on the basis of some category of subject-matter, but by a *displacement of attention along a series* of ideas linked by temporal simultaneity."[72] Both Eliot and Freud thus reproduce the mechanics of montage (the horizontal serializing of disassociated signifiers). While they respectively strive for "objective correlative" or "suitability of determinant," the hysteric body subverts linear plot in its kinesthetic "displacement of attention."

Eliot articulates his theory of the "objective correlative," a demand to repress materials "in excess of the facts," in the context of his complaints against Hamlet, who "fails" as a character because he is possessed of "a feeling which he cannot understand" ("Hamlet" 58). Eliot's complaints about "the stuff the poet could not drag into the light" are indicative of his uneasy awareness of inversion circulating in the culture at large.[73]

"The Love Song of St. Sebastian," a manuscript poem Eliot sent to Conrad Aiken in 1914, shows the "double orientation" Freud refers to in cases of hysteric susceptibility to inversion. Accompanying the poem, Eliot enclosed a defensive claim that "there's nothing homosexual about this . . . but no one ever painted a female Sebastian, did they?"[74] Eliot was most likely familiar, as Christopher Ricks notes, with the homosexual "cult" of Saint Sebastian, specifically "[t]he combination of nudity and the phallic arrows" in Wilde's earlier presentations of this figure.[75] After an orgy of self-flagellation, Eliot's St. Sebastian choreographs his lover in a lowered position as he prepares to strangle her: "I would come with a towel in my hand / And bend your head between my knees" (*Inventions* 68). Eliot calls up the homoerotic legacy of St. Sebastian, but then displaces it by transmuting a "passive" role into an "active" one, "mangling" (as the poem puts it) the female bearer of dissociated desires. The poem, in its hysteric act of defending against sexual "aberration," visibly denotes it.

As the next section demonstrates, this double activity reemerges in *The Waste Land*. The particular resistance to female corporeality in the poem leads to an emblematic "séance" for a body in bits and pieces, a performance of fragmentation as unconscious material or as involuntary reflexes. "Objective correlatives" reduce to a "heap of broken images," related to bodily waste ("broken fingernails of dirty hands," "carious teeth," "wrinkled dugs"). Moreover, Eliot's cinematic methods, linked to the "displacement" mechanisms of hysteria, enable what I call a Tiresias complex, the resisting and staging of sexual undecidability. The hysteric and the automaton enter Eliot's writing as bodies *in* his work and *as aesthetic enactment*, and in the process subvert clearly defined sexual identities.

TIRESIAS COMPLEX

Much more explicitly than Pound, Eliot both embodied and performed male hysteria. Rejected from volunteering for the war effort on fitness grounds and thus left behind in a mostly evacuated London, Eliot no doubt came face to face with the fact that he fell into a demographic composed of women, the elderly and the sick. Eliot's exclusion from the trenches might well have exacerbated a survivor guilt over the millions dead in the First World War, and more personally, over the death of his friend Jean-Jules Verdenal, who died in battle in 1915.

The diffuse angst of "Prufrock" as well as Eliot's self-dubbed "'nervous sexual attacks'" correspond time-wise with his brief but passionate friendship with Verdenal from 1911–12 in Paris (when he began composing "Prufrock").[76] His mourning for Verdenal does not seem to abate. He recounts in 1934 an emblematic memory from the summer of 1911: "I am willing to admit that my own retrospect is touched by a sentimental sunset, the memory of a friend coming across the Luxembourg Gardens in the late afternoon, waving a branch of lilac."[77]

Eliot's grief appears mixed with homosexual panic when considered in light of James E. Miller's conjecture that the poet's intense attachment to Verdenal spurred his hasty marriage to Vivienne Haigh-Wood just a month after hearing about his friend's death.[78] In addition to prolonged grief and homosexual panic or perhaps as a result of them, Eliot consulted a psychiatrist in 1921. His symptoms consisted of what he called "an aboulie [lack of will] and emotional derangement which has been a lifelong affliction."[79] According to Wayne Koestenbaum, Eliot "suffered from a paralysis similar to the literal immobility that afflicted Freud's patients," and he completed *The Waste Land* while under psychiatric care in a Lausanne sanitarium only by defying his doctors who forbade intellectual activity (the advice given to the famous female hysterics, Alice James, Woolf, and Charlotte Perkins Gilman).[80] It is important to keep these biographical details in mind in order to see the relationship between Eliot's cinematic writing and hysteria.

Eliot understood that film could be a means of embodying his cultural and personal anxieties. In October 1914 (during his year at Merton College, Oxford on a travelling fellowship granted by Harvard), he wrote to his cousin Eleanor Hinkley that "he would have liked to have gone in to the training corps . . . but they won't take a foreigner."[81] In the same letter, he shared his latest amusement, derived from American sources: "Just now I am working on my great ten-reel cinema drama, EFFIE THE WAIF . . . to be staged at vast expense, the first reel to be in the mountains of Wyoming."[82] Unlike Crane's "Chaplinesque" which wrings its handkerchief for "a kitten in the wilderness," Eliot ridicules such pathos, the all-too-familiar diffuse emotion he scorned in his Romantic predecessors. The ensuing scenario shows how thoroughly familiar he was with popular film melodramas, which often centered upon the immigrant's assimilation troubles and triumphs.

Reel one, set in Medicine Hat, Wyoming on Christmas Eve, features Spike Cassidy ("the most notorious gambling house proprietor in the county"), who upon returning home from the saloon after shooting a man, finds "a small bundle on his doorstep." By reel two, Spike, "reformed by the sweet insidious influence of the child," and by virtue of film editing, has become mayor and the richest man in the county. However, Seedy Sam returns after a long absence from the town, demanding that Effie marry his simpleton son Peter, or else he will expose the now virtuous mayor's past. Eliot then introduces Walter Desborough, who has hailed from one of "Harlem's oldest and richest families." The family's money has been lost, leading to the father's death from "shock"; Walter is thus forced to go west to seek his fortune. "As the canal boat carries [Walter] westward up the Erie he turns and gazes at the Statue of Liberty disappearing on the horizon," Eliot narrates, providing the emblematic immigrant icon, with the comment "(not strictly accurate geography, but a fine scene)."

The scenario invokes many stock elements of film melodrama – the struggle between vice and virtue, the return of the repressed "villain," the angelic waif without a mother threatened by an unfit marriage ("so rudely forced"), the crucial westward trajectory and its concomitant fantasy of striking it rich in the frontier. Another letter to Hinkley enumerates "all the comic and villainous characters who fall in love with EFFIE" against the backdrop "chiefly on the plains" for "(you must have either the plains or the desert if you expect a good pursuit)."[83] The panoply of Effie's suitors include "DANCING BEAR the chief of the Pottawottobottomies, a terrible fellow, given to drink, and no end treacherous" and "Traihi Sheik" for "[y]ou simply have to have either a red Indian or an East Indian."

While Eliot certainly jibes at the screen's stereotyping portraits, his mock film scenario registers an uneasiness with the large-scale immigration America had recently sustained. My point in elaborating upon Eliot's "ten-reel cinema drama" is to establish his flirtation with the medium of film, which provided an imaginary space where he could articulate anxieties over the shifting matrices of class, race, gender, and sexuality. He combines the cultural obsessions of popular film with the developing experimental tactics of Griffith, whose own desire to preserve a hegemonic white masculinity culminated in *Birth of a Nation* (1915), the most widely seen silent film. Eliot would associate the First World War with the disruption of racial, ethnic, and national boundaries, amplified by the Treaty of Versailles, which fragmented Europe and the Middle East.[84] He dramatizes this state of affairs in *The Waste Land* with the non-sequitor: "I'm not a Russian woman at all, I come from Lithuania, a true German" (written in German).

By the time Eliot transcribes *The Waste Land*, his anxieties over racial and gender identity, coincident with his personal experiences of loss and sexual repression, seem to have induced hysteric symptoms. How they transmute into the modern montage poem par excellence is what concerns me here. If "film since Griffith has been something . . . we accept as a fragment" (*Memory of Tiresias* 26), Eliot almost "invented" the fragment upon which modernist poetic composition relies. Eisenstein compares Griffith to Dickens; inadvertently, Eliot does the same, considering his original title for *The Waste Land*, derived from *Our Mutual Friend*: "He Do the Police in Different Voices." Through its quick shifts between images, its kaleidoscopic polyphony, its unexpected juxtapositions (including popular slang alongside literary allusions), the poem disrupts the monumental and vertical "long-shot" of the literary history it extols. By layering and superimposing allusions, the text demands that the reader, akin to an hysteric medium, put together its frame-by-frame fragments, and then Penelope-like, the poem undoes or decomposes itself after every reading.

Eliot enacts the "method of parallel action" and the "displacement of time-continuity" made famous by Griffith, most evident in the palimpsest film, *Intolerance* (1916), with its "complex cutting" and its "incredibly frenetic barrage of images, some of them of only a few frames' duration."[85] (The heightened self-reflexive montage of *Intolerance* was in a sense Griffith's reply to what he considered to be the unwarranted attacks upon the "racist content" of *Birth*.) As if using Eliot's "mythical method," *Intolerance* counterpoises four story-lines and time periods (Ancient Babylon, France in the Middle Ages, Christ's Crucifixion, and the present) each punctuated with the image of a "static receptacle," a woman (Lillian Gish) rocking a cradle, with a fragment taken from Whitman: ". . . out of the cradle endlessly rocking." Temporal counterpoint along with a series of abject female bodies also structures *The Waste Land*; these bodies (like the maternal Lillian Gish, an icon of film melodrama, akin to Eliot's Effie) link disjunctive temporal rails (including the literary past of Shakespeare with a contemporary pub scene).

In contrast to the female bodies in the poem's foreground, the mythic and spectral Fisher King with his testicular wound haunts the poem's slashed dioramas. Male wounding animates a "masculinity crisis," engendering a "displacement of attention" to other bodies that trouble sexual definition, especially the absent "off-screen" Tiresias, another oblique but focal figure. An ambiguous footnote to *The Waste Land* instructs us that "Tiresias, although a mere spectator and not indeed a 'character,' is yet the most important personage in the poem . . . What Tiresias *sees*, in fact, is the substance of the poem" (*CPP* 52). This direction to consider an invisible spectator leads us towards the cinematic, but also to a double-sexed viewer, a figure "throbbing between two lives, / Old man with wrinkled female breasts" (*CPP* 43). The body of Tiresias in this way recalls Swinburne's "Hermaphroditus," whose composite gender disallows any fulfillment.[86] Eliot's identification with Tiresias, however, allows him to participate in both the active and passive roles in the "bisexual" fantasy Freud ascribes to the hysteric. Meanwhile, his off-screen spectator "*sees*" and therefore brings into being the "substance of the poem," which as I develop, is identified with a host of female bodies.[87]

Rather than maintaining a spectator's distance from the visceral, Eliot specifically identifies his own body with the poem, when he writes Aiken: "It's interesting to cut yourself to pieces once in a while, and wait to see if the fragments sprout."[88] This stark but cavalier assertion recalls a "fragment" written in 1911: "I am put together with a pot and scissors / Out of old clippings / No one took the trouble to make an article" (*Inventions* 71). "The best way to do it is with scissors," Hitchcock would later comment, glossing not only criminal acts of violence (mostly committed upon female "substance") but montage itself.[89] Eliot's confession to Aiken, of course, finds its place in the poem's grim jest about the casualties of war: "'You who were with me in the ships at Mylae! / That corpse you planted last year in your garden, / Has it begun to sprout?" (*CPP* 39). The poem invokes corporeal mutilation and psychic shock, but also forges an hysteric identification with the vulnerable female body.

The poem's body is refashioned as it were from the severed nerves, broken synapses and amputated "parts" cut from a vast literary corpus and grafted together without apparent order. Perhaps reflecting the sanitarium in which it was completed, *The Waste Land* implicitly confesses to its own artful yet almost neurological in-coordination, recreating a sort of intricate gothic scientific experiment where Eliot is both dissecting surgeon and mutilated flesh. The poem is not only cut and pieced from other texts but owes a "debt" to Pound, who cut the poem in half.[90] Pound describes Eliot's work as "Uranian" (a term for homosexuality) and his own editing of *The Waste Land* as a "caesarian Operation."[91] This operation is a metaphoric bypassing of the uterus as well as a way of Pound's identifying Eliot as patient and himself as doctor.

The poem questions the very notion of authorship not only because of Pound's editing (Eliot dedicated the poem to Pound as "the better craftsman"), but because of the less visible debts to his wife's annotations, which remain occluded.[92] The section "Game of Chess," for instance, makes it unclear whose "nerves are bad tonight." Like the unseen slain woman in *Secrets*, Eliot's wife is the poem's representative disowned female body, fractured into multiple women. In his note about the "spectator" Tiresias, Eliot claims as well that "all the women are one woman."

More often than not, Eliot's portraits of women reveal an acute discomfort with their flesh, and hinge upon his identification with hysteria. Notwithstanding his own discomforts with female corporeality, Pound excised one of the most disturbing renditions in Eliot's manuscript, one that specifically links the female body to film. As though casting for a "ten-reel cinema," Eliot had catalogued women as "types" (including the "plain simple bitch" and the "strolling slattern in a tawdry gown"), and then zoomed in upon Fresca, who "in other time or place had been / A meek and lowly weeping Magdelene."[93] Alternately, she is a debased version of Venus, a "can-can salonnière" steeped in decadent aesthetics: "Women ~~grown~~ intellectual grow dull, / And lose the mother wit of natural trull. / Fresca was ~~baptised~~ in a soapy sea / Of Symonds – Walter Pater – Vernon Lee" (*Manuscript* 27).

What makes Fresca an even more significant deletion is an extended conceit, wherein Eliot parallels Aeneas recognizing his mother (Fresca/ Venus) with the "rabble" viewing a film star:

> He ~~recognized the goddess by her supernatural grace~~
>   the goddess by her smooth celestial pace.
>   pact
> So the ~~close millions~~
>   close rabble
> ~~The sweating rabble~~ in the cinema
>   ~~Thousands,~~
> ~~Know~~ Sees ~~on the screen,~~
> ~~Can recognize~~ a goddess or a star.
>   silent rapture
> ~~In reverent~~ In ~~reverent~~   ~~heaven~~   (*Manuscript* 29)

Eliot's distaste for the "sweating rabble" is as much a rejection of "low culture" as it is an hysteric response to female flesh, here specifically its maternal incarnation.

Fresca's absence from the final version of *The Waste Land* erases the explicit connection between embodiment and the "silent rapture" of film, but the implicit connection persists. Moreover, the remaining women, either violated virgins or neurasthenic vamps, are emblems of sexuality gone awry. These bodies relay hysteric identification as well as the modern male's "wounding." Women, we recall, are demonized in this period for their newly acquired liberties; psychoanalysis constructs them as already castrated, and experimental psychology reveals them as perhaps more vulnerable to conditioning than men.

Space will not allow me to explore all of the women Eliot invokes to represent his anxiety over fleshiness that is "[s]usceptible to nervous shock" ("The Hippopotamus," *CPP* 30). Among his violated virgins are Philomel "so rudely forced" and the mad Ophelia drifting off to her suicide. Among his carnal bodies, a proletariat harpy, the pub room Lil, with her multiple abortions and rotting teeth (recalling Pound's "old bitch gone in the teeth" in "Mauberley"), awaits her "demobbed" husband's return from war. And on a larger scale, a female chorus to his apocalyptic vision of broken bridges and falling towers, is the "[m]urmur of maternal lamentation," the rampant "hooded hordes swarming / over endless plains." This chorus recalls the wide-angle panoramas in Griffith's *Birth of a Nation*, including the repeated image of the hooded rush of the Klu Klux Klan avenging their threatened masculinity.

Yet another female figure, the "typist home at teatime" awaits her "young man carbuncular" in "The Fire Sermon," the third section of the poem where Eliot first specifically names Tiresias. What in fact does this off-screen, blind Tiresias *see* in this scene? He mediates, almost narrates as if through inter-title, the typist's "modern" single life as she comes home from work to her "food in tins" and "her drying combinations." Tiresias pans and scopes the room, cataloguing the typist's undergarments:

> On the divan are piled (at night her bed)
> Stockings, slippers, camisoles, and stays.
> I Tiresias, old man with wrinkled dugs
> Perceived the scene, and foretold the rest –
> I too awaited the expected guest.   (*CPP* 45)

The visionary's close observation of the typist's personal life (knowing the dual function of her divan, for instance) hinges not upon desire for her but upon identification with her (he "too awaited the expected guest").

What Tiresias apparently "foretells" in the "violet hour" is the degraded sex-scene that will unfold with the arrival of the young man. The clerk "assaults" and "encounter[s] no defence," while the neurasthenic typist remains detached from both body and mind (what would be evidence of a "weak nervous system" in Pavlov's interpretation of the hysteric): "Her brain allows one half-formed thought to pass: / 'Well now that's done: and I'm glad it's over.'" This mechanical encounter fails as heterosexual romance: "She smoothes her hair with automatic hand, / And puts a record on the gramophone." The typist's automaton gesture does not make her the "mechanical vamp" Huyssen identifies in Lang's *Metropolis*; rather, her desultory movements evoke a sexual anesthesia not unlike the sexual wounding of the more hidden yet omnipresent Fisher-King.[94] At this juncture, Tiresias confesses his identification with the sexually numb typist:

> (And I Tiresias have foresuffered all
> Enacted on this same divan or bed;
> I who have sat by Thebes below the wall
> And walked among the lowest of the dead.)
> 					(*CPP* 44)

As if using the film "tricks" of flashback and forward motion, Tiresias is both the indifferent bearer of "assaults" in this modern scene and a transgender outlaw who "walked among the lowest of the dead."

Tiresias's sexual reversibility suggests why he must remain an off-screen, impossible "blind" spectator and not a character caught up in the action. The undecidability of his sexual identity goes to the heart of Freud's view of male hysteria as closely related to inversion. From this perspective, Tiresias also numbers among the inverts of Krafft-Ebing's *Psychopathia sexualis* (1886) or falls within Otto Weininger's continuum of "all sorts of intermediate conditions between male and female – sexual transitional forms,"[95] but Eliot seeks to disembody his mythic spectator to veil this possibility. In the myth, Hera blinds Tiresias for claiming authority over "what women want" and for his "false" claim that women enjoy sex more than men. But as a surrogate for the typist on her divan, Tiresias clearly knows this as false.

Capable of projecting himself into the typist's position, Tiresias is contiguous with other female figures etched into the poem, such as "the hyacinth-girl," who elicits and manifests the most sensualized response in the poem ("Your arms full, and your hair wet / I could not speak"). This transient speaker's passion is stopped (like many of the poem's other personages – most violently among them, Philomel with her tongue cut out) so that he/she, in a gender confusion built into the poem, is "beyond or before speech" (Sachs), claiming one of hysteria's "most powerful images – the swelling uterus lodged in the throat."[96] Such stifled speech converges with Eliot's worry about emotions or events that lack an "objective correlative," including perhaps Verdenal waving a lilac branch. Aside from signaling an hysteric mode, the "hyacinth girl," like Tiresias, potentially supercedes gender categories, mediating the male homoerotic desire present in the story of Hyacinthus and Apollo, a myth beloved among Eliot's Decadent predecessors.

Tiresias's blindness further acts out a "refusal" to acknowledge either "castration" or sexual indeterminacy. In this sense, taking on the role of Tiresias, with his vestigial "wrinkled dugs," satisfies a desire both to *become* a female body and then to erase this body by regaining a male form. Eliot's double-oriented figuration not only depends upon the abject female bodies canvassing the poem, but also insists upon renewed virility. The poem plays out its hysteric "Tiresias complex," both by relying upon and disavowing sexual indeterminacy. This dynamic parallels Eliot's relationship to film: he generally disregards it as a medium worthy of serious aesthetic consideration, yet relies upon its techniques to reorder temporality and to imagine the forms embodiment could take.

Perloff observes that *The Waste Land* stands as a "brilliant culmination of the poetic revolution that began with 'Prufrock,'" marking an explicit departure from an avant-garde sensibility (*21st-Century Modernism* 39). She also reminds us that Eliot expresses his antipathy to film in a 1923 issue of the conservative *Criterion* (under his editorship): "'cinema,'" he laments, "'has perpetuated and exaggerated the most threadbare devices of stage expression.'" According to Perloff, he thus disdains "the art form generally held . . . to constitute the new cutting edge" (*21st-Century Modernism* 40). Yet in typically contradictory fashion, Eliot writes that "[i]t is the rhythm, so utterly absent from modern drama, either verse or prose, and which interpreters of Shakespeare do their best to suppress, which makes Massine and Charlie Chaplin the great actors that they are."[97] These two comments encapsulate the intense ambivalence he felt towards film as well as corporeal experience. Chaplin's body is a case in point. Eliot most likely admired him not only as an emblematic inventor of modern rhythm but, with his out-of-date, tattered Victorian garb and genteel inclinations, as resistant to the rabble and rubble of the contemporary. To some extent, Chaplin figures forth Baudelaire's dandy, flourishing as "the last flicker of heroism in decadent ages," whose encounters with mass culture are incongruous and isolating.[98] As the next chapter develops, Stein praises Chaplin's dislocated, and in some sense anti-lyrical, movements. In the manuscript *Waste*

Land, Eliot disparagingly associates the "swarming" London population with "the jerky motions of these ~~poor cheap~~ toys" (37). Given these conflicting encounters with modernity, I propose that Eliot could not entirely erase from his thinking the mechanics of film – with its sensate, rhythmic possibilities, nor could he obliterate his female effigies, from Effie to Fresca. At the same time, his cutting-edge methods of cinematic dissociation are what paradoxically enable Tiresias's ambiguous sexuality and "hysterical" desires.

CINEMATIC UNDERGROUNDS: PROJECTING THE BODY

Both Pound and Eliot, as exemplary high modernists, excavated literary history in part to insulate themselves from the assaults of a "threadbare" culture. *The Waste Land*, in particular, claims its exalted cultural legacy in an effort to stave off identification with the feminized post-war body, but in the process, this legacy itself becomes a form of the repressed making its return. As if in double exposure, Eliot recreates the ghostly motion of those who have died in the war: "A crowd flowed over London Bridge, so many, / I had not thought death had undone so many"(*CPP* 39). These "apparitions" take their place alongside the poem's many uncanny bodies, "neither living nor dead." Even Eliot's literary allusions ultimately function as a series of phantom limbs: they haunt as pieces that mechanically persist even though they have been severed from their original textual "bodies."

Eliot's desire to re-enter the past suggests the work of psychoanalysis, which often configures its enterprise as necessary excavation among the wreckage of memory. In this way, he seems to regard himself as at the cultural helm (albeit precariously) as well as the "medium" sifting through high culture. Likewise, Freud insists that the analyst has the primary authority in digging out and interpreting the patient's "ruins."

The unconscious as archeological site is linked in the modernist imagination with the *place* of cinema. As Laura Marcus observes, silent film itself is "a form of hieroglyphics, a thinking in pictures rather than words," that was "[f]uelled by the discoveries and translations of Egyptologists and the opening of Tutankhamun's tomb in 1922" (*Cinema and Modernism* 102). I have thus far suggested that the cinematic "tomb" perhaps overlays the "chambers" of sensual embodiment in "Prufrock," the passive womb in the "Metro," and the "caverns" swallowing up the spectator in "Hysteria." Further, Eliot was both uncomfortable with and inclined to the "feminine" or passive role, a position potentially assumed by the film viewer in a dark room, "chained" to the flickering of images on the screen. Even more provocatively the screen itself becomes feminized, identified with Prufrock's nervous enervation, and in *The Waste Land*, with the "silent rapture" of a silver screen goddess.

Like Eliot, H. D. identifies a "deterioration" in modern culture, linking it to the specter of mass destruction: "London, Paris and Vienna" all reverberate with a "dissociation or disintegration between soul and body" ("Beauty" 30). Despite H. D.'s affinities with "mythic" modernism, her version of tradition regains sensuous incarnation through cinematic representation. Film's "cutting edge" links her to the past and resuscitates the present. In fact, she configures the film chamber as "a sort of temple" where we are awaiting "our Aeschylus, our Sophocles, our Euripides," a place where a fragmentary "bit of chiffon" can evoke erotic possibility. She describes "sinking" into the cinema as an underground space where fusion and identification transpire:

> Then we sank into light, into darkness, the cinema palace (we each have our favorite) became a sort of temple. We depended on light, on some sub-strata of warmth, some pulse or vibration, music on another plane too, also far enough removed from our real or intellectual stimulus. We moved like moths in darkness, we were hypnotized by cross currents and interacting shades of light and darkness and maybe cigarette smoke. Our censors, intellectually off guard, permitted our minds to rest. We sank into this pulse and warmth and were recreated.[99]

This "sub-strata of warmth" offers an almost pre-symbolic reprieve from the censoring intellect as well as an opportunity to be re-embodied.

In her study of a masochistic film aesthetic, Gaylen Studlar revises Metz's phallic model of cinematic experience, and offers I think a more appropriate direction for understanding H. D.'s own model. Rather than offering a "prosthetic" to cover over castration, watching a film "revives the memory trace of plenitude (screen/breast) and metonymic fetish of the original symbiotic attachment."[100] The resulting "loss of ego boundaries [is] analogous to the child's presleep fusion with the breast."[101] With this in mind, it is striking that Eliot makes the screen a maternal signifier in the excised scene of Aeneas viewing his mother as defamed film goddess. Enchanted with the film theatre's "sub-strata of warmth," H. D. is evidently more inclined to enjoy the symbiotic relationship simulated by the spectator's relationship to the figurative "screen/breast." Yet she too rejects rapturous wholeness or "reality": "we were almost as one" and we are "accepting yet knowing those symbols were divorced utterly from reality." Hieroglyphic signification, as Iampolski asserts, is "established on the ruins, as it were, of mimesis" (*Memory of Tiresias* 27).

H. D. clearly comprehends and internalizes the dissociation Eliot makes so palpable, but she draws upon mechanical reproduction to create new possibilities for somatic experience. For her, poetry's resourcefulness with the fragment is a matter of regeneration: "[t]here is already enough beauty in the world of art, enough in the fragments . . . to remake the world" ("Beauty" 31). These fragments ultimately do not sediment continuity with the past, but rather ameliorate and transform an inevitable dissociation.

In writing about her first dazzled sighting of Garbo in Pabst's *Joyless Street*, she is struck by the opening shot's post-war amputee, "the sombre plodding limp of a one-legged, old ruffian" ("Beauty" 30). Against the backdrop of this dismemberment, Garbo "stepping, frail yet secure across a wasted city" provides H. D. with an erotic cathexis or bisexual possibility: "Beauty and the warrior were at rest" ("Beauty" 30). As will be more fully developed in chapter 4, cinema offers her a locus for shifting between masculine and feminine positions of desire and identification.[102]

Furthermore, H. D.'s work imagines an alternate relationship between viewer and viewed to the ones framed by Baudelaire's "disembodied spectator" and later by Pound's Imagist optics. To illustrate this contrast, the first-person lines "I have seen beautiful feet / but never beauty welded with strength"[103] become in a related poem "our feet cut into the crust / as with spears" ("Huntress," *CP* 24). Consider in another instance the "camera work" in "Loss," her version of the modernist blazon: "I wondered as you clasped / your shoulder-strap / at the strength of your wrist" (*CP* 23). Meter breaks with the change from "clasped" to "strap," suggestive of an erotic dwelling upon the part. H. D. freezes time, but focuses upon an activity and potential for action (as opposed to the passive "to-be-looked-at-ness" Mulvey ascribes to Dietrich). In her "sub-strata of warmth," the division between viewer and viewed potentially breaks down in a projection of a bisexual space, where the body's "beauty with strength" anticipates her idealization of Garbo as "beauty and warrior." If Eliot enters and exits this space with his double-sexed spectator Tiresias, H. D. remains long enough to develop an alternative to Eliot's erotics.

Nevertheless, like Pound and Eliot, H. D. is anxious about embodiment, and she particularly rejects the corporeal when it pretends to wholeness. Thus, she resists the "talkies" because "speaking was too natural." To further complicate matters, she complains of the "mechanically welded" face and voice, the production of "a sort of robot," and in the same breath, declares that she does not "*like* her ghost-love to become so vibrantly incarnate" ("Movietone" 21).[104] A "robot" *and* "vibrantly incarnate"? This contradiction perhaps points up H. D.'s own hesitations in naming her "ghost-love" or same-sex desire. Garbo, H. D.'s screen idol, embodies bisexuality but is more attractive to H. D. when she remains ethereal.

In each of the underground cinemas of Pound, Eliot, and H. D. the fragmented body can be displaced as the "film's body." The material elements that constitute the "mechanical apparatus" of film (celluloid, screen, and projection among them) form part of the vocabulary of resistance to and enactment of a reorganized corporeality. More specifically, "projection," if understood both in its mechanical and psychological forms, can facilitate the hysteric's bisexual fantasy of being both active and passive.

With the film projector in mind (H. D. publishes two "Projector" poems in *Close Up*), she writes that "[t]he fascinating question of light alone could occupy one for ever."[105] She uses similar language to connect herself with Sappho's body: "the history of the preservation of each line is in itself a most *fascinating* and bewildering romance" (emphasis mine). There is an implicit parallel between Sappho's fragile persistence on papyrus and the physical projection of light upon celluloid, what Artaud calls the "epidermis of reality."[106] H. D.'s "romance over ruins" is repeated in the "romance over celluloid,"[107] a material capable of projection and duplication yet flammable and perishable like Sapphic fragments. The projector's light has the ability to cut out, embody, and eroticize a montaged part. While modernist texts often disown the involuntary or discontinuous impulses of corporeality unanchored from a controlling intellect, the body reasserts itself as ghostly other through the skin of celluloid and in its displacement upon the screen. For instance, in Eliot's "Preludes," the ghostly other manifests as a "thousand sordid images" which "flickered on the ceiling."

In a psychophysiological sense, the images that insinuate themselves upon us are processed by the cerebral cortex. The "hyper-suggestibility" that Pavlov detects in hysterics is due, he assesses, to a breakdown in the "alert, active state of the cerebral hemispheres, its unceasing analysis and synthesis of external stimuli."[108] In his study of the effect of overwhelming shock in causing hysteria and war neurosis, Freud is similarly compelled by the subject's loss of "selective" or filtering capacity. He distinguishes the cortical processes as "internal excitations" from the stimuli emanating from the external world. While what he calls the "stimulus shield" protects the self against excessive external agitation, from the "inside there can be no such shield."[109] However, the psyche has "projection" at its disposal as a way of "dealing with any internal excitations which produce too great an increase of unpleasure."[110] In projection, these "excitations" of "unpleasure" are disavowed, treated "as though they were acting, not from the inside, but from the outside."[111] Hence, projection externalizes the unbearable "stuff" of anxiety, and film in this context becomes an ideal forum for disavowal and projection in their psychological meanings.

Projection in its mechanical meaning similarly erodes boundaries. Sobchack argues that the "cinematic apparatus" is an "extension of the spectator's being" so that "[i]t is no accident that the normal mode of perceiving a film is by sitting in front of rather than behind the projector" (*Address of the Eye* 177). In this way, the light projecting upon the screen emanates as if from the spectator's own body. H. D.'s first "Projector" poem eulogizes this process where this light becomes the return of Apollo who "is god and / song" in "new attribute."[112] She interrupts this third-person poem with "I have returned," thus identifying with the position of the projector (Pound's virtual position in "Metro"), imagining herself behind the streaming light as the male god.

H. D.'s "Projector II" allegorizes, if rather heavy-handedly, the film experience as our displaced existence elsewhere, our dissociated bodies coming back to haunt us as if in an hysteric's "séance." In my reading, the Freudian hysteric here converges with mechanistic automatism through the projector itself. Note how in the following portion of her poem, punctuation acts as perforation; her lines are gripped frame by frame as if in the projector's claw:

> we sleep and are awake
> we dream and are not here;
> our spirits walk elsewhere
> with shadow-folk,
> and ghost-beast,
> we speak a shadow-speech,
> we tread a shadow-rock,
> we lie along ghost-grass
> in ghost shade[113]

As prosthetic extension of the body and as a means of psychic excavation with its potential to "raise a living thing / draw to screen," the projector reanimates our "ghost bodies."[114] Film projection makes it possible to inhabit a hybrid consciousness – hypnotized and yet awake. The projector's displacement into another realm as "ghost body," like the displacement of attention enjoined by hysterical response, blurs the boundary between the lived body and the apparition. In other words, the mechanism of cinematic projection visceralizes a "dissociation of sensibility."

Expression and perception, Sobchack argues, are reversible in that, like human beings, film functions as both object and subject. Rather than constituted as only object, film "in the lived sense" also embodies the dislocated viewer. The film and the spectator "meet on shared ground but never identically occupy it" (*Address of the Eye* 23). In this way, the mechanical becomes co-extensive with the body in H. D.'s projector poems and recreates corporeality as both whole and in pieces. In "having sense" and "making sense," film "returns us to our senses" (*Address of the Eye* 13). Yet how are these senses inhabited if the film in question, self-consciously subverts our narrative or sense-making capacities? Sobchack proposes that Léger's *Ballet Mécanique* – a film I examine in chapter 5 – "present[s] a visible but physically uninhabitable world" but one that we still regard "with a situated and finite eye" (*Address of the Eye* 209). However, it is this experimental film's very embodied power that, in rendering the body indeterminate, allows for erotic reinvestments of the sort I will be exploring in later chapters. Film externalizes the dislocating movement of turning the inside into the outside, of transplanting the body of the viewer into the "other." Representations of the "uninhabitable" body "falling to pieces" do not necessarily create a desired aesthetic distance, but by eradicating illusory wholeness or a seamless mimesis, provoke unexpected identifications.

CABINET OF DR. CALIGARI

Projection is a mechanism not only for disavowal but also for identification with the dislocated yet potentially eroticized fragment. In this way, cinema can be the ground for reenacting the "dissociation of sensibility." Such a reenactment transpires within the "uninhabitable" realm of Weine's *Cabinet of Dr. Caligari*, which draws together a number of motifs I have pursued thus far. Sitney regards it as an exemplary "trance film."[115] As a "kind of allegory for film per se,"[116] *Dr. Caligari* reveals how cinema can both anaesthetize and activate sensory experience. It depicts the return of the repressed body, blending the psychoanalytic and mechanistic versions of the hysteric and the reflexive body present in *Secrets of a Soul* and *Mechanics of the Brain* respectively. Further, the film enacts its own masculinity crisis or "Tiresias complex," displaying while simultaneously eschewing an indeterminately sexed body.

Weine includes a framing device in *Dr. Caligari* that Kracauer famously argues "convicted its antagonist of madness," whereas the original story by Hans Janowitz and Carl Mayer "exposed the madness inherent in authority."[117] The framing device purports to give us the point of view of a narrator (the androgynously named Francis), but then undercuts his reliability – he ends up in an asylum while the authoritarian doctor turns out to be a benign figure whose demonic powers have only been hallucinated.

In spite of the framing device's attempt to enforce boundaries between madness and sanity, *Dr. Caligari* (similar to *Secrets*) unfolds like a "hypnogogic hallucination" (Freud's phrase for dream experience).[118] The film's off-kilter psychic landscape created through acute angles, pointedly artificial stage-sets, and dizzying camera movements disrupts naturalist representation and a stable point of view. It thus typifies an avant-garde Expressionist aesthetic in its "sense of crisis and structural ambiguity" along with its perpetuation of an "inability to distinguish clear and fixed identities and events."[119] In a 1922 review, Lionel Landry complains that the film's décor prohibits the "possibility of drawing of two parallel lines"; moreover, its "bewildering vertiginousness of hyperspace is a new hashish that overturns all aesthetic principles."[120] Interestingly, Pound condemned the film because he thought it merely "cribbed its visual effects" from modern art.[121]

The film's "unframed" plot pivots upon the trope of extreme bodily anesthesia. Dr. Caligari, posing as a "showman," induces an hypnotic trance in Cesare, who appears as if he were a trained subject in a behavioral experiment. When not contained by the cabinet, Cesare acts out the doctor's murderous desires. Emerging from a coffin-shaped cabinet, he is stiff, uncertain, his face in heavy make-up and his hair wild.[122] The queer-identified Conrad Veidt plays Cesare, thus heightening the possibility that this body might also be a homosexual body, the "third sex" brought to life.

As emblematic of a disavowed indeterminate sexuality, Cesare (much like Tiresias) is simultaneously absent and present. In his cabinet, Cesare mimics a corpse or automaton, and when he commits the doctor's crimes, a dummy substitutes for him in the cabinet.[123] Meanwhile, the narrator Francis, with the aid of Jane, investigates the suspicious doctor and also saves Jane from Cesare's knife. The film in this way encompasses the hypnotized body and the deranged one, motivated by unconscious impulses, with the "narrator" mediating between them. *Dr. Caligari* thus reproduces a kind of hysterical séance where the narrator as investigative "viewer" may act out all the roles – doctor, somnambulist, dummy, and inmate in the film's "living theater of pathology."

Caligari/Cesare is a familiar version of the modernist double, but particularly striking is the doubling the film articulates between the hypnotized body of the film-viewer and that of the repressed and projected Cesare-side of Caligari. *Dr. Caligari* interpolates the spectator with the spectacle, Cesare – a mute, suggestible specter, a post-war body, knocked out of his senses. The film foregrounds the ghostly element of the bodies projected on the screen as well as in the act of perceiving these bodies; under hypnosis, or alternatively at the cinema, the "body itself submits to a sort of temporary depersonalization which takes away the feeling of its own existence."[124] (We recall as well Eliot's credo of "depersonalization" or even H. D.'s "temple" of "half-light" forgetfulness.) As Kracauer assesses: "The moviegoer is much in the position of a hypnotized person. Spellbound by the luminous rect-angle before his eye – which resembles the glittering object in the hand of a hypnotist."[125]

The film makes somatic displacement, like the hypnotic effect it induces, visible. Outside is not readily distinguishable from the inside, and the framing device underscores these overlapping borders: if Francis is truly the mad one, whose desires are being enacted by Cesare? His own? Our own? By the time we see Francis confined in an asylum, the film has already drawn us into identification with him and his "projections" upon Caligari. Thus, our suspicions of the doctor linger – suggestive of a cultural legacy of suspicion of medical practices aimed at controlling the body. Particularly in post-war Germany, the use of "suggestion" and hypnosis increasingly carried ominous associations. *Dr. Caligari* provides a metaphor for the Cartesian body awry, the dangerous consequences of detaching physical movement from consciousness. In effect, it recreates modern "reflex theory" where "even when the brain is wholly out of action or destroyed and the indi-vidual remains unaware of the whole process" (McDougall), the body still performs involuntary responses. Are we, *Dr. Caligari* asks, acting without will and gratifying the wishes of another's more powerful body? Does the film, as Kracauer interprets it, predict the rise of the fascist body? Is the modern subject merely an automaton or somnambulist, mesmerized by the "whir and thud of various hypnotic appliances"? ("Beauty" 25)

Dr. Caligari expressly reveals the dangers of hypnotism, inclusive of the methods practiced by both psychoanalytic and experimental psychology. Yet it also points towards another version of the hypnotic as not fully governed or limited by rational or fixed categories. Under hypnosis or in a trance, the body potentially loses its "essentialist" cohesion and sexual-ity. The "body etherized on a table" may enact what the mind does not otherwise acknowledge, including its "ghost-love" or sexual indeterminacy.

Marianne Moore perhaps recognizes some of this loosening of "realms of experience" in *Dr. Caligari* when she writes to Bryher in 1921. After declaring that she has "seen a wonderful movie" and encouraging Bryher and H. D. to see it, she specifically exults in the film's "entrancing" geometries:

All vertical lines slant, and the shadows on stairs, on attic floors and through casements, are wonderful. Cesare, the somnambulist on appearing – although standing with legs side by side – looks as if he had but one leg. Later, when he is roused from a trance in total darkness against the back of his cabinet, wedge-shaped lights slant down from his eyes at [Jane], the heroine, the exact shape of a dagger that he uses later when intending to kill her.[126]

Moore is characteristically giddy about artifice, abstract shapes, and dismembered parts. The dagger-shaped [Jane] as fetish doubles for the threatened phallus. Cesare is not only an emblematic automaton but also a male hysteric, his dagger a sign of his castration and sexual anesthesia.

Does Cesare's indeterminacy, however, exclusively indicate castration and a culturally despised passivity? Through its elaborate doubling and reversal of identities implied by the alternating pairs Cesare/Caligari, Caligari/Francis, Francis/Cesare, Jane/Cesare (along with the viewer doubled with each one), the film exposes that the body is malleable and transitive, mutating into both passive and active roles. Further, it both elicits and dramatizes "projection" through "permeability," the way "exterior facts are continually being transformed into interior elements and psychic events are exteriorized."[127] In this way, the film's Expressionist aesthetic does not promote "distantiation" but rather creates an intra-subjective space, not unlike H.D.'s depiction of cinematic experience as an in-between zone for "ghost bodies."

In *Dr. Caligari*, the body is never full-frontal or whole. As Moore observes: "the forms of the satanic doctor and Cesare often slant up in a shot deliberately out of focus."[128] These bodies exist therefore in their exaggerated partiality. The film's "ghost realm" allows the witnessing of the stylized "not-me" on the screen, opening up horizons of so-called "undepictable" embodiment. Part of the appeal of experimental film, as we will see in the various effects that modern poets reproduce, is its ability to refashion the kinesthetic body. Virginia Woolf interprets what is really a flaw in the print she saw of *Dr. Caligari* – a "shadow shaped like a tadpole" at the edge of the screen: "For a moment it seemed as if thought could be conveyed by shape more effectively than words."[129] Woolf's "tadpole moment" alerts her to the spectral materiality of film. Modern lyric bodies, written over by shock and dissociation, are re-pieced together through montage; this process may revive sensation *and* recreate fractures. Like the dissociated bodies of *Dr. Caligari*, Eliot's Tiresias belongs to an "uninhabitable" landscape. He can thus express and disown multiple, fractal desires, including those based on identification with femaleness.

The mechanism for simultaneously identifying with and disavowing reappears in Eliot's comments about Stein's poetry. On the one hand, "[it] can, for anyone whose taste has already been disciplined elsewhere, provide a valuable exercise for unused parts of the mind."[130] On the other hand, he writes that there "is something precisely *ominous* about Miss Stein . . . Moreover, her work is not improving, it is not amusing, it is not interesting, it is not good for one's mind. But its rhythms have a peculiar hypnotic power not met with before. If this is of the future, then the future is, as it very likely is, of the barbarians."[131]

Eliot's double response to Stein inadvertently registers the "ominous" ghosting represented in *Dr. Caligari* as well as his own hysteric montage poetics. Indeed, Eliot and Stein may be "two sides of the same coin" (*21st-Century Modernism* 45). *The Waste Land* is surely reverent of high culture, but it also mauls and mutilates its booty. Among the poem's fragments are clips of "non-sense," which subvert mimesis and even resemble the rhythms invoked by Stein's cinematic poetry. With his hypnotic and disjunctive rhythms – "Twit twit twit / Jug jug jug jug jug jug"; "Weialala leia / Wallala leialala"; "la la"; "Drip drop drip drop drop drop drop"; "Co co rico co co rico," it looks as though Eliot were exercising "unused parts" of the dissociated mind. Such hieroglyphs invoke somatic fragmentation or what Kristeva would call "semiotic motility," showing us that we are "not quite one" with either the word as substance or the evasive image;[132] these syllables vibrate with reflexes, motions, and "the irregularity of the part."

In the next chapter, I return to hysteria and automatism, but focus upon Stein's "intercepted cinema of suggestion" that "urges the reactions of the reader."[133] Stein's hysteric repetitions become occasions for comedic gesture and the pleasures of amnesia. She replaces the indeterminately sexed body of Cesare with herself as Caesar, cutting into myths of cohesive embodiment.

CHAPTER 2

"Delight in dislocation": Stein, Chaplin, and Man Ray

I cannot repeat this too often any one is of one's period and this our period was undoubtedly the period of the cinema and series production. And each of us in our own way are bound to express what the world in which we are living is doing. ("Portraits" 177)

Stein "cannot repeat too often" that her writing had been "doing what the cinema was doing." Kenneth Macpherson, editor of *Close Up*, recognized Stein's cinematic style when he widely recruited "anything [she] might send" because "the kind of thing [she] write[s] is so exactly the kind of thing that could be translated to the screen" (*Cinema and Modernism* 14). Stein appeared in three issues of the journal, and in 1927 her portrait "Mrs. Emerson" (first published in 1914) was placed next to a piece by Man Ray about his first full-length experimental film, *Emak Bakia*.[1] The journal's juxtaposition of these seemingly disparate texts opens up an unexpected dialogue between them.

This chapter traces a number of significant parallels between Stein's writing and experimental film in this dialogue between Stein and Man Ray. The cinematic aspects of her work have been overshadowed by her more explicit relationship to modern painting. While cubism could effectively "prevent a coherent image of reality,"[2] cinema made palpable a serialized embodiment and time-sense, finding its equivalent in Stein's anti-narrative disjunctive forms. Thus, *How to Write* presages: "Painting now after its great moment must come back to be a minor art."[3]

Modern painting constituted one aspect of a continuum that, in Stein's search for an aesthetic of dislocated embodiment, involved a radical movement away from art governed by the single frame, or even the multiple frames permitted by photography, and towards the successive flux of film. Transcending the limits of the frame, the medium of film embodied Stein's notion of movement as "*a groping* for a continuous present" and "an inevitable beginning of beginning again and again and again."[4] This "groping" suggests a bewildered tactility, a nuance directing us to Stein's fragmented, repetitive, often comic, textual bodies.

Stein praised cinema for its dual ability to focus and fragment attention through the continuous supplanting or erasing of one image by another, its ability to capture the temporal displacement of "existing." In cinema, every successive image "has each time a slightly different thing to make it all be moving" ("Portraits" 179). Stein's "continuous present" or inevitable "beginning of beginning again" enacts what Maya Deren later defines as the "telescoping of time" in "a continuous act of recognition," which functions "like a strip of memory unrolling beneath the images of the film itself, to form the invisible underlayer of an implicit double exposure."⁵ With the relentlessly rolling picture, memory becomes a form of disintegrative erasure where "one second was never the same as the second before or after" ("Portraits" 195). In the same vein, Jean Epstein (a film theorist contemporary with Stein) proclaims: "there is no real present . . . [it] is an uneasy convention. In the flow of time it is an exception to time"; "cinema," he continues, "is the only art capable of depicting this present as it is."⁶

In using the elements of succession and variation, amnesia and recurrence, film simultaneously seemed to solve and heighten the apparent conflict between inanimate mechanical reproduction and "existing," and as such it emerged as Stein's prototypic medium for embodying the vital crisis of a "continuous present." Stein's refusal to exalt the European literary past came with a willed forgetfulness – as if the shock of the present obliterates the capacity or desire to remember – to produce an expansion of bodily, sensory pleasures. In contrast to Eliot's monumentalism, Stein recognized in cinema her own desire to depict the "present as it is" and to expose the falsity of history as a linear, teleological progress with its concomitant faith in transparent mimesis. As an "outlawed" art (to use her word from "Composition as Explanation"), the medium of film incarnated a "solution" to the burden of inherited tradition as well as a means of escaping constrictive forms of female embodiment. Her sensate lyric body and her remaking the figure of the hysteric depended upon the disintegration of memory and attention.

This chapter explores the fragmented, repetitive bodies of Stein's poetics in light of the techniques developed in modernist experimental films. I argue that Stein's depictions of the hysteric and comic body emerged in part out of her sense that the First World War signified an absolute rupture from previous modes of embodiment and memory. Her conception of hysteria as a form of mechanical, circumambulatory movement converges with modern comedy, iconicized for her by Chaplin's gestural slapstick.

His spasmodic gait, perfected during the First World War, simulated a traumatized body: the gesticulatory tics and motor incoordination of either the war neurotic or the male hysteric. At the same time, "[Chaplin's] basic principle of never going beyond the moment," a principle operating as well in Stein, fashioned a comic body propelled by amnesia or the "sin of repetition."[7]

The considerable attention Stein devoted to the often interchangeable, cultural representations of the hysteric and the comic originated in her early study of experimental psychology at Radcliffe in the 1890s (which culminated in her first publication, a co-authored article, "Motor Automatism"), and in her abiding fascination with Chaplin, whose bodily semiotics she associated with her poetry. I further argue that the hysterical and comedic body overlap through Charcot's formulations and Henri Bergson's definitions of comedy. Finally, I trace Stein's cinematic revision of these cultural tropes of bodily dislocation by juxtaposing Man Ray's *Emak Bakia* with her "Mrs. Emerson."

INCOMPLETING NARRATIVE: "THE WHOLE IS INSIDE THE PART"

Before I develop the specific relationships between the diverse figures of Stein, Man Ray, and Chaplin, it would be useful to rehearse how Stein's poetic practice more particularly converges with film montage. This convergence links the modern dislocated, automaton body with the subordination of plot to somatic, disjunctive rhythms, and comedic derailments. Invoking rhythm and the "concept of intervals" to explain montage, Eisenstein explicitly claims that poetry emerges from the "reconstruction of the event in montage fragments" where "the plot is no more than a device" ("Dialectic Approach" 60–1). Echoing Flaubert's ideal of a book "about nothing," charged by the "force of its style," Eisenstein emphasizes that dramatic tension revolves around "the methodology of form – not content or plot!" ("Dialectic Approach" 49). The kinship between Stein's poetry and film hinges not only upon the subordination of plot to rhythm, but also upon the fragment in its jostling of other fragments, and its consequent evisceration of attention and memory. Stein's montage insists upon the body in flux, composing itself through "collision" and the corporeal part as detachable from the whole.

As discussed in the last chapter, the shocks of modernity not only made the "possibility of lyric poetry questionable" but also led to the recreation of new lyric modes. According to Benjamin, Baudelaire's "traumatophile" capacity to place "shock experience at the very center of his artistic work" both enabled the poet's unique success and raised the stakes for the modern poem, forced to compete with the emergent film medium ("Motifs" 163). Elaborating further, Benjamin observes that cinema more capably induces and simulates an automatic "reaction to shocks," since the "rhythm of production on a conveyer belt is the basis of the rhythm of reception in film" ("Motifs" 175). Chaplin's body in *Modern Times* (1936) is notably co-extensive with the factory's assembly line.[8]

Stein's aesthetic delights in "shocks" and repetitive rhythms. She alludes, however, to the potentially numbing effects of mechanical repetition in *The Making of Americans* (1903): "If they get deadened by the steady pounding of repeating they will not learn from each one even though each one always is repeating the whole of them they will not learn the completed history of them, they will not know the being really in them."[9] When composing *Making of Americans*, Stein still aimed toward "completion" rather than the fractal. Paradoxically, her self-acknowledged "failure" to produce "a complete history of everyone who was or is or will be living" animates her portraits.

By 1908, Stein began to doubt the idea of producing the "complete history" and began her portrait writing. As will be clarified through "Mrs. Emerson," Stein's portraiture renders the automatism stemming from overwhelming shock the "kin-aesthetic" ground of her modernism. Like Benjamin's cinematic "conveyer belt" with its mechanical repetition, Stein's writing reproduces a shocked body, not "deadened" but renewed by movement where "each time the emphasis is different just as the cinema has each time a slightly different thing to make it all be moving" ("Portraits" 179). Moreover, Stein's fractured "time-sense" reflects the way modernity's accelerated pace impinges upon attention and "remembrance" (the crystallizing of experience through contemplation or narrative). As Benjamin notes, reflex takes over as protection against excessive stimuli. In this way, modern consciousness can be said to approximate the mechanism of the camera's fluttering shutter, where attention is held temporarily at the expense of contiguity. Visceral shock jolts the body into grasping experience while simultaneously threatening to obliterate its memory. By contrast, Proustian memory (as Benjamin portrays it) commits itself to disinterring what is uncovered by the "mémoire involuntaire," that which has "not been experienced explicitly and consciously, what has not happened to the subject as an experience" ("Motifs" 160).

If it is necessary for Proust to chance upon an object that will unfold unconscious memories, Stein makes a comic art out of willed stumbling

for its own sake. Plot becomes a ruse. Her writing forgets itself as it per-
ambulates. In this way, Stein enacts a consciousness embodied through
automatic gesture and reflex, immersed in the porous breakdown of continuity and the body's cohesion. Her writing – a kind of shock-absorber –
resists remembering: "We in this period have not lived in remembering, we
have living in moving being necessarily so intense that existing is indeed
something, is indeed that thing that we are doing" ("Portraits" 182).

From Stein's phenomenological standpoint, "memory plays no part" in
the corporeal experience and act of attention of "feel[ing] anybody else."
Knowledge and embodiment dissipate under the glare of reconstructive
temporality. As if echoing Stein, Merleau-Ponty succinctly states: "To perceive is not to remember" (*Primacy of Perception* 13). The act of remembering
for Stein encumbers vital "existing," whereas cinematic movement provides
"a movement lively enough to be a thing in itself moving" and "does not
need that there are generations existing" ("Portraits" 171). Deleuze similarly
observes that "cinema does not give us an image to which movement is
added, it immediately gives us a movement-image" (*Movement-Image* 2).
With Stein, movement becomes "the thing in itself" so that in her "cinema,"
the image, even when repeated, is always in the process of being erased rather
than being fixed. Stein's attempt to evoke the "act of existing" in writing
comes up against the piecemeal act of reproduction in what amounts to a
continuous mode of double exposure where the body emerges in reiterated
fragments and traces.

If Stein considered the time-sense of *Making of Americans* an "assembling
the whole thing out of its parts," what inevitably emerges is how the "whole
thing" resides in the holographic "part." Precluding ultimate cohesion, Stein
articulates in "Salad Dressing and an Artichoke" this governing motif: "A
whole is inside a part."[10] The act of assemblage indicates the disassembled
character of the "whole," composed of contiguous parts where "no two
pictures are exactly alike" ("Portraits" 177). While a painting may be seen as
a whole in a moment in time, cinema cannot be reflected upon "all at once,"
but rather through what Loy calls the "disintegration and reintegration" of
parts in Stein's "intercepted cinema of suggestion."[11]

The "period of the cinema" consequently became for Stein the period of
the volatile fragment, of the reflexive body that does not quite hold together
or congeal. "[I]t is not possible," she writes of her era, "to choose a completed sentence a completed thing."[12] Oddly, Stein responded with terror
the first time she saw her "speaking body on screen" in a 1930s newsreel. This
visual "shock," she elaborates, was due to "a slightly mixed-up-feeling": to

watch a "talking picture" was discordant, "never having heard anybody's voice speaking while a picture is doing something."[13] I speculate that Stein's difficulty emerged from seeing herself as a whole animate body, a reproduction that did not match her sense of dislocated corporeality. Moreover, Stein delights in the fragment as the whole, or bodies erotically "together in pieces."[14] While film perpetuates a continuous motion or present, its smoothness relies upon repetition and displacement.

ALL OF A PIECE: WARS SHE SAW

Wars I Have Seen makes evident that Stein regarded the two major state prosecutions at the end of the nineteenth century, namely the Dreyfus Affair and the Wilde Trial, as resonant with her own anxieties about naming, camouflage, and visibility. These trials were paradigmatic for her of the movement from a comfortable "naturalism" to the identification and suspicion of "unnatural" bodies. Stein anxiously reflects: "I had never conceived the possibility of anybody being in prison, anybody whose business it was not naturally because of natural or accidental crime to be in prison . . . Oscar Wilde and the *Ballad of Reading Gaol* was the first thing that made me realise that it could happen, being in prison."[15]

As a Jewish lesbian, she was not likely to feel like an inheritor of literary tradition or "naturalist" theories of the body. Even though Stein probably never discussed the exact details of her sexual orientation, her intimate relationship with Alice B. Toklas was an "open secret." After all, the inclusion of Toklas in the Stein's Paris menage in 1910 caused a rupture with her brother Leo and ultimately led to the international bestseller, *The Autobiography of Alice B. Toklas* (1933). Nevertheless, her lesbianism placed her outside both the mainstream and the male line of succession, an "outlaw" position that fueled her competition with her male peers, particularly Eliot, Pound, and Joyce. In order to seize a place for her own dislocated body, Stein replaced the nineteenth-century vision of an omnipotent hero with herself as a comic transgender Caesar, wielding her scissors upon history. As such, she fights a campaign to "kill off" (as she puts it) the corpus of the nineteenth century with its myths of progress and heroic conquest.

While written during the Second World War, *Wars I Have Seen* casts the First World War as a significant part of the "epistemic" upheaval which changed the world where everything had been "all of a piece" into one *in* pieces.[16] The hero on his mountain top, surveying a scene amenable to will and "perspective," could no longer be sustained:

There was nothing more interesting in the nineteenth century than little by little realising the detail of natural selection in insects flowers and birds and butterflies and comparing things and animals and noting protective coloring nothing more interesting, and this made the nineteenth century what it is, the white man's burden, the gradual domination of the globe as piece by piece it became known and became all of a piece, and the hope of Esperanto or a universal language. (*Wars* 10)

Stein further asserts that it took until 1943 for the nineteenth century "to slowly come to an end" when, through the technology of mechanical reproduction, "anybody can hear everything and everybody can hear the same thing, so what is the use of conquering" (*Wars* 10). Esperanto gives way to the circular motion of the film loop as well as to a categorical crisis for the dominant body or "the white man's burden." Stein implies that modern war was not only culminating evidence of the breakdown of a universal body politic, but paradoxically "brings us up to the present because it heightened the act of living" (*Wars* 12).

With its mass production of munitions and new mediating technologies, including airborne warfare and poisonous gas, the First World War broke with the formal conventions of previous wars. As a "total war," the First World War established both a distance and applied, as it were, a zoom lens to the individual experience of horror, making Stein's numbing tautology convincing: "the time-sense that is at present the most troubling is the thing that makes the present the most troubling." In its simultaneous absorption of the spectator into a "continuous present" of moving images, the viewing of film, to some extent, paralleled the experience of the "shell holes" of the battlefield. Paul Fussell argues that the First World War was a theatrical rather than a cinematic war.[17] Yet the technology of cinema also found metaphors in the technologies of warfare. The early tinting of lenses suggested the discoloration of mustard gas, while the cranking and loading of the camera mimicked the readying of the machine gun and canon. Both the machine gun and the camera had the ability to shoot on a semi-automatic basis; moreover, these "prosthetic" devices required (and merged with) the hand to produce rapid fire. The impact of cinema was felt, if not fully theorized, within the theatre of war.

If Stein's "imaginary cinema," as Sitney calls it, "is not essentially a mode of visual representation" but rather enacts a "flexibility of rhythm," she also plays with and against the regimentation of bodily comportment in war (*Modernist Montage* 163). The body became a machine in the corpse-grinding war, and recalling the stupor of Cesare in *Dr. Caligari*, the soldier was often kept "marching unto somnambulism."[18] King Vidor's *The Big*

Parade (1925) recapitulates what Bryher calls the "sweeping of everyone into something they did not clearly understand, the enlistment through sheer mass hypnotism."[19] Vidor's film approximates kinetic rhythms – from the recruiting anthems that successively lead to foot tapping, to marching in parade, to the snaking convoy to the front, to the body in close-up pulled, as if mechanically, into no man's land.

One of Stein's two unpublished film "scenarios," "A Movie," probably inspired by her friend Apollinaire wounded in battle, particularly illuminates the interface between war and film. It begins with an enigmatic "sound poem,"[20] followed by a comic narrative of an American painter in France who becomes a taxi driver and then a driver for the French war effort. Stein's "hero" trains his Bretonne housekeeper to be his automaton double (a comic version of Cesare) and to assume his place at the front when he wants to sleep. "A Movie" thus becomes a feminist reworking of the male's responsibility to go to war. (The maid's shouldering of war duty mirrors Stein and Toklas's driving during the war for the American Fund for the French Wounded). At one point in the scenario, the "funny little taxi" has a "grand smash," yet by the end, it has been "mended." The "movie" concludes with a comic parade:

After many other adventures so famous has become the american painter, Bretone femme de menage and taxi that in the march under the arch at the final triumph of the allies the taxi at the special request of General Pershing brings up the rear of the procession after the tanks.[21]

Stein thus injects comedy into the war's lexicon of somatic trauma and dissociation. During the First World War, the film theatre (rather than the drawing-room where women "talk of Michelangelo") epitomized the way bodies "come and go" (as Sassoon's "Picture Show" would have it). Film was an important vehicle of both propaganda and comic distraction. Max Linder and Chaplin comedies that showed the buffoonery of battle were particularly popular at home and among the troops.

War heightened Stein's sense of how "bound" we are "to express what the world in which we are living is doing," shaping her recreation of automatism and hysteria, those specters at the periphery of nineteenth-century Enlightenment ("Portraits" 177). Within Stein's version of embodiment, much like the perspective of a soldier in the trenches, no plateau or privileged position exists above or outside of the moving "thick of things." Both Stein's physiological research and her experimental poetics, as we shall see, located the body as bound, if not unified, by "an enormous number of threads" to the phenomenal world.[22] Cinematic representation likewise confirmed that "space is traversed and inspected" rather than regarded from a superior or fixed point, and implicated – at least for Stein and Man Ray – the body's propensity to fragmentation.[23]

While many other texts might serve to demonstrate Stein's cinematic writing, I invoke "Mrs. Emerson" (written during the First World War) as exemplary of "a collection of repeated references," filmicly scored."[24] Stein's "willingness to detach words from referential meaning" and to arrange them in abstract designs can overshadow the sensual dimension of her poetics.[25] Her writing often mimics scientific "objectivity," or as I earlier posed, actively *resembles* narrative logic. What we must not lose sight of, however, is the fact that Stein extends Eliot's imperative of "impersonality" to a comic extreme; much like Keaton's deadpan yet absorbent face, her very withholding is an imprimatur of bodily receptivity.

Attempting to account for Stein's apparent disembodiment, Catherine R. Stimpson suggests that Stein writes "a ghost-ridden, ghost-written language" where "[s]oma must become somagram," an encrypting of bodily identity, specifically her "monstrous" weight and lesbianism.[26] Rather than masking her corporeality, Stein defines it as unfixed and fragmented, yet intensely materialized; her erotics accordingly are charged with detours. Nicholls writes that Stein "invents another version of modernism by circumventing the image altogether and by exploring precisely that self-sufficiency of language which had seemed decadent to the 'Men of 1914.'"[27] In this way, "Mrs. Emerson," like many other Stein pieces, is abstract while being urgently visceral: "I do not share unless you are coming unless you are coming to caress country" ("Emerson" 28). The line practically tumbles over its insisted reciprocal desire.

Many avant-garde films could be invoked in connection with Stein, yet Man Ray's anti-mimetic *Emak Bakia*, created as an example of "automatic" filmmaking, is particularly apt in that it typifies a tension between abstraction and embodiment prominent not only in Stein but in most experimental films of the period. And, in accord with Stein's writing, *Emak Bakia* dramatically places the "human body on equal footing with objects."[28] Man Ray insists upon the materiality of film, aligning an often "shocking" montage with his own body, willing its construction.

Neither Stein nor Man Ray in their apparently "pure" anti-narratives forsake corporeality; rather they focus upon the body in its momentary segments, reflexes and gestures. As popular icon, Chaplin is here the copula binding the gestural body, modernist comedy, and experimental representation. North writes that Chaplin's success among writers in fact resides in his ability to overcome the "gap between the sense and the abstract intellect."[29] Like Chaplin and Man Ray, Stein abandons the illusionist ambitions of theatre, and instead foregrounds non-purposive gestures and their mechanistic reproduction. By triangulating these figures, I reveal how Stein bridges or combines an embodied slapstick with an apparently abstract film aesthetic, producing an "hysteric" body that claims its non-normative sexuality.

Stein, as I have said, devises an aesthetic indebted to film's capacity to track the shock of a "continuous present." Similarly, Man Ray describes *Emak Bakia*, as adamantly serial and partial, as "[a]series of fragments, a cinepoem with a certain optical sequence [that] make up a whole that still remains a fragment" ("Emak" 40). A still of repeating frames from the film illustrates this emphasis on the part (fig. 5).

Just as Man Ray is "adamant that there be no script,"[30] no progress in *Emak Bakia*, "Mrs. Emerson" perversely breaks from linearity in a repeating, circular "communication":

If heating is beside the meal and the selection of masterpieces makes communication, communication is ardently rechosen, communication is suddenly respected, communication is suddenly resumed, communication is suddenly rested, communication is suddenly respected, communication is suddenly chosen communication is suddenly chosen. (25)

The passage "selects" its parallel abstract strips, its measured "beats," while dramatizing the passive or involuntary. This "scene" resembles the opening of *Emak Bakia*: a brightly lit merry-go-round calls attention to the distracting and inscriptive capacity of film, what Hedges calls "its own status as writing motion in lights (kinematographein and photo-graphein)."[31] In "Mrs. Emerson" what "is suddenly chosen" is a merry-go-round score knitting together words buried in other words in a linguistic dislocation (as with "rested" in "respected"). Visual correspondences supercede the visibility of signification. Stein reminds us that her language is "selected" and "chosen," yet both words recur so often here and elsewhere that they begin, paradoxically, to appear automatic.

Stein's phenomenology can be traced to a textbook by William James, *The Principles of Psychology*, assigned to her at Radcliffe in 1893. Here James asserts what would become a touchstone in Stein's writing: "Selection is the very keel on which our mental ship is built."[32] He also asserts that in the process of selection "forgetting is as important a function as recollecting"

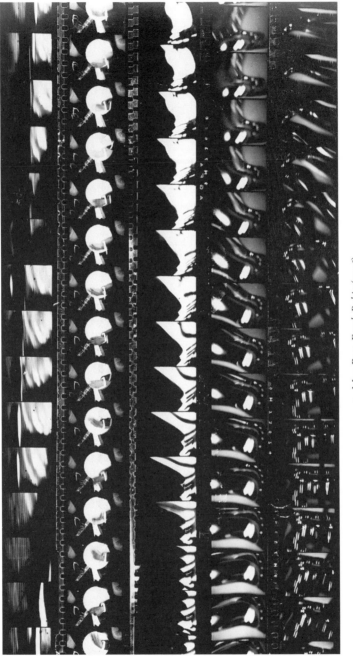

5. Man Ray, *Emak Bakia* (1926).

(*Principles* 445). If "framing is the art of choosing" (*Movement-Image* 18), the necessary exclusion required in film composition, then both "Mrs. Emerson" and *Emak Bakia* demonstrate that the mounting of a shot necessarily partakes of the selective body's finitude, dislocated by a complex intertwining of reflexive and voluntary action.

While both the titles "Mrs. Emerson" and *Emak Bakia* (the name of the estate of Man Ray's patron derived from a Basque proverb meaning "leave me alone") evoke proper names, neither follows a single character.[33] In Stein's piece, a first-person voice operates as a free-floating, even anaesthetized, body of shifting negations and denials ("I do not believe in wretches") without a narrative; this plotless body reverberates as a "collection of repeated references" to an ongoing tension without objective correlative ("I am getting rather anxious. / Really I am getting rather anxious") ("Emerson" 18, 25, 28). Her "I" alternates with a "she" or "he" so that pronouns become merely instrumental or "somagrams" (to re-use Stimpson's word) in an elaborate comic séance. Nowhere does "Mrs. Emerson" (only a ghost "Transcendentalist") materialize, and "characters" appear and quickly evaporate. "Mrs. Evangeline Henderson came in" only to vanish immediately ("Emerson" 23). But where one body disappears another transmogrifies.

Like Stein's writing, Man Ray's film denies a stable "bodily ego" through its own ghostly effects, including the use of spiraling smoke to make still objects look mobile. Further, both "Mrs. Emerson" and *Emak Bakia* resist propriety and continuity, and yet self-consciously foreground the evanescent and fragmentary rhythms of embodiment. Hedges points out that "pellicule" (Latin for "little skin") designates "the idea of celluloid as skin," a fact resonant for Man Ray who "would typically write on his film"; given this technique, each shot marks a temporal shedding of bodily surface.[34]

Although Man Ray's literal relationship with Stein ended abruptly, their estrangement casts further light upon their artistic crossing. Sitney observes that Man Ray's photograph (used for the frontispiece of the successful *Autobiography of Alice B. Toklas*) features Alice in a doorway and eclipses Stein "deep in shadows as she sits writing at a table" (*Modernist Montage* 153). And Man Ray recollects in his *Self Portrait* that his "portraits of Gertrude Stein were the first to appear in print, to give her small circle of readers at the time an idea of how she looked."[35] At this time, he exchanged some prints for Stein's "portrait of [him] in prose"; with the subsequent publication of *The Autobiography*, she required publicity photographs, but when Man Ray sent a "modest bill," Stein refused payment on the grounds that "we were all struggling artists" (*Self Portrait* 260). Their exchange of portraits paradoxically led to an irrevocable breach in their relationship.

Stein's meeting with Chaplin, on the other hand, suggests an imagined identification. She viewed her art as a necessary precursor to his, or at least as a simultaneous mirror of it, recording Chaplin's emblematic significance for the Parisian avant-garde crowd: "The clowns had commenced dressing up in misfit clothes instead of the old classic costume and these clothes later so well known on Charlie Chaplin were the delight of Picasso and all her friends."[36] Stein extolled Chaplin's early gestural films before and during the First World War rather than his later more narrative ones. After they met in the 1930s, Chaplin recounted Stein's admiring imago of his work as a kind of avant-garde film loop: "She would like to see me in a movie just walking up the street and turning a corner, then another corner, and another" (quoted in *Modernist Montage* 159). In her estimation, she vies with the comedian for an inaugural role: "'he wanted the sentiment of move-ment invented by himself and I wanted the sentiment of doing nothing invented by myself'" (quoted in *Modernist Montage* 160); implicitly, she saw herself as initiator of both. However, Chaplin gets the last word in his 1954 talkie, *Limelight*, where in half-ironic homage he repeats Stein's hieroglyphic "A rose is a rose is a rose."

Stein's admiration of Chaplin might be linked to her notion that the "rhythm of anybody's personality" overrides the sentiment of narrative since "events are not exciting" ("Portraits" 174). In this context, she praises, for instance, Dillinger for his "intensity" rather than for his actions ("It wasn't what Dillinger did that excited anybody"). Similarly, she is attracted to the anti-hero Chaplin who frequently, especially in his early films, assumes an "outlaw" persona, antagonizing and evading the police through innovative bodily maneuvers.

When Chaplin screened in Paris, "'the little tramp'" or Charlot as he was called, emerged as "the new hero of the literary avant-garde," the very "embodiment of modernity" in his "resistance to meaning."[37] Benjamin observes that Chaplin's films "stand in complete opposition to films based on action and suspense."[38] In 1928, French film critic Robert Aaron paired Chaplin with Man Ray in their "delight in dislocation" as "they create peculiar breaks in the narrative, each of which strangely never returns to what went before."[39] Likewise, Jean Epstein remarked upon Chaplin's "pho-togenic neurasthenia," observing that his "entire performance consists of reflex actions of a nervous, tired person."[40] And for Louis Aragon, such narrative and somatic dislocations reflected the "discovery of the mechan-ical and its laws . . . to such an extent that by an inversion of values each

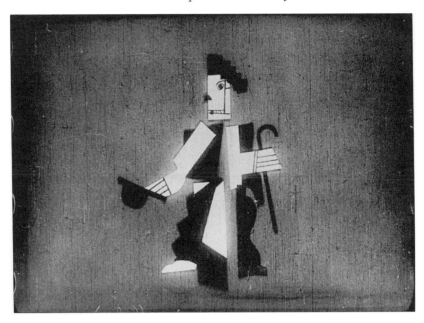

6. Fernand Léger, *Ballet Mécanique* (1924).

inanimate object becomes a living thing for him, each human person a dummy whose starting-handle must be found."[41] Chaplin often becomes a "dummy," subverting the very "laws" that seem to govern him.

This small compendium of Chaplin as dislocated body makes sense of his consequence to avant-gardists like Stein and Man Ray. Accordingly, Fernand Léger memorializes the cubist Chaplin as living machine in *Ballet Mécanique* (fig. 6).[42] So too, one shot in *Emak Bakia* uses a diagram of a jumping man from one of Marey's motion studies, a borrowing that accents automatic locomotion in dissolution. Importing one of his collage-sculptures made of cogs and wheels for another image, Man Ray's ambivalent sign *Dancer / Danger*, made kinetic through the spiraling of smoke, suggests Léger's earlier mechanical and endangered (about to fall apart) body. This mechanistic trope owes precedence to Chaplin himself, who Benjamin reflects, is "his own walking trademark" with his spasmodic, non-purposive gait.[43] Deleuze regards Chaplin's volatile trajectory as a function of time: "Charlie is caught in the instant, moving from one instant to the next, each requiring his full powers of improvisation" (*Movement-Image* 169).

In counterpoint to his often expanded mobility, Chaplin at times appears cataleptic, unable to hold himself up and at the mercy of others; suddenly animated, he can as suddenly lose all motor command. "'[It seems that Chaplin] cannot walk. He cannot put one foot in front of the other. He cannot move forward,'" Willy Hass remarked in 1923.[44] In other words, Chaplin operates like a disabled Model T, unable to be cranked up and started. He is thus akin to the prototypic modern hysteric suffering alternating symptoms of paralysis and unexpected movements, or in Pavlov's dichotomy, between states of extreme inhibition and excitement. Interestingly, William James earlier described a condition that would be exhibited by Chaplin, observing that when a person loses attention, he is somehow immobilized, or partially anesthetized, so that "he cannot start" (*Principles* 134).

Chaplin's elliptical gait is symptomatic of the modernist obsession with non-teleological movement, and specifically Stein's somatized rejection of a monumental, static past. Her peripatetic lyric movement, turning a corner and then another corner, reflects the modernist drive to uncover an embodied practice of knowledge, aptly summarized by Nietzsche's notion that "[p]hilosophy itself was to be written walking – or, preferably, dancing."[45] Such modern embodiment roots itself in discontinuity and the corporeal "incapacity to grasp all": "There is nothing beyond the multiplicity of perspectives, positions, bodily forces" (*Volatile* 128).

Yet Nietzsche's delight in dance misses the nuance introduced through film's exposure of the body's loss of control and propensity to automatism. Chaplin may assume the sudden ability to skate with acrobatic grace in *The Rink* (1916), but his elastic body is never rendered entirely volitional (fig. 7). Similarly, in the opening of *The Tramp* (1916), the comic is successively knocked down by a motor car; no sooner does he elaborately dust himself off, than he is once more struck down, as if only aware of and purely reflexive to the discrete moment. Each repeated motion forgets itself: Chaplin must continually "pull himself together" with each tumble. As in avant-garde film, "what matters" in silent film comedy is "that the units follow each other uninterruptedly, not that their succession implements a plot."[46]

Chaplin is in this way representative of Stein's circumlocutory comic mode, her swerving from plot, her ability to "keep centre well half full" ("Emerson" 23). Indeed, locomotion, intentionally of a mistaken or circular kind, recurs in her writing. These comic one-liners exemplify her pleasure in resemblance and rejection of continuity: "Call me semblances. / I call you a cab, sir," she quips in *Lifting Belly* (32). "What do you do to stop. / What do you do to go on. / I do the same," she continues, followed a few lines later with "what do you do to turn a corner" (*Lifting* 23). Stein's language, like Chaplin's circular movements, characteristically encourages

7. Chaplin in *The Rink* (1916).

rhythmic propulsion along with relapsing (this process of "stop," "go on," "the same").

The modern trope of the evasive hysteric, from Charcot's "theater of living pathology" and its series of portraits to Freud's frustrated attempt to "daguerreotype" Dora, shapes the dislocated bodies of Chaplin and Stein. Chaplin's "broken stroke" belongs to the iconography of hysteria, reverberating as a crisis in sexual embodiment, particularly of masculinity, related to war trauma and to other historical upheavals, including women's greater mobility, often coded as hysterical "acting out." Hake writes that Chaplin's "renunciation of male sexuality" was apparent to German audiences during and after the First World War: "Hunched over, Chaplin stands as if he is always ready to receive a blow . . . This experience of alienation, and the unconscious protest against it, finds an emotional outlet in what could be called male hysteria."[47]

This assessment of the emasculated "hysteric" comedian resonates, of course, beyond German reception. Stein's awareness of the Wilde trial and the Dreyfus Affair, as I have implied, made her aware of the dangers inherent in questioning normative identity. Chaplin further highlighted the possibilities of "traumatophile" automatism as well as of gender indeterminacy in somatic comportment. The modern figures of the hysteric and the automaton, as we have seen in the previous chapter, became means for mediating anxieties about sexual definition.

Stein early on in her studies at Radcliffe invoked the hysteric as cultural commodity. Nevertheless, she purposefully ignored the psychoanalytic model of the unconscious and the primacy of dreams (so prominent in surrealism).[48] In contrast, Man Ray was much more closely affiliated with the surrealist version of the unconscious. His work, however, also calls upon the "mechanistic" vision of the comic/hysteric body prominent in Stein.[49] Rather than the hysteric formulated by Freud, Stein's diagramming of reflexive responses in *Making of Americans* anticipated Pavlov's lesser-known version of hysteria: "the excitatory processes are weakened, while the inhibitory prevail."[50] Further, her training with experimental psychologists, William James and Hugo Münsterberg, molded her view of the reproducible hysteric body.[51]

The multiple cultural renderings of the hysteric act as a tributary of influences, indirect and direct, upon Stein. Her unique reformulation of the wandering womb syndrome as peripatetic dislocation found confirmation in the "hysteric" methods of film where the comic body is montaged "together in pieces" (*Lifting* 27). A version of the comic/hysteric drifts, detached from plot, into the end of "Mrs. Emerson" where an "inhibitory" ennui of refusal erupts:

> This is a little climb in when.
> Not to-day.
> Yesterday, not some day.
> Yesterday.
> Wretched creature.
> Wretched reason for winter.
> Really not at all.
> ("Emerson" 29)

Stein's "wretched creature" is suspended ghost-like, akin to "the apparitional lesbian" who is "always somewhere else."[52] Detached from any comprehensive plot and thriving by negation, the body Stein depicts exists as if only through the flashing hints and gestures of experimental film.

Man Ray's mistress and model, Kiki of Montparnasse, the most recognizable "whole body" in *Emak Bakia*, turns "upside down" at the end of his film, her vacancy and distraction, italicized by staring eyes painted on her eyelids that suddenly, mechanically flutter open. Kiki as female "dummy" underscores the problematic representation of woman as passive object. In another sequence, Man Ray submerges her head in the liquidity associated with dreams: he reverses the subordination of somatic rhythms to the mind, but nevertheless conflates the feminine with unconsciousness. Somnambulism and waking are often interchangeable in Stein's writings so that in "A Movie," her Breton proxy has an edge over the sleeping painter and yet crashes the taxi, or in another portrait, "[s]he could be as she sleeps and as she wakes all day."[53] Stein's early experiments with automatism pursue these vacillations between will and loss of control, rewriting the hysteric as open to unexpected fracturing and adjustment.

MOTOR AUTOMATISM AND HYSTERIA

The dislocated bodies or comically "wretched creatures" Stein constructs in her lyric experiments resonate with those she discovers in Chaplin and Man Ray. Likewise, these bodies correspond to the hysteric and automaton figures she studied while completing her experiments at Radcliffe in the 1890s. Hysteria, she was to conclude, is contiguous with automatism, a link that Charcot had adumbrated through his "portraits" of patients, who were compelled to enact repetitive postures and gestures. As Pavlov further conjectured, such hysteric bodies were prone to amnesiac states and high levels of suggestibility. William James tied the automatism described by Charcot with mental "distraction," confirming the "connection between the apparently anaesthetic skin and the mind in some Salpêtrière-subjects" (*Principles* 133). Hysteria apparently imprinted mental processes upon bodily surface. James, echoing Janet's insistence upon mental weakness, provided Stein templates for understanding the dislocated body, as when he characteristically writes that "an hysterical woman abandons part of her consciousness because she is too weak nervously to hold it together" (*Principles* 137).

However, distinct from her teachers, Stein avoided confounding hysteria with femaleness. Rather than "womb wandering," Stein's 1903 flaneuse Melanctha possesses a polyvalent sexuality and meanders of her own volition.[54] While Freud fixated on sexual anesthesia as central to hysteria, he also suggested that the hysteric attack was a kind of autoerotic indulgence in so far as it spelled a refusal of normative coitus. From this point of view, Chaplin's gait, turning one corner and then another, transforms into a free-floating erotogeneity. Chaplin frequently engages in autoerotic poses, giddy with his own self-caressing; his famous "ballet" in *The Rink* is charged with erotic "impossibilities." Likewise, Stein's sexual body purposefully resists codification and assumes the fluidity she finds in cinematic depictions of comic, dislocated corporeality. Paradoxically, Stein's model of hysteria invokes automatic repetition as a mode of forgetful, non-teleological sexuality.

After conducting experiments in automatic writing under the supervision of Münsterberg, Stein's 1896 "Motor Automatism" (published in the *Harvard Psychological Review*) belonged to the emergent field of experimental psychology. She published this piece with Leon Solomons along with an addendum "Cultivated Motor Automatism: A Study of Character in its Relation to Attention," written solely by Stein. These articles tie bodily sensation with a "crisis of attentiveness" and memory.[55] Ultimately, Stein's comic sensibility relies upon acts of willed automatism that heighten the dislocations within reiterative gesture.

In order to more fully comprehend Stein's link to both Chaplin and Man Ray, I will look in some detail at these first publications. Wagner-Martin describes these scientific articles as an early discounting of "automatic writing."[56] Stein confirms her disavowal in *The Autobiography*: "Gertrude Stein never had subconscious reactions, nor was she a successful subject for automatic writing."[57] As I have mentioned, she endorses William James's notion of "consciousness as a selecting agency" (*Principles* 85). Yet what these articles make evident is the convergence of this selective capacity with bodily automatism.

Thus while "Motor Automatism" insists upon the "limits of normal automatism" and the acts of so-called normal people as opposed to those of hysterical subjects, the article determines that automatism permeates everyday activities of the non-hysterical subject.[58] (Stein and Solomons, I should note, are the sole "normal" experimental subjects in the first article.) It is this everyday automatism, always available as a mode of being as it were, that will become visibly realized in Chaplin's comedies and Man Ray's film. However, Stein and her co-author more dramatically link hysteria to the phenomenon of "double personality," the experience of dissociation often figured by the detachment of motor impulses from proprioceptive consciousness ("Motor Automatism" 9).

Stein's conclusions about automatism and double personality, intriguingly, are well illustrated in Chaplin's films, where he often plays two different characters or reveals this division within the "self-same" body, abandoning clear boundaries. In *Behind the Screen* (1916), for instance, he becomes inexorably bound to the switch that controls a trap-door or oubliette he "operates" so much so that he oils his body as well as the forgetful mechanism.

Significantly, Stein and Solomons anchor "the feeling of personality" in an "expectation represented by the group of feelings we have called, for convenience, the motor impulse" ("Motor Automatism" 26). They assert that the "writing of a word at dictation" involves "the formation of a motor impulse" that "consists of a melange of visual and kinesthetic material – whatever ordinarily innervates our writing – as well as other elements not easily described" ("Motor Automatism" 14). The absenting of consciousness from motor impulses leads then, as the article formulates it, to automatism, or in more severe cases, to hysteria. This enmeshment of the psychical with the kinesthetic as well as the rift between these domains constitutes the basis for the "cinematic" comedy Stein realizes in her lyric experiments.

In the first experiment, Stein and Solomons instruct their subject to "get himself as deeply interested in a novel as possible" and at the same time to ready himself to take dictation ("Motor Automatism" 10). They conclude that "although the arm does not really move spontaneously, yet any movement once started up tends to continue of itself" unless "deliberately checked by the will of the subject" ("Motor Automatism" 11). Induced automatic writing leads to an experience of the "extra personal" or, as Stein and Solomons more bluntly put it: "It is not he but his arm that is doing it" ("Motor Automatism" 11). The subject, when sufficiently distracted, loses a sense "of intention or desire," producing the "tendency to movement from purely sensory stimuli, independent of any conscious motor impulse or volition" ("Motor Automatism" 12–13). Such dissociation between "personality" and attention forms an early example of the automatism issuing from modernity's sensory bombardment, prefiguring Chaplin's jerky reception of shocks as well as his autoerotic seizures of pleasure.

Furthermore, the experiment implies not only that bodily movement or reflexive sensation can become separated from consciousness, but also questions the efficacy of memory and its coincidence with motor impulses in the act of writing. Knowledge emerges through "sensations from the arm"; the subject

was conscious that he just had written a word, not that he was about to do so. While mere scribbling went on the subject would scarcely be conscious that he was doing anything . . . Small words would usually be completely written before the subject knew about it. ("Motor Automatism" 12–13)

These observations denote ruptures or "lapses in consciousness"; only belatedly does the subject remember the activity of his arm. Thus memory does not function to bolster identity, but contributes to unfastening it.

Knowledge comes late, after the fact, in the "memory after image" ("Motor Automatism" 15). Similarly, simultaneous action – reading and taking dictation at once – further fractures the body, both attentive and distracted in its dispersal among activities. This is a familiar comic scenario for an over-stimulated modern subject. In *Sunnyside* (1919), Chaplin exhibits forgetfulness and even autoerotic absorption resulting from multiple actions: herding cows while reading a book, he follows his motor whims and wanders into a ditch. This kind of "intended" distraction is most evocative in the context of Stein as well as theories of hysteria. Freud considers "seemingly accidental clumsy movements" as "governed by an intention . . . which cannot in general be credited to our conscious voluntary movements"; they have, he assesses, "their violence and their unerring aim – in common with the motor manifestations of the hysterical neurosis."[59]

"Motor Automatism" is Stein's attempt to separate voluntary from involuntary processes as well as to "cultivate" both. While written collaboratively, the essay is prescient of Stein's penchant for repetition, and her endowing this poetic strategy with somatic impetus and "unerring aim." For instance, consider this characterization of "unconscious memory and invention":

> A marked tendency to repetition. – A phrase would seem to get into the head and keep repeating itself at every opportunity, and hang over from day to day even. The stuff written was grammatical, and the words and phrases fitted together all right, but there was not much connected thought. The unconsciousness was broken into every six or seven words by flashes of consciousness, so that one cannot be sure but what the slight element of connected thought which occasionally appeared was due to these flashes of consciousness. But the ability to write stuff that sounds all right, without consciousness, was fairly well demonstrated by the experiments. ("Motor Automatism" 21)

In this passage, repetition does not provide cohesion; rather it appears to produce a series of discrete reflexive motor impulses. While Stein will blatantly disavow repetition ("I am inclined to believe there is no such thing as repetition"), she nevertheless relies upon its rhetorical doubleness as both present and already absent, as that incremental variation that occurs with each new "insistence that in its emphasis can never be repeating" ("Portraits" 166, 171).

Such "insistence" or "marked tendency to repetition" discombobulates sense rather than fortifying it; "flashes of consciousness" dilate and disrupt coherence. Anticipating Eisenstein's delineation of a montage technique exceeding plot, "Motor Automatism" claims that grammatical writing which "fits together" is not necessarily "connected thought."[60] A shifting in tempo and rhythm reflects a visceral fluctuation between distraction and belated attention, demonstrated by this semi-confessional observation: "Miss Stein found it sufficient distraction often to simply read what her arm wrote, but following three or four words behind her pencil" ("Motor Automatism" 21). By writing about herself in third person, she enacts an automatism that bears out her "scientific" findings.

The language of "Motor Automatism" echoes William James's "Stream of Consciousness" (1892) where consciousness is "a kaleidoscope revolving," with the flight between repeating images taking precedence over a resting upon a final or static assemblage of them.[61] His depiction of a mobile consciousness engaged in continual rearrangement, governed by shifts between "magical rapidity" and "relatively stable forms" also anticipates Man Ray's "kinematographein" and experimental rotation of the camera in *Emak Bakia*.[62] Stein and Solomons in this way anticipate the kinesthetic vertigo of anti-narrative cinema.

In her aim to "cultivate" conditions of dislocated embodiment, Stein's follow-up article, "Cultivated Motor Automatism," includes more subjects. This investigation of automatic writing delineates two types (foreshadowing her attempt to classify all human types in *The Making of Americans*): Type II is more prone to automatism, and hence "much nearer the common one described in books on hysteria" than Type I.[63] Assuming a kind of Charcotian role, Stein oscillates between guiding the hands of her Type II subjects and releasing them to their own impulses. She choreographs or cultivates the "decidedly rhythmic character" of their motility:

> At first there was a continued return to the old movement or to no movement, but gradually came an *aimless indefinite movement*, then again the old, then the new, and then again an uncertain movement, then a more decided revision of the new, then a slight return to the old, like the struggle between two themes in a musical composition until at last the new movement conquered and was freely continued. ("Cultivated" 28; emphasis added)

Her "Type II" proto-hysteric subjects verge on "aimless" slapstick. She describes one such subject, dynamized by mechanical automatism: "He had a spontaneous movement of a circle made with the swing of the whole arm. He began these circles, gradually increasing in speed, not breaking into any other movement, just a continued rush of circles" ("Cultivated" 32). (This kind of "arc de cercle," Freud alleges, signifies an "energetic disavowal" of sexual intercourse.)[64]

"Real automatism," Stein and Solomons assert, occurs "whenever the attention is sufficiently distracted" ("Motor Automatism" 14). Hysteria, at the far end of Stein's continuum with daily automatism, becomes truly the favored disease of modernity with its onslaught of shock and stimuli. Furthermore, if hysteria, as Stein and Solomons reiterate, is a "disease of attention," then film becomes an aesthetic equivalent with its paradoxical capacity to hypnotize and to diffuse sensory experience, to hold and to divert attention ("Cultivated" 26).

Stein and Solomons thus summarize their findings: "Our problem was to get sufficient control of the attention to effect this removal of attention. In hysteria this removal of attention is effected by the anesthesia of the subject. We would not, the histerique can not, attend to these sensations" ("Cultivated" 25). In its distinction between willed and involuntary loss of attention or anesthesia, the article points towards the avant-garde's purposeful oscillation between control and "purposeful derangement of the senses" (to invoke Rimbaud's influential phrasing). This oscillation appears at its apex in *Emak Bakia*, which progresses through broken synapses and flashes rather than narrative connectives.

Significantly, Stein functions in the first experiment as "double personality," as both "directorial" subject and experimental "subject." Man Ray likewise directs *Emak Bakia* and represents his role as director with an image of his own eye superimposed upon a shot of the camera. Chaplin, apart from his stint with Mack Sennett, also assumed the dual role of directing and performing in his films. His very comedic movements manifest an intricate cooperation between automatism and will, between what, as Merleau-Ponty puts it, "we carry with us, in the shape of our body, an ever-present principle of absent-mindedness and bewilderment" and the conscious manipulation of the corporeal (*Phenomenology* 27). As "operators," Stein and Solomons will their own distraction, yet they also suggest that "habits of attention" often partake of involuntary impulses, a dialectic that underpins both *Emak Bakia* and "Mrs. Emerson."

Anticipating her writing experiments where she simultaneously engages in "loosening" and directing attention, Stein's "experiments" in physiology underscore the shrinking line between attention and bewilderment.[65] The object or gesture in isolation – like the man's swinging arms in "Cultivated Motor Automatism" – is part of an unfolding montage, necessitating its own evanescence and susceptibility to distraction. Or as Merleau-Ponty describes the fragile, contingent motion of attention: "the miracle of consciousness consists in its bringing to light, through attention, phenomena which re-establish the unity of the object in a new dimension at the very moment when they destroy it" (*Phenomenology* 32).[66] Stein's own process of "bringing to light" and subsequent destruction of phenomena, her method of illuminating an object only to eclipse it, recurs throughout her writing. It is perhaps most recognizable in *Tender Buttons*, a text rampant with dissociation ("a closet does not connect under the bed") and comedic slippage geared to reorient vision by blocking it. For instance, under the heading "EYE GLASSES" she blinds: "A color in shaving, a saloon is well placed in the centre of an alley."[67]

As I have earlier suggested, Benjamin correlates modernity's eviscerated attention specifically with cinematic experience. Asserting an apparent contradiction between distraction and habituation – "the distracted person, too, can form habits" – Benjamin argues that "[r]eception in a state of distraction . . . finds in the film its true means of exercise" ("Work of Art" 240). Yet the "exercise" of mechanical reproduction can heighten modes of attention. In this way, avant-garde film sought to use the medium to jolt or propel the spectator into altered states and conditions. William James inadvertently invokes this agenda when he refers to the "cure" of some Salpêtrière-subjects; along with "suggestion," he states, "[a] still better awakener of sensibility is the hypnotic trance . . . in which the lost sensibility not infrequently becomes entirely restored" (*Principles* 132).

Oddly, the technique for inducing a state of "distraction" entails procuring a dogged single-mindedness, an ingredient also evident in comedy. For instance, the reunited country couple on their way to a fairground in the comic portion of F. W. Murnau's *Sunrise* wander entranced with one another into city traffic, magically oblivious to the barking horns and the threat of oncoming traffic. This "process shot," enhancing the film's dream-like artifice, uses two different pieces of film, "pasting" the figures crossing the street on to another strip of film that acts as background. Many other examples might be drawn from the opportunistic "tricks" of silent film comedies (in addition to Chaplin's). While much less "mechanistic" in his physical bearing, Harold Lloyd, for instance, often enlists his concentrated distraction. In *Never Weaken* (1921), he maneuvers an unfinished skyscraper by focusing on one immediate obstacle at a time; or in *Safety Last* (1923), he famously hangs by the minute hand of a building clock for what seems to be a "continuous present." In such instances, the passivity of the comic combines with his bodily pragmatism, the moment-to-moment ability to cope with every new turn of gravity's screw.

The "dream state" likewise encouraged by Man Ray's *Emak Bakia* exists side by side with its "awakening" measures, including the literal shaking of the camera in some sequences. When James admits that "[t]here is no such thing as voluntary attention sustained for more than a few seconds at a time" and that such attention is a "repetition of successive efforts," he is unwittingly adumbrating the conditions of film reception (*Principles* 273). The close-up exemplifies cinema's ability to block what "the aims of the surrounding world force on our involuntary attention" through the focusing and isolating of detail.[68] At the same time, the act of framing and selecting intimates all that threatens to over-saturate or blind attention. Stein's experiments at Radcliffe offered her an early opportunity to visualize the psychological equivalent of these film techniques in the hysteric, often comic shifting between will and automatism.

Initially as scientist, Stein assumed the incipient transgender role of "Caesar," a nickname she dons that diversely alludes to her imperious bodily presence, to the epidermal act of "cesarean section" as alternative to conventional childbirth, and to a cinematic cutting and scissoring of words. Building upon her early role as "experimenter," she recreates hysteria as amnesiac bliss in "seizures" and in discontinuous parts, elliptically (even epileptically) demanding: "connect me in places" (*Lifting* 25). The name Caesar nicely matches with the hypnotic Cesare in *Dr. Caligari*. In her Radcliffe experiments, she operates on both sides of the cabinet as doctor and as passive automaton.

COMIC/HYSTERIC BODIES: CHARLOT/CHARCOT

Hysterical bodies suffering the "disease of attention" at Charcot's Salpêtrière Hospital deflect narrative, enacting the non-purposive gesture characteristic of what I am calling modernist comedy. Elisabeth Bronfen summarizes Charcot's reading of the "hysterical body" as a "somatic performance of traces of a psychically traumatic shock" that disrupts coherent plot: "It articulates through an unjust image, speaking deceptively, obliquely."[69] The body abstracts itself as "the radical nothing that experiences of loss entail."[70] It is this "radical nothing" that converges with the comic mode typified for avant-gardists by Chaplin in his "resistance to meaning." Suggestively, the second phase of the hysterical attack, as mapped by Charcot, is the "period of grand movements, of contortions and body dislocations," what he "came to call the clown phase (période clonique)."[71] The hysteric body, framed by Charcot and his followers, becomes in this light closely related to the comic body in modernist cultural discourse.

Henri Bergson's extended essay "Laughter: An Essay on the Meaning of the Comic" (1911) confines itself mainly to the theatre for its exempla, but nevertheless reveals how these two bodies, the comic and the hysteric, overlap in the cinematic aesthetics of Stein, Chaplin, and Man Ray. (Bergson, incidentally, had been among the attendees at one of

Charcot's public lecture/performances of hysteric bodies.) As if echoing the research findings of Stein and Solomons, Bergson considers the body's repetitive automatism as signifying the loss of an otherwise necessarily "constant alert attention" to the needs of the moment and as a slip into absentmindedness.[72] In such a state, the body comically abjures its "tension and elasticity" in unwilled mechanical acts: "The attitudes, gestures and movements of the human body are laughable in exact proportion as that body reminds us of a mere machine" (*Laughter* 32).

Bergson's description squares with Chaplin's comic techniques, which often replicate mechanical behavior. In *The Rink*, Chaplin turns his cane into a crank, a prosthetic extension of his body, using it to wind up his rival. This "winding" is common for Chaplin who himself moves as if he has been wound up; *Modern Times* will exaggerate this condition when he unknowingly ingests great quantities of cocaine instead of salt.

Comedy, Bergson further contends, "consist[s] in looking upon life as a repeating mechanism, with reversible action and interchangeable parts" and persists only as life "forgets itself" (*Laughter* 94). The forgetful body as "repeating mechanism" engages in its "automatic ballet," Deleuze's phrase describing *The Italian Straw Hat* (*Movement-Image* 42). Chaplin exemplifies the automaton, without will and vulnerable to breakdown, but he just as suddenly becomes balletic, sweeping others into a hypnotic state (much in the way that Stein assumes dual roles in her scientific experiments). For instance, in *Behind the Screen*, he engages in a self-consciously conventional fight, with its automatic chase, knockdown, and bouncing back. By mechanically and then gracefully mirroring the boxing moves of his rival, Chaplin temporarily mesmerizes his opponent into bodily forgetfulness.

As I have already noted, Stein often poses as an amnesiac, cultivating strategic repetition both to italicize the dissociated part and to focus upon the present: "Now to date now to date. Now and now and date and the date."[73] In the same portrait, she proclaims: "Let me recite what history teaches. History teaches" ("Completed Portrait" 25). The joke here relies on the way her repetition undermines itself as the sentence jerkily springs back to its initial iteration. Stein refers to a camera's attentive "selection" in its circular use of aperture and emphasis: "Shutters shut and open so do queens. Shutters shut and shutters and so shutters shut and shutters and so and so shutters and so shutters shut and so shutters shut and shutters and so" ("Completed Portrait" 21–2). Caught up in the rhythmic blinking of the shutter mechanism itself, the passage intentionally neglects to provide a clearly delineated image but rather creates the forgetfulness of a "continuous present." She counts and hypnotizes, as if using a metronome in one of her physiological experiments: "One. / I land. / Two. / I land. / Three. / The land." Ironically, she derives this semaphore from Longfellow's poem memorializing Paul Revere's night ride, but here she disrupts smooth movement.

In order to prevent an otherwise blurring effect, "the strip of film," as Münsterberg delineates, "must be drawn before the lens by jerking movements so that the real motion of the strip would occur in the periods in which the shutter was closed."[74] Experimental film – and Stein's writing – foregrounds this "jerking" mechanical movement, unnoticeable in conventional narrative film, which as Garrett Stewart puts it in another context, represses the material joining of images in a "successive overlapping flow."[75] Stein's language at times itself verges on opaque blur, borne out by her elimination of commas because, as she puts it, "they stopped you." The present urgency of "[n]ot to-day" ("Emerson") as well as the phrasing of "shutters shut and so and a so" ("Completed Portrait") accommodates the "[c]lick, clack, lack – in that double absentation of the forgone and the just gone past."[76]

With the bodily pun of convulsive "shudders," Stein's portrait of Picasso emerges in autonomic flickers: "He he he he and he and he and and he and he and he and and as and as he and as he and he" ("Completed Portrait" 23). Incremental, mirroring repetition of this kind (and the giggling "he he he he") calls for supreme attention by the reader and threatens a comic forgetfulness, the consequence of slipping up by covering the same ground. Yet in repeating, Stein enacts the infinitesimal recuperations necessary for slapstick. According to Bergson, such useless activity, the result of becoming a "repeating mechanism," turns comic, albeit abyssal, pivoting on the "radical nothing" of hysteria: "To cover a good deal of ground only to come back unwittingly to the starting-point, is to make a great effort for a result that is nil" (*Laughter* 80).

The abstract opening of "Mrs. Emerson," both abstract and irregular, is a particularly striking example of how Stein requires our "distracted attention." Her reiteration of "the regular way" ironically forges the hazardous twists and turns of the moment:

The regular way of instituting clerical resemblances and neglecting hazards and bespeaking combinations and heroically and heroically celebrating instances, the regular way of suffering extra challenges, the regular way of suffering extra changes the regular way of submitting to examplers in changes, the regular way of submitting to extraordinary celebrations, the certainty, because centre well half full whether it has that to close when in use, no not repeatedly, he has forgotten. ("Emerson" 23)

In "celebrating instances" and "neglecting hazards," the unanchored subject in this prose poem paragraph "has forgotten." Repetitions compel attention to "suffer" and "submit" to "extra challenges"; the wayward circle closes just when the "way" has been forgotten. The transcendent singularity of the nineteenth century ("heroically and heroically") has "submitted" to divagatory automatism. As with Stein's rhythmic discontinuities in the passage above, Chaplin's forgetful body belies its strategic miscoordination. By "neglecting hazards," he ignores and yet embodies the ever-present possibility of coming apart, stumbling into an unexpected abyss or "suffering extra changes."

Stein's famous tag – "A rose is a rose is a rose" – becomes a form of "regularity," a perpetual film loop of comedic and useless gesture (memorialized by Chaplin in countless films). It also suggests "la construction en abîme," a term "borrowed from the culture of heraldic insignias, where it referred originally to a coat of arms that contained a copy of itself reproduced in a smaller size" (*Memory of Tiresias* 36). Directing us to the disassociated "hologramic" impulse in her work, Stein's line acts as "heraldic insignia" ("when this you see remember me") of the literary tradition she buries (the associations of the rose with female chastity). The part or increment refers to a whole that is first and foremost a part. As in the passages from "Picasso: A Completed History" and "Mrs. Emerson," she provokes the "abyss" or quick sand of reiterative fragmentation.

Bergson defines such deliberate aimlessness and partiality of gesture as that which expresses itself "without aim or profit" and which "slips out unawares, automatic . . . [as] an isolated part of the person is expressed, unknown to, or at least apart from the whole of the personality" (*Laughter* 129–30). Chaplin's body of "interchangeable parts" bespeaks how mechanical behavior can reflect an excess of "somatic compliance," the gesture erasing or impeding purposeful movement. By obsessively repeating articles and divesting a sentence of a subject in a phrase such as "[a]nd also and so and so and also" ("A Completed History"), Stein also enacts a comic and hysteric rhythm that suspends resolution, does not "get anywhere"; there is perhaps no surprise in finding "so" in "also," but in sequencing and parsing these phrases she makes deliberately unexpected re-turns and compels attention by subtly altering her phrasing.

Calling *Emak Bakia* "automatic cinema," Man Ray similarly interprets "the sentiment of movement" as selectively fractured in a turn away from mimetic expectations. While not obviously comic, this avant-garde film diverts itself in the repeating fragment, "turning a corner, then another, and another." The comedic, exemplified here through Chaplin was, as I have indicated, a significant resource for avant-garde filmmakers. Artaud more generally writes of *The Seashell and the Clergyman*: "The mechanics of this type of film, even when applied to serious subjects, is modeled on something rather similar to the mechanics of laughter."[77] Man Ray's film likewise devolves upon the mechanics of the comically bewildered body.

In the bodily syntax of hysteria, like that of the comic gesture or any of its "grand movements," the part becomes detachable and reiterable as, according to Grosz, "[t]he intensity of one zone is displaced onto another bodily zone" (*Volatile* 77). In Grosz's revision of hysteria, "there is a lability of meaning for the various bodily organs, zones, and processes. Any one zone of the body can, under certain circumstances, take on the meaning of any other zone" (*Volatile* 78). Both Stein and Man Ray transpose bodily regions to produce a liberating forgetfulness, a kind of anesthesia that permits the erotic and bodily equivalent to aesthetic dislocations, or "the coming together of disparate surfaces" made possible by experimental montage.[78]

EMAK BAKIA / "MRS. EMERSON"

Man Ray explains of *Emak Bakia*: "its reasons for being are in its inventions of light-forms and movements, while the more objective parts interrupt the monotony of abstract inventions or serve as punctuation" ("Emak" 40). In the heightened "shutter" action of the film, body parts punctuate other defamiliarized images. For instance, a shot of Kiki with her arms on a table is followed by a swish pan of rotating lights reflected and blurred by mirrors. The film further "invents" almost every available cinematic device, including superimposition, out-of-focus, animation, reversal, double-exposure, and rayograms, in order to degrade the mimetic image and to underscore its mechanical materiality, its moment-to-moment piecing.[79] Throughout, a "revolving kaleidoscopic" movement, in particular night shots of a brightly lit merry-go-round, decenters as it hypnotizes the viewer to the point of dizziness or anesthesia. This physical effect approximates the "neonate" plunged in its "whirring, ever-changing flux of experiences" (*Volatile* 31). Each film rhythm registers as gestural fragment.

After its swirling title shot, *Emak Bakia* begins with a side-view of Man Ray looking through a camera with several lenses that rotate; a reflection of the cameraman's physical eye, upside down and directed at us, is superimposed on one of the lenses (fig. 8). In this way, *Emak Bakia* capsizes what would soon become in mainstream film the 180 degree rule that decrees that the camera must "deny its own existence as much as possible, fostering

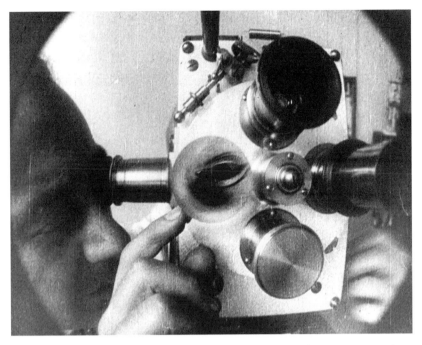

8. Man Ray, *Emak Bakia*. Still of camera of multiple lenses with eye superimposed.

the illusion that what is shown has an autonomous existence, independent of any technological interference, or any coercive gaze."[80]

At the outset of the film then, Man Ray draws attention to the fact, as Sitney observes, that "films are shot through lenses," and represent the world seen "through layers of glass" (*Modernist Montage* 29); multiple lenses and filters mechanically intervene between eye and object. The camera does not see or attend, but disassembles. *Emak Bakia*, "automatic" as it claims to be, purposefully reinforces this trope of the disassembling eye throughout. Later, for instance, Man Ray's blinking eye (like the multi-eyed camera) superimposes upon a car headlight, further melding the human and the mechanical into anthropomorphic mutant. In this sense, Man Ray as director undermines his own cohesiveness, placing his fractured body on a par with the film's representations of the fragmented female body.

Emak Bakia foregrounds the cinema as the machine of our time: capable of rendering simultaneous experience, testing the threshold of interior and exterior realms, and producing the mechanically-lived body through motor impulses anchored, but not quite firmly and cohesively, in consciousness.

This body remains without full volition. In his recounting of being driven in his patron's racing car, Man Ray describes his risks in making the film as bodily ones, as vacillating between chance and conscious will:

> I was using my hand camera while [Rose Wheeler] was driving eighty or ninety miles an hour, being pretty badly shaken up, when we came upon a herd – why not show a collision? I stepped out of the car, followed the herd while winding up the camera and set it in movement, then threw it thirty feet up into the air, catching it again. . . . There were other more carefully planned sequences; a pair of lovely legs doing the popular Charleston dance of the day, the sea revolving so that it became sky and the sky sea. (*Self Portrait* 220)

Man Ray initiates or plans a "collision" and then tosses his camera into space, as if enacting a comic stunt as well as the automatism which, according to Stein and Solomons, is concomitant with voluntary and willed impulses. *Emak Bakia* vivifies this detachment of automatic gesture from consciousness, reinforcing that "the whole is inside the part."

By visceralizing the fragment as reflexive motion, the film reveals the body as bound to a principle of comic bewilderment. In all of the film's "useless" activity, it swerves away from cohesive narrative, and in the process, meshes the abstract with the somatic. One sequence features a close-up of a series of women's legs, only seen partially, as they step off a car's running board; as if to disembody their movement, we then see a quick ghost image of the same legs. Belated recognition is part of the film's erasable memory. Through double-exposure, Man Ray underscores the autonomic processes or the idea of "double personality" where even if the primary consciousness is unaware of an object, it "gets a 'negative after-image' of it when he looks away again, showing that an optical impression has been received" (James, *Principles* 138). The double-exposed spectral legs of *Emak Bakia* recur in their disappearance and non-purposive motion. In another shot, Man Ray presents a sensual image of the legs and torso of a sun bather (never the whole body) on the beach; in the next shot, he focuses on the rising and lowering knees moving up and down as if automatically. The abstracted image merges with one of somatic immediacy.

The rapid motion of the camera, sometimes spun or shaken, denotes a body both orchestrating its convulsions and "neglecting hazards." After an image of the ocean turning and revolving, inverting the sea with the sky, the camera reveals fish swimming under the water in double exposure. The final shots of the film present Kiki's upside-down gaze, further suggestive of the unconscious and the dreaming body. By reproducing the opening shots of his own eye displaced upon the camera lens, he blurs the divide between cameraman or "operator" and specular subject. Yet Man Ray presents Kiki as figuratively dead. As she opens her eyes, he raises her from the dead. She has been an unconscious automaton, and now upsets our expectations of bodily inertness, again demonstrating the "double personality" that Stein refers to in cases of hysteria. And, as Benjamin suggests, we become implicitly such automatons when viewing a film, subject as we are to the modern "disease of attention." *Emak Bakia*, like other experimental films, both "cultivates" and resists psychical displacement by highlighting the very motor impulses that make the viewing of a film possible. Paradoxically, the film incarnates a dislocated consciousness, distracting while honing our attention.

Like Man Ray's film, Stein's "Mrs. Emerson" reads as a "cinepoem," demanding that we attend to the piece's mechanical apparatus, and to her insistence upon non-purposive circularity. Apparently rejecting transparency for a screen's opacity, she writes: "I will repeat I will not play windows" ("Emerson" 25). With the heightened self-consciousness of an experimental film being pieced together, Stein counterpoints what she "means" and "believes" and "wills" (words familiar to her from William James and repeated throughout) with disjunctive images, as with the gender subversive: "I mean to believe that soldiers order pearls" ("Emerson" 28). (In *Tender Buttons*, "a real soldier has a worn lace a worn lace.")[81] Delighting in dislocation and multiple lenses, she breaks up attention: "They remembered mentioning, they saw eight angles, they meant to do mending" ("Emerson" 29). "Mending" is willed stitching that offers only intermittent remembering. The fragment thrives.

Stein's physical engagement with her text involves "mounting" a series of inconclusive resembling shots, as in this telling passage:

I thought that I would state that I knew certainly that she was so seen that if her eyes were so placed not violently not verbally so placed. She is not agreeable. She is not so agreeable. I think it is what I said what I recognized in mounting her. I mounted her there. Deliberate. She has a son not a son he was a thicker one. I go on. Begun. Bessie is like Bertha. ("Emerson" 24–5)

Where is the body being mounted? The passage will "go on." Stein retracts, modifies and then returns to a groove of sonic and comic gesture – "son" "son" "one" "begun." Carolyn Burke has pointed out the sexual overtones of "splice" in relation to Mina Loy, Stein, and Moore in its "modalities of joining and separation, union and disunion" ("Getting Spliced" 100). Here the act of "mounting" (without fixing upon a particular "bodily zone") becomes embodied and erotic. Rather than the mounting of a camera on a tripod from a distance, Stein implies the deliberate, physical work of film editing. (Vertov explicitly links sewing with film editing, eroticizing both activities; in fact he juxtaposes a store-window dummy at a sewing machine with the gleeful movements of a woman operating the treadle.)[82]

What is "placed," as Stein puts it, displaces the "transparent eyeball" (alluded to by Emerson in her title and recalling the many lenses of Man Ray's camera), initiating one in a series of mis-recognitions or slippages in attention. Instead of mounting a singular subject, "Mrs. Emerson" introduces a number of resembling and reassembling shapes (as does *Emak Bakia* in its semi-anagram title): "Mrs. Evangeline Henderson went in. She said that this morning. She said that in listening. No I will not be funny" ("Emerson" 23). Such comic sentences or refusals pivot upon language as mechanistic and serial, epitomized by the cinematic "conveyor belt" of hysteric, incessantly displaced motion: "Please copy this. Others able to copy this. Others able to copy this after" ("Emerson" 26). Likeness ("Bessie is like Bertha") or "exact resemblance" ("Completed Portrait") depends on slipped distinction. Stein's "copying" mechanism, so central to her poetics, reverberates in the "repetitiousness of [Chaplin's] movements" which, as North pinpoints, "makes the whole process of copying, without which the movies are unimaginable, visible, and in so doing it highlights the inherent instability of every object and person in a film."[83] To "exact" a resemblance is to highlight its status as reproduction.

"I cannot see I cannot see I cannot see. I cannot see," Stein reiterates, as if bound to an automatic refusal or hysteric occlusion ("Emerson" 24). The "I/eye" founders so that she returns to fractured refrain and likeness, to the pleasure "of getting nowhere," suggestive of the celebrated scene in *The Circus* when the police chase Chaplin into a fun-house of multiplying mirrors where he temporarily becomes mesmerized by his own unrecognizable reflection. When Chaplin finally exits to evade the police, he camouflages himself as a mechanical adornment, perfectly in sync with the amusement park's "real" automaton. One of Stein's fun-house mirror sentences reads: "I say I do know Bessie. Bessie resembles Bertha. Paula resembles Bessie. Bessie resembles Bertha Bessie resembles Bertha. I do not offer to determine whether Paula and Bertha and Bessie are distinctly separate" ("Emerson" 28). The spring in this genealogy loses its tension in willed automatic gesture and retraction. Continuity, figured through negated and claimed kinship, flickers forth in hysteric jerks: "My sister she is not my sister she is my sister" ("Emerson" 24). Bertha, it should be noted, is the name of Stein's older sister, and with the early death of their mother, Bertha took on the traditional female role of caretaker. As Wagner-Martin indicates, "[w]atching Bertha taught [Stein] that she would rather not lead a woman's life."[84]

Stein thus mounts a skewed "family photo," animated by disavowal and a paternal crisis: "Will you give this to your fathers. It is natural without children natural. They didn't expect that Hannah would be in it. They didn't expect that he would seem to be sat upon a single piece of cardboard box" ("Emerson" 27). "Mrs. Emerson," in this way, is a kind of "caesarian section," refusing "natural" reproduction and lineage. Instead, it presents an Emersonian father as tramp who "would seem to be sat upon." The piece accelerates in this centrifugal revolving: "One of his brothers the man was descending by his brother. They thought nothing of it naturally one would have objected. They seemed searchful. It gives you some arrangement you see" ("Emerson" 27). Which brother is which? A typical comic scenario of doubling and searching abandons plot to mechanistically give us "some kind of arrangement," "fathers" that are "brothers," words refracting in resemblance and deflating the paternal (recall Stein's "killing off" the nineteenth-century "hero"): "I do not care to remember what I do not feather. I do not remember whether a flavour is farther" ("Emerson" 27). The text recalls itself in its father-feather-flavour-farther rotation, producing something akin to Man Ray's rotating prisms in *Emak Bakia*. By not building towards resolution, "Mrs. Emerson" reinforces an amnesiac dislocation rather than temporal continuity.

Like Man Ray's manipulation of "light forms and movements," as he calls them, Stein yokes incohesive bodily parts and sensory experience through synesthesia. William James recognized the abilities that come with the limits of the hysteric's anaesthetic body, its proneness to synesthesia: individuals who "saw the impression received by the hand, but could not feel it" could nevertheless translate the image into another of the senses (*Principles* 134). This correlates with the capacity of silent film to engender or enhance sensory experience. "Mrs. Emerson" in this vein crosses erotogenic zone with color: "I do not say that green is believed to be that color. I do not say that green makes lips." Or alternately, she compactly registers the ephemera of movement, "Water is coloured by the sudden departure of all the interested readers of a newspaper" ("Emerson" 25). Contiguous scraps of "a newspaper or a packet of cigarettes," Aragon comments, "moved" the cubist artist and then found their way into the "décor" of films.[85] Stein is here compelled by the conjunction of the abstract with the visceral experience of an evanescent text: "departure" becomes tinted and physical. *Emak Bakia* also interleaves shades and texture in an effort to visualize sensation. When Man Ray's camera turns the ocean upside-down, its circular sweep blends an image of sand with sunbathing flesh.

In another passage that mimics automatic writing, Stein's roving subject displaces the visual, and kinesthetically confesses: "I can't help it. I can't help hearing carrots. I do help it. I do help it fastening chocolate. A secret time in spinning" ("Emerson" 29). "[S]pinning" and "fastening" point to the lingo of threading film on the projector's reels along with the manual fastening required by editing; in this context, these activities also imply a body being spun and spliced. The humor of what can't be helped emphasizes the automatic, the way sensory experience (such as the chocolate "fix") provokes and can unravel or re-coordinate bodily reflex even as the mind desires control: "I hope that I select that I retain" ("Emerson" 25). Part of the drama of the phenomenology of fragmentation resides in this unfastening of the Cartesian inheritance that subordinates the body's powers and frailties to the mind's ostensible control, its capacity to "retain" and archive the past.

While "Mrs. Emerson" illustrates the effort of consciousness to will selection, Stein insists upon wandering within corporeal mapping: "I do not select to have similar sounds. Bertha can be surrounded. Bertha can be surrounded by so much saliva" ("Emerson" 26). The unexpected jump to "saliva," a sign of autonomic Pavlovian process (a process visible in the canine experiments of *Mechanics of the Brain* referenced in chapter 1) "surrounds," working against willed, deliberate activity. Mechanical gesture or utterance draws into the forefront the choreography of "kin-aesthetic" experience, its lapses and recoveries. The body imagined here simultaneously forgets and recalls its temporal conditions in what Stewart dubs "continual splicing on the run" or "cinema's intrinsic dismemberment."[86]

The last lines of "Mrs. Emerson" provide what could be the scenario for a short abstract film with its "delight in dislocation," its comic non-purposive shot-by-shot measure:

> I wish I had a certain rain.
> Then a little barometer.
> Then a dry cellar.
> Then a dog which means to be old.
> Then all the exceptional white.
> Then a climbing bell.
> Then more water.
> Then all over it.
> I wish I had to go and get her.
> ("Emerson" 29)

Stein makes physical motion, serial and suspended, stand out against "exceptional white." Desire ("I wish") and volition ("to go and get her") simultaneously resume. It is as if she is thinking of the dislocated body, figured here as a Pavlovian dog, responding to "a climbing bell," its response a "beginning of beginning again," or "all over it." In *The Fireman* (1916), a bell also automates Chaplin's mechanical body usually to no avail, yet his body performs its reflexes and habits even as he forgets their purpose. And, over and over, Man Ray's camera animates a detached motion (Kiki's eyes opening and shutting for instance) only to join it with other gestural fragments.

Referring in many of her writings to her dogs (Basket I and Basket II), Stein draws a comparison between human and animal reflexivity. Reflex habituation has its comic undertow partly because humans do not want to be conscious of it as such: "I liked habits but I did not like that habits should be known as mine. Habits like dogs dogs have habits but they do not like to be told about their habits . . . I can remember very well not liking to be told that I had habits" (*Wars* 7).[87] Acknowledging the human tendency to repetitive habituation, *How to Write* begins by forgetting this: "Qu'est-ce que c'est cette comedie d'un chien."[88] Yet as her teacher James argued, an individual's capacity for "attention" can only really be grasped *before* it becomes habit.[89] Her writing, like avant-garde films, tries to reclaim initial responses, before the grooves of habit and bodily reaction have been imprinted or fixed. Her investigations in "Motor Automatism" reverberate throughout her writings, directed at her own habits and affects, and so "Three Sitting Here" recommends: "One of the things to know is why they love me so and what it is that tires my attention."[90]

What Bergson finds comedic, the use of the mechanically repeated fragment or monomaniacal trait, takes on new valence in Stein's cinematic enactment of a crisis of embodiment. Apparently disavowing "the voice" of theatre in favor of silent film's gestural body, she declares: "I do not see why a voice is necessary" ("Emerson" 26). She also refers to "silent rugs" and "late carpet," evoking the tactility of a film screen and the mounting of fabric ("Emerson" 26). Stein, we recall, resisted seeing her "talking body" in the 1930s newsreel, its "unnatural" meshing of her voice with her bodily image. Thinking specifically of Chaplin films, she favored silent film over the emergent talkies: the former "could change the rhythm but if you had a voice accompanying naturally after that you could never change the rhythm you were always held by the rhythm the voice gave them."[91] For Stein, "voice" inhibited the rhythmic discontinuity of experience, the hysteric body's "labile" transpositions of multiple, moving parts. Experimental silent film offers "an escape from actuality,"[92] and in the context of early comedies, there is "freedom from reality bestowed by silence."[93]

Stein consciously perceived herself as cutting away from the visual to write a form of divagatory cinema with the body as idiosyncratic "repeating mechanism." As the pseudo-objective "scientist," she reconstructed the hysteric as comic, variable body of a continuous present. I have mentioned already the famous scene of Chaplin crazed by the automatism induced by the conveyer belt in *Modern Times* as well as his tendency to autoerotic behavior. Even when off the clock, he continues to re-enact the gesture of turning a wrench on the assembly line so much so he ends up chasing a woman with this wrench because her dress presents rather large buttons. The joke is that his response results from automatism and a truncated field of vision, not sexual excitement; at the same time, the scene suggests how attention can be re-directed and "buttons" diversely activated.

Within Stein's universe, the body might be retrained or animated by a non-teleological sexuality of "tender buttons." If the hysteric fit is itself culturally constructed "as a sort of spasm of hyper-femininity, mimicking both childbirth and the female orgasm,"[94] then Stein reproduces this "spasm" in parsed, extended invocation:

Cow come out come out cow come out come out cow cow come out come out cow cow come out cow come out cow come out come out cow cow come out come out cow cow come out cow come out cow come out cow come out cow cow come out cow come out.[95]

In this paradigmatic passage, Stein transmutes the cultural legacy of hysteria as the frustrated wandering uterus. Mechanical reflex deflects the embodied equation of women and "biological destiny," including Freud's notion of normative femininity as a necessary forsaking of "presence" for "lack," or at best, the substitution of the phallus with the infant.[96] Finally, Chaplin's comedic/hysteric body bridges Stein's work with other avant-gardists, including Man Ray. The spasmodic dance away from causal plot reverberates in Stein, unhinged from destination, a gestural body of malleable mechanics. Williams admired Stein's rhythmic movements as evidence of a "breakdown of attention" where her "writing must always be considered aimless, without progress."[97] As the next chapter develops, Williams is similarly compelled by "breakdown," but his cinematic aesthetic depends upon the visual economy Stein refuses.

CHAPTER 3

W. C. Williams and surrealist film: "a favorable distortion"

In his introduction to *Imaginations*, Webster Schott observes that "[Williams's] writing snaps pictures like a marvelous image machine."[1] Indeed, Williams constructs a poetics based upon the visual image in movement. Seeking to become a "mirror for modernity," his aesthetic early on "admitted the whole armamentarium of the industrial age," including "the phenomenal growth of movie houses."[2] At the same time, he recognizes cinema's violent potential to "cleave," uproot and dislocate the spectator's body: "cleaving away the root of / disaster which [movie houses] / seemed to foster."[3] The poet's "cleaving" (one of his touchstone words) – with the double meaning of cutting away from and adhering to – is much like the methods of film editing where celluloid is cut cleanly and its surfaces sewn or glued together. "Cleaving" also suggests how Williams forges a visual path in a continual process of "creation and destruction."

As a doctor/poet, Williams assumes a visual "authority" over the body (identified with the fictive as well as real scientist figures discussed thus far – Charcot, Freud, and Stein who had medical training); yet his poems insistently propose a male spectator disarrayed by his own desires.[4] Williams proposes that the artist "must be his own spectator" (an idea he borrows from his favorite painter Juan Gris), a position that reflects a relentless self-consciousness. In the poems of Williams discussed here, he creates an imagined, self-reflexive spectator. By becoming "his own spectator," Williams plunges into a dialogue with cinematic discourse. As spectator of himself, Williams can shift between subject and object, seer and seen, undermining the scopophilic pleasure Mulvey identifies as integral to patriarchal cinema.

To some extent, Williams reinforces the notion theorized by Freud that bodily identity accrues through visual knowledge. The girl's "castration complex" emerges from her having glimpsed her brother's or playmate's penis and recognizing her "own small and inconspicuous organ."[5] As Lacan frames this pivotal crisis, the phallus for both sexes becomes "the privileged signifier" in "the advent of desire."[6] In the psychoanalytic model that informs Williams and many of his modernist peers, having the phallus or not having it organizes vision and is inextricably tied with access to desire itself. This seems to confirm what film theory has repeatedly demonstrated: the "dominant cinematic apparatus is constructed by men for a male spectator."[7] What distinguishes the male spectator in Williams's poems, face to face with his "primally dislocated limbs" (Metz), is the way he masochistically enhances the tropes of his own fragmentation, a method illuminated by a similar enactment on the surrealist screen. Williams shares multiple obsessions with surrealist film, particularly its rupturing the very "ocularcentric tradition" that makes his spectator possible.[8]

In part, Williams undercuts the primacy of the male gaze by championing tactility and tapping into the fantasy of a pre-oedipal sexuality. Moreover, he valorizes the sub-cutaneous, insisting (semi-smugly) that those who do not understand new forms of poetic expression "know nothing of physiology of the nervous system and have never in their experience witnessed the larger processes of the imagination" (*SA* 123).[9] In other words, the "larger processes of the imagination" coordinate with the "larger processes" that mediate porously between the skin and less visible bodily function. Williams aims for poems of somatic immediacy so that we may "smell, hear and see afresh," goals that are not inseparable from those of surrealism.[10]

Surrealist films, burgeoning in advance of and concomitantly with dominant commercial film, possessed qualities of a heightened visual immediacy while enacting a "breach between the image and its referent."[11] As if invoking the motifs of surrealism, Benjamin theorizes that modernity in the form of violent shocks "hit the spectator like a bullet" and demanded a tactile film medium "based on changes of place and focus which periodically assail the spectator" ("Work of Art" 238). Williams demands a similar "assailing" aesthetic which breaks with calcified rationalism or with a disembodied poetics "designed to keep up the barrier between sense and the vaporous fringe which distracts attention from its agonized approaches to the moment" (*SA* 89). Rooting himself in the "lived body" and the visible "natural" world, he simultaneously rejects representational practices which, as he puts it, strive for "the beautiful illusion." Instead, he seeks in his "agonized approaches to the moment" to expose the separation of "things of the imagination from life" (*SA* 107). Likewise, surrealist films viscerally cross the "barrier" or "vaporous fringe" between viewer and viewed, commanding the primacy of the phenomenological body and its "skin ego," while denying it coherence.

The basis for his physical yet disjunctive poetics stems from his training as a doctor and his exposure to a variety of theories about "male creativity."

These theories led Williams towards both a surrealist aesthetic and the cinematic spectator he designs in *Kora in Hell* (1917). His poems develop "cleavage" as a cinematic term of art to rupture seamless "wish fulfillment" and to bind the spectator's "endless desire" with the "measuring eye." The desires of this eye, linked to the camera's purported omnipotence and fallibility, are figured in this chapter respectively by Dziga Vertov's *Man with a Movie Camera* and Keaton's *Sherlock, Jr.* The breach between spectator and fantasy, exemplified by Keaton's performance, is pivotal in the surrealist films I explore, namely Luis Buñuel's *Un Chien Andalou* (1929) and Germaine Dulac's *Seashell and the Clergyman* (1927). The bodily dislocations featured in these films, particularly in Dulac's more feminist work, ultimately point away from a visual to a more tactile erotics, one already articulated by Williams's *Spring and All* (1923). The poems in this volume reveal how Williams tracks, risks and cuts into his spectator's desiring eye.

"THE MALE PRINCIPLE" AND SURREALIST SEX

Williams boasts naivete in his *Autobiography* when he claims that even after forty years of medical practice he had not known "the derivation of the adjective venereal is from Venus" until "only yesterday" reading Chapman's *Illiad*.[12] Yet his medical training exposed him to contemporary psychological theories attempting to account for sexual behavior, including that of the "deviant" body, variously promulgated by Weir Mitchell, Krafft-Ebing, Ellis, and Freud. In his last year at medical school, Williams read Otto Weininger's *Sex and Character*. Weininger (a student of Freud) conjectured that woman as "substance, subject to man's genial capacity for forming her" is "wholly sexual in her nature"; "woman herself," he put forth, "is only part of the Universe, and the part can never be the whole; femaleness can never include genius."[13] He imagined that a primitive bisexuality persisted in human beings, which if not kept in check could reassert itself as "degenerancy." In Weininger's view, women along with non-Aryan races were less evolved and thus prone to bisexuality.[14] The trouble with women, he further believed, is that they are simultaneously anchored to their reproductive capacities and more sexual than man: "The parts of the male body by stimulation of which sexuality is excited are limited in area, and are strongly localized, whilst in the case of the woman, they are diffused over her whole body, so that stimulation may take place almost from any part."[15]

I have already pointed towards the long tradition behind these particular formulations of the hystericized, dissociated body. The male principle, as Plato framed it, functions as the active shaping force; the female, without "genial" spirit, is merely the material receptacle, "the receiving principle" which is "only to be entered, never to enter."[16] When women "enter" cinema, the discourse of the body radically alters. Williams, however, often appears at home with an extreme division of male and female principles as well as with Weininger's "evolutionary" theories, as when he refers very starkly to Kathleen McBride (nursemaid for the Williams children during the First World War) as an "exquisite chunk of mud" ("K. McB.," *CP* 106).

Pound further acted as purveyor of "seminal" theories for many male modernists, including Williams. The masculine brain, Pound claimed, was "'a sort of great clot of genital fluid held in suspense or reserve.'"[17] Pound's translations in "I Gather the Limbs of Osiris" (1911–12) identify the disassembled Egyptian god as "'the male productive principle in nature' who became when his scattered limbs had been regathered the god of the dead (of Homer, of the Seafarer poet, of Arnaut Daniel), but also 'the source . . . of renewed life.'"[18] The reclaiming of literary tradition, in other words, can help repair a depleted or threatened masculinity.

Echoing Weininger's notion of the masculine "genial spirit," Pound hypothesized that "'the brain is thus conceived not as a separate and desiccated organ, but as the very fluid of life itself.'"[19] Pound also introduced Williams to Rémy de Gourmont whose *The Natural Philosophy of Love* elevated sexuality in all its varieties, naturalizing the so-called perversities of adultery and homosexuality. Notwithstanding his frankness about sex, de Gourmont reduced women to either vampires or as lower entities capable only of reproduction. As a poet and novelist, de Gourmont's influence was widespread, dovetailing with other cultural fantasies that equated femininity with primitive corporeality. While Williams was attracted to the idea of "the third sex," an idea gleaned from both de Gourmont and Ellis, he could be stunningly homophobic in his depictions of lesbians whom he apparently regarded as "the knife of the times."[20]

With this backdrop in mind, Williams's spectator is seemingly "cut to the measure" of masculine desire. As discussed in chapter 1, Nicholls argues that Baudelaire codified "the objectification of the other," particularly the female body, as the ground upon which the modernist male gaze constitutes a "contrasting disembodiment." Williams certainly repeats this act of visual objectification as well as Eliot's olfactory repulsion to women (Pound crossed out the "hearty female stench" of the Fresca section in *The Waste Land*). In "The Wanderer" (1914), the poet flaneur is lost in the crowds and glimpses his female muse: "And then, for the first time, / I really scented the sweat of her presence / And turning saw her and – fell back sickened!" (*CP* 29). In "The Cold Night," the obstetrician Williams exults over "the

bare thighs of / the Police Sergeant's wife – among / her five children,"
expecting "out of the depths of / [his] male belly" to delight in her procre-
ativity and his invasive speculum: "In April . . . / In April I shall see again –
In April! / the round and perfect thighs / of the Police Sergeant's wife"
(*CP* 154). (To underline that this sexual act is also a rebellion against paternal authority, he reiterates in this very short poem the husband's title as
police sergeant.) As another example, the doctor's lustful thoughts, "put
over and under and around" a little girl who is his patient would, he confesses, "burn [her] to an ash" if she knew ("The Ogre," *CP* 95).

Williams thus veers into monopolizing upon his "rights" as a voyeur
physician. Yet he also frequently questions his visual license and legitimacy –
part of the pleasurable unpleasure of his particular avant-garde, surrealist
aesthetic. For instance, his "Portrait of a Woman in Bed" gives voice to a
disgruntled patient: "The county physician / is a damned fool / and you / can
go to hell!" (*CP* 87). His poems, in fact, often muddle the division between
his self-reflexive spectator and the female patient. Williams reenacts what
Modleski refers to as Freud's "sadomasochistic dialectic" that "enables the
male subject simultaneously to experience and deny an identification with
passive, victimized female characters."[21]

This same duality in representing the female body also dramatically
emerges in surrealist films, even when asserting forms of the "male principle." Lautréamont's proto-surrealist metaphor for the beautiful as "the
chance meeting of a sewing machine and an umbrella on a dissecting table"
invokes the conventions of sex, yet defamiliarizes them. Thus, it must
be kept in mind that the surrealists were engaged in subverting clearly
defined binaries. As Breton fantasizes in his famous manifesto, surrealist practice would eventually overcome all "contradictions" (including the
division between male and female) in an ultimate "future resolution of
these two states, dream and reality . . . into a kind of absolute reality, a
surreality."[22] The "transitional" eroticism of surrealism allows Williams to
deflect or suspend dominant cultural figurations of male desire. His pleasures perversely hinge upon the very cleavage that ensures his detachment
from fulfillment.

A SURREALIST FILM AESTHETIC

As far-reaching as surrealism's influence has been, the term, as Roger
Shattuck cautiously but capaciously puts it, "refers to literary–artistic
activity that centered in Paris in the Twenties and profoundly affected
two generations of poets and painters in Europe. Beyond this point, any

concurrence of opinion on the nature and significance of surrealism goes to pieces."[23] In spite of the difficulty of pinning the Surrealist movement down, Mary Ann Caws identifies among its key features an "openness to the contingent" and otherness: "To find ourselves, but to find ourselves other, and then still other, this is central to the surrealist enterprise."[24] This love affair with mutability and the perpetual "recreation of the self in movement" goes hand in hand with the surrealist undermining of Cartesian rationality through a focus upon unconscious and dream states (*Surrealist Look* 22). As the poet of movement par excellence (composing many of his poems while driving his car), Williams shares these characteristics with surrealism as he finds himself other, continually other through the desires of his migrating and embodied spectator.[25]

Williams had many affiliations with surrealism, among them his translation of Philippe Soupault's novel *Last Nights of Paris* which traces the divagatory wanderings of a French prostitute. This text, like the poems I examine, alternately recapitulates an "omnipotence of desire" or "amour fou," phrases coined by Breton. Further, like the surrealists, Williams protests against poetry mired in the need for symbolism and for imitation, but as others have noted, he insists that "abstraction and reality should coexist."[26] The drive toward reality is not irreconcilable with avant-garde aims to escape transparent mimesis; surrealist film, in contrast to other forms of experimental cinema, managed to unsettle "reality," but still tantalized with the semblance of narrative cohesion.[27]

The surrealist agenda to undermine the "institution" of art itself attracted Williams to the avant-garde. In fact he wrote much of his poetry in opposition to what he considered the overly academic poetics of Eliot. Williams thought that Eliot, "by looking backward," had "betrayed" the vital well spring of modern poetry.[28] *Spring and All* is an attempt to rescue kinesthetic immediacy.

Part of surrealism's ideological lure was its claim that art could not only create visceral effects but also approach an unmediated "reality." Krauss relates Breton's attraction to photography to his belief in the camera's "blindness," its automatic registering of images.[29] Further, automatic writing (one of surrealism's key practices) was meant to achieve a "direct presence." Motivated by this rejection of "logocentrism," surrealist filmmakers fantasized about a return to a pre-discursive realm where its primary means, "the image, faithful guardian of a gesture or a fugitive expression, attains all of its eloquence in the silence that rules over it."[30]

Kora in Hell (1918), with its "dislocation of sense, often complete," brings together the dislocated body, surrealism, and cinema. He allies his writing to "pre-historic rock-paintings" that "had to wait six thousand years or more for the invention of the camera obscura" in order to render "the most delicate and expressive posture of running" (*KH* 9). He further invokes cinema as Kora's underworld, comparing its flickers to those of a distracted mind, "the floating visions of unknown purport": "In the mind there is a continual play of obscure images which coming between the eyes and their prey seem pictures on the screen . . ." (*KH* 67). In this volume, Williams significantly identifies with a mythic Kora: "I thought of myself as Springtime and I was on my way to Hell" (*KH* 4). In other words, he expects his own poetic rebirth to be mediated by this emblematic female muse. Yet he claims "mal-adjustment" within and along the flux of embodiment, in "an anthology of transit" that is "held firm only by moving rapidly from one thing to the next" (language he uses to praise Moore's verbal propulsion).[31] His mythic transit points towards cinema's capacity to make the body "continually other" (to use Caws's phrase) and to intensify sensation in the spectator.

The descent and regeneration Williams imagines operates through cinematic metaphors. His writing is like a film camera, rendering the "approach" of "THE BEGINNING" as an endless time loop running itself into exhaustion:

> that huge and microscopic career of time, as it were a wild horse racing in an illimitable pampa under the stars, describing immense and microscopic circles with his hoofs on the solid turf, running without a stop for the millionth part of a second until he is aged and worn to a heap of skin, bones and ragged hoofs – (*KH* 81)

This passage calls to mind Marey's experiments with chronophotography. What is morphologically impossible in "real time" becomes realized in cinematic time. A "microscopic" examination of the "illimitable" in early "scientific" film intersected with surrealism: the hyper-documentation of natural processes in compressed sequence dislocates them from a banal verisimilitude. (Dulac incorporated time-lapse photography of "a grain of wheat sprouting" in one of her most experimental films, *Themes and Variations*.)[32] These temporal dislocations have kinetic impact upon the spectator, and approximate what Artaud described as a "shock designed for the eyes, a shock drawn, so to speak, from the very substance of our vision."[33] Such visual "shock" would, Artuad thought, create a "pure," intuitive cinema that "moves the mind by osmosis and without any kind of transposition in words."[34] Similarly, Dulac argued that "the shock of what is seen . . . depends on the judicious choice of isolated expressions developing a theme" where "inner life made perceptible by images is, with movement, the entire art of cinema" ("Expressive Techniques" 306, 310).

The opening of *Spring and All* recalls *Kora*'s sped-up "wild horse" with its giddy temporal deformations. Williams condenses and accelerates history (and implicitly literary history) into an apocalyptic moment: "All thought of misery has left us. Why should we care? Children laughingly fling themselves under the wheels of the street cars, airplanes crash gaily to the earth. Someone has written a poem" (*SA* 180). Like Stein snuffing out the nineteenth century, Williams abandons the past through cinematic techniques of simultaneity and quick alternations between images. Like the surrealist film that "aimed at liberating the unconscious of its spectator" and the "reordering of perceptions" through "structures of aggression," he assaults the reader.[35] This destructive gesture crystallizes Breton's famous disconcerting claim that the simplest surrealist act would be to go out into the street, revolver in hand, and fire at random into the crowd.[36]

Poem 1 ("By the road to the contagious hospital") of *Spring and All* further enacts surrealist cinematic principles – and the forms of shock delineated by Artuad and Dulac. He offers a compressed and sped-up hallucinatory close-up: "Now the grass, tomorrow / the stiff curl of wildcarrot leaf" (*SA* 183). The clarifying snapshot or freeze frame is characteristic of Williams's aesthetic (think of his red wheelbarrow "glazed with rain / water"). But he corrodes, as does the surrealist, the lyric as an autonomous moment outside of time in favor of "the inevitable flux of the seeing eye toward measuring itself"(*SA* 192).

Williams traces "the seeing eye" in Poem 1 even as the self-reflexive spectator's "inner life" disappears into the scene. Line-breaks pay no heed to convention, measured instead by the cleaving eye in movement, most likely from the perspective of a motor vehicle. The poem opens with the eye panning the landscape, organized by prepositions, and then cut up before any image is complete:

> By the road to the contagious hospital
> under the surge of the blue
> mottled clouds driven from the
>
> northeast—a cold wind beyond, the
> waste of broad, muddy fields
> brown with dried weeds, standing and fallen

Within the span of the poem, a contagious, "dazed spring" turns translucent, as if coming to consciousness from sleep: "One by one objects are defined – / It quickens: clarity, outline of leaf" ("Poem 1," *SA* 95). The poem slows its speed, and with its "judicious choice of isolated expressions" irises in on objects. In this way, Williams practices découpage, which Buñuel defines as "the preliminary operation in cinema consisting of the simultaneous separation and ordering of the visual fragments contained amorphously in a cinematic scénario."[37] "Separation and ordering," as Buñuel explains and as the poem demonstrates, involves metamorphosis: "Excising one thing to turn into another. What before was not, now is" (*Unspeakable* 132).

As this brief survey suggests, the poet's efforts to "excise" and reorder resonate as part of a surrealist credo as well as a credo of regenerating sensation. However, Williams does not share Breton's belief in the "self's eventual unity" or faith in an unmediated cinematic reality. He writes of Moore's work as if of his own: "there must be edges";[38] edges texture a poem while underscoring what is missing through the act of excision. Any desire to abolish the separation between the body and the text founders upon his insistence that he "must be his own spectator."

Caws observes of surrealism that "an obsessive speed, desperate to get things down, verged upon hysteria in its wish to close the gap between perception and the subsequent representation" (*Surrealist Look* 30). While Williams exhibits an almost "hysterical" effort in *Spring and All* to remain in the present, his spectator thrives upon the discomfiting split between the "measuring eye" and the world it measures. Likewise, the surrealist films he anticipates might seek to "close the gap between perception and the subsequent representation," but in this very wish, they ultimately accent the gaps, rifts, and ruptures engendered by "optical shock." A surrealist aesthetic somatizes processes of fantasy and desire, visibly induced by the spectator himself.

SUTURE AND CLEAVAGE: THE *MISE-EN-SCÈNE* OF DESIRE

Williams confessed that he "accepted all the help [he] could get from Freud's theory of the dream" as wish fulfillment, acknowledging that "the subject matter of a poem is always phantasy."[39] The elucidation of fantasy can be likened to "the mechanism for producing film images" for it "imitates the functioning of the mind while dreaming."[40] Artaud makes an important distinction, insisting that his scenario for *Seashell* replicates "the mechanics of the dream 'without being a dream itself.'"[41] Of course, the surrealists (in contrast to Freud) did not attempt to elucidate the unconscious through the "light of day," but rather *consciously* provoked the unconscious to seep into or overturn rational categories. The dark cinematic chamber became one location for this seepage.

The contiguity between dream processes and film as a "conscious hallucination"[42] reverberates with Freud's notion that the "primary function of phantasy" is "the *mise-en-scène* of desire."[43] This enactment of fantasy, when read through cinematic production, appears to be more complicated and less linear than the attempt "to recover the hallucinatory objects that are bound to the very earliest experiences of the rise and resolution of internal tension."[44] As Laplanche and Pontalis elaborate: "Even when they can be summed up in a single sentence, phantasies are still scripts (scénarios) of organized scenes which are capable of dramatisation – usually in a visual form."[45] By activating his spectator's desires and by participating in what he calls "a revolution in the conception of the poetic foot,"[46] Williams underscores the process of visualizing and embodying such "scripts," short-circuiting their status as seamless wish-fulfillment.

In implanting himself as the desiring spectator, Williams invites the reader into his kinesthetic field as partner. *Spring and All* specifically genders his reader/spectator masculine: "In the imagination, we are from henceforth (so long as you read) locked in a fraternal embrace, the classic caress of author and reader" (178). Invoking a Whitmanian tactility, his project nevertheless persistently hinges upon the visual, accentuating "the absence of the object seen," a feature which as Metz theorizes, "defines the specifically cinematic scopic regime" (*Imaginary Signifier* 61). Metz further argues that "voyeuristic desire, along with certain forms of sadism" requires "the infinite pursuit of its absent object," but that its necessary "principal of distance symbolically and spatially evokes this fundamental rent."

Metz's spectator, like Williams's, is implicitly gendered male. Thus, his psycho-cinematic crisis is predicated upon the cultural fantasy of castration, the "fundamental rent," which the spectator desires to overcome. According to Freud, the male body enters into the oedipal contract and symbolic order by recognizing his mother's castration: this produces the fear that he might suffer the same fate if not careful; his sexual existence becomes a shoring against this potential dismemberment. The fetishism of women's body parts in cinema represents an "endeavor to find the penis in women," to allay the anxiety associated with lack.[47]

According to Kristeva, the refusal to acknowledge castration becomes a continual covering over this "nothing to see" with the objects of art.[48] Williams, however, deploys the fetish object to clarify his embodied spectator's insistence upon a "fundamental rent." Rather than depicting the female form as "phallus-like so as to mitigate woman's threat," he turns towards the orifices that expose bodily permeability. Even further, he identifies his creative process with the disparaged maternal; in the prologue to *Kora*, his own mother is both a "ravished Eden" and "indestructible as the imagination itself" (7). (He recounts that his mother was subjected to uncontrollable "seizures," induced by trance states in which she believed she was in contact with the spirit world.)[49] Rather than rejecting the "nothing to see," Williams incorporates it, unmasking bodily "lack." Like the surrealistic films I will discuss, his poetry obsessively returns to a "rent" within the "classic caress."[50]

The female body in *Spring and All* is the ground upon which his gaze pivots and ostensibly the figure for his desire, dislodged from the self-same "fraternal embrace." Yet Williams occupies a more complex position in relation to this dynamic. In contrast to surrealist film, classical narrative cinema ultimately erases the marks of the spectator's entry into the scene by creating seamless continuity through camera techniques. The shot/reverse shot, for instance, would permit the viewer to alternately identify with an individual figure in the film (narcissism) or with the movement of the camera (voyeurism). Stephen Heath defines suture as the process that establishes "the relation of the individual-as-subject to the chain of its discourse where it figures missing in the guise of a stand-in."[51] In other words, as the camera conceals the "absent field" from which it emanates arbitrarily to structure the "interlocking shots" as a chain of signifiers, the spectator fills in the gap, "suturing the wound of castration with narrative."[52]

Suture ensures that the spectator becomes interpolated in the film without friction. Annette Kuhn summarizes: "The process of subjectivity constantly is seen as both ongoing and dynamic in that the subject is constantly being 'sewn-in' to, or caught up in, the film's enunciation."[53] Williams, however, discloses this process of "sewing" and suturing so that the need for narrative closure always recedes before the "stand-in" act of desire itself; further it is precisely that which is missing, the "absent field," which gains the poet's attention as well as identification. Suturing in its medical definition is evocative for Williams both because of his profession (he specialized in obstetrics and pediatrics) and his very bodily aesthetics: wounding and incision precede suture.

His poems enact and expose a "cleavage," which much like the notion of suture, points toward a self-referential gap between signifier and signified in the act of montage. In medical usage, cleavage additionally indicates cell division or segmentation of the ovum. Breasts figure prominently in his poems, and thus "cleavage" in its colloquial usage is also invoked and sexualized. Note the exemplary beginning of "Spouts" and its voyeurism deflected in the very act of seeing, from its first mid-air line: "In this world of / as fine a pair of breasts / as ever I saw / the fountain in / Madison Square / spouts up water" (*CP* 169). In a "cleavage" of "seeing," he overlays the apparent focal point of the breasts with the phallic fountain. The poem then ends with typical deflation: "and rising there / reflectively drops down again." There is no attempt to obfuscate the imagined spectator's frangible condition. The breasts – detached from the body for optical shock – lead to the spectator's almost immediate detumescence.

"Good Night" (1917) clarifies the poet's manipulating the *mise-en-scène* of desire to cast himself as diminished spectator. It opens with a series of close-ups that situate the poet so that "all is in order for the night": his eye moves from "a glass filled with parsley – / crisped green" to "a pair of rubber sandals." A seductive visual fantasy interrupts the scene: "– three girls in crimson satin / pass close before me" (*CP* 85–6). Perloff observes that "it is lineation rather than the pattern of stresses that guides the reader's eyes so that objects stand out, one by one, as in a series of film shots."[54] In this film score, the spectator is characteristically at a window "frame." But this spectator, *Spring and All* insists, will have "bitter and delicious relations and from which he is independent – moving at will from one thing to another – as he pleases, unbound – complete" (121). This traversal from "one thing to another" verges on misogyny as much as on "bitter" masochism, rendering his independence always precarious (the sentence is itself left unfinished).

Silverman argues in the context of Freud's "A Child is Being Beaten" that the male masochist can take on multiple identifications in "a sequence in which the subject has his own part to play and in which *permutations* of roles and attributions are possible."[55] Further, the male masochist's willed instability "magnifies the losses and divisions upon which cultural identity is based, refusing to be sutured or recompensed. In short, he radiates a negativity inimical to the social order."[56] This describes the Williams spectator, who in his anarchic surrealism, roves "from one thing to another" and assumes multiple positions, particularly ones which "magnify his losses and divisions."

Masculine desire, as Williams often depicts it, operates as a relentless push against stasis that disfigures and crosses "respectable boundaries" and frames. Yet this push also disfigures the boundaries that gender the body. "Transitional" (1914) speaks to his potential for inversion and androgyny (looking forward to the sexually indeterminate characters in *Un Chien* and *Seashell*). After declaring, "I am too much a woman," the poet becomes disoriented: "Am I not I – here?" (*CP* 40). "Portrait of the Author" (1921) continues to question the "here-ness" of his somatic imago in a love song to another man ("O my brother"). The poem describes an "estranged" erotic bond (without yet using the disjunctive forms of surrealism):

> Every familiar object is changed and dwarfed.
> I am shaken, broken against a might
> that splits comfort, blows apart
> my careful partitions   (*CP* 173)

We can hear the Whitman overtones in this self-portrait where "lilac blossoms are driving [him] mad with terror," but also the speaker's confessed dislocation in the face of his longings.

There is reason to assume that the sexual desires of Williams's spectators are multiple and "transitional." "Danse Russe" (inspired by Nijinsky's performance in 1916) indulges in an erotics outside usual heterosexual boundaries while his "wife is sleeping / and the baby and Kathleen / are sleeping" (*CP* 86). Dance here exceeds both mimetic and sexual fixity. Erotic indulgence, however, is conditional, framed by a series of "if" phrases:

> [i]f I in my north room
> dance naked, grotesquely
> before my mirror
> waving my shirt round my head

With the shades drawn, he is watching himself watch himself, and his gaze becomes keenly autoerotic, breaking off provocatively:

> If I admire my arms, my face,
> my shoulders, flanks, buttocks
> against the yellow drawn shades, –

The pleasurable secret moment of "waving [his] shirt round [his] head" is tinged with the masochism that comes with a sense of himself as both seer and seen. A final question, suspended between two lines with one ending in negation, asserts neither narcissistic satisfaction nor complete faith in his masculine "genius": "Who shall say I am not / the happy genius of my household?" The break in the penultimate line ends with a frustrated "I am not."

As we will see, poems from *Spring and All* emphasize what is missing from their dislocated frames. Cuts between images (often highlighted by dashes and extra white space) as well as permutating prepositions disallow fantasies of omnipotence. Williams is not fond of the "dissolve" where "images that are linked are related to each other so that the movement from one to the other is not jarring" (Dulac, "Expressive Techniques" 311). Animated objects (unlike the still-life "glass filled with parsley" or "rubber sandals" of

"Good Night") become more evidently "jarring" through the poet's erotic reveries.[57] Concrete objects regularly assume an estranged quality because they embody conflicted desires. Thus his "wife's new pink slippers" with their "gay pompons" are disorienting and tantalizing; "shivering," he will "watch them / descending the stair" and then "talk to them / in [his] secret mind" ("The Thinker," *CP* 167). His "secret" objects for satisfaction (the girls passing before his window in "Good Night," the potential for autoerotic satisfaction in "Danse Russe," the delight in the fetish in "The Thinker") become more keenly out of reach in *Spring and All.*

    The staging of *mise-en-scènes* of desire in this later volume incorporates several characteristic elements of surrealist film: the cathexis to bodily parts or objects without conventional romantic meaning; anxiety over bodily stability, particularly, a preoccupation with castration; and erotic obsession that reveals gender unhinged or reoriented by desire. As Linda Williams makes evident, such thematic concerns with dislocated morphology become formal dislocations where "desire functions much less as a subject-content than it does as a form."[58] Likewise, the poems of *Spring and All,* while not exclusively surrealist, mesh thematic with formal dislocation – in emphasis of the fracture between the poet as embodied spectator "taking in" and "taken in," cutting and cut by his own desires. In cinematic language, "the very movement of the spectator as subject in the film" depends upon the gaps or absences covered over by narrative coherence.[59] Williams's aesthetics demand a "cleavage" from mimesis as well as the "wound of castration" to both direct and disarray the spectator's erotic energies.

TRANS-FIXED SPECTATOR

The poet's kinesthetic spectator self-consciously initiates the processes by which his erotic dis/figuration occurs. I invoke two divergent figures to illuminate the poet's assertion and undercutting of visual pleasures: Vertov and Keaton (the latter much beloved by the surrealists, including Artaud). This apparently unlikely combination confirms the surrealist impulse of my own text, yet these figures are more connected than might at first be imagined. Keaton was famous for undertaking elaborately difficult physical feats in front of and with the camera. This kind of daring in filmmaking reaches a crescendo in *Man with a Movie Camera* which self-reflexively features a cameraman in every possible position taking shots: under a train, between trolley cars, on a high tower, in an air balloon, in a fast-moving car.

As already intimated, Williams creates a kinesthetic spectator who tests ordinary temporal and spatial limits as when he renders objects from a window, or speedily motors past them. In this way, he shares with Vertov an indefatigable drive towards mastery of all visual odds through the circumambient "kino-eye."[60] This camera eye mechanically takes in what the physical eye cannot: "Kino-eye means the conquest of time (the visual linkage of phenomena separated in time). Kino-eye is the possibility of seeing life processes in any temporal order or at any speed inaccessible to the human eye."[61]

Vertov's camera penetrates both public and private places otherwise inaccessible. For instance, his zoom lens records the intimacies of marriages, funerals, and births. At one point he provides a close-up on the facial expressions of a woman in labor, cuts away to an exterior tracking shot of mourners, and then zooms back in on the emerging baby with its bloody umbilical cord. Accordingly, Vertov hails the "assault on the visible world" by his "high-speed eye":

> Kino-eye is understood as 'that which the eye doesn't see.'
> as the microscope and telescope of time,
> as the negative of time,
> as the possibility of seeing without limits and distances,
> as the remote control of movie cameras,
> as tele-eye,
> as x-ray eye,
> as "life caught unawares," etc., etc.

Williams (who himself facilitated many births) is as well exuberant about art's potential to derange, telescope, close in, and transform, but in his more surreal directions, he makes his "measuring eye" fallible. "I raise my head and / Sight leaps twenty miles," he buoyantly claims in an early poem, yet a few lines later his "desires" undercut him: "'But my desires,' / I say to myself / 'Are thirty years / Behind all this'" ("Idyl" 1914, *CP* 49). Indeed the "flashback" quickly superimposes upon the desired future in a cinematic reordering of experience; this reordering, however, comes with an insistence upon the spectator "caught unawares" and equally assaulted.

Man with a Movie Camera stresses the materiality of its own making, situating the camera/voyeur in the film as a self-reflexive subject. In fact, the film portrays multiple women (waking up as well as at sewing machines, telephone switchboards, and film editing machines) bound together by threads, cords or wiring to a larger community. Yet Vertov highlights the camera's abilities to make these women *visible* and to interpolate them in an overweening fabric of the seen. His almost aggrandizing self-reflexivity emerges in *Movie Camera*'s framing device: it begins with filmgoers entering a cinema and taking their seats, and ends showing an inset screen with the cameraman we have followed throughout, motorcycling towards us with his "kino-eye."

While Williams also accentuates the materiality of his poems and their "measuring eye," he continually deflates its "x-ray" ambitions. In this way, he approximates Keaton's role of fallible spectator; the comedian maintains his stony gaze, but repeatedly shows his desires rebuffed in an almost willed masochism. Like *Man with the Movie Camera, Sherlock Jr.* makes the cinematic apparatus necessary to its plot, but foregrounds the deflated scopophilia necessary to Williams's self-reflexive spectator. Keaton plays a projectionist who crosses between his private fantasy and the screen's threshold, what Deleuze calls the "frame of frames" (*Movement-Image* 14). Like so many of Williams's scenarios, Keaton's traversal hinges upon lack; even in his fantasy, he remains "junior." The projectionist falls asleep, and then imagines and "projects" the detective career and the romantic relationship he desires upon the screen. Assimilating a surrealist aesthetic, *Sherlock Jr.* asserts the primacy of dream, its ability to take the upper hand over ordinary consciousness. However, in one shot near the end, Keaton – as if in recognition of the fragile staging of wish-fulfillment – wistfully examines the perforations and gaps of a strip of film (trailing off from the projector) (fig. 9).

Perez conjectures that Keaton reveals his "discomfort with the disjunctions of film editing" when he is placed in the alternate screen world, crafted as if it were a Griffith film with its "disconcerting cuts."[62] Yet Keaton's persistent bodily notation of bewilderment functions similarly to the cutting he apparently disdains. The very premise of the movie rests upon the "split screen," devised by the film framed within the film. Instead of Vertov's unstoppable "kino-eye," Keaton's embodied viewpoint is necessarily fractured. The projectionist, with his projector as prosthesis, is truly not, as his distance from the screen might suggest, in a position of visual privilege. Like Williams, Keaton does not supply a solacing "fantasy of omnipotence," which the psychoanalyst Barbara Low considers one of the dangers of cinema. According to Low, film "helps to maintain [the spectator's] omnipotence and narcissism, leading to a regressive attitude."[63] She warns of the "more serious consequence" of psychic "disintegration" that could result form this attitude. In the case of Keaton (as well as the surrealist), disintegration does not confirm the ego's sense of autonomy or control; rather it denotes an alternative film style while deflecting absolute wish fulfillment.

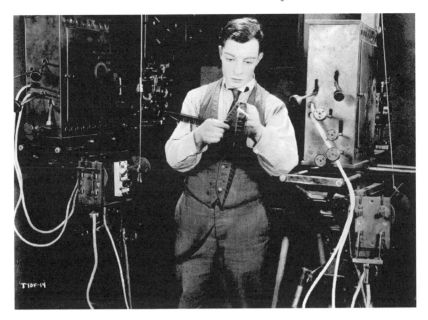

9. Buster Keaton in *Sherlock Jr.* (1924).

"Spring Strains" (1917), with its abrupt cuts between images and its "swift convergings" (like Vertov's camera-work), maps a sexualized landscape left incomplete, pointing outside its line-by-line frame, readjusted through the use of dashes and white space. Like Keaton in his projectionist booth, Williams displaces his erotic fantasy as cinematic scenario, beginning with its long shot and then contracting to a close-up that implodes upon itself:

> In a tissue-thin monotone of blue-grey buds
> crowded erect with desire against
> the sky –
>
>   tense blue-grey twigs
> slenderly anchoring them down, drawing
> them in –
>
>   two blue-grey birds chasing
> a third struggle in circles, angles,
> swift convergings to a point that bursts
> instantly!   (*CP* 97)

Visual grandiosity ("crowded erect with desire") and an energetic dereliction (through present participles and line-breaks governed by movement rather than sense) find their equivalent in sexual boasting that "bursts instantly." This "bursting" is much like Keaton's "romantic hero" or ego-ideal in *Sherlock Jr.* who awakes from his fantasy of omnipotence to find his projectionist's chamber in disarray.

As was the case with Poem 1 ("By the road to the contagious hospital") of *Spring and All*, "Spring Strains" installs a pivotal shifting gaze (more will be said of this mobility later) without directly establishing an "I/eye," yet the spectator directs the poem while seemingly absent from it. The temporal and spatial ruptures which the camera permits accord with Williams's desire to be anchored both outside and inside (as his own spectator) of his poetic compositions, thus procuring a potentially masochistic depletion. Buñuel tellingly writes (and he could well be referring to more than his own surrealist films and to one of Keaton's comedies or to a Williams poem) that "'the inexplicable impossibility of fulfilling a single desire, often occurs in my movies.'"[64] But it is not simply unfulfilled desire that circumscribes the eye measuring itself in Williams; rather the self-conscious spectator initiates and cultivates his own dis/figuration.

"The Attic Which is Desire" (1930) is overtly a visual poem, situating a spectator whose desire dictates the angle of his gaze. Here is the opening:

> the unused tent
> of
>
> bare beams
> beyond which
>
> directly wait
> the night
> and day –
> Here
>
> from the street
> by
>   * * *
>   * S *
>   * O *
>   * D *
>   * A *
>   * * *
>
> ringed with
> running lights
>   (*CP* 325)

With the flexibility of wish fulfillment, Williams places his attic spectator both inside and outside ("from the street") through pre-positions that both orient and disorient. Often Williams allows a preposition to command a single line or shot so that it becomes a visible pirouette in angle ("of" to "beyond" to "by" here in "Attic"). The eye, as if mediated and reflected by "the darkened pane" of cinema, "is transfixed" by the neon sign and follows its "running lights."[65] The middle of the poem with its soda advertisement, a projection of the poet's "parched" desires, opens the abyss discovered in the body's "unused tent."

Insofar as "relativity applies to everything," Williams derails conventional identification through the permutations of an imagined spectator's gaze.[66] As transfixed spectator, Williams dwells upon the threshold (the place where the wish-fulfillment breaks down), the slippage between embodiment as moment-to-moment movement and its delayed representation; somatic presence is rushed after, mediated, cut up by multiple angles, and then pointedly rearranged. The bodily imperative of Williams's poetry ("a thing known passes out of the mind and into the muscles") is not incompatible with the act of separation and resuturing, the "sewing in" of the spectator (*KH* 74). Similarly the morphological mutations sustained in surrealist film (as we shall see with Buñuel and Dulac) devolve upon somatic edges, accentuated and deformed by desire.[67]

UN CHIEN ANDALOU / SEASHELL AND THE CLERGYMAN

Much of what "happens" in *Un Chien* and *Seashell* occurs without explanatory diegesis or logical connectives. We provide the connections; we provide what is missing. But there is an important paradox here: these films frustrate, almost against the grain, the spectator's impulse to establish continuity and coherence. Likewise, Williams himself jealously guards "what is missing," in a perverse form of fetishism. How do the often abrupt segues between images – calling attention to their cleavage – inform desire? Desire, as a function of fantasy, can make the impossible possible and, at the same time, subject the body to uncontrollable dislocations. The unraveling and mutation of the body, and by extension the male spectator, in the films of Buñuel and Dulac sets the stage for closely related poems in *Spring and All* that dwell upon a loss of fantasized bodily omnipotence.

Both *Un Chien* and *Seashell* were collaborative efforts. Dali apparently provided the initial idea for *Un Chien* but had limited impact in shooting the film.[68] The collaboration between Artaud and Dulac was much more vexed. He wrote the original scenario, but had virtually no involvement with the filming. Apparently dissatisfied with the outcome, Artaud and his male colleagues insulted Dulac at the premiere of the film.[69] While both

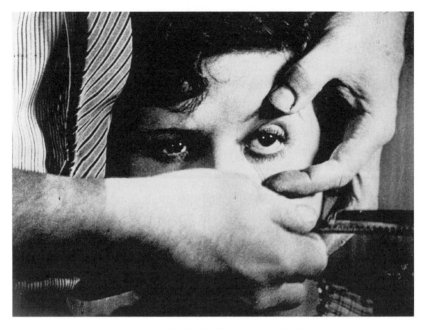

10. Luis Buñuel, *Un Chien Andalou* (1928).

Un Chien and *Seashell* strategically undercut visual prowess even as they fragment images of the female body, Dulac's direction revises the axiomatic identification of a decidedly masculine spectator.

Un Chien upholds even as it decenters a phallic economy of desire. The shocking close-up of the blank, unblinking stare of a woman's eye as a man (Buñuel himself) makes a razor incision blatantly violates the female spectator (fig. 10).[70] This opening appears to identify the director of the film with sadism. Yet as Linda Williams points out, the eye cutting is "symbolic of the entire act of the film's creation," and by "blinding us to the possibility of seeing through the figure" it "forces us to look at the work of the figure itself."[71] This "figure" follows a sequence of shots depicting the "bisection of circular shapes by horizontal lines" – a man sharpens a razor on a balcony and cuts his thumbnail, a cloud drifts past the moon, and then the eye is cut. This linkage of images acts as "a self-reflecting comment on the very process of making metaphors" so that "form rather than content dictate the ground of the association" (*Figures of Desire* 72). The female eye here "bears" the surgery, and the spectator involved in "making metaphors" appears constructed as solely masculine. However, the film never really confirms or solidifies its metaphors; as Michael Wood suggests, its images are joined "by simple succession: *then, then, then, then. We invent the missing syntax, supply all the connectives.*"[72]

Buñuel's disassociating narrative, almost impelled by the eye cutting, derides vision: "the eye seemed to many Surrealist artists less an object to be revered, less the organ of pure and noble vision, than a target of mutilation and scorn, a vehicle of its own violence."[73] Thus the prologue to *Un Chien* assaults the rational Cartesian subject, and in this way potentially aligns both male and female spectators with the acts of mutilation and being mutilated. The "camera's look" is never "disavowed in order to create a convincing world in which the spectator's surrogate can perform with verisimilitude" ("Visual Pleasure" 47). Instead, the camera scars vision itself, and in this somewhat twisted process, questions the very privileges it seems to bestow upon the male gaze.

Williams similarly employs the trope of cutting to dislocate the form of his spectator's desire; his eye fractures in the process of observation, recording a body's and the poem's thresholds. Like Buñuel's film, Williams conjoins "geometry of line" with "illogical detail" (characteristics of surreal cinema).[74] His "circles, angles / swift convergings" structure a scene "crowded erect with desire," yet his most beloved punctuation, one that interrupts logic or suture and slashes away at "demoded meanings," is the dash as linguistic precipice or visible splice. As if echoing Stein's unfastening of the rose as emblem of female chastity, "[t]he rose is obsolete," he declares, "to engage roses becomes a geometry – // Sharper, neater, more cutting" (*SA* 107).

Un Chien likewise alerts the viewer to an awareness of our over-determined figurations and the possibility of overhauling them: "We tend to say that the clouds slice or cut the moon which they do not readily do – it is already a figure of speech to say so" (*Figures of Desire* 91). Likewise Williams observes himself falling back upon readymade "figures of speech" and then exposing them as such:

Crude symbolism is to associate emotions with natural phenomena such as anger with lightning, flowers with love it goes further and associates certain textures with

In keeping with his concept of the imagination as "a cleavage through everything by a force" (*SA* 139), his observation about "crude symbolism" purposely leaves us cut off, dangling in the act of troping.

The aggressiveness of Williams's cleaving establishes the gaze as potentially turned upon itself, intent upon what it is missing. For instance, in a poem about a child patient, her very body bespeaks this deflection: her

11. From *Un Chien Andalou*.

arms "wrap themselves / this way then that / reversely about her body!"
He finally questions: "Why has she chosen me / for the knife / that
darts along her smile?" ("Sympathetic Portrait of a Child," *CP* 94–5). The
doctor and patient become doubles so that he both wields the knife and is
under it. Likewise, *Un Chien* interpolates a purportedly masculine viewer
as "reversely" under the razor. The "seeing eye measures itself" (as Williams
promotes) and in effect becomes sliced in the process of seeing. As we will
see in *Spring and All*, what complicates this slicing for the male spectator in
Williams's poems is his doubleness – both "outside" of and "reversely" identified to some extent with the "mutilated body image" culturally inscribed
upon women's bodies (*Volatile* 60).

I devote much attention to the inaugural scene of *Un Chien* because the
film forces us to recall the slit eye when it offers up other morphological
traumas. In a later sequence, an androgynous woman ("shot steeply from
above, encircled by the iris diaphragm" fig. 11) pokes an amputated hand
with a stick. A crowd surrounds her and she remains a spectacle until a

policeman "picks up the hand, which he carefully wraps and places in the box that the cyclist was carrying" and gives it to her (*Unspeakable* 164). From up above, a man and woman look from the balcony at the street scene unfolding below. The scene's "geometry of line" and "illogicality of detail" bind a permutation of looks: the iris widens from the close shot of the hand to the androgyne to the crowd and then to the balcony spectators.

This trajectory of looking culminates in another "mangling" and this time of the woman observed in the street:

> Cars pass by at vertiginous speeds. Suddenly one of them runs her over, mangling her horribly.
>
> Then, with the decisiveness of a man completely within his rights, the character (upstairs in the room) approaches the young woman and, after looking lasciviously into the whites of her eyes, he grabs her breasts through her clothes. Close-up of lascivious hands on her breasts, which emerge from under her dress. We then see a nearly fatal expression of anguish reflected in the character's features. Blood-streaked drool runs from his mouth onto the young woman's uncovered chest.
>
> The breasts disappear and transform into thighs that the character continues to feel up. (*Unspeakable* 165)

The "accident" joins the violent death of a sexually ambiguous figure with desire, impelling the regressive and slobbering "mad love" of "the character" now "assailant" (thus Buñuel designates him as both protagonist and antagonist). Here the "assailant" fitfully grasps his female companion's breasts only to find his hands emerging from them. He then pursues her in a rather protracted chase wherein the woman successfully rebuffs him. When she attempts to lock a door on him, his hand becomes caught in the jamb at the wrist. This scene, of course, calls up the image of the severed hand (or looks forward to it depending on how one makes sense of the film's temporal movement).

Desire is continually frustrated in the film's erotic encounters, such as the one detailed in the scenario above. Close-ups contribute to a loss of distance and perspective, emphasizing the body's besieged thresholds. There is no attempt to cover over castration anxiety, and the female body fragments, but in its mercurial transformations evades the male grasp. Further, the bloody saliva slipping from the "character's" mouth indicates a loss of bodily control and the binding of the "nearly fatal" with the deflated romantic. Like Keaton's lackluster hero, the "character" is abjectly suspended between interior and exterior realms. Williams's Poem xvi, akin to Buñuel's anti-romantic eroticism, constructs an anti-blazon, or incantation to the body as wound and "toppled" edifice:

> O tongue
> licking the sore on
> her netherlip
>
> O toppled belly
> (*SA* 129)

The close-up of the sore on the woman's "netherlip" slips into a disjunctive stanza: "Elysian slobber / from her mouth / upon / the folded handkerchief" (129). Like so many of the poets I examine in this book, Williams examines how involuntary reflexes impinge upon embodiment; here they purposefully destabilize the division between the spectator and the female body in bits and pieces.

Similarly, *Un Chien* reveals the "character" in "rapt attention" of his own dissolution. At one point, he studies a wound in his hand. The woman then "*sees for herself* what he has in his hand. Close-up of the hand, in the center of which ants crawl as they emerge from a black hole" (*Unspeakable* 164; emphasis mine). What she "sees for herself" is the culturally constructed "wound of castration," as well as her own "mutilated body image." The "black hole" transforms into "armpit hair" which then "fades into a sea urchin whose movable spines vibrate gently" (164). This genitalizing of the armpit attaches the fearful "black hole" to the female body, here an oceanic Medusa figure with "movable spines."

In its visualizing this process of endless substitution (repeating yet submerging one image with another), the film somatizes the character's fear of "the nothing to be seen" by appropriating one of the woman's sexual signifiers: "When the character takes away his hand, we see that his mouth has disappeared . . . Hair begins to grow where his mouth used to be. On noticing this, the young woman stifles a cry and looks quickly at one of her armpits, which is completely depilated" (*Unspeakable* 169). The woman's look of horror ("seeing for herself") shifts to the character's gaze, temporarily identified with the camera's. His gaze moves from "a small black stain," metonymic with the woman's underarm, recreating an image of female fatality: "The death's head on the wings of the moth fills the entire screen."[75] These shots perhaps make all too clear the way cinema can be "constructed according to the unconscious patriarchy."[76] But they also imperil the male spectator's corporeal stability, calling attention to the film's dismembering tactics, its compulsive framing and displacing the "wound of castration" to multiple body parts: the hand, the underarm, the mouth. At the end of *Spring and All*, Williams feminizes and racializes his spectator's wound as "[b]lack eyed susan" who is "rich in savagery":

> Arab
> Indian
> dark woman
> ("Poem xxvii," *SA* 151)

Recall as well how Williams depicts his mother's body as stand-in for the ravished site of imagination – and thus in some sense an internalized source for the poet's modes of identification.

The preoccupation with castration and cleavage likewise permeates the earlier surrealist film, *Seashell and the Clergyman*. While it would be impossible to do justice to the significance of Dulac's contribution to feminist film history here, I must make a brief detour to demonstrate how her other work dovetails with Williams's bodily poetic of thwarted desire. It is important to note that only part of her career, namely the making of *Seashell*, directly binds her to surrealism. Her films covered the gamut from narrative to pure abstraction, such as her *Cinegraphic Study of a Arabesque*, which she would call "[a] visual symphony, a rhythm of arranged movements in which the shifting of a line, or of a volume in a changing cadence creates emotion."[77] Previous to her non-narrative films, she made several feature-length "Impressionist" works such as *Death of the Sun* (1920), which used "objects, lights, and shadows . . . calculating their intensity and rhythm to match [her] character's physical and mental state."[78] These narrative films, including one of elaborate love triangles, *La Belle Dame sans merci* (1920) and *The Smiling Madame Beudet* (1923), dwell upon the "inner life" (particularly that of her female protagonists) through dissolves, superimposition and distortion, which lend a "surreality" to her *mise-en-scènes* of desire.

Like Williams (and Buñuel), Dulac's province is fantasy – how it can manipulate temporal and spatial obstacles as well as its irreconcilable clash with social expectations. For Dulac, the medium of film itself expresses this duality. For example, her Madame Beudet is unhappily married to a conventional bourgeois man whose "laugh that sets his wife's nerves on edge, this laugh must fill the entire screen" ("Expressive Techniques" 310). Trying to block out the demands of her "vulgar husband," she is frequently lost in reveries over the poetry of Baudelaire and the music of Debussy, mirroring how Dulac's imagined audience might be entranced by her film composition. Daydreaming over a magazine (with its various advertisements of escape – an image of an automobile and one of an airplane disappearing into the clouds), Madame Beudet pauses at the picture of a trim and fit tennis-player. Dulac cuts out this fantasy image, animates it and superimposes it upon the "real" scene of marital tension, so that the tennis player emerges out of the flat picture and momentarily removes M. Beudet from the scene. The actualizing of interior states moves to a further extreme in *L'Invitation Au Voyage* (1927), where her character's divagation in a nightclub (populated by heterosexuals side by side with transvestites and interracial couples) results in multiple erotic fantasies. "Superimposition is thinking, the inner life," Dulac writes ("Expressive Techniques" 311). Her film devices highlight mental and bodily states as often blurred with the world where, as with many poems of Williams, her character's fantasies are ultimately circumvented.

If Dulac's films primarily attend to the dislocating locus of female desire, more relevant here is her recasting of the crisis of masculinity, so prominent in *Un Chien*, as closely tied to morphological fluidity. Instead of identifying with the camera's perspective in cutting into the body (the camera follows Buñuel's point of view in the slitting action), *Seashell* takes on the hetero-pathic point of view of the body being acted upon. Silverman explains that the "heteropath, who identifies excorporatively . . . surrenders his or her customary specular parameters for those of the other," whereas the idiopath "turns upon the ingestion of the other, and the resulting triumph of the subject's proprioceptive frame of reference."[79]

Heteropathy (as defined by Silverman) is akin to Dulac's "fusion of the shot" as opposed to Artaud's or Buñuel's preference for "optical shock." While Dulac apparently follows Artaud's scenario quite rigorously, her "forms" of dislocation rely upon soft-focus and distortion of images; the images, while originating with Artaud, specifically undercut the spectator's ability to attain distance or to fix an image. Representative of Artuad's rhetoric, he writes in his scenario (as if anticipating Buñuel's film) that his clergyman "'tears off [the woman's] bodice as if he had wanted to lacerate her breasts'" (quoted in *To Desire Differently* 129). Dulac's "version" transforms the bodice "into a carapace of shell-shaped armor" (*To Desire Differently* 119). Such a shift calls upon the iconography of an oceanic pre-oedipal phase.

The cinematic experience, as many have theorized, can recapitulate a return to the fantasized womb. While on one level the film clearly enacts an "oedipal drama" and the consequent castration theme present in Artaud's scenario, Dulac's methods accentuate the amniotic and fluid. The tactile supercedes the visual, recalling "the darkness or invisibility of the maternal sojourn [that] conditions and makes vision possible" (*Volatile* 104). *Seashell*

12. Germaine Dulac, *The Seashell and the Clergyman* (1927).

begins with a clergyman, compulsively filling beakers and test tubes, measuring a liquid from an oyster shell, a kind of relic of the "maternal sojourn."
He no sooner pours the liquid than he smashes the beakers, establishing
a cadence of shattering, with the heap of glass growing larger and larger
beside him.

Seashell follows the perspective of this androgynous clergyman's seemingly endless pursuit of a woman, whose clothing, including a whalebone
bustle, clearly gender and date her; the "ideal" femme of the turn-of-the-
century, she is often paired with the authoritative general who sports a
protruding saber at his side. The clergyman early on discovers them, as if
in a primal scene, after he walks, trance-like, through a series of doors that
successively open in déjà vu. Throughout the film, his bodily comportment
reflects anguished or diminished conditions: he runs after the couple with
his arms akimbo or stiffly out to the sides.

As in *Un chien*, bodily mutations underscore castration anxiety. In one
instance, Dulac's camera follows the clergyman's vertiginous course through
Paris on his hands and knees; the angle of the shot makes it appear that he
has lost his limbs (fig. 12). The camera has heteropathically identified with
the mutilated (and crawling) body: we have its perspective, not the camera

13. From *The Seashell and the Clergyman.*

as prosthetic gaze or knife. Williams often adumbrates a body, amputated and dwarfed by its own motion, taking its perspective: "the poet in
desperation turns at right angles and cuts across current with startling
results" (*KH* 17).

Dismemberment as a formal principle in Dulac's film is inextricably bound to a castration crisis. Yet *Seashell* also attempts to dissolve
this psychological dynamic altogether. The general's face, at one point,
expands almost beyond recognition as if in a fun-house mirror. When the
clergyman attempts to strangle the general (who has morphed into a priest),
the two men merge, and an enlarged image of the clergyman's face diag-
onally superimposes over the image (fig. 13). In her "Impressionist" films,
Dulac was fond of "[t]he psychological shot, the large close-up" with "the
very thought of the character projected onto the screen"; here the close-up
distorts the part so that "thought" cannot be quite rationalized and commu-
nicates, as Artaud might say, through "osmosis" ("Expressive Techniques"
310). Subsequently in this scene, cracks of blood arterially erupt on the
general/priest's head and then disappear, culminating in the skull splitting
in half, yet again to reunify. The head here loses shape or liquefies, thus
linking it to the film's seashell imagery.

While such imagery has no fixed significance, it functions as icon for the fantasized lost "chora," what Kristeva designates as the anarchic imaginary preceding the symbolic phase of identity formation. Later in the film, a dark globe is placed in the center of a room under glass like an object of art; housekeepers busy themselves dusting it. This object transmutes into a seashell (like the one from the opening scene), and suddenly the housekeepers disappear, the disoriented clergyman holds the shell and has become headless – a more extreme version of the vanished mouth in *Un Chien*. Cixous observes that women "only keep [their heads] on condition that they lose them – lose them, that is, to complete silence, turned into automatons; decapitation is part of women's condition or legacy under patriarchy."[80] Here the clergyman's temporary headless condition fuses with a prospective female gaze, suggested by the reflexive dynamics of castration and decapitation.

The head in *Seashell* is not the most elevated organ, as with Pound's notion of the seminal brain. The clergyman drops and shatters the shell (emblem of the absent head) with its swishing liquid, discovering himself reflected in it. In this sense, the head's simulacrum has an affinity with what H. D. identifies as "jellyfish consciousness," experienced as "a cap, like water, transparent, fluid yet with definite body," a consciousness that has "long feelers [that] reached down and through the body."[81] This receptive "jellyfish" state is likewise connected to the realm of the imaginary.

Near the end of the film, the clergyman imbibes his own reflection. Flitterman-Lewis argues that this moment (not written into Artaud's scenario) accords with Dulac's inclusion of "a reciprocity of vision that blurs the distinction between characters," manifested earlier through a merging of the woman's gaze with the lusting gaze of the clergyman (*To Desire Differently* 130). This "reciprocity" implies that any effort to shore up the bodily ego dissipates in the very liquid that the clergyman attempted to measure in the first sequence. Such liquefaction affronts scientific rationalism.

The film's image of the globe/seashell calls to mind the figure of the mermaid, the "shape-shifter" Mélusine (a favorite of Breton), whom Caws identifies as a "model" for "surrealist feminism": she is "invincible because she changes, being the victim of no categorization" (*Surrealist Look* 20, 28). Dulac's film calls upon this motif of mutable identity. Operating with similar dynamics, Poem xx in *Spring and All* is an incantation to the sea's body ("ula lu la lu / is the sea of many arms"). The ocean beckons with the typical siren song of destruction, yet the chorus of dissolution evocatively splits: "Underneath the sea where it is dark / there is no edge / so two –" (136).

The poem discovers its twosome edge, representative of divisible flux, rather than the obliteration of boundaries. In this context, the "chora" does not passively receive or conform to the masculine economy, but also shapes and de-forms the spectator's body.

Un Chien, like Dulac's film, makes similar efforts to unfix embodiment. Like the androgynous clergyman of *Seashell*, the bicyclist in *Un Chien* who has an accident wears a white mantelet that flaps effeminately in the wind. He carries a striped box that contains the severed hand from a previous scene. Kovács argues that "the elusive Surrealist object," respectively the box and the seashell in the two films, are coded specifically masculine: "The seashell is thus linked to the alchemy of the clergyman, but no more explicitly than is the striped box to the life force of the man in *Un Chien Andalou*."[82] Yet these objects exist in excess of the male creative principle and of singular "objective correlative."

After the woman on her balcony witnesses the bicycle accident, she races down to the body and passionately kisses the fallen man. The film then returns to the woman's upstairs room, and Buñuel notes that "the bed, that is to say, the cover and pillow are lightly rumpled and depressed, as if in fact a human body were lying there" (*Unspeakable* 164). This androgynously garbed specter lies on the bed like a "patient etherized upon a table," recalling as well Cesare in his cabinet. The box (also lying on the bed as one of bicyclist's "accessories") is the closed receptacle or coffin bearing the hand as severed phallic signifier. It can be seen as male accessory or "stand-in" for desire as well as signifying female genitalia.[83] In this sense, the box in *Un Chien* (like the globe in *Seashell*) refuses to fully disclose its sexual contents.

Part of what connects Williams to these surrealist methods of denotation is his attraction to the improbable object, precisely described and diffusely eroticized, that resists full mimetic transparency. In Poem XII of *Spring and All*, he gives us this elusive fetish:

> The red paper box
> hinged with cloth
>
> is lined
> inside and out
> with imitation
> leather

This box becomes an elaborate machine with its "engineers / that convey glue / to airplanes" (*SA* 123–4). Williams suggests that his spectator, often assailed by what cannot be assimilated, identifies ("inside and out") with the indeterminate, animate yet absent image. As the next section demonstrates, the reader, like his spectator, is expected to supply missing parts and yet retain or interiorize the impression of their absence.

It is impossible to ignore "what is missing" or to "suture over castration with narrative" in either *Un Chien* or *Seashell*. Likewise, the refusal of a coherent bodily image or text emerges in *Spring and All*. This volume disarrays contemplation through its hybrid prose and poetry, disjunctive line-breaks and dashes, its dizzying perspectives established through multiple prepositions, and its incongruous image juxtapositions. Its typographical "tricks" (upside-down chapter headings, chapter numbers out of order, broken off sentences, interrupting upper-case letters) in surrealist spirit all jolt the text's spectator into motion. These techniques purposely deflect wish fulfillment and disarray the male bodily ego in its *mise-en-scène* of desire.

Poem IX of *Spring and All* self-consciously exposes the permeability of the spectator whose desires leave him off-balance and with "his losses magnified." Williams begins the poem by questioning the act of writing and then exclaims his desire:

> What about all this writing?
>
> O "Kiki"
> O Miss Margaret Jarvis
> The backhandspring
> (SA 113)

In his serial invocations, Williams calls upon Man Ray's mistress of Montparnasse "Kiki" (featured in *Emak Bakia*) and then the nurse with whom he had an affair when he interned at the French Hospital in New York. The poem quickly establishes that the seeing subject is not separable from his surreal, estranged atmosphere:

> In my life the furniture eats me
>
> the chairs, the floor
> the walls
> which heard your sobs
> drank up my emotion –
> they which alone know everything
> (SA 113–14)

This "narrative" of loves gone wrong pivots upon a dread of being "eaten" by female desire, and at the same time, testifies to the necessary (even tantalizing) gaps in this poetic body. His disavowed desires return to him in the nurse's sobs which "soaked through the walls / breaking the hospital to pieces." He depicts the nurse as hysteric; her violent emotion seemingly takes over every object. Yet each embodied object in this "broken" hospital retains the spectator's own erotic secrets, which pervade the atmosphere.

The spectator's fragmented articulations mobilize several permutations in perspective:

> Drunk we go forward surely
> Not I
>
> Beds, beds, beds
> Elevators, fruit, night-tables
> breasts to see, white and blue –
> to hold in the hand, to nozzle
> (*SA* 114)

The poem zooms in on a part of the nurse's body, the "breasts to see," among the other "objects" of the broken scene. Seeing becomes tactile. "To nozzle" (Williams makes "nozzle," the spout of a hose, into a verb) indicates a mechanizing or dissociating of the breasts. The nozzle, in effect, alternately protrudes as phallic. Caws refers to Man Ray's use of "the wheel and its knob as a particularly erotic device, a female/male juxta-or super-position . . . this picturing of Picabia and his steering wheel, the knob of which he will later transpose in the glass circle overlay upon a naked female breast."[84] As in this example, the breasts in Williams's poem alternately shift between and unsettle gender specifications and beyond objective correlative. The breasts take on an "undifferentiated erotic referent."[85]

The parceling of the female body in Poem IX points toward similar scenes in *Un Chien* and *Seashell*. As in these films, the scenario unfolds the underside of wish fulfillment so that the desiring spectator loses his impervious pretense to visual "ironic superiority." By the end of the poem, his attempt to separate himself from the scene unfurls in an erotic somersault ("my legs, turning slowly / end over end in the air!"). Like the "character's" predicament in Buñuel's film, the "omnipotent desire" of the male gaze incessantly comes up against its own dereliction. The spectator's "partitions" (to use a word from "Portrait of the Author") are blown apart so that he becomes the object of his own gaze, watching his own watching. He is both there and not there. This is a poem where "the furniture eats [him]" much in the way perhaps that the vibrating tentacles of the sea urchin in *Un Chien* threaten incorporation.

The spectator's permeability in Poem IX increases to such an extent that he becomes a wrap, an extra skin, of the female body. His eye figuratively cloaks the body of the other rather than fixing it from a distance, suggestive of the blurring of bodies in *Seashell*:

> I watched.
>
> You sobbed, you beat your pillow
> you tore your hair
> you dug your nails into your sides
> I was your nightgown
> I watched!   (*SA* 115)

The gap in the second "I watched" creates a space for the gaping spectator to perceive himself falter as he tries to regain distance. With this visible gap, Williams reestablishes "the space the fracture which forever separates [the voyeur] from the object" (Metz, *Imaginary Signifier* 60). This fracture occurs incrementally, as a figure in movement as it were, across the poem's widely flung spaces.

The spectator nevertheless momentarily collapses the distance between himself and his lover's body, achieving a nearness (at the threshold of her skin) that obliterates his capacity to watch at a distance. Tactile contact surmounts visual perspective when he becomes his lover's nightgown. Freud claims that a piece of clothing or undergarment can act as a fetish object, yet here the fetishist becomes the sexualized object or image himself. The crossing between positions in this *mise-en-scène* evokes Merleau-Ponty's "double sensation," his claim for "the fundamental reversibility" between touching and being touched, seeing and being seen (*Volatile* 100). The seer, in other words, is always imbricated in the seen. By watching himself watching, Williams potentially assumes a position akin to the female spectatoress observing her cleaved eye in *Un Chien*.

Poem IX oscillates between disconnective present-tense assertions ("In my life the furniture eats me") and more coherent flashback (the "backhand-spring" somatized throughout the poem). Such use and misuse of temporal markers, much like the disassociating continuity in *Un Chien* established through inter-titles ("Once upon a time . . ."; "Eight years later"; "About three o'clock in the morning"), further represents the spectator's bodily disarray. The poem's temporal hybridity is "ballistic," jarring the "romantic" register of its *mise-en-scène* of desire:

> Wrigley's, appendicitis, John Marin:
> skyscraper soup
>
> Either that or a bullet!
>
> Once
> anything might have happened
> You lay relaxed on my knees –
> the starry night
> spread out warm and blind
> above the hospital –
>
> Pah!
> It is unclean   (*SA* 113)

The spectator/doctor wants to eject the "unclean" emotions that threaten to overwhelm him, yet the form of the poem, with its quick temporal reversals, dashes, and exclamations, disrupts such borders. The "broken pieces of the city – / flying apart at his approaches" implies that the spectator *has* a ballistic effect in his "agonized approaches to the moment" akin to the nurse's breaking the hospital furniture with her sobs. After all, he does ultimately wear her nightgown (unlike Tiresias who merely catalogues the typist's underclothing).

In Poem IX ("What about all this writing?"), Williams takes on a variety of erotic permutations in his withdrawal from and immersion in the sob-ridden scene, evoking the simultaneous positions possible in the masochist fantasy of "A Child is Being Beaten," particularly from a female perspective.[86] Contrary to Freud's belief that "the voyeur does not look at his eye," Williams does examine his own scopophilic drive, exposing the tenuous borders of his imagined spectator, even to the point of assuming the "feminine position."

Poem XI ("In passing with my mind") exemplifies this self-conscious looking that traverses the screen of other bodies and cuts into the body of its own visual practice. I quote it here in full:

> In passing with my mind
> on nothing in the world
>
> but the right of way
> I enjoy on the road by
> virtue of the law   —
> I saw
>
> an elderly man who
> smiled and looked away

> to the north past a house—
> a woman in blue
>
> who was laughing and
> leaning forward to look up
>
> into the man's half
> averted face
>
> and a boy of eight who was
> looking at the middle of
>
> the man's belly
> at a watchchain—
>
> The supreme importance
> of this nameless spectacle
>
> sped me by them
> without a word—
>
> Why bother where I went?
> for I went spinning on the
>
> four wheels of my car
> along the wet road until
>
> I saw a girl with one leg
> over the rail of the balcony
> (*SA* 119–20)

The moving car becomes the poet's camera governed by the pull of the shot. If Baudelaire inaugurates the "art of taking a walk," Williams launches the "art of driving a car" as a means of observing the "seeing eye" in flux and disarrayed. One of his earlier "self-portraits" aligns vehicular exhaust as cellular (and emotional) disintegration: "Wheels stir you – / Up behind them! / You tissue out" ("Self-Portrait 1," *CP* 42). In another instance, he fantasizes a girl who "[l]eaned on the door of my car / And stroked my hand" ("Revelation," *CP* 39). More disturbingly in "The Young Housewife," he observes a woman as he "pass[es] solitary in [his] car" and compares her to a fallen leaf only to sadistically note that the "noiseless wheels of [his] car" crush a bed of fallen leaves (*CP* 57). The car in these earlier poems, like the camera, mediates his bodily identity so that he can confirm his position vis-à-vis the sexual divide.

The spectator of Poem XI, line 4, however, turns the "virtue of the law" against itself, interpolating himself in the unfolding scene. In "passing with [his] mind," he appreciates his visual privileges and cleaves his "right of way." (This sounds much like the "character" in *Un Chien* who is "completely in his rights," or so the scenario reads, perhaps ironically.) Here the spectator both passively takes in multiple pieces of a moving "nameless spectacle" which "sped [him] by them" and shatters a unified perspective. Each of the "couplets" in this silent viewing ("without a word") enact a shot, framed as it were by the space left between each one, allowing the driver to cleave away from each successive image. Nevertheless, his pleasure is broken by prepositions: "I enjoy on the road *by*." The process of putting these lines together that resist suture makes the poem cinematic as well as erotically charged. Here both the optical shock of the "defective" one-legged figure as well as the poem's disjunctive form, can be a fetish in Freud's thinking, but in this context it deflects the desire to cover over unsettling gaps. The fracturing of lines really serves as much as it severs erotic pleasure.

While the poet's gaze is central in this poem, "I saw" embeds itself in a web of other "limited" perceptual trajectories (those of an elderly man, a woman in blue, and a boy of eight) that ultimately threaten to spin out of the spectator's control. "Why bother where I went," he asks. A chance encounter for Williams can easily reach centrifugal saturation as in Poem XVIII: "No one / to witness / and adjust, no one to drive the car" (*SA* 133). Poem XI ends with a partial climax (as if completing the initial "I saw"), but this eroticized vision remains tauntingly incomplete:

> I saw a girl with one leg
> over the rail of a balcony

Williams here literalizes enjambment – a word that derives from the French "jambe" for leg, thus linking his "revolution in the conception of the poetic foot" to its metaphoric bodily significance. The dismembered part overtakes the narrative whole. On the one hand, the ending potentially enacts a sadistic amputation. On the other, it arrests perceptual mastery and returns the spectator to his "dislocated limbs."

This final shot of the "one leg" and the poem's use of "vertiginous speeds" on "the four wheels" replicate the ethos of surrealist film. These elements foreground the restive spectator and keep narrative in a formal "condition of imaginative suspense" (*Figures of Desire* 206). By highlighting the girl's vulnerability – and with a trick shot, her possible handicap – he anticipates to some degree the problematic eye-slitting scene in *Un Chien*. The suspense of the poem potentially becomes a function of the distance required by voyeurism and "some forms of sadism," to reiterate Metz's argument. However, in the unfolding of the scene, the poet reveals his own eye cut up by its action, and stopped short by the final freeze-frame. The spectator is indeed out on a limb by the end of the poem. Like the spaces between incomplete stanzas, the framing of the last one depends upon the spectral missing leg to see through to the spectator's contingent relationship to the visual field, predicated on absence rather than self-presence.[87]

The "one leg / over the rail" constitutes both an allurement for the driving spectator and a displaced image of castration. It thus underscores the disunitary experience of the phenomenological body rather than the solaces of plenitude. Disfigurement becomes both a physical manifestation of lack and a narrative fissure so that the "part" becomes erotically volatile where "the cinema is a body . . . a fetish that can be loved" (*Imaginary Signifier* 57). Yet we are not meant, I believe, to supply the missing leg, but rather retain it as a phantom which becomes "a kind of libidinal memorial to the lost limb" (*Volatile* 41). The stunning moment at the end of xi ("In passing with my mind") remains phantom; and because of the multiple perspectives offered throughout the poem (including a "half / averted" gaze), it implies another point of view from the balcony rail. In a poem such as xi, Williams verges, as he had in Poem ix ("What about all this writing?"), upon collapsing the distance between his cleaving spectator and the dismembered scene.

Spring and All makes a workable cleavage between a poetic in which "reality plays a part" and the surrealist destructive exuberance for "new names for experience" (*SA* 204). This tension structures Poem x ("The universality of things") which bridges the "unclean" borders of Poem ix ("What about all this writing?") and the poem with its one-legged girl. It attempts to detach vision from sensory experience but confesses to mutability:

> the favorable
>
> distortion of eyeglasses
> that see everything and remain
> related to mathematics –
> (*SA* 118)

The animate eyeglasses are a parable for the spectator's desire to be the absent Euclidean viewer who can "see everything" from some privileged point-of-view along with his desire to turn himself into "his own spectator." This hinges upon a necessary absent presence created by the resting, anthropomorphic eyeglasses: "they lie there with the gold / earpieces folded down." In the process, this poem almost forsakes the ocular.

Williams is capable of the hyper-clarity of a moment such as Buñuel's close-up of the insects pouring out of the hand wound or his own freeze frame of the one-legged girl. In the lines already quoted from the beginning of Poem 1 of *Spring and All*, he engages in shots that both isolate images and smudge the borders between them:

> By the road to the contagious hospital
> under the surge of the blue
> mottled clouds driven from the
>
> northeast—a cold wind beyond, the
> waste of broad, muddy field—
> brown with dried weeds, standing and fallen

The lines in this stanza overtake each other through the repeated use of "the," blurring and suspending an incomplete image; the "mottled clouds" that are "under the surge" will later give way to a clarity, but here suggest the rush to the hospital. Likewise, Dulac's distortion and fusion of images, however, exemplifies a continual usurpation of poetic ground (as well as the ground of the gendered body), methods present in Poem x ("The universality of things").

Poem x follows its desire, creating a montage of the broken yet contiguous particulars of this "reality. It opens with oral and visual attraction that subverts any "fixed denotative code" (*Figures of Desire* 74), each stanza an opening and a refusing:

> The universality of things
> draws me toward the candy
> with melon flowers that open
>
> about the edge of refuse
> proclaiming without accent
> the quality of the farmer's
>
> shoulders and his daughter's
> accidental skin, so sweet
> with clover and the small
>
> yellow cinquefoil in the
> parched places   (*SA* 117–18)

The "favorable distortion" brought about by the eyeglasses in Poem x makes visuality instrumental in the contiguity of bodily identities.

The shoulders of the farmer and his daughter with her "accidental skin" are of a piece with the desired "candy / with melon flowers" and the yellow five-fingered plant (this series of images is another version of the moon-thumb-eye displacement in *Un Chien*). Where are the tenor and the vehicle in this unfolding figuring? After all, the farmer's "shoulders" lie on the same line as the daughter. Erotic desire cathects to the fabric of these interwoven images (like the nightgown in poem IX, "What about all this writing?") rather than to a single object.

"Cinquefoil," like much of this poem's mutating vocabulary, conjures up a "tactile seeing" and the "foil" echoes the daughter's ephemeral skin. But her skin is also – after the intrusion of spectacles in the next stanza – linked to the materiality of the visual "frame":

> the most practical frame of
> brown celluloid made to
> represent tortoiseshell –

This stanza captures some of the disorienting verve of surrealism's hybrid conjunctions and Williams's own startling conjoinings ("That is why boxing matches and / Chinese poems are the same" *SA* 102). Celluloid here evokes the cellular skin of the farmer's daughter as well as of the material used in creating film. The camera (or these glasses made of celluloid) zoom in upon "[a] letter from a man who / wants to start a new magazine / made of linen." The poem's emphasis upon texture converts the visual into the tactile.

Williams foregrounds the "accidental skin" of his poems so that, as we have seen elsewhere, the body becomes "the threshold or borderline concept that hovers perilously and undecidably at the pivotal point of binary pairs" (*Volatile* 23). Invoking the "edge of refuse," Williams draws attention to how the daughter's skin and the "tortoiseshell" glasses operate as threshold images. The "refuse" returns in the incomplete reflection offered by the glasses:

> All this is for eyeglasses
>
> to discover. But
> they lie there with the gold
> earpieces folded down
>
> tranquilly Titicaca—

The last phrase is meant to shock: not only does the poem's camera move from the doctor's office to one of the largest lakes in the world, the proper name of the lake is humorously improper, combining the disparaged breast with waste material. The poet's dislocated spectator, with his recumbent eyeglasses, shifts within embodied flux. In following the path of his cleaving desire, Williams reveals the spectator's body identified within and fragmented by all it both desires and wants to disown.

In his traversal of a scene, Williams contrasts to Stein's movement, which as the previous chapter delineates, does not establish a central spectator with an identifiable visual trajectory. Yet like Williams, Stein invokes a car metaphor as sexual body. Her Ford ("Aunt Pauline") does not specifically signify shifting visual permutations, but rather embodies not getting anywhere: "the motor goes inside and the car goes on, but my business my ultimate business as an artist was not with where the car goes as it goes but with the movement inside that is of the essence of its going" ("Portraits" 194). Stein's pleasure in circulating without destination has erotic consequences; orgasms are not the end of pleasure but part of the "essence of its going" so that the body, as Irigaray affirms, has *"sex organs more or less everywhere"* akin to Whitman's "instant conductors."[88]

In splicing incongruous objects to reconstruct a poem's body, Stein calls upon Lautréamont's metaphor for the beautiful as "the chance meeting of a sewing machine and an umbrella on a dissecting table." Williams (as will Moore with her "various scalpels") partakes as well of the pleasure at the "dissecting table." Yet unlike Stein who "hysterically" enjoys the "psychic montage" created from either/both the sewing machine or umbrella (objects in fact that recur in *Tender Buttons*), Williams indulges in the unpleasure of sewing and unsewing himself as spectator in a mobile topography. H. D., as I next demonstrate, will rework the female body's "traumatic dislocation" created by the "scopic regime" Williams both cleaves to and away from. She overtly assumes and deforms the culturally despised roles of femme fatale and hysteric to imagine alternate forms of embodiment.

CHAPTER 4

H. D.'s borderline bodies

For Williams, the "camera obscura" records psychic "mal-adjustment" in the "agonized present," allowing him to shake up the visual economies he calls upon. H. D., on the other hand, identifies this same instrument as the "dark room of memory," a place for excavation and reproduction of the personal and collective past.[1] While the films she appreciated were generally more narrative than abstract, she closely binds the cinematic apparatus, its projection of interior experience, with the work of psychoanalysis. From her early Imagist poetry to her explicit involvement with film beginning in the mid-twenties, H. D. refashions female embodiment through montage.[2] Her vexed and intimate relationship with psychoanalysis is a pivotal element in this refashioning. As Friedman maps it, H. D.'s relationship to Freud dated back to 1909 when she and her first love, Frances Gregg, perused Freud in German. H. D. underwent therapy with Freud for three months in 1933 and for five weeks in 1934, memorialized in *Tribute to Freud* (1956), a work that retrospectively connects psychoanalysis with cinema.[3] H. D. reworks those aspects of Freud's theories that pathologize "detoured" female sexuality, and simultaneously edits in those that make such detours possible, namely his ideas about dream mechanisms, bisexuality, and hysterical identification.

In *Tribute*, H. D. writes that Charcot had been "concerned with hysteria and neurotics this side of the border-line," dividing them from "the actual insane"; this "border-line," she argues, is really "a wide gap," "an unexplored waste-land, a no-man's land between them."[4] This crucial assertion implies H. D.'s frustration with the limited taxonomy available for naming the "border-line" bodies in a psychic "no-man's land" or an all-inclusive "kingdom of hysteria." H. D. might well be echoing Radclyffe Hall's *The Well of Loneliness* (1928) where her "famous heroine learns early in life 'that the loneliest place in this world is the no-man's-land of sex'" (*No Man's Land* 218). Such a landscape of isolation and anxiety leads the lesbian, as Gilbert and Gubar argue, to seek out places where they "could commune with others who, like her, felt other than their bodies" (*No Man's Land* 217). To feel "other" in this context is nonetheless an embodied experience. This chapter argues that cinema for H. D. is the medium most capable of articulating borderline bodies, including those sexual inverts invisible to Charcot and newly "recognized" by Freud as well as by modern sexologists.[5]

Freud's inspired breakthrough while studying with Charcot, H. D. conjectures, was his interpretation of hysteria as gestural narrative: "He noted how the disconnected sequence of the apparently unrelated actions of certain of the patients yet suggested a sort of order, followed a pattern like the broken sequence of events in a half-remembered dream" (*Tribute* 118). She envisions Freud wandering through a Saltpêtrière ward among the delusional Caesars and Hannibals, and can "*see* even, as in a play or film, those characters, in their precise setting" (*Tribute* 116). Moreover, H. D. assumes the perspective of Freud, underscoring the "relativity" of his identity to that of other "performers": "I, Sigmund Freud, understand this Caesar. I, Hannibal!" (*Tribute* 121)

As H. D. further meditates upon the "characters" at Saltpêtrière, she blurs the boundary between the hysteric and the visionary; for in her logic, who can dispute with the enactment of "Caesar," for instance, as an imagined identity like any other? In other words, hysteric identification can be a form of visionary performance, specifically a cinematic embodying of multiple identities. In H. D.'s "mythic" poetry, "not only can we recall the men and women of antiquity, but the gods themselves" ("Restraint" 30), she frequently projects herself into alternate bodies of both sexes. We might think of Stein's "mutation" into Caesar, or Eliot's slippage into "I Tiresias" or the "Hyacinth girl." This hysteric mode of unfixed and plural identity is also a dominant feature in the Expressionist films H. D. admires in the 1920s.

H. D. assimilates a sexual in-between zone into her poetic and cinematic vocabulary so that she can dramatically recast the pathological bodies of hysteria and sexual inversion, including her own bisexual "lived body," as vital incarnations within a "broken sequence of events." In fact, these bodies, reconstituted and enacted as figurative bodies in her texts and in modernist films, become visible through an erotic cathexis to the fragment. Further, the poetry and film reviews she published in *Close Up* articulate a version of the spectator that allows for multiple, necessarily fractal identification and desire.

In *Sea Garden* (1916), her first volume, stylized images of slashed or torn bodies, while usually not affixed to a specific identity, are precursors to her later embodiments and montage methods. Her relationship to the image, articulated against the backdrop of the modernist depiction of hysteria, war trauma, and sexual indeterminacy, reflects a complicated investigation of cultural "forms" of female embodiment. These forms ranged from Freud's misogynist notion of female development as contingent upon the "discovery that she is castrated" to his more liberating claim for a universal "bisexual disposition."

Paired with the practice of "cutting" she modifies from Pound's Imagism, her early poems rely upon synesthesia and fusion to enact the dynamics of "hysteric" identification and desire, and as such point towards her relationship to the screen as a figure for the maternal. Yet the "sub-strata of warmth" of cinematic experience, as I suggested in chapter 1, does not provide a satiating wholeness; rather, it heightens her sense that cultural bodily identities are malleable. H. D. "performs" and interacts with a myriad of interlocking fragmented female bodies extending from the mythic Sappho, Helen, and Eurydice to film figures, including Joan of Arc (Dreyer 1927), Lulu in *Pandora's Box* (Pabst 1929), and her own character of Astrid in *Borderline* (1930).

The larger argument of this chapter works towards establishing the missing link between the hysteric and the femme fatale, each embodied through stylized "symptomatic acts" and gestures. In her landmark essay, Joan Rivière attempts to account for women who desire to occupy a masculine position: they "put on a mask of womanliness or femininity as a defense to avert the anxiety and retribution feared by men."[6] Shrouded and sensationalized into visibility, the "improper" body of the hysteric and the femme fatale, in their exaggerated poses of the feminine, can be beards for queer sexuality. Doane writes that the femme fatale elicits "a certain discursive unease, a potential epistemological trauma" and as such "harbors a threat which is not entirely legible, predictable, or manageable."[7] Both the femme fatale and the hysteric, fabricated in excess of all facts, puncture "objective correlative"; simultaneously, these figures sustain the period's interest in indeterminate corporeality. H. D. both identifies with and desires the figure of the "unwholesome" femme fatale, derived from the legacy of Decadent poetry, and later developed in Expressionist film. The so-called destructive energy of the femme fatale – in her violation of heterosexual imperatives – coalesces with the deviant desires of the bisexual.

BETWEEN HALLUCINATION AND PATHOLOGY:
A BISEXUAL APPARATUS

It is oddly fitting that H. D.'s introduction to Freud took place in the context of her pivotal homoerotic relationship with Gregg. In *Paint It Today*, her posthumously published fictional account of her troubled "coming out," she configures their coupling as "wee witches."[8] H. D. thus allied herself with both sexual diminution and subversion, an alliance that spurred her search for more viable modes of female embodiment. She later assumes a Medusa-like role when she acts in the film *Borderline* (1930), thus performing an avenging response to untenable bodies, including those outlined by psychoanalysis.

Between H. D.'s initial interest in Freud in 1909 and the beginning of her analysis with him in 1933 (a date which coincided with the demise of *Close Up*), H. D. suffered a number of breakdowns and psychological traumas. Friedman aptly describes this string of losses as "the palimpsest of disaster involved in the interconnected shock waves brought on by war, death and betrayal in love" (*Psyche* 29). In brief, H. D. experienced a stillbirth in 1915, coinciding with the sinking of the Lusitania. Her husband Richard Aldington enlisted in 1916. Subsequently, he engaged in a succession of adulterous affairs. Yet as Laity observes, H. D.'s early thwarted romance with Gregg who "betrayed" her twice (first with H. D.'s erstwhile fiancé Pound and then with a surprise marriage to Louis Wilkinson) "cut closer to the bone than Aldington's desertion" (*Fin de Siècle* 136).

Compounding these betrayals in love were the deaths wrought by war: her brother was killed at the front, a trauma that most likely precipitated her father's death in 1919. H. D. and her illegitimate child almost died in 1919 as a result of double pneumonia. She recovered from this "series of shocks" under the care of Bryher when they traveled to Greece in 1920. While she would never directly declare herself a lesbian, H. D.'s most significant relationship between 1919 and 1961 was with Bryher, who with the help of Ellis diagnosed herself as a sexual invert or member of the "third sex."[9] At the same time, H. D. acknowledges in "The Master" that Freud made it possible for her to identify her bisexuality: "I had two loves separate" (*CP* 453).[10] This line suggests that her double love was "separate" from the world but also divided in itself, a state apparent in her re-citing of Sappho: "I know not what to do, / my mind is reft:" ("Fragment Thirty-six," *CP* 165). Again and again, her poems fantasize about sex change: "If I had been a boy, / I would have worshipped your grace" ("Toward the Piraeus," *CP* 178).

H. D. underwent her sexual traumas, like many other modernists, in the context of war traumas. Friedman tells us that she "partially regarded her analysis with Freud as training that she could use to help other war-shocked people" (*Psyche* 22). Film itself served as a kind of therapy in its "condensation" of dream images; it could also "shock weary sensibilities" and otherwise "doped" consciousness ("Borderline Pamphlet" 117). Further, H. D.'s avant-garde aesthetics shaped and were shaped by re-definitions of sexual relations in the postwar period. These interrelated "shock waves" made finding adequate representation of physical and psychic ruptures imperative. As she writes in *The Gift*: "shocks can, like avalanches, uncover buried treasure."[11] H. D. regarded the cinematic apparatus as one means of excavating lost mythic realities, particularly those that might recover and recharge the "lived body."

H. D. would retrospectively describe the visionary "hallucinations" she experienced in 1920 as "the series of shadow-or of light-pictures I saw projected on the wall of a hotel bedroom in the Ionian island of Corfu" (*Tribute* 61). One of her visions is of "the three-legged lamp stand" as a "tripod of the classic Priestess or Pythoness of Delphi," who ecstatically "pronounced her verse couplets" (*Tribute* 75). H. D.'s vision of the priestess, speaking in rhythmic language and held up by the tripod (the classic support of the camera), binds poetry, filmmaking, and bisexual desire. While she asserts that she was the one "granted the inner vision," she admits that her ecstasy depended upon the presence and aid of Bryher, whom she compares to the Pythoness: "Or perhaps in some sense, we were 'seeing' it together, for without her, admittedly, I could not have gone on" (*Tribute* 72).[12] *Tribute* elevates cinema to a visionary art, while underscoring that "seeing things" devolved upon "'two women alone'" together in the birthplace of Sappho.

As *Tribute* unfolds, Freud regarded H. D.'s Corfu hallucinations, and implicitly her correlation of them with cinema, as "a dangerous tendency or symptom," indicating that she "desired union with [her] mother" (60, 44). Early ego development for Freud hinges upon the infant's separation from the mother, particularly from "what he desires most – the mother's breast."[13] In successful "development," the "sexual object proper, that is, the male organ" becomes the organizing principle of identity and desire.[14] As H. D. wrote to Bryher, Freud thought she was "stuck at the earliest pre-OE stage, and 'back to the womb' seems to be [her] only solution."[15] Needless to say, H. D was deeply ambivalent about Freud's theories of normative female identity, which devolve upon the resolution of a crisis of castration: "she has seen it and knows that she is without it and wants to have it," and thus "in a flash" discovers her difference as deficiency.[16] Accordingly, if the female does not accept her anatomical diminu-tion, she inevitably compromises her heterosexuality, either becoming a sexually inhibited hysteric or a "masculine woman," prone to lesbianism or regression to maternal attachment. (Or as Rivière formulates it, the masculine woman is compelled to masquerade as ultra-feminine to escape negative social repercussions.) Freud put the possibilities for deviance in place, while predominantly configuring them as undesirable. Meanwhile, H. D. eroticizes what Freud construed as "regression," adamantly insisting that *"woman is perfect"* ("The Master" *CP* 455). H. D. exults in sensuous female embodiment, resisting the overbearing somatophobic as well as homophobic strains within modern culture.

H. D.'s praise of Moore and her later displeasure with Carl Dreyer's 1927 *Joan of Arc* summarize to some extent her ongoing schism with Freud and her search for a revitalized eroticism. She compliments Moore for being a "master swordsman" who presumably overcomes sexual anesthesia through poetic "turn and counter-turn"; by contrast, Dreyer's film intensely disturbs H. D. because the director wielded the scimitar all too well in his film editing ("Joan" 19). Moore, in this opposition, is the successful "mannish" woman poet, while Joan (played by Renzée Falconetti) figures as the immobilized, masochistic body, or in other words, Freud's "normative" femininity taken to logical extremes. H. D. sought to undo this paralyzing dichotomy by formulating a bisexual apparatus – one extended by cinema.

Like psychoanalysis, other theories of deviant sexuality, had their own crippling effects. Most relevantly here, the sexologist Karl Ulrich defined the female invert as a "male soul trapped in a female body," and in effect, supplied a visual correlative for sexual "difference," reproducing the misogynist hierarchies framing the mind/body dialectic. The "male soul" was trapped in the wrong body.[17] In spite of his problematic and limited understanding of female sexuality, what Freud (in contrast to sexology) offered H. D. were mechanisms of *bodily* identification and desire, incarnated through a cinematic aesthetic.

Freud's theories both pathologized and opened up a "no-man's land" of sexual embodiment. De Lauretis clarifies this contradiction in Freud's work: "perversion, and homosexuality, in particular, has a peculiarly paradoxical status; both central and yet disruptive; necessary and yet objectionable; . . . regressive or involuntary and yet expressive of an original intensity of being."[18] Particularly suggestive here is Freud's notion in *Three Essays* that the sexual instinct is not tied to a specific object; rather "it is only by means of effective restriction and other kinds of modification" that bodies "approximate" the "ideal norm."[19] Yet even with his acknowledgment of only relative norms, Freud was more inclined to accept "the universal bisexuality of human beings" and that "the libido normally oscillates between male and female subjects" than cases of full-blown homosexuality.[20]

Cinema, and to some extent Freud's theories, provided poets with an "original intensity of being" and even a vocabulary for mediating a bisexual erotics. H. D.'s hallucinatory visions at Corfu specifically use filmic language to express "two loves separate." H. D. had multiple erotic attachments beyond Gregg and Bryher, including her brief, passionate affair with Peter Rodeck on the boat to Greece in 1920, her relationships to Kenneth Macpherson (who Bryher married in 1927) and Sylvia Dobson in 1934 as well as her active fascination with Paul Robeson.[21] It is no surprise that desire and identification circulate in multiple directions in the films H. D. most admires.

I have discussed in chapter 1 H. D.'s exaltation of the projector for its recreation of "ghost bodies." In her "projector" poems, she identifies herself with both Apollo as the god of light and the "feminized" screen, suggesting that these identifications cross into each other. *Tribute* further portrays her visions as acts of projection that establish a meeting-ground between internal and external experience. Her hieroglyphic "writing on the wall" realizes and choreographs "an extension of the artist's mind, a picture or an illustrated poem, taken out of the actual dream or day-dream content and projected from within (though apparently from outside)" (*Tribute* 76). In this context, the projector is a metaphoric prosthesis "externalizing inside stimuli," while the screen becomes, as Pabst calls it, a "psychic medium."[22]

With this sense of projection in mind, cinema operates in her writings as a possible threshold space for both the bisexual as "separate" in a "no-man's land" and "the apparitional lesbian" who is "always somewhere else."[23] For her, film spectatorship is an "inter-action," an exchange of borders, and a "healing in blur of half-tones and hypnotic vibrant darkness . . . half-light" ("Movietone" 23). Film may diminish bodily boundaries, temporarily dissolving the division between mind and body.[24] H. D. resisted the "talkies," we recall, because sound technology she believed would limit the play between the other senses; or put in another way, sound might foreclose a polymorphous erotogenicity before "restriction" and "modification."[25] The silent cinematic apparatus could thus provide a spectral zone for "ghost-love" and sexual borderlines. Yet as her poems from *Sea Garden* reveal, the hyphenated language of "half-tones" does not engender utopian pre-oedipal fusion, but rather stages a bisexual tension between active and passive impulses along with her own version of "dissociation of sensibility."

G. W. Pabst's 1924 *Joyless Street*, H. D.'s "first real revelation of the real art of the cinema" epitomizes a cultural "disintegration or dissociation" where "body and soul" are not on "speaking terms" ("Beauty" 26). Yet it is Garbo's face and fugitive gestures, as if in hysteric performance, that signal a sense of "whole destruction"; she bears the "whole history of oppression in her eyes" ("Beauty" 30). Operating with a similar aesthetic, Dulac frequently indulges in close-ups of her female protagonist's faces, often to the point that almost the entire screen merges with the skin. The whole is inscribed on the body's malleable surfaces; and for H. D., magnetized by Garbo, the soul is not, as sexology might have it, trapped in the body, but etched there. Film is, after all, the medium most suited to self-consciously manipulate Freud's concept of the "bodily ego" as the "projection of a surface."[26] This surface projection, as Grosz elaborates, represents the "skin ego," a surface literally retraced and rewritten by libidinal desires (*Volatile* 20).[27]

It is precisely because film is not solely immediate, but instead mediates a layered and epidermal consciousness that Garbo's body, for instance, can mesh with the iconic Helen of Troy, or with the Sapphic fragment which vibrates as "shadow-print" or metaphoric film piece ("Fragment 113," *CP* 131). Yet there are "enough fragments in the world to remake the world," she writes in reference to Sappho. Hence, she cuts up the figurative body to recreate it.

SLASH AND CUT: THE BODY'S LANDSCAPE

The re-shaping of cultural fantasies of female embodiment was necessarily a hazardous enterprise for H. D., given the Imagist mandate for "hard" and "dry" verse. As discussed in chapter 1, Pound's credo of Imagism was implicitly a reaction formation to the "vague" excesses and emotions of Decadent predecessors. In effect, bodily experience had to be contained by "direct treatment" of the object and reined in by concision, or with what Lindsay described as "Doric restraint." H. D. appeared to fulfill completely these aesthetic criteria, and thus Pound applauded *Sea Garden* for its "restraint" and classical ethos.

The Imagist model of poetry is readily adaptable to film practices. For instance, Bryher extols Eisenstein's *Potemkin* for its "power of compression of the Homeric phrases and the siege of Troy."[28] "Cutting," Bryher writes of Soviet film composition, "is considered far more important than the story."[29] More significantly, H. D. theorizes in *Close Up* that "the evocative detail or part" is what makes for the "classical" in cinema: "a part has always been important, chiseling and cutting, shaping and revising" ("Restraint" 33). Accordingly, she pleads that "it is not necessary to build up paste board palaces, the whole of Troy, the entire over-whelming of a battle fleet" ("Restraint" 33). She addresses the potential poet/filmmaker: "You and you and you can cause Odysseus with one broken oar to depict his woefulness" ("Restraint" 34); she succinctly commands: "Sweep away the extraneous" ("Restraint" 31). In *Helen in Egypt*, she will signify her heroine's fleeing presence through a "broken sandal." Her ideal film consists of "one centralizing focus of thought cutting and pruning the too extraneous under-brush of tangled detail. Someone should slash and cut" ("Restraint" 33). These directions echo the Imagist credo, while exemplifying the embodied activity she enlists in *Sea Garden*, where "someone" does "slash and cut."

H. D. kept the iconic initials that Pound bestowed upon her at the British Museum tearoom along with her attraction to "Hellenic hardness." "True modernity," she writes, "approaches more and more to classic stan-dards" ("Restraint" 31). But Imagism, finally, does not entirely account for H. D.'s "excesses" of erotic expression. Her excavation of the classical past is sensuous and romanticized ("spare us from loveliness" *CP* 28), enabling her to construct "metaphoric landscape/bodies and language for trans-gressive desire she gleaned form the sexually diverse 'Greece' of Victorian Hellenists such as Pater, Wilde, and Swinburne" (Laity, *Fin de Siècle* 42). As Collecott writes, H. D. gravitates to Sappho in her emblematic role as decadent "femme fatale for both Swinburne and Baudelaire."[30] Yet H. D. calls upon Sappho's "broken" representations as part of her classical style and to specifically express the heightened language of a lesbian eros. (Bryher had apparently memorized *Sea Garden* before meeting H. D., apparently recognizing its Sapphic eroticism.)

Sea Garden mediates a variety of bodies, only some specifically named and gendered, that are scarred and slashed versions of a "skin ego," with its "articulation of orifices, erotogenic rims, cuts on the body's surface, loci of exchange from inside and the outside" (*Volatile* 37). Scene after scene create the effects of elemental exposure and wreckage, "where sea-grass tangles with / shore-grass" ("Hermes of the Ways" *CP* 30). Images of torn flowers, broken shells, scattered leaves and petals constitute a somatic cartography where fragment and part supplant nostalgia for the "whole."

Her first volume represents a "series" of poetic forms and bodies that have "weathered" if not mastered shock. Like the mediating isthmus of a "stim-ulus shield," the poems themselves appear to have survived and sustained trauma. Freud's "stimulus shield" is an elaborate filtering mechanism, "a borderline between inside and outside," that "screens" out excessive stim-uli and provides "a special envelope" for the "receptive cortical layer."[31] This "cortical layer" is precariously positioned: "this little fragment of liv-ing substance is suspended in the middle of an external world charged with the most powerful energies; and it would be killed by the stimula-tion emanating from these if it were not provided with a protective shield against stimuli."[32] While Freud struggles to separate the death instinct from the libidinal instincts in *Beyond the Pleasure Principle*, the two are intertwined, making the ego's "shield" assailable and porous.[33] H. D. similarly defines her aesthetics as both resilient and subject to violent incursions: "beauty remain[s] through mutilations."[34] Her poems are figurative bodies, imprinted and "flayed" by sensory experience.

To catalogue some of H. D.'s broken figures in *Sea Garden*: in "Storm," "each leaf is rent like split wood"(*CP* 36); "a wild-hyacinth stalk is snapped" ("Pursuit," *CP* 11); a "brittle flower, / one petal like a shell / is broken" ("Sea Iris," *CP* 36); there are "grated shells / and split conch-shells" in "The Wind Sleepers" (*CP* 15); a white violet "fragile as agate, / lies fronting all the wind / among the torn shells / on the sand bank" ("Sea Violet," *CP* 25); "[t]he shrivelled seeds / are split on the path –" in "Mid-day" (*CP* 10); and "each leaf / cuts another leaf on the grass" in "Evening" (*CP* 19).

H. D.'s "making new" of literary tradition resides to some extent in her revision of the cultural history of flowers (like Stein does with her rose). Rather than identifying them with an idealized, dematerialized female purity, the flowers signify as mutilated "lived bodies," and overtly belong to a no-man's land, refurbished through Greek scenery. Yet hers is always a bodily landscape as much as it is a literary one. Further, the ruptured bodies scattered throughout *Sea Garden* reflect H. D.'s hyper-awareness of war ravages. A borderline topography registers as well a crisis of sexual indeterminacy and possible fear of persecution. Thus her dangerous no-man's land, cut into by edges, is at least double. In "The Shrine," for instance, "there is no shelter in that headland, / it is useless waste, that edge, / that front of rock" (*CP* 9).

"Sea Rose," the first poem in *Sea Garden*, slashing into the feminized rose of literary and cultural tradition, presents a mutilated body. With its sequenced image, the poem operates as though by the shot by shot layering of film:

> Rose, harsh rose
> marred and with stint of petals,
> meagre flower, thin,
> sparse of leaf   (*CP* 5)

Distinctly defying Victorian norms of female gentility, the poem zooms in upon the "harsh" beauty of female genitalia, specifically the "meagre" clitoral organ that Freud's oedipal model disdains. Repetition produces a passionate invocation of the slashed, "unloved" body.

The permeable bodies of *Sea Garden* often do not propose an "I"; rather these poems reinvest in a bodily ego as "frontier-creature."[35] In "Hermes of the Ways," her mythic figure is "facing three ways" and, situated in the midst of an exhilarating if painful tumult, cries: "Heu, / it whips round my ankles!" (*CP* 38) Likewise, her sea rose is "caught in the drift," and her "Sea Lily" shows the marks of violent sensory immersion.

Yet the poetic medium itself strips and carves into these "frontier" bodies, giving them "hard edges" and showing them as "little fragment[s] of living substance." Her sea lily, for instance, is a "[r]eed, / slashed and torn," rendered centrifugal in bits and pieces through a passive voice: "Myrtle-bark / is flecked from you, / scales are dashed" (*CP* 14). She characteristically eroticizes the fragmented, scriptable body:

> Yet though the whole wind
> slash at your bark,
> you are lifted up,
> aye – though it hiss
> to cover you with froth.
> (*CP* 14)

Slashing is here inscription. An exclamatory "aye" signals a reflexive "I" and emphatic desire for that which is dramatically "lifted up."

As if in a dialogue with both Freud and Pound, the poems in *Sea Garden* evoke an extreme passivity, while assuming a cinematic stance in their active principle of cutting. For instance, she is at once paralyzed and ready to dismember the addressee (quite possibly Pound) of "Garden":

> If I could break you
> I could break a tree.
>
> If I could stir
> I could break a tree –
> I could break you.
> (*CP* 24)

These verb-energized lines and their swift, broken tempo suggest that she is poised to break out of the dry timber of Pound's Imagism and his straight-jacketing mythology of her as his Dryad. (In his earlier courtship with H. D., Pound addressed her as his tree-like muse in a collection of poems, *Hilda's Book*.) Rather than *being* a Dryad, she can surround herself with border-line "[d]ryads / haunting the groves, / nereids / who dwell in wet caves" ("Acon," *CP* 32).

"Sheltered Garden" cogently expresses this dialectic between actively carving out and masochistically identifying with torn bodies. The speaker urgently longs for some "sharp swish of branch" to break into her

anesthetized physical condition: "I have had enough. / I gasp for breath."
This scenario accords with what I have been describing as the modernist
craving for immediacy and physical sensation and the experience of various
states of numbness, nervous exhaustion as well as somnambulism. In the
climactic stanza, almost every line-break occasions a present-tense verb,
which can be read as quick directives for motion in a film scenario:

> I want wind to break,
> scatter these pink-stalks,
> snap off their spice heads,
> fling them about with dead leaves –
> spread the paths with twigs,
> limbs broken off,
> trail great pine branches,
> hurled from some far wood,
> right across the melon-patch,
> break pear and quince –
> leave half-trees, torn, twisted
>
> (*CP* 20)

H. D. refuses the domestic confinement of "normal femininity" with its
"border-pinks, clove-pinks, wax-lilies." Instead, she would rather see "limbs
broken off" and assume the so-called "masculine" active role. At the same
time, she identifies the female body with a "twisted," fractal topography.

Her early poems, then, often turn the chisel upon the bodies they invoke;
they are in fact among the influences upon the "cutting" scenes I will address
in *Borderline*, where H. D. literally assumes the knife. In these poems, she
can occupy both positions of slasher and slashed, evincing an eroticism
accommodated by Freud's "Hysterical Phantasies" (1908). His "series of
successively exhaustive formulas" conclude with a ninth principle: "An
hysterical symptom is the expression of both a masculine and a feminine
unconscious sexual phantasy," thus encoding a "bisexual meaning of a
symptom."[36] He writes of this double fantasy in a case where "the patient
pressed her dress to her body with one hand (as the woman) and trying to
tear it off with the other (as the man)."[37] Freud's paper a few year later,
"General Remarks on Hysterical Attacks," however, intimates the complex-
ities in his otherwise reductive assessment of hysteric displacement: "The
attack becomes obscured by the patient's undertaking the parts played
by both the persons appearing in the phantasy, this through *multiple
identifications*."[38] In other words, double identification might easily become
plural, as H. D. herself hints in her depiction of the inmates (as well as
Freud) in Charcot's clinic.

H. D.'s early poems with plural addressees – often indeterminately sexed – suggest that her bisexual eroticism has a less fixed or axiomatic form than "Hysterical Phantasies" might suggest. In "Pursuit," for instance, she tracks "deep purple / where your heel pressed" (*CP* 11); alluding to the myth of Apollo pursuing Daphne without naming it, she obscures the gender of her speaker. Alternately, the libidinal "chase" becomes explicitly "Artemesian": "blunt your spear with us, / our pace is hot / and our bare heels / in the heel-prints –" ("Huntress," *CP* 23).[39] In "The Gift," her speaker follows a beloved and is like "the street-child" who "clutched / at the seed-pearls you spilt / that hot day / when your necklace snapped" (*CP* 16). "You know the script –," she writes; it is a script narrated through broken images invested with libidinal intensity: "a comb / that may have slipped, / a gold tassel, unraveled, / plucked from your scarf" (*CP* 16).

H. D.'s identification with the torn fragment (or mediating isthmus) as an aesthetic and erotic mode extends back to Sappho and forward to the condensed, sensuous "prints" of film images. Her landscapes can eroticize Sappho's body *as fragment*. "Fragment Forty-one," for example, uses as an epigraph the barest quotation with ellipses (". . . thou flittest to Andromeda. – Sappho"). The poem is classical and excessive, even melodramatic; the unrequited lover must yet "stumble toward / [Aphrodite's] altar-step": "though my flesh is scorched and rent, / shattered, cut apart, / slashed open" (*CP* 182). "Eros" (written after Aldington's betrayal in 1917) puts it bluntly: "What need – / yet to sing love, / love must first shatter us" (*CP* 175). It foregrounds the masochistic element of heterosexual desire and evokes what Laity calls the "erotic thralldom" in H. D.'s tumultuous relationship to Gregg. Ultimately, the desire *to be fragmented* identifies her with Sappho's poetic body, delivered to Aphrodite's "altar-step," to "the white slab of her house."

What I call a martyrdom of the image in *Sea Garden* becomes a form of vital dissociation, or what Bersani refers to as "productive masochism," linked to Freud's "view of the libidinized ego as an essentially shattered ego."[40] For H. D., it is as if the "violence from without" both numbs and awakens the body to its senses. The search "to forget, to find a new beauty / in some terrible / wind tortured place" in "Sheltered Garden" encodes a double desire – forgetting tradition and embodying a sexualized shattering for the sake of a "new beauty" (*CP* 19). This "terrible" place with its "half-trees torn, twisted" resonates with her romantic inheritance and with the extremes in German Expressionist film scenery. She later admires, for example, the setting of *The Student of Prague* (1927): "The little tree twists and bends and makes all the frantic gestures of the little tree at the cross-roads under which Faust conjured the devils."[41] The technology of film delivers landscapes imbued with bodily attributes, making possible an enactment of the multiple desires of her poems, including the desire to break out of restrictive aesthetic and sexual norms.

It becomes progressively alien to think of *Sea Garden*, prescriptively cinematic, as "Imagist," at least in Pound's restricted sense. In spite of its trim, concise lines, hers is a vocabulary of tumult and rift. The volume's "hyperbolic pitch of emotion" has affinities with Expressionism;[42] her sweeping gestures borrow from the melodramatic masochist. The body is "ruined" or "flayed" or "shattered" by love. What later becomes her prostration before a screen idol like Garbo reverberates in her early work so that she confesses: "I fell prostrate / crying" ("Orchard," *CP* 28). In "Mid-day," she shows no restraint: "My thoughts tear me, / I dread their fever. / I am scattered in its whirl" (*CP* 10). Patrice Petro argues that "melodramatic conventions in Weimar cinema, including excessive visual and narrative repetition, sexual ambiguity or androgyny, and a heightened emotional appeal," are what attracted female audiences.[43] H. D.'s sensuous language not only resuscitates a disparaged romantic lineage but also interpolates sites for alternate spectators.

RHYTHM OF A SCIMITAR: BECOMING AND REFUSING JOAN

H. D.'s address in "Sea Rose" to the discarded, wind-swept flower "caught in the drift" raises a disturbing opposition. Her landscapes are "borderline" bodies, caught between two elements (here the sea and land) and recreated through collision. She evokes the defiant energy of the moving image, yet the image is frequently emblematic of a passive female body: "Stunted, with small leaf, / you are flung on the sand" ("Sea Rose," *CP* 5). This duality is, of course, a central problem for feminist film theory which considers the problematic place of the female spectator, whose processes of identification are often fraught by images of women in "stunted" or otherwise compromised postures. In her developing ideas about the spectator, H. D. struggles to re-define the parameters of female embodiment through an "inter-action" with the screen; in other words, she articulates a female body's desire while adumbrating the film image's own phenomenological agency. Within the cinema of the period, however, it is extremely difficult to claim these apparently irreconcilable goals.

Just a year before making *Borderline*, H. D. criticizes Dreyer's "remorseless cruelty" to the spectator of *The Passion of Joan of Arc*: "we are left pinned like some senseless animal, impaled as she is impaled by agony" ("Joan" 132).

While she admires the film's artistry, H. D. significantly feels "cut up": "Do I have to be cut into slices by this inevitable pan-movement of the camera, these suave lines to left, up, to the right, back, all rhythmical with the remorseless rhythm of a scimitar?" ("Joan" 19). Strangely, what H. D. questions in Dreyer's style, his use of violent cutting, could be asked of *Sea Garden* as well as of her wielding the rhythmic scimitar in *Borderline*.

Raymond Carney asserts that Joan shares an "expressive marginalization," manifested through her non-narrative gestures, with Dreyer's other female protagonists.[44] Yet for H. D., Dreyer places the spectator in an intolerable position. Like one of her many borderline bodies, she is "flung on the sand," but unable to resist, slash back or engage in "productive masochism." Nevertheless, the film inadvertently illuminates H. D.'s complicated endeavor to theorize a bisexual spectator in both poetry and film.

H. D.'s review reveals her sense of a compulsory bodily identification, demonstrating what Béla Balàzs calls "spectatorial abduction" where film identification "alters the terms of bodily reference."[45] Rudolf Arnheim claims there is a "tiresome sense of dislocation" in *Joan of Arc*.[46] For H. D., the film's relentless cutting is *physically* wearing and mortifying: "Jeanne stressed and stressed and stressed, in just this way, not only by the camera but by every conceivable method of dramatic and scenic technique" ("Joan" 19). Simultaneously brooding and fracturing close-ups are among Dreyer's unsettling effects. Owing to the film's kinesthetic power, H. D. is not "allowed comfort," has "curious nerve reactions," and must "clench her fists" ("Joan" 16).

H. D. admits that she "can NOT watch this thing impartially and it is the first film of the many that I have consistently followed that I have drawn away from" ("Joan" 20). Yet she both withdraws from the film and feels specifically, intensely addressed by it. She does not, in short, leave the theatre. Instead, H. D. observes her painful, transfixed identification with Joan's subordinated point of view: "I must stare up at, see in slices . . . the judges and the accusers of Jeanne, *as if seen by Jeanne herself from below* the overwhelming bulk of ecclesiastical political accusation" ("Joan" 19; emphasis mine).[47] She describes the "wind-hardened" face of Joan, and in recalling the bodies of *Sea Garden*, confirms her vexed attachment to this "small, intolerably sturdy and intolerably broken" figure. The camera angles corner her (she feels "shut in") so that she absorbs all of the scimitar strikes aimed at Joan.

This "spectatorial abduction," most likely heightened by the fact that Joan of Arc is one of the few women history identifies as heroic, clearly represents for H. D. a set of missed opportunities.[48] Carney argues that the film's minimalist plot pivots upon "the attempt to 'name' Joan as a heretic, and her answering efforts to avoid being so named."[49] Yet if the "mere act of 'naming' is dangerous to her ontological health," not being named makes her embodied existence an impossibility. It is not only as heretic that Joan is "poised precariously on the margins of social discourse."[50] Indeed, H. D. recognizes herself in the visionary warrior and potentially bisexual Joan, but Dreyer's phenomenological portrait forces her into a negation of that identification.

While H. D. emphasizes Joan's bisexual possibilities – she is "the merest flash of a sturdy boy figure" and "medieval girl warrior" ("Joan" 17–18), Dreyer focuses upon the saint as immobilized hysteric: "Jeanne already numb and dead, gazes dead and numb at her accuser and fumbles in her dazed, hypnotized manner" (19). H. D. praises cinematic art for its ability to *embody* and transform hysteric displacement into visionary experience, but Dreyer thwarts this possibility. His Joan is "kicked towards the angels," as if she is one of Charcot's hysterics, whose visions are regarded as symptom or hallucination ("Joan" 22).

The shearing of Joan's hair, as if fitting her for an asylum, is a crucial visual correlative for H. D.'s troubled identification with Dreyer's Joan. Figure 14 shows an agonized Joan with tears on her cheek, her head cuffed between an executioner's fist and scissors. She looks as if she has been subjected to the traumas and cruelties of war. Finally, Dreyer's "scimitar" resonates as punishing Joan's "apparitional" bisexual body.

In effect, Dreyer deprives Joan and the female spectator of any active dynamism. Joan becomes a one-dimensional, scriptable surface. She has no stimulus shield; she is all stimulus shield. The ultimate "frontier-ego," her "hardened" skin cannot swerve from the imprint of an unforgiving paternal judgment. Thus Dreyer short-circuits what might make her a most valuable possibility for the female spectator, particularly for H. D., whose search for "beauty with strength" consumes her poetics. Yet by means of H. D.'s review, we recall that the historical Joan was engaged in bloody battles, that she wielded the sword, even as she claimed to prefer the shield.[51]

I have argued so far that H. D.'s early poems establish her as "shearsman of sorts" (a phrase of Wallace Stevens in "The Man with the Blue Guitar") *and* as slashed body, the latter in some sense culminating in Dreyer's representation of Joan. What are the spectator's alternatives to a prolonged catalepsy ("numb and dead, dead and numb") and torturous bodily constriction (Joan is of course shackled for most of the film)? The "defiance" inspired by the film leads H. D. to speculate upon "that other Jeanne,"

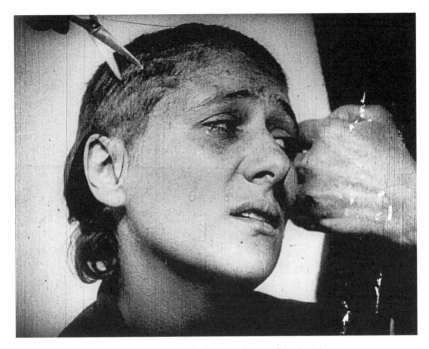

14. Carl Dreyer, *The Passion of Joan of Arc* (1928).

the more robustly defiant one *not portrayed* by Dreyer. In this way H. D. manages to reclaim the "negative" of the Joan she disavows.

By alluding to the bisexual possibilities of Joan and then tracing their derailment, H. D. adumbrates how the female spectator *might be* redrawn through cinematic identification. The review directs us back to her earlier cinematic portraits; for instance, two blazons ("The Contest" and "Loss") create alternate identifications for the female spectator. "The Contest" depicts an ostensibly male body, "chiseled like rocks / that are eaten into by the sea" (*CP* 12):

> The ridge of your breast is taut,
> and under each the shadow is sharp,
> and between the clenched muscles
> of your slender hips.
>
> From the circle of your cropped hair
> there is light,
> and about your male torso
> and the foot-arch and the straight ankle.
> (*CP* 13)

Read next to the less gender-specific portrait in "Loss," the "cropped hair" reverberates as a potentially transvestite element. The speaker of "Loss" once more notes the addressee's "beautiful feet," but is overawed by "beauty welded with strength." While not specifically portraying Joan's experience, "Loss" eroticizes a bisexual martyred body in a scene of sacrifice:

> And I wondered as you clasped
> your shoulder-strap
> at the strength of your wrist
> and the turn of your young fingers,
> and the lift of your shorn locks,
> and the bronze
> of your sun-burnt neck.

The speaker places herself as spectator in the poem: "I wonder if you knew how I watched, / how I crowded before the spearsmen –"(*CP* 23). This might just as well have been addressed to Joan. Likewise, "Prisoners" depicts a lover waiting for a last glimpse of her fellow "wretch," who is "about to be crushed out, / burned or stamped out" (*CP* 34). The *mise-en-scène* admits to masochism: ("Why do I want this? / I who have seen you at the banquet / each flower of your hyacinth-circlet / white against your hair"). Yet this poem, obfuscating the gender of speaker and addressee, traces out trajectories of desire and identification not possible in Dreyer's *Joan*.

For H. D., Joan is a visionary, actualizing dual identifications: "I am a priestess. / I am a priest" ("The Dancer"; *CP* 260). Through H. D.'s bisexual apparatus, "opposite qualities such as active/passive or masculine/feminine coexist within a single individual" (*Psyche* 58). Joan's hallucinations have been cited as "dangerous symptoms," but rather than being construed as merely hysteric they have come to signify a psychotic refusal to separate interior realities from external ones. As I later elaborate, H. D. nevertheless draws upon a psycho-cinematic blurring of inside and outside in her creation of the femme fatale.

DAZED AND REVITALIZED

When H. D. leaves *Joan of Arc*, she sees the movie poster and continues to feel obliged to identify with the character's oppressed body. Her response to this film dramatizes the danger of women's irresistible "imbrication with the image" (Doane, "Masquerade" 426). The other side of such imbrication is the possibility of "healing in the half-light." After all, H. D.'s "ideal" cinema encourages merging and proximity along with half-ness, fissures, shadows. The screen, as Judith Mayne argues in another context, can be simultaneously "a figure of permeability and division."[52]

This duality governs H. D.'s phenomenology of film viewing in which the borders between film and her "lived body" are not clearly defined. Yet the "healing" H. D. desires requires the disjoining of usual sensory tracks to forge alternate ones. Thus, fusion can be itself a form of "psycho-somatic" fragmentation. The beginning of H. D.'s review of *Expiation* (1928) is worth quoting at length to denote her corporeal merging with the film, even before she enters the cinema:

> I was precipitated suddenly, after the sinuous run along the edge of Lake Geneva, unto the cobbles of the formal irregularities of the Square of Saint Francis at Lausanne . . . I was tumbled out and dazed and exulted at the head of a sort of dimensional dream-tunnel. I was precipitated between so to speak, built-up and somewhat over-done little shops with windows and wares; oranges, boxes of leeks, lettuces on the pavement; bright green shutters. Dazed and revitalized by the run, I plunged down this street somewhat reeling, making jig-jag to find just how those shadows cut just that block (and that block) into perfect design of cobbled square and square little doorways till I found myself at the entrance of a slice of a theatre, the Palace of Lausanne. ("Expiation" 38)

Notably, H. D. is "revitalized" and "precipitated" by film. But what makes this passage extraordinary is its rendition of a mode of seeing. H. D.'s vision, both slicing and "cobbled," is highly attuned to both external sensory details and to her interior "dream-tunnel." Significantly, she arrives at the "slice of theatre" in the middle of *Expiation*; following a plot, it would seem, is less important than the transitive movement between external and internal experience.

Echoing her painful merging with Dreyer's Joan, she writes that *Expiation* "takes the human spirit acting and re-acting . . . *further* than it can go." She refers to the film's casting its protagonists into an elemental landscape familiar from *Sea Garden*: "Rain soaks and pours and pours and soaks and the elements have these at their mercy" ("Expiation" 41). What distinguishes *Expiation* from *Joan* is that oppression by the imagined natural world is of an entirely different order than oppression by paternal "law." As we saw in her early poems, the tumult of a "wind-swept" and "terrible" scenario can revive the senses. Two poems, "Oread" and "The Pool," illustrate her incipient "theory" of the film spectator as prone to fusion with the screen image and "precipitated" by montage.

"Oread" (1914), often cited as *the* Imagist poem, does not "contain" an image but reveals its permeability. The poem's communal speakers (Greek mountain nymphs) invoke a reversibility between inside and outside almost to the point of destruction:

> Whirl up, sea –
> whirl your pointed pines,
> splash your great pines
> on our rocks,
> hurl your green over us,
> cover us with your pools of fir.
>
> (*CP* 55)

These verb-motivated injunctions merge sharpened substance ("your pointed pines") with fluid reflection so that no clear-cut separation exists between the erotically charged setting and the plural body. The poem is clearly not meant as a depiction of film phenomenology. Yet when read in the context of H. D.'s cinematic sensibility, its "mobile consciousness" points toward the mediating, porous, and reflexive film screen.[53] The last line blurs subject and object much in the way the screen has the potential to override divisions between the viewer's body and the tactile, immediate image ("your pools of fir"). Unlike Joan's passivity in the face of corporeal subordination, this poem's multiple speaker ("we") calls for a "shattered ego." In "Oread," a shatter effect paradoxically heightens a state of fusion.

"The Pool" (a poem closely related to "Oread") does not provide a cohesive or completely tangible image:

> Are you alive?
> I touch you.
> You quiver like a sea-fish.
> I cover you with my net.
> What are you – banded one?
>
> (*CP* 56)

Revising the Narcissus myth, the poem shows the indeterminately sexed body intervening within an act of reflection and "banded" by it. The self-interrogation ("are you alive?") establishes an intermediary space for the spectator – who rather than chained down, slips through the banded net, an act visualized by the dividing dash. Thus the contact proposed by the poem ("I touch you") does not "suture" self-presence.

According to Sobchack, subject and object are reversible in cinematic experience so that a film and its spectator "meet on shared ground but never identically occupy it" (*Address of the Eye* 23). "The Pool" insists upon such reversibility and division. In other words, it is possible to read it as taking the point of view of the net as film screen addressing the spectator

("I cover you") as well as the reverse. In "Oread" and "The Pool," fusion and cutting are two sides of a resistance to a finely demarcated bodily ego. Joan, by contrast, is all too vividly outlined, pinioned by the camera's gaze.

On route to the Lausanne theatre, H. D. situates herself in the fluctuating environment ("plunged down this street somewhat reeling, making jig-jag to find just how those shadows cut just that block") through the "shared ground" of a cinematic phenomenology. Film accomplishes the reversibility of subject and object in part through the play of shadow and light upon external surfaces. While "The Pool" does not overtly address the function of light, its bodily ego is banded by shadow; skin is a net, not a solid surface. (A still from *Potemkin* in *Close Up* shows "a curious effect of light and shadow" upon a saluting sailor, as if casting a net over his face and torso.)[54]

"Oread" and "The Pool" break away from a bounded bodily ego by crossing lines dividing the internal from the external. In other poems, light constitutes and deconstitutes the body in the "over-weaving of semi-phosphorescent light" ("Restraint" 39).[55] "Light speaks, is pliant, is malleable," she writes ("Restraint" 38). In fact, embodied landscapes emerge in *Sea Garden* through the subtle manipulation of light, what Eisenstein calls "tonal montage" where "optical light-vibrations (varying degrees of 'haze' and 'luminosity' . . . light-vibration" induces emotional effects ("Dialectic Approach" 76). For instance, "[t]he light passes / from ridge to ridge"; alternately, "shadows dart / from the cornel-roots –" and "each leaf / cuts another leaf on the grass, / shadow seeks shadow" ("Evening," *CP* 18–19). The play between light and shadow in her poems, prominent as well in Expressionist films, creates psychological nuances, revealing the way bodily identities can merge and potentially reclaim new outlines.

Thus she praises those moments (much like her own in *Sea Garden*) in *Student of Prague* that reveal "things we can't say or paint at the sight of windows half-closed in moonlight" so that character is consequently "symbol, asterisk, an enigma," not a determinate identity ("Conrad Veidt" 41). *Sunrise* is another exemplary film that vividly links ambient atmosphere to embodiment. The film relies upon hypnotic studio settings of "desolate marshes" so that "it takes the eye a long time to discern their artificiality."[56] Murnau's use of low-level lighting and chiaroscuro creates a bodily reality even as it dematerializes it: the glowing moonlight reflected in the marsh disperses its light so that bodies lose their outlines within the energized natural elements, an activity reminiscent of "Oread" and "The Pool."

At the same time, *Sunrise* recreates the binary sexual tropes of vamp and virgin, those limiting possibilities for female identification prevalent in modernist texts and films. In one scene, the Circe-like vamp from the city, shot in a radiant moon-glow, dances tarantula-like among the swaying reeds, luring the "naïve" husband into a plot to murder the more domestic country wife. Friedberg tells us that Macpherson's *Foothills* (1929) was modeled on the plot of *Sunrise*, with H. D. playing the role of the city woman (*Cinema and Modernism* 213). As Janet Bergstrom observes, the City Woman is "exclusively sexual" and the other "desexualized, ethereal."[57] These abstract bodies haunt H. D.'s attempts to undermine sexual polarization along with the consequent split between mind and body inherent in this dialectic. Yet in spite of its conventional female figures, *Sunrise* generates an "atmosphere" where bodies can be refashioned. H. D.'s poems likewise employ fusion and splicing to conjure a transformational "half-light." The seeming obligatory alternatives between enacting the victim or the vamp, however, continue to frustrate H. D. For example, she asks of the portrait of Mary Magdelene in Cecil B. de Mille's *King of Kings*: "Why must a supposedly fascinating woman . . . find it necessary to stress and over stress and restress all the vamp qualities of the most illiterate penny dreadful charmer? *Must* beauty always dress itself in scarlet, drag sumptuous velours about apparently naked limbs?"[58] This is language familiar from her review of *Joan*. Why must "apparent" female embodiment be granted at the expense of mind, she questions. *Pandora's Box* provides an alternate figure through Louise Brooks – the "innocent vamp" whose pre-oedipal kinesthetic body evades conscription, promising some kind of union between body and soul.

PROJECTING AND DISSECTING THE FEMME FATALE

Doane explains that texts of modernity are drawn to the femme fatale because she "is a clear indication of the extent of the fears and anxieties prompted by shifts in the understanding of sexual difference" (*Desire to Desire* 1–2). The popularity of this figure in texts during and after the First World War revealed an exaggerated duality: an "apocalypse of masculinism" and an "apotheosis of femaleness" (*No Man's Land* 262). H. D.'s poems, "Eurydice" and "Helen," are important strata in the delineation of the femme fatale as pinioned between these extremes. The 1917 revisionist "Eurydice" lucidly represents the problem of female embodiment as a visual one: to be a female body in modern culture is to be either disembodied or excessively carnal. "Helen" (1924), building upon this dialectic, traces the visual mechanisms present in creating the femme fatale and then retraces the body as a figure for bisexual desire.

In seeming opposition to the femme fatale, the mythic figure of Eurydice is the chaste wife, the mourned-for bride of the poet Orpheus. She is a mute body readily linked to figures like the disembodied Madonna-like wife in *Sunrise*, who is nearly murdered by her husband. As Cixous writes, "silence is the mark of hysteria. The great hysterics have lost speech."[59] What the hysteric Eurydice shares with the classic femme fatale is that she seems "totally devoid of thought, a blank surface" (*Desire to Desire* 152), a quality that likewise reverberates in H. D.'s Helen and Pabst's Lulu. In her "blankness," the femme fatale externalizes the body as scriptable, both fulfilling and thwarting masculine fantasies.

The culturally constructed femme fatale in her "hyperbolisation of the accoutrements of femininity" poses a threat to gender norms (Doane, "Masquerade" 427). H. D.'s bisexual apparatus makes visible her donning a variety of masks, including one where "womanliness is a mask that can be worn or removed" (427). Each of these "masks" (Eurydice, Helen, Lulu, and Astrid) bear projections of male anxiety about female embodiment. As Huyssen exposes, the mechanical femme fatale in *Metropolis* is unambiguously the product of male fantasy literalized as "technological artifact": "woman, in male perspective, is considered to be the natural vessel of man's reproductive capacity, a mere bodily extension."[60] In some sense, Lang's "robot" is the one H. D. imagined in "Mask and Movietone" – an artificially constructed female identity, an automaton vamp who would be more at home in the soul starved talkies. H. D.'s mythic "masks" recover a gestural "aura" or "original intensity of being," an aim that may seem at odds with film technology, yet H. D. believed that "[m]iracles and godhead are not out of place on the screen" ("Restraint" 35).

In her "half-light," Eurydice as poet-as-absence replaces Orpheus as the prototypic poet-as-presence whose legendary grief has fuelled his creations. Significantly, the poem returns to an underground like Plato's cave, a setting that adumbrates the "impossible place of woman's desire," in order to re-project her embodiment.[61] H. D.'s "revitalization" of Eurydice depends upon a "vibrant darkness."

The poem opens en medias res, after Orpheus has descended to retrieve Eurydice and has failed to restore her to the lit upper world. At the very last moment, he disobeyed the commandment of Hades and gazed back at Eurydice, thus dooming her to the underworld. For all intents and purposes, the dead or intangible female body becomes the basis of Orpheus's poetic legacy and fame. H. D. assumes Eurydice's perspective and mythic identity to undo the accreted work of male fantasy, revising the psychoanalytic model of female sexuality as lack.

By sequencing the poem into six scenes, H. D.'s recursive and broken narrative defies the stasis of the "held shot" or the abstracted female body.[62] It begins in backwards motion:

> So you have swept me back,
> I who could have walked with the live souls
> above the earth,
> I who could have slept among the live flowers

"Swept back," Eurydice is the "object of the motion rather than its originator."[63] Anticipating Tiresias who has "walked among the lowest of the dead," she indulges in the masochist's penchant for dwelling upon the inciting detail. Her questions amplify and reiterate:

> what was it that crossed my face
> with the light from yours
> and your glance?
> what was it you saw in my face?
> the light of your own face,
> the fire of your own presence?

Eurydice, as screen image, looks back, specifically addressing the male spectator who would rely upon the female body as immobile specter to shore up his identity.[64] In short, she transforms herself from the object of the gaze into the spectator.

At the poem's outset, Eurydice mourns what amounts to a "psychic blindness": "everything is lost, / everything is crossed with black, / black upon black." Merleau-Ponty describes how a body needs a "background" to stake out its spatiality: "Bodily space can be distinguished from external space . . . because it is the darkness needed in the theatre to show up the performance, the background . . . against which the gesture and its aim stand out" (*Phenomenology* 100–1). With a similar kinesthesia in mind, Page du Bois argues that in reading Sappho we "are always conscious of the possibility of dismemberment, of the fragility of wholeness, of corporeal and psychic integrity, even as our identity is fashioned *against the background* of such dismemberment" (emphasis mine).[65]

In the middle of the poem, Eurydice enumerates what has been "lost," retracing her corporeal surface, texture and movement:

> Fringe upon fringe
> of blue crocuses,
> crocuses, walled against blue of themselves,
> blue of that upper earth
> blue of the depth upon depth of flowers

Eisenstein remarks that "movement in film resides in the fact that two motionless images of a moving body, following one another, blend into an appearance of motion" ("Dialectic Approach" 49). Superimposition through repetition is the strategy that here allows Eurydice to inhabit, as if for the first time, a sensate world.

By the penultimate stanza, Eurydice requires a "background" for her recreated "dismemberment":

> Against the black
> I have more fervour
> than you in all the splendour of that place,
> against the blackness
> and the stark grey
> I have more light

By placing Eurydice "against" a backdrop of "stark grey," H. D. re-animates loss as poetic sufficiency: "At least I have the flowers of myself." Among the garland of flowers that now apparel her body are crocuses and hyacinths, bits of light and color that flash across the poem's screen. In particular, her face is the "reflex" of "hyacinth color / caught from the raw fissure in the rock." (We must remember that silent films were often tinted to create atmospheric effects.) "Hyacinth color" (like the violet tinting of *The Waste Land*) signifies for H. D. an entire homoerotic tradition, and in "Eurydice," recalls Sappho's "Epithalamia" honoring a bride in the name of Aphrodite.[66]

The poem ends with Eurydice as ethereal wife transfigured into the femme fatale brandishing her "terrible" body:

> and the flowers
> if I should tell you,
> you would turn from your own fit paths
> toward hell

Eurydice has changed the terms of her visibility ("I have the fervour of myself for a presence"). A final reversal of spatial arrangement (she is no longer looking in the same direction) commands that "hell must open like a red rose / for the dead to pass." This act of inversion, accomplished through a cinematic layering and repetition of images, is an act of defiance against literary as well as sexual conventions. The dead/not dead Eurydice, as we shall see, is an incipient figure for H. D.'s defiance in *Borderline*.

"Eurydice" situates the viewer and the subject of the view within an underworld. Likewise, *Joyless Street* – the film H. D. claimed as most pivotal to her film experience – takes place in the dark shadows of a street, emblematic of post-war poverty and despair. The film makes it clear why the defiance of Eurydice is so hard won. In reviewing *Joyless Street*, H. D. fixates upon Garbo but also directs us to the film's allusion to the myth's dismemberment scene: "The performance began with a street (will I ever forget it) and the somber plodding limp of a one-legged, old ruffian. Just a long, Freudian, tunnel-like, dark street. . . . Nothing within sight, nothing to dream of or ponder on but . . . the butcher's shop with its attendant, terrible, waiting line of frenzied women" ("Beauty" 30).

The film crosscuts scenes of the very poor lined up before the butcher's door (Garbo sinks down in exhaustion waiting for her allotted slab of meat) with scenes of crooked investors enjoying the excesses of a fine hotel. One of the most extraordinary aspects of *Joyless Street* is not only its deft social criticism, but its elaborate rendition of multiple women figures – each struggling with the forms of embodiment available to them. The women of the street are commodities on par with the butcher's dangling carcasses of meat. Their hunger drives them to prostitution, despair or madness. The daughter Maria (played by Asta Nielson) of the one-legged veteran (whose peg leg induces a double take) is desperate to leave the street and her abusive father. From the outset, she behaves as if in a trance; she is dressed in a baggy plain dress and moves clumsily. She will not – as another woman (a mother with a starving baby) does – give way to the butcher's advances to gain a necessity. Instead, she leaves home and tries to join the upwardly mobile man she loves (Egon), asking him to marry her. He claims he first needs money for a stock investment, spurring her decision to prostitute herself to supply him the cash. She allows herself to be seduced by a wealthy investor, and while they are consorting, she overhears Egon in the other room. Through a key-hole, we see a bare-backed woman, the film's femme fatale, in an embrace with Egon. Before the film clarifies through flashback and repeated images that Maria has strangled this other woman, we watch her descend into a state of complete traumatic shock – not knowing precisely why. She lets herself be made into an image of male fantasy; she is gaudily outfitted, her hair is made to look electric, and her make-up starkly outlines her face, never smiling and staring into space.

In spite of H. D.'s fixation upon Garbo in this film, Nielson offers an important link to H. D., for whom the absent gaze can represent a visionary trance as much as a symptom of cultural breakdown. She is, in short, another vivid expression of "dissociation of sensibility," performing a body that has been divested of all desire. Garbo manages, as H. D. suggests, to resist corruption and thus gains the poet's desired identification. Yet Garbo as "icy mermaid" is never entirely untrammeled by the street's bodily demands. She resides on a continuum of the other women: the femme fatale, the hysteric, and the starving mother, who ends up stabbing the butcher with a train of hungry women behind her. The mother is the emissary of a communal vengeance, and thus in the film's "making new" conjures up the frenzy of the Maenads. Of course, the Maenads who dismember Orpheus do so because he does not return their desire. In *Joyless Street*, the butcher (oppressive arbiter of who eats and who doesn't within the patriarchal economy of the street) is butchered as retribution for his bartering of food for enforced sexual power. Yet both female murderers end up being punished, with the mother being burned to death. The femme fatale, the wronged woman and the starving mother merge as sacrificial bodies, receptacles filled and then emptied.

Building upon the claiming of an "absent presence" in "Eurydice" and in dialogue with the abject forms of embodiment in *Joyless Street*, "Helen" mediates both the cultural body of the femme fatale and bisexual desire. Helen is also the name of H. D.'s mother's, and according to Freud, motivated her trip to Greece in 1920 (*Tribute* 65). The poem's Helen is alabaster, linking her to the notable "pearl-like quality of [Lulu's] skin" in *Pandora's Box*.[67] Her skin signals not only a receptive "blank" but a palimpsest, layered with at least three superimposed bodies: the mythic Helen as femme fatale, H. D.'s mother and the idealized Garbo in *Joyless Street*. Indeed, this composite figure is a recurrent "fix" in her refashioning a poetic body.

Mandel directs us to the poem's film method: "The poem contains, as does a held shot of a living image, a cinematic dynamic of tension within stasis."[68] "Helen" in this way presents a dead woman in bits and pieces, anticipating H. D.'s destiny as Astrid in *Borderline*.[69] Like a camera, the poem pans the living/unliving body of Helen, composing her through syntax dependent on delayed appositions and dissecting takes:

> All Greece hates
> the still eyes in the white face,
> the lustre as of olives
> where she stands,
> and the white hands. (*CP* 154)

By disrupting expected syntax, the body part is constituted as a fragmentary afterimage ("and the white hands"); the part persists as if a phantom limb, a "kind of libidinal memorial" (*Volatile* 41). H. D. adopts the male "heroic" gaze that traces the physiognomy of the "femme fatale," desired only when mortified and broken. In the process, she simulates a "montage of male eyes"[70] that constructs a statuesque "vamp," caught as if in several freeze frames. Yet the "still eyes" are the poet's own, a shade away from the gaze of the female hysteric (including Nielson in *Joyless Street*): "I stare / till my eyes are a statue's eyes" ("Trance," *CP* 244).

"Helen" thus reveals how male desire can project fatality upon an apparently passive object of beauty; in fact the poem ends with a condition of "idolatry" clearly spelled out. Love of Helen's body appears to depend upon her being "laid" and dead:

> Greece sees unmoved,
> God's daughter, born of love,
> the beauty of cool feet
> and slenderest knees,
> could love indeed the maid,
> only if she were laid,
> white ash amid funereal cypresses.
>
> (*CP* 155)

Yet by inhabiting Greece's "hating" and lusting or indifferent gaze, H. D. superimposes another possibility for the female spectator or for the gaze "moved" by the "beauty of cool feet," participating in what Bergstrom calls a "less goal-oriented way of looking."[71] Such looking potentially interrupts narrative coherence and deflects the oedipal imperative.

The fragmenting of the female body can be read against the grain by reconnecting the mythic Helen to her Sapphic roots. As Du Bois suggests, Sappho's body cannot be fully reconstructed. The erotic charge in H. D.'s poem lies within its lingering over Helen as tableux, suspended between animation and death, who returns a look from eyes with "lustre as of olives." Hysteric in her fractured gestures and femme fatale in her alluring but desecrated beauty, Helen is the apparitional object of female desire.

H. D.'s review of Pabst's *Joyless Street* (written just a year after "Helen") literally identifies the queer icon Garbo with Helen, intimating how they escape the heterosexual fix: "Well beauty has been slurred over and laughed at and forgotten. But Helen of Troy didn't always stay at home with Menelaeus" ("Beauty" 32). Simultaneously, H. D. bestows upon Garbo a "purity," specifically distinguished from Gish's sexlessness, that nevertheless implies a self-enforced anesthesia: "Helen walking scatheless among execrating warriors, the plague, distress, and famine is in this child's icy, mermaid-like integrity" ("Beauty" 31). This "Helen" sounds much like Dreyer's Joan, but rather than "kicked towards the angels" she walks among them. In her double narrative of Garbo as Helen, H. D. shows her as abducted and ruined by the "Ogre" of Hollywood, made into a "masquerade of femininity": "Miss Garbo has been trained . . . wigs, eyelashes," losing her "almost clairvoyant intensity" ("Beauty" 31). She revisits this plot line in her epic *Helen in Egypt* (1952) where she proposes (via Stesichorus) that Helen never went to Greece but was always a specular "phantom," an hallucination of male desire.[72] Lulu in *Pandora's Box* stands between the poles of disembodiment and martyrdom with her eroticized innocence.

EXPRESSIONIST BODY: FROM LULU TO ASTRID

H. D.'s absorption in film was at its apex in the late twenties when she lived in Territet, a Swiss town near the German border, with Bryher and director Macpherson (in a marriage of convenience with Bryher). It was in this period that the menage edited *Close Up* (1927–33), which sought to foster the most innovative ideas percolating about avant-garde cinema. The trio produced *Borderline* in Territet in 1930.

Coincident with living in Territet, Bryher and Macpherson made frequent trips to Berlin where they participated in the gay subcultures proliferating in the Weimar Republic as well as the steady emergence of repressive laws aimed at these subcultures.[73] These excursions helped to shape the group's sexual aesthetics, providing H. D. with a wide repertoire of female images, including the femme fatale, the cross-dresser, and the "monster as Medusa,"[74] each to some extent either encoding or explicitly enacting sexual deviance.

Bryher and Macpherson no doubt witnessed first hand the hydraulic mechanism at work in Weimar aesthetics. Nicholls elucidates: "Subjective emotion seemed to suffer a constant repression, and in its boldness and grandiosity Expressionist art sought to direct that emotion as a transformative energy against social constraints."[75] As such, an Expressionist aesthetic reflects the symptomatic cultural struggle between authoritarianism and transgressiveness that Kracauer identifies in his *Caligari to Hitler*.[76] As we shall see, this polarity recurs in both Pabst's *Pandora's Box* and in *Borderline*.

On one of his trips to Berlin, Macpherson wrote to H. D. about several meetings with Pabst, one from Hotel Adlon in Berlin after seeing photos: "one of Pabst himself, young, very very very very Lesbian, and he is DeeeeelI-IIIIIghted to mit (sic) you."[77] Bryher (on this same trip) wrote to H. D. that she and Macpherson "are both in love with Pabst."[78] Macpherson also reported Pabst's reaction to *Wingbeat*: "what he reeeeeally liked about the film was that YOU showed up the utter futility of the Hollywood tradition, and that beauty was something quite different. And I am wondering if he still wants Louise Brooks for Lulu."[79] Even if this flattering speculation is far afield, there is a dramatic inverse connection between Lulu and H. D.'s later screen embodiment in *Borderline* as Astrid, a femme fatale stripped of all charisma.

The inverted connection between Astrid and Lulu can be traced to H. D.'s unremitting admiration of Pabst – from *Joyless Street* to his having "vanquished the border-sphere" in *Secrets of a Soul*. Within Pabst's "border-sphere," the body has a porous relationship to the unconscious. For H. D., Pabst repeatedly stakes a place for the versatile representation of female embodment. Unlike Dreyer's Joan whom she cannot love, H. D. will "love and always will love [Pabst's] most modest feminine creation."[80] Hypnotized by the director's finesse with lighting, these creations "move and glow before him like sun-flowers to the sun."[81]

Finally, Pabst's film style, often criticized as "feminine" for its "decadent" attention to surfaces and atmosphere, meshes with H. D.'s "half-light" aesthetics. Petro writes that "Pabst's films are not only imbued with an atmospheric 'moodiness'; they are, more fundamentally, precisely about the transitory, fleeting, impermanent condition we call 'mood.'"[82] Moreover, Pabst supplies pliable settings to accommodate diffuse desires, including Lulu's "polymorphous perversity."

Like *Borderline*, *Pandora's Box* enacts the double weave of expression and repression of Weimar Expressionism that Nicholls and Kracauer so aptly describe. In fact, *Pandora's Box* "puts into play the signifiers of sexual transgression – incest, androgyny, lesbianism, prostitution" (*Desire to Desire* 144). The femme fatale motif binds the feminine as castration threat and dangerous other, and as such belongs to an Expressionist legacy that both transgresses "the normative" in its concentration upon the sexual and perpetuates an oedipal model of desire. In scripting this figure, *Pandora's Box* stitches in subversive desires as an "in-between" warp within the weft of cultural repression.

The inspiration for *Pandora's Box* was a play of the same name by Frank Wedekind written between the years 1892 and 1901. The German government banned the play as immoral. Even though its cast of characters includes an open lesbian, Countess Geschwitz, what most enraged reviewers was Wedekind's portrait of Lulu's seemingly guiltless sexuality. In response to the banning of his play, Wedekind claims that the "tragic central figure of the play is not Lulu, as the justices mistakenly assumed, but Countess Geschwitz. Apart form an intrigue here and there, Lulu plays an entirely passive role."[83]

While he amplifies upon Lulu's polymorphous sexuality, Pabst also gives a prominent place to Geschwitz (considered the first overtly lesbian character to appear on screen). She is driven and ultimately thwarted by her desire for Lulu; yet unlike the men who seek to possess Lulu, she does not disown these desires. For example, in Lulu's wedding reception scene, Geschwitz openly takes Lulu by the arm and dances with her. Pabst records Geschwitz's minute expressions of longing, disappointment, and pleasure. Thus Pabst simultaneously reveals Geschwitz "burdened with the curse of abnormality" (Wedekind's words) and makes a space for an alternate sexuality as an identificatory possibility.[84] Ultimately, Geschwitz raises the lesbian possibility, but also acts as foil for Lulu's more "illegible" sexuality.

Pabst diverges from Wedekind's play by exaggerating this femme fatale's sexual indeterminacy and her disruption of narrative cohesion. As a result, he was severely criticized by a *Close Up* reviewer who argued that *Pandora's Box* fails because it cannot live up to Wedekind's play without "the words"; Lulu is too much body, "limited by her senses": "Sexuality alone in her remains vital."[85] Pabst's version of Lulu disappoints this critic precisely because she is not the traditional femme fatale: "In vain one looked for the legendary urging and gaining in her, that men desire and fear with a woman." However, by expanding upon Wedekind's notion of the "completely passive" Lulu as victim of "fatal destiny," Pabst succeeds in making her childishly "innocent," the tabula rasa of her skin absorbing and deflecting the projection of male fear and desire.

Symptomatic of Lulu's polymorphous sexuality, the "plot" is a "broken sequence" or series of non-narrative episodes, portraying Lulu engaged in non-teleological movement – ecstatic dance, acrobatic arabesques, or more loosely swinging her limbs. Her movement does not advance the narrative but rather suspends temporal sequence. During these non-teleological episodes, Pabst uses close-ups of Lulu to clarify her role as the receptacle for "the constant demands and desires of the other characters" (*Desire to Desire* 146). These desires inevitably interrupt her movement and return the film to its "plot." Yet like other women in Pabst's films, Lulu's kinesthetic expressivity reflects a temporary escape from the barter system visibly oppressing female sexuality.

A good example of Lulu's non-teleological embodiment occurs near the film's beginning. Lulu dances in front of a painting which represents her dressed as a boy in harlequin costume, an image that reverberates with the film's depiction of several key Weimar venues: carnival, cabaret, café life, and the "revue." In "Helen," the contrast between stasis and movement highlights the camera's potential to animate and to kill the phenomenological body. Here the painted version of Lulu as transvestite points to the film's wider delineation of sexual variance – which in oedipal logic becomes associated with fatality. The men in the film lust after Lulu, projecting their desires upon her while fearing her polymorphous body. Like Helen of Troy, Lulu becomes the "innocent" bearer of disowned desire. Criticized by film reviewers for "doing nothing" (as Brooks herself recounts), Lulu is appealing precisely because she provokes an "epistemological trauma" and resists clear-cut notions of embodiment.

Lulu is caught within a skein of desires, geared to pin down and contain her sexuality. A "respectable" man (Dr. Peter Schon) struggles to overcome his unstoppable lust for Lulu, considered dangerous and undesirable because of her bohemian marginality. He is "forced" to marry her (after his fiancé catches him enveloped in Lulu's arms). On their wedding night, he discovers his son Alwa (also compelled by irrepressible desire for Lulu) with his head on her lap. Into this primal scenario, Schon has toted a gun, hanging limply by his side. After he rouses his son and sends him away, he mounts a murderous rage.

However, what this scene foregrounds is not Schon's jealousy of his son, but Lulu's ability to experience bodily sensation in the forgetful present (an ability Stein might admire). The screenplay reads: "Catching sight of herself in the looking-glass . . . She has already forgotten her terror." Enraged, he watches her oblivious of him:

Lulu stands in front of the mirror admiring herself: slim, white, innocent. (Now her hands reach for the shoulder clasp and she begins to slip off her dress.)
Dr. Schon is staring in horror at this display.
   But Lulu turns back happily to the mirror and takes off the pearl necklace. She runs it caressingly through her fingers before laying it in the jewel case.[86]

To emphasize her self-absorption Pabst places Lulu beside Schon in the mirror. In shadow, he appears as a "death's head," seeing his own absence. Petro reads this moment as a "self-consciously modernist gesture" that "reveals that woman is there by virtue of the other, that she is a projection of male desire, and that male desire is dependent on a certain image of female sexuality."[87] Yet the ghostly reflection of Schon in contrast to Lulu's vital pleasure before the mirror suggests the "femme lesbian" who "adopts an ambiguous position in relation to the gaze of the camera/spectator. She is on display, actively designed to lure the gaze; the crucial difference is, however, that the spectator is shut out from her world."[88]

This mirror scene in fact leads to Schon's deranged injunction – "Kill yourself, it's the only way to save us!" Presumably by "us" he means father and son along with other men not yet under her spell. Schon forces her to grip the gun, shoving the barrel against her breast. After a protracted struggle, she manages to defy him, turning the gun against her assailant. Lulu acts in "self-defense," her role as "murderer" clearly foisted upon her.

After Lulu is found guilty of the murder of Schon (as well as guilty of all crimes against men in her role as Pandora), she escapes captivity with the help of her vaudeville friends. Immediately able to throw off her widow's veil (slipping it off as simply as her wedding gown in the inciting mirror scene), she flips through fashion magazines, she twirls and pirouettes, she takes a bath, she looks in the mirror. In Wedekind's play, she exclaims: "When I looked at myself in the mirror I wished I were a man . . . my own husband." (In "Towards the Piraeus," H. D. repeats this conditional: "If I had been a boy" *CP* 178; conversely, Eliot writes "Then he had been a young girl" in "The Death of Saint Narcissus" *The Manuscript* 95.)

The central crisis of Pabst's film appears to be the centrifugal force pulling Lulu away from her own sexual fluidity. Lulu's ultimate "pinning down" occurs when Jack the Ripper brutally murders her. He is the perverted extreme of the masculinity crisis, acting as a "scourge" of London women. Pabst emphasizes Jack's cracked, post-war demeanor: pale, hungry and twitching, he meekly smiles when entering Lulu's room. In the last scenes of the film, the camera zooms in upon Jack's "symptomatic act" of opening and closing his hand as well as upon the glinting knife he uses to slay Lulu.

This knife is a precursor to the one Astrid wields in *Borderline*, one that is turned against her. Lulu's death presents a very difficult moment for the spectator. The character Brooks portrays, complicit with the commodity culture that markets her, is similar to H. D.'s portrait of Helen as fatal beauty. To identify with Lulu is to identify with kinesthetic vibrancy as well as with the near impossibility of surviving as such. The femme fatale's body unleashes a variety of erotic energies that must be repressed by the cultural narrative of oedipal desire.

BORDERLINE EXPRESSIONISM: REDEFINING
HYSTERIC / FEMME FATALE

Borderline borrows from an Expressionist aesthetic through its thematics of degeneration and alienation along with its concomitant style of disjointed montage and exaggerated, distorted perspectives. Both *Pandora's Box* and *Borderline* test the thresholds of an increasingly repressive culture, but the latter film more insistently dislocates an oedipal narrative. This dislocation emerges in part through the film's rescripting of the femme fatale as "an articulation of fears surrounding the loss of stability and centrality of the

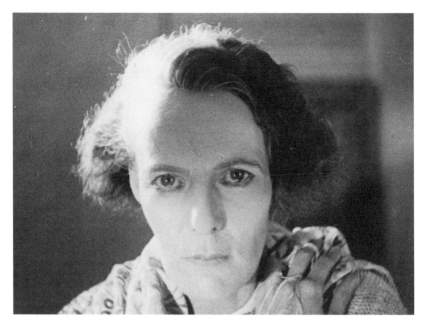

15. From *Borderline* (1930).

self, the 'I,' the ego" (*Desire to Desire* 1–2). What *Borderline* underscores, in contrast to *Pandora's Box*, is the failure of compulsory heterosexuality, particularly its role in the enforcement of racial categories.

H. D. assumes a perversely unlikable role in her portrait of the self-confessed racist Astrid. The film gestures towards making Astrid into a femme fatale but then undercuts the allurement of this position by showing close-ups of H. D.'s piercing, Medusa-like eyes (fig. 15). In contrast to the effervescent, acrobatic Lulu with her mesmerizing, seductive gaze (fig. 16), Astrid is crimped and pinched, her exaggerated movements and facial expression signs of intense bodily discomfort and angst. H. D. rejects Dreyer's "remorseless rhythm of a scimitar," yet here she deploys the scimitar in her role as Astrid. She does not embody the glamorous femme, fabricated to cater to delusive fantasies; her enactment punctures this "masquerade."

Reflecting the influence of Eisenstein's theories, the film makes joltingly vivid the fact of sexual and racial division, while exposing how predictable metonymies might be shifted and realigned from a visceral vantage. The collective realm becomes intersubjective for Eisenstein with the "creating spectator" actively engaged in the piecing together of shots in intellectual montage. Accordingly, the spectator, interpolated through the editing,

16. G. W. Pabst, *Pandora's Box* (1928).

becomes part of the process of conflict within and between shots. This use
of montage is perhaps why Pabst called *Borderline* "the only real avant-garde
film" (quoted in *Cinema and Modernism* 389). Unlike Pabst's seamless editing style, here the act of montage more evidently disrupts cultural fantasies
as it attempts to refashion them. Destructive and potentially liberating,

the act of cutting is a means of reconstituting embodiment. Cutting is an aesthetic device with corporeal meaning. In *Borderline*, it underscores the instability of gender and racial categories.

If Astrid dissects with both her gaze (mirroring the camera eye) and later the knife, she is dissected and exposed in her enacting the white modernist's cultural displacement of desires upon blackness. *Borderline* reanimates the figure of the femme fatale by self-consciously racializing it, shifting the film's erotic locus from H. D. to Paul Robeson. As such, the film invokes the femme fatale as an index for how sex and race impinge upon each other. As Petro comments, the "New Negro" is often conflated with the "New Woman" in modernist texts.[89]

In counterpoint with an escalating repression in Weimar culture and the corresponding lock-down of sexual and racial difference, *Close Up* defined itself in diametric opposition to the Hollywood mainstream, bringing to the surface issues of cultural appropriation and fetishism. The journal's demise in 1933 coincided with Hitler's rise to power. Along with Eisenstein's ideals of a "collective" fuelling its progressive agenda, and Bryher's articles against war, promoting education and dismantling censorship, *Close Up* devoted an issue to black cinema in August 1929. In this issue, Robert Herring argues for a "pure" Afroamerican cinema, protesting: "Not black films passing for white, and not, please, white passing for black" (quoted in *Cinema and Modernism* 34). Herring, a queer who played a queer in *Borderline*, was instrumental in bringing the Robesons into H. D.'s circle and into the film itself.

The complex erotics of the close-knit trio (Bryher, H. D., and Macpherson) became further complicated with the inclusion of the Robesons. Apparently, Macpherson (bisexual like H. D.) had a number of relationships with black men in the late twenties. Friedman speculates: "Robeson himself may have been the object of Macpherson's attraction for black men. Macpherson's fascination with Robeson's beauty as a body to film is evident in his stills, sketches, and montage for *Borderline*."[90] After the film, H. D. memorialized her sexual feelings towards Robeson in several poems, including "Red Roses for Bronze," where she problematically imagines him as a "bronze god" (1931) sitting for her in an artist's studio so that she can "sate / [her] wretched fingers / in ecstatic work" (*CP* 211).

Borderline expresses multiple trajectories of desire (many pointing towards Robeson) even while it shows the cultural suppression of these trajectories. The film, living out its own hysterical fantasy, enacts "*multiple identifications.*" The café manageress (played by Bryher), frequently arm-in-arm with the barmaid (Charlotte Arthur), presides as lesbian "overseer"

17. From *Borderline*.

(fig. 17). The barmaid is the bisexual copula: she is most physical with Bryher but openly flirts with Pete (Robeson). (Both Bryher and Arthur are stand-ins for H. D.'s bisexuality.) At the film's end, the queer piano player (Herring) tips his hat in sad farewell to Pete whom he has desired throughout, keeping a picture of him on his piano ledge. He removes the photo and tucks it under his jacket near his heart, a gesture signaling the repressive stifling of alternate modes of desire and racial affiliation.

Personal pathology operates overtly within the film's matrix of desires as cultural pathology. Astrid's gestures in particular encapsulate a rising fascism and racist ideology, cinematically legitimated by arguably the most influential and popular silent film, *Birth of a Nation* (1915). In brief, the first half of Griffith's three-hour movie depicts the chaos of the Civil War (with shots of hand-to-hand fighting and the arbitrary, feeble borders between combatants), and a budding romance between a Southerner (whose brain-child will later be the KKK) and a Northerner (played by Lilian Gish). The second half of *Birth* demonstrates how Emancipation "looses" social anarchy, centering its horror upon the threat of miscegenation, the inciting "cause" of the Klan's formation. A mulatto politician, Silas Lynch, who along with pledging to "build an African empire" by giving blacks more power, tries to force himself upon Gish, while a black man Gus (played by a white man) pursues a white Southern woman until she hurls herself from a rock to her death. Unlike *Borderline*, there are no *real* black actors. As Michael Rogin articulates: "Inadvertently underlining the status of the black menace as white fantasy, *Birth*'s rapist and its mulatto seductress were whites in blackface."[91]

Borderline, however, reverses Griffith's myth of American identity as the virulent protection of white womanhood from "primitive" black sexuality; it exposes the ambivalent desire for the black body across gender lines along with the white body's pathological refusal to recognize its "border" existence, permeable and contiguous with other bodies.

The short "libretto," passed out at the premiere of *Borderline* to out-line its fairly conventional but confusing melodramatic plot of sexual jealousy, belies its experimental method and reconfiguration of cultural fantasy:

> In a small 'borderline' town, anywhere in Europe, Pete, a negro, is working in a cheap hotel café. His wife, Adah, who had left him some time previously, has arrived also in the same town, although neither is aware of the presence of the other.
>
> Adah is staying in rooms with the white couple Thorne and Astrid. Thorne is a young man whose life with Astrid has become a torment to them both. Both are highly strung, and their nerves are tense with continuous hostility evoked by Thorne's vague and destructive cravings. He has been involved in an affair with Adah, and the film opens with the quarrel which ends their relationship.
>
> At the "climax" of this film in a prolonged argument between the white couple, Thorne stabs Astrid in "self-defense." The programme notes read: 'The negro woman is blamed . . . Thorne is acquitted . . . the mayor, acting for the populace ordered Pete to leave town. Pete is a scapegoat for the unresolved problems, evasions and neuroses for which the racial "borderline" has served justification.' (*Cinema and Modernism* 218)

The plot strategically hinges upon Thorne's initial revoking of his bi-racial relationship. With its opening shot of Thorne violently pushing Adah (Eslanda Robeson) away from him counterpoised with a shot of Adah's "look" at Thorne (and at us), the film immediately de-legitimates the cultural claim of white "purity." Adah is throughout depicted as poised, thus discounting the claims of female black sexuality as out of control. Her relationship to Thorne is never explained, except as a function of Thorne's assertion of power over her.

Astrid, a racist neurasthenic, has actually called Pete to the "borderline" town," motivated by her jealousy of Thorne's relationship with Adah. When

Astrid confesses in the café that she has drawn Pete into a vortex of emotional entanglements, an inter-title in large letters, the only shot in the film of its kind, reads: "*PETE?*" This moment foregrounds Pete's disruptive function within the narrative: after all, he is, like the femme fatale, the most desired character in *Borderline*.

Perhaps the only character more undesirable than Astrid is an old woman, garbed in Victorian clothing and physically twisted with hatred. Her hatred is instrumental in Pete's ultimate removal. Allied with Astrid, she declares with her bodily movements as well as through inter-title: "If I had my way not one Negro would be in the community." Instead of presenting an idealized version of white women (as does Griffith's *Birth of a Nation*), the film shows their complicit hatred of this troubling "other," much in the way H. D.'s Helen is "hated by all Greece" because of her "beauty" and illegible sexuality.

Astrid draws Pete into conflict not only to provoke Thorne's jealous reaction to his black rival but also to destroy the relationship between Adah and Pete. Contrary to Astrid's expectations, the black couple reunites in shots of Adah walking to meet Pete through the town's liminal archways. Later we see Adah look at herself and us through her compact: the mirror isolates her eye, which stares back at us. Her "indirect" look interrupts our identification with the white gaze. She sports a hat with thin black lines, an image chiming with almost every image in the film; her fashion item acts as semaphore of racial borders and her interference of them. Adah's mulatto skin, her indirect gaze, and her hat all signal a border sphere. In a society where erotic and racial difference is rapidly becoming punishable, it is no wonder that blame will be wrongly cast upon Adah for both the affair and for Astrid's eventual death.

Bryher is another liminal character who accentuates the permeability of boundary lines. She wears male attire and smokes a cigar. If Adah is a cross between races, Bryher represents a cross-pollination of the sexes. (Unlike Geschwitz, however, she does not appear doomed by her "abnormality.") When she reads the notice from the mayor ordering Pete to leave town, she models a self-critical reaction in an inter-title as she looks upward towards Robeson: "What makes it worse is that they think they are doing the right thing. We're like that." "They" shifts to "we" as Bryher admits her complicity with racism. Like Frau Bernburg in the anti-fascist *Maedchen in Uniform*, Bryher, the barmaid, and the piano player enact what Ruby Rich calls "repressive tolerance." Notably, Pete has the film's last words and look; he sardonically mirrors Bryher's, repeating them with a difference, looking at her and then at the camera: "Yes. We're like that."

The multiple desires circulating in the film function in concert with and against the potentially transgressive biracial relation between Thorne and Adah. Macpherson attributes *Borderline*'s lack of popularity with British audiences to "its unexplainedness – like something seen through a window or key-hole."[92] This "key-hole" quality emerges from the film's eruptive sexual energies. *Borderline* further confirms how the fear of losing racial purity directly impinges upon sexual anxieties. This fear of "impurity" foments the rise of fascism and its anti-miscegenation laws intended to "protect" the Aryan race. Furthermore, laws against miscegenation become contiguous with the persecution of "deviant" sexuality in the emergent Nazi regime.

Without going any further, it is important to acknowledge *Borderline*'s serious limitations in its representation of race. Eslanda writes in her diary that she and Paul "'ruined [their] make-up with tears of laughter" over Macpherson and H. D.'s "'naïve ideas of Negroes.'"[93] The film engages in what Petrine Archer-Straw calls "negrophilia," the avant-garde's co-opting of blackness as a form of transgression and as "a sign of their modernity, reflected in the African sculptures scattered in their rooms."[94] Robeson is given a body, but he also functions as mythic, shots of his head against lofty clouds (fig. 18). He is thus distinguished from the white characters, whose bodies are obsessively posed in agonized close-ups of their immobilized body parts, twisted postures, and catatonic gestures. This binary of white angst-ridden body and an implied transcendent black soul is an attempt to reverse the cultural polarity between the "black body" and "white soul," paralleling the subordination of the female body to male mind in modernist texts and film. Strikingly, Robeson starred in the all black cast of Oscar Micheaux's 1924 *Body and Soul*, evocatively playing the diametric roles of two brothers: the evil minister who commits rape and the truly spiritual man-of-science. As we have seen in H. D.'s desire to fuse body and soul through Garbo, this binary haunted her.

Seeming to confirm the split between body and mind, H. D. writes that the film's black couple has more "integrity" than the neurotic whites: "they dwell on the cosmic racial borderline" ("Borderline Pamphlet" 221). For Hazel Carby, *Borderline* reflects the "desire of white modernists for an unambiguous essential masculinity that came to be located in the black body."[95] The film, however, should not be viewed solely as an expression of skewed worship, for it simultaneously subverts the desire for either wholeness or an essentialized bodily identity.

As Carby understands it, *Borderline* relies upon "an almost obsessive use of close-up, in which light and shadow from taut skin and flickering muscle

18. From *Borderline*.

are used to evoke mood and meaning."⁹⁶ These aesthetics extend beyond Robeson's body, resonating with Expressionist techniques as well as with H. D.'s own notions of Hellenic embodiment. "Loss" lovingly attends to "the sharp muscles of your back / which the tunic could not cover –" (*CP* 23); in 1931, H. D. "sculpts" Robeson's bronze body: "sensing underneath the garment seam / ripple and flash and gleam / of indrawn muscle" (*CP* 212).

Carby further asserts, singling out the director, Macpherson: "The subjectivity dissected and exposed by his camera work was in effect a product of his own modernist desires and anxieties surrounding the formation of masculinity in the modern world. Its racialization was a mediating device."⁹⁷ Yet while the filmmakers wield the "dissecting gaze," the white protagonists and creators of the film also become dissected. Racialization becomes more than a mediating device; it is in fact how we become bodies, how we are defined as such. The film's experimental methods, particularly its attention to the fragmented bodily ego as "frontier-creature," bring into radical relief the very processes that form and install gender and racial fantasies.

Race is a vehicle, as Carby suggests, for mediating the sexual transgressions of the white characters. Indeed, the erotics between the participants of *Borderline* were as complicated as those figured forth in the film. By undercutting the heterosexual imperative from several directions, the film represents how these transgressions converge to mediate race. The borders of sex and race overlap. The femme fatale, revealed as empty in herself and completely fabricated, becomes here the prototypic gender and racial scapegoat.

As in the case of Lulu, the camera gives Pete a body, but it also deprives him of the agency of desire. Rather than H. D. occupying the role invested with desire, Robeson becomes the provisional fulcrum of erotic attention, a body to be inscribed upon with convergent multiple desires. The piano player cherishes a picture of him; the barmaid courts him; and even Thorne tries to possess him through a symbolic handshake; but especially, as Carby notes, the camera's gaze, which pans lovingly across his skin, provides multiple close-ups of his hands and upward-gazing face. (This posture notably mimics Joan's tortured look towards the "angels.") Here the compelling desire for and hatred of the femme fatale (both Helen and Lulu meet their death because they are receptacles for unwanted desires) slides into connection with eschewed biracial desire.

Lulu is Dionysian, expressive sexual force; Pete is both bodily and otherworldly, ironically Olympian, given the muscular men displayed in the café's Swiss travel posters. However, it is in the realm of embodiment that Pete is banished from the small-town café existence. Lulu, the fatal dynamo of erotic energy, similarly exceeds her surroundings. Astrid dies as a result of her "excess" (like Lulu she is stabbed), but again Astrid is not the film's femme fatale; instead, the film makes this trope more problematic, and through Robeson, manifests culture's expulsion of a feminized racial other.[98] Unlike Lulu, Robeson suffers banishment, a form of legal death. The feminizing of his character emerges from the cultural conflation of the abject and disavowed with the feminine. As I have argued throughout, film itself represents an emblematic disavowed and desired body in modernist consciousness. In this context, the conflation between the unloved body and the "new woman" serves to reify racial boundaries.

Nevertheless, the film turns cultural assumptions upside down (largely through Robeson). In contrast to mainstream Hollywood film and even so-called experimental film, white sexuality and desire have no glamour in *Borderline*. In fact, the white characters are consistently depicted in unattractive, distorted postures. As we have seen in other silent films, psychic states of dissociation are somatized through "[p]rojection of the conflict onto the whole expressive bodily system" (Eisenstein, "Dialectic Approach" 53). Disavowal of desire, in Freudian terms, manifests itself in "expressive" bodily symptom. Thorne is often portrayed in slumped paralysis. In one dislocated shot, for example, he lies wriggling on the floor, while a bottle of liquor is spilled on his face by an unidentifiable hand. Numerous shots of hands in isolation appear throughout as a sign of lost agency (think of Helen's hystericized "white hands"). By cutting up the body in rapid sequence, the camera reveals the body's "projection of a surface" as divided and disrupted by multiple lines of desire.

While the film almost deifies Robeson, the camera caresses him almost to the point of soft porn, building upon his cultural capital as sex symbol. The film thus idealizes, objectifies, and fragments Robeson, associating him with the femme fatale. As Silverman emphasizes in another context, the intractable cultural gaze fixes him: "We cannot simply 'choose' how we are seen."[99] In her reading, the cultural "screen" functions as a mirror, as the "repertoire of representations by means of which our culture figures all those many varieties of difference," images that "do not always facilitate the production of a lovable body."[100] Nevertheless, the same camera that objectifies Robeson also opens up a space from which he "looks back" at the white gaze.

Silverman proposes that unlike the gaze (operating like the camera's eye to construct and privilege the white male body as "ideal"), "the look" can undermine the dominant processes of fabrication. Robeson "looks back" at white audiences from a space mapped and freighted with "gesticulatory gesture" that makes it difficult to maintain essential identities ("Dialectic Approach" 53). "Pure" racial or sexual identity is foreclosed, as we will see, by the film's avant-garde montage. The film questions and displaces the authority of the gaze, its own misguided liberalism and enmeshment within dominant ideologies. Ultimately, cutting (figurative and literal), a device anticipated by H. D.'s early poems, becomes the central character of this film.

CUTTING OUT THE BODY: BECOMING MEDUSA

Unlikable as Astrid is, she emblematically severs the screen's ideals of whiteness and heterosexuality. A pivotal scene shows Astrid aggressively wielding a knife (implicitly also the phallus) as she cavorts about a claustrophobic interior, replete with objects endowed with hieroglyphic meaning (a stuffed gull, for instance, with its beak holding the ace of spades). Even as Thorne finally turns the knife upon her, Astrid's activity protests against the film's "negation of the feminine."

Doane theorizes: "Through their structuration as sight, the woman, illicit sexuality, and death display an affinity and the woman is guaranteed her position as the very figure of catastrophe" (*Desire to Desire* 148). Here the "catastrophe" located in the to-be-looked-at-ness of women shifts between female and male, black and white bodies. The camera significantly focuses on Astrid's eyes as piercingly tortured in "seeing," while the "to-be-looked-at-ness" apparently shifts to Robeson's body, a surface exalted and then expunged. Portrayed as the bearer of chaos and the female "dark continent," he must be strategically revoked in order to maintain borders of racial and sexual identity. The two interrelated scenes I here examine disclose the performance of this triple action of cutting, marking, and "purging."

Early on, we see Thorne with a knife, initially pointed towards his hand. The close-ups of hands as I have said highlight how hysteria somatizes psychic trauma, reinforced through meticulous attention to parts of the body. The wielding of the knife, however, also draws attention to film cutting as bodily inscription and dissection. One of the film's most painstaking, almost masochistic, devices is the use of clatter montage, which H. D. describes as not the "mechanical super-imposition of short shots" but the "meticulous cutting of three and four and five inch lengths of film and pasting these tiny strips together" ("Borderline Pamphlet" 230). This self-conscious splicing of minute film pieces binds shots of Pete in waterfall settings with Astrid's later knifing scene: "[t]he same sort of jagged lightening effect is given with Astrid with her dagger" ("Borderline Pamphlet" 230).

Jean Walton argues that such oppositional montage (shots of Pete rapidly intercut with the waterfall and H.D with the knife) gives Astrid access to creative power while naturalizing Pete, yet the technique in itself reveals bodies (white and black) as subject to fragmentation.[101] This strategy pointedly interrupts a smooth viewing of the film. H. D.'s wielding of the knife is not an easy assumption of creative power. The film, as Friedberg tells us, was cut and edited largely by Bryher and H. D. while Macpherson was ill. This adds edginess to H. D.'s claim that the "super-imposition of short shots" was not a matter of "facile movement of a camera" but rather "a meticulous jig-saw puzzle technique in the best of the advanced German and Russian montage" ("Borderline Pamphlet" 230). Like the film's disruption of a fixed center of desire, this collaborative practice disturbs notions of single clear-cut auteurship.

After teasingly impinging the knife upon his hand, Thorne rests it against his visage as a dividing line, an act which reveals his self-destructive impulses staking out the limits of his body. In between shots of Thorne with the knife, we intercut to a panning of Robeson's body; the deployment of the knife thus becomes an act of violent impingement upon an(other's) body. This sequence shifts to a shot of the café barmaid using a pair of scissors to gleefully fashion a costume. Bodies, this film emphasizes, are "cut out," in the interdependent sense of formation and exclusion.

In the *mise-en-scène* between Thorne and Astrid that follows, every bodily gesture connotes tension: Thorne curled up on the bed, and Astrid putting a record on the gramophone, her shawl extending before her, metonymic with the stuffed gull's wing by the window, an image of impending death. When Thorne threatens to leave, Astrid "hallucinates" the flashing face of Adah superimposed on his suitcase and becomes "hysterical," collapsing to the floor. Significantly, she plays dead before she is actually killed, alerting us to the convention of catastrophe associated with the femme fatale. This simulation of death echoes "Helen," creating the uncanny position where the border between the living and the dead is uncomfortably indecisive. When Thorne returns to examine Astrid's still figure, her eyes pop open and in cobra position, she arises to claim a violent agency usually reserved for a male antagonist.

In the ensuing sequence, the knife reappears as Thorne uses it to sharpen a pencil at phallus level. The camera then cuts to the racist old woman outside looking up at their window, carrying a basket of phallic-shaped leeks. In this scene, we are also given a glimpse of a vase of Narcissus and a book fluttering open. The choice of flowers comments upon the scripted, self-centered relationship of the white couple as well as upon the thwarted desire to sustain bodily borders as impervious.

Seizing the knife from Thorne, Astrid darts towards his body, making little cuts on his face, showing the body as screen, a scriptable surface. As we recall from poems in *Sea Garden*, "cuts on the body's surface create a kind of 'landscape'" (*Volatile* 37). With her choreographed marks upon Thorne's skin, Astrid vivifies the trope of the castrating female body as well as establishing the detachability of the phallus from "symbolic" function.[102] For Thorne to see Astrid with "his" phallus severely deflates his sense of bodily omnipotence. In an effort to repress his anxieties, Thorne wrests the somatized knife away and instead of merely disabling Astrid, he stabs her, perpetuating the narrative that usually accompanies the femme fatale. As viewers, we experience the déjà- vu of her earlier prone body.

The cutting, however, is not over. We crosscut to a sequence of shots with the barmaid, polyvalent in her sexuality, flirting with Pete. She cuts him a white rose to put behind his ear, placing the knife between her lips. The pair performs a gender inverted courtship scene: she bows to the feminized Pete, with his flower and a serving-tray behind his head, making it appear as though he were a gypsy dancer with a shiny tambourine. (The gypsy was another non-Aryan ethnic group terrorized by the Nazis.) As the barmaid takes the knife from her lips, the scene disjunctively cuts to an image of Thorne's knife being dipped into a basin, blood spreading in the water. Thus, the sexing of Robeson (even from the sympathetic point-of-view of the barmaid) is related to Thorne's "crime of passion," confirming the sacrificial status of the black body.

After Thorne murders Astrid, he bandages himself, goes to the police, and successfully pleads "self-defense." Legally, his attempt to preserve a phallic presence becomes a justification for killing Astrid. Indeed, this is visibly an act of "*self*-defense." (Unlike the convicted Lulu, Thorne is able to convince the legal authorities of his "rights.") His disavowed vulnerability notably leads not only to Astrid's death but also to the destruction of Pete and Adah's relationship.

The film's avant-garde clatter montage along with the dwelling upon the gestural body "falling to pieces" does not allow its spectators to uncritically accept Thorne's phallic privilege. Quick cuts disrupt a continuous narrative, while the framing and composition of shots reveal the horrific consequences of an imprisoning "screen" as the cultural gaze. In particular, the old woman's point-of-view, often emerging from behind a beaded curtain, intrudes and dissipates the potential liberation offered by the café scene, a border space for sexual liberty and repression. While Astrid as "castration threat" dies in the previous cutting scene, the apposite café montage confirms the slippage between the borders of sex and race.

A group of men playing cards in the café insult Adah; when Pete defends her, he is ostracized, thus provoking a struggle. After Pete hits one of the jeering men in defiance, the other men in the café rise, lifting their fists in a racist coalition. This communal gesture implies that the Aryan race will prevail. The café scene is spliced with a discontinuous image that repeats several times: the old woman lifts and shakes her arms behind a fire. Her gesture (and the café patrons) not only presages the emergent Nazi regime's notorious book burnings, but more broadly, the "cleansing" of border figures in order to constitute an homogenous, unified racial corpus.

Use of self-conscious montage foregrounds the cutting out of Pete and Adah from the white landscape, while it also enacts anxieties regarding bodily and psychic integrity related to ideas of racial "purity." This film explicitly concerns itself with gender divisions as they install the phallus or the lack of the phallus as organizing construct. As Carby suggests, Thorne's anxiety over his masculinity meshes with his uneasiness about race. The only depiction of Thorne's biracial affair shows him towering above a disheveled Adah who he has pushed to the floor. Disowning sexual transgression then leads to the violent reinstitution of racial borders. Adah and Pete function not only as receptacles for the disowned, but also as surfaces where conflicting desires meet. The body then, this avant-garde film amply elucidates, is not closed off, but visibly inscribed.

THRESHOLDS AND "LOOKING BACK"

Thresholds, metaphoric and literal, are prominent throughout *Borderline* as they are in *Sea Garden*. There are two threshold scenes featuring Thorne and Pete which reveal that the body functions as permeable threshold. The first one occurs early in the film, after Adah returns to Pete. A sweating Thorne, expressing the gestures of breakdown, confronts Pete across the threshold. He has rejected Adah, but must now assert his imaginary "possession" of her through racial dominance. He appears as if he is about to spring upon Pete, while Pete looks back at him with cool equipoise. Bryher (who has followed Thorne to Pete's room) manages to wrest Thorne away to shield Pete from the white man's violence. The striped design on her sweater accentuates a ritualized gesture of her arms, extended before her, after she ejects Thorne.

Following Thorne's acquittal, he and Pete reenact the threshold scene. Once more he makes eye contact with Pete (but this time the camera lingers upon their exchange) in the liminal space of the doorway. In this shot-reverse-shot, when Pete gazes back at Thorne, the camera gives us a close-up of Pete looking at us. In both scenes, Pete not only stares Thorne down, but us as well. This is not typical. As Carby remarks of another scenario: "the black subject is not allowed to look back at the viewer."[103] Like the earlier threshold scene, this one emphasizes the distribution of power over racial lines, but here the camera also dwells on Pete's gaze to interrupt the narrative's flow. He smiles sardonically at Thorne, with a gaze suffused with the knowledge of a systematic racism marking his body as container of white desires.

Furthermore, the handshake in *Borderline* reinforces the lack of legal rights available for blacks. The taboo against miscegenation is here linked with an erotically charged gesture. As the camera reveals the white hand outside of the black one, we have a phantom sexual encounter. But there is no unity in difference; rather this moment seems to seal oedipal law, confirming for Thorne his "triumph" over Adah and Pete as well as Astrid. The threshold scene serves as a microcosm of racial borders. Moreover, it underscores the fact that Pete has been "framed" by Thorne. Yet the doorway is visibly double, and this doubleness opens up the possibility of a reframing. For Walton, Robeson is excluded from Freud's symbolic order: "The erotic is the phallus for which 'civilized' white protagonists compete against a background of 'natural,' black supporting characters."[104] Pete does not, however, recede to a background. The film refuses a singular point of view and the repetition of this scene undermines Thorne's dominant position.

The femme fatale, both elevated and abject, represents a perfect gage of the double process of repression and expression prominent in Weimar film. *Borderline*, like *Pandora's Box*, overtly recasts the femme fatale by dismantling the myth of a unitary, bounded ego. The intersection and multiplicity of desiring subjects makes a strictly oedipal narrative intentionally slippery to locate.

The film engages the spectator in the very process of cutting out borders and the necessary reconfiguration of them. H. D.'s "Borderline Pamphlet" articulates the film's aesthetics as part of Macpherson's (and implicitly her own) strategy to question the cultural mechanics of fixing identity borders: "When is an African not an African? When obviously he is an earth-god. When is a woman not a woman? When obviously she is sleet and hail and a stuffed sea-gull. He says when is white not white and when is black white and when is white black? You may or may not like this sort of cinematography" ("Borderline Pamphlet" 111). The film fetishizes Robeson but also engages in an activist exposure of racism and implicitly of a rising fascism. Bodies are literally cut out in the sense of expulsion and as they are constructed by the gaze of dominant culture. These facts come into relief when we consider the place of *Borderline* within cinematic history, most significantly and uniquely as a response to Griffith's *Birth of a Nation* as well as numerous film renderings (including Pabst's) of the femme fatale. Further, when we consider *Borderline* within the context of modernist poetry, it takes up the very motifs and anxieties over racial and sexual identity Eliot treats so pervasively within *The Waste Land*. Eliot's ambivalence to film – played out with the aid of film's fragmenting devices – enacts an emblematic resistance to the "dark continent" of the female body as well as to a rising democritization. Using the avant-garde techniques inherited from Griffith, H. D. and her cohorts deploy montage in part to reveal this cultural resistance as well as to highlight the processes whereby we might refashion how embodiment becomes instantiated.

Borderline calls attention to cinema's power to shape and reshape cultural fantasies. For H. D. in particular, film has an additional "visionary" function that allows for multiple identities and forms of female embodiment. By making herself the monstrous figure haunting the modernist male psyche in *Borderline*, H. D. assumes the role of "femme noire."[105] In her epic *Helen in Egypt*, the alabaster Helen turns "noire" in the reiterated "Helena, Helen hated of all Greece" who "lived / on [her] slice of Wall / while the Towers fell";[106] her power resides in her ability to fully enact her abject role and to translate herself into an illusory effect as if upon a flickering screen. In H. D.'s earlier femme fatale, her portrait of Gregg, "[i]t was her eyes, set in the unwholesome face; it was the shoulders, a marble splendor . . . unholy splendor." H. D. moves from marble to the kinesthetic medium of film in her rendition of the "unwholesome" femme fatale.

She covers over her own role as "monster" creator in her "Borderline Pamphlet," when she writes:

The camera has for the most part been the property of monsters, like those three Gorgons in the wasteland, holding a precious legacy, one human EYE between them. Would it be altogether inept to say that Mr. Macpherson and his young colleagues are just the least bit like Perseus who snatches the EYE from the clutch of the slobbering and malign Monsters? (15)

The "malign Monsters" ostensibly are those who produce mainstream films; in making this equation, she echoes the high modernist disdain for femininity and mass culture, and her own contempt for the "vamping" of Garbo. Yet in depicting the handmaidens to Medusa, she avoids the question of who possesses "the EYE," of who controls the gaze? This "promotional" pamphlet never acknowledges her own and Bryher's extensive work on *Borderline*. In fact, she elevates Macpherson as sole heroic maker of the film. Most notably, he becomes a Perseus slaying the Gorgons and thieving their shared eye; he becomes "a hard-boiled mechanic, as if he himself were all camera, bone and sinew and steel-glint of rapacious grey eyes" ("Borderline Pamphlet" 226). According to de Lauretis, the shield belonging to Perseus is a figure for the movie screen, with the image of a slain Medusa inscribed therein – a means of protection from the castrating female

gaze.[107] Nevertheless, H. D. slashes away at the fabric of phallic omnipotence within the film, undermining a full triumph over the femme fatale,
figured by Pete who escapes, if not unscathed, the small town's neurasthenic
vortex.

Although Astrid, like Lulu, is slain in the end, her knifing activity points
towards her "repressed" role in editing *Borderline* and outside the film
towards the visual economy where women "regularly lose their form in
monstrosity."[108] Bryher and H. D. become invisible seamstress/slashers. Yet
finally, H. D. occupies multiple positions (like the dissociating hysteric) –
acting, editing, viewing. In the embodied language of post-war trauma, she
describes watching Macpherson: "It is funny to watch him work if you have
a mind for just that sort of humour. Like watching a young gunner alone
with his machine gun. It is as if one knew all the time the sniper would at
the last get him" ("Borderline Pamphlet" 225). The film, like H. D.'s poetry,
protests against "the negation of the feminine" perpetuated in overlapping
modern psychoanalytic, literary, and cinematic narratives.

To some extent, H. D. recapitulates the modern dilemma of the dissociated female body through the trajectory she supplies for Garbo, moving
from anesthetized or chaste goddess to Hollywood vamp. Yet H. D. reveals
the processes that make and unmake these bodily tropes. Finally, she places
these figures as if in a series: an "ideal" Garbo/Helen, a cross-dressing Joan
"kicked towards the angels," an innocent yet errantly sexual Lulu, and the
return of the repressed Medusa in Astrid.

Finally, H. D.'s early poems testify to the body's "transgressive" desires.
They exceed Eliot's claims to impersonality, objective correlative or disembodiment (which he himself exceeds) explicitly in their use of cinematic
methods that unfix singular erotic identification or desire. The psycho-
cinematic image can become a hysteric displacement of an eroticized bodily
part. This accords with Freud's concept of hysteria as "sustaining the image
in opposition to speech."[109] Sapphic fragments converge with the luminous
details provided by Freudian dream interpretation as well as with the emo-
tionally freighted images later produced by the melodramatic Expressionist
films of Pabst, the director she most admired.

Like Williams, H. D. is compelled by the part that isn't there, thus her
interest in the one-legged veteran in *Joyless Street*, and the "wan soldier" who
"back from the last war, / feels healing, electric, in a clear bar, / where an
arm should be" ("The Dancer," *CP* 441). H. D.'s cinematic language raises
the stakes to a social imperative of "healing" and bodily expression, such
that the "priestess" of modern dance, Isadora Duncan, is a "poem / writ

in the air," where she might "[l]eap as sea-fish / from the water, / toss [her] arms as fins" (*CP* 450). As we will see in the next chapter, Moore also engages in experimental slashing of cultural fantasies of female embodiment to find new forms – often those which conjoin animal and human, like H. D.'s finned Isadora. Her poems are geometric and abstract, creating idiosyncratic hybrid bodies whose parts vibrate anew.

CHAPTER 5

Marianne Moore: film, fetishism, and her Ballet Mécanique

Marianne Moore writes to Bryher in 1933: "I doubt that there is anyone living who is more enthusiastic about movies than I am" (*Selected Letters* 296). If this assertion verges on hyperbole, it recommends that we re-read Moore with the cinematic in mind. Like H. D., Moore was moved by what the eye cannot see except through mediating devices, extending from scientific equipment to that of the cinema. H. D.'s fascination with camera lenses and the projector resulted to a degree from her early exposure to her father's work as renowned astronomer and her grandfather's "close up" research in micro-botany, specifically freshwater algae. In fact, he identified "thousands of species of minute living components of the green scum that gathers on lakes and ponds."[1] From the damp pools of algae to the Medusa might seem a long trek, yet H. D. links these entities through their fluidity (for after all the medusa is also a jellyfish whose habitat is the Bay of Napoli). There seems to be an even longer trek from H. D.'s effort to establish a visual aesthetic that accounts for female sexuality outside of the oedipal model to Moore's poetic projects. Yet by scrutinizing material bodies, Moore extends the imaginative limits of embodiment. She takes pleasure in animal documentaries, seemingly at another extreme from experimental film, merging the mechanical with the bodily, the artificial with the natural, "non-fiction" with poetry in order to engender hybrid bodies. She is equally engaged by "the lion-cage scenes and and tight-rope incidents and a mirror maze" in Chaplin's *The Circus* as she is by apparently objective "data" about elephants that she discovers in a lecture-film called *Ceylon, the Wondrous Isle* (*Selected Letters* 191).[2]

This chapter analyzes an exemplary poem, "Those Various Scalpels," with its significant analogies to the anti-narrative aesthetics of Léger's *Ballet Mécanique*, famous for its cubist animated constitution and deconstitution of Chaplin's body (see fig. 6). Ultimately, the avant-garde mechanics of her montage, including a lineation based on syllable count, represents a somatic poetics. My argument builds towards a reading of two films she reviewed and admired, Leontine Sagan's *Maedchen in Uniform* (1931) and Melville Webber and J. Sibley Watson's *Lot in Sodom* (1933). These films not only mark the end of the silent era and are therefore suitable as a conclusion, but are also explicitly homoerotic. Part of my aim is to dispel the perception of Moore as a predominantly cerebral poet who "never was known to have fallen in love" ("The Frigate Pelican").[3] Like the other modernist poets I have discussed, she uniquely bridges (without integrating) the often-divorced realms of mind and body through strikingly cinematic means.

Rather than invoking the hysteric body developed in previous chapters, I delineate a fetishist practice in Moore's orchestration of multiple fragments, which she catalogues, joins, and eroticizes. These fragments are drawn from quotations from disparate texts ("'business documents and / school textbooks'"), mechanics, fabrics, objects, and the overlapping realms of animals and humans (as with "the immovable critic twitching his skin like a horse / that feels a flea, the base- / ball fan, the statistician – " in "Poetry").[4]

Before developing Moore's form of fetishism, I want to first review the reception of her work, which overwhelmingly cast it as disembodied and asexual. Moore was consistently praised for her impersonal, restrained, unsentimental poetics. In his review of Moore and Loy, Pound lauded "these girls" for their "logopoesis" – "the play of intellect among words"; he was happy to detect only "traces of emotion" in Moore and none in Loy.[5] At the same time, Pound subtly criticized Moore for her "spinsterly aversion," a phrase no doubt more inspired by her lifestyle (never marrying, living with her mother all her life) than by her writing style.

Of all her peers, Williams most clearly celebrated her embodied avant-gardism. But his comprehension also faltered before her sexuality: he configured her alternately as his virgin "saint" of poetry, or erased her gender altogether, placing her as a scientist in a photographic laboratory of words, removing their smudges. At another extreme, he described her poetry as "clarifying in its movements as a wild animal whose walk corrects that of man."[6] And finally, in his eulogy for her "escape" from the cliché symbolism in poetry at large, note both his pleasure in her artistic method of "cleavage" and his conception of Moore in the role of universalized male artist as romantic sufferer:

Marianne Moore escapes. The incomprehensibility of her poems is witness to at what cost she cleaves herself away . . .
    The better work men do is always done under stress and at great personal cost. (*Spring and All* 101)

Williams was not alone in masculinizing Moore; in fact, Moore refers to herself as such, and her mother and brother also generally designated her by the male pronoun (*Selected Letters* 4). Eliot, on the other hand, claimed that her poetry is distinctively "feminine," and "one never forgets that it is written by a woman" – which in her is "a positive virtue."[7] As we shall see, Moore escapes, Houdini-like, the cuffs of modernist classifications – particularly in relation to gender identity and embodiment.[8]

Like Williams, Eliot favorably responded to Moore's "incomprehensibility," but appeared slightly put off by her lacking "immediate poetic derivations" and by not being able to "fill up [his] pages with the usual account of influences and development."[9] He admired, however, her versatile diction garnered from "the jargon of the laboratory and the slang of the comic strip" (*Gender of Modernism* 148). Eliot further remarked upon her use "of minute detail" in favor of "emotional unity," pointing out that her penchant for "detailed observation, for finding the exact words for some experience of the eye is liable to disperse the attention of the relaxed reader" (151). As if anticipating that Moore would be construed as excessively cerebral, he defended her by placing the burden upon the reader: "To the moderately intellectual the poems may appear to be intellectual exercises; only to those whose intellection moves more easily will they immediately appear to have emotional value" (151). Accordingly, Moore produces a "bewilderment consequent upon trying to follow so alert an eye, so quick a process of association" (151). By stressing the need for an optic response to Moore's effects of "bewilderment," Eliot called upon language that applies as well to experimental films: "she succeeds at once in startling us into an unusual awareness of visual patterns, with something like the fascination of a high-powered microscope" (151). Eliot was attuned to her "scientific" leanings, her identification with the investigative behaviorist who observes sensations and involuntary responses, such as "[h]ands that can grasp, eyes / that can dilate, hair that can rise / if it must" ("Poetry" 72). After all, in college she adored biology (and failed English), and like Stein, thought about studying medicine.[10] The persona of the laboratory scientist equipped with prosthetic lenses underlies her embodied poetics. It is largely her high-powered "scopic detailism" (Emily Apter's phrase)[11] and her "startling," idiosyncratic effects that designate an aesthetics of fetishism.

Following a generation of bewildered, if appreciative, modernists, Randall Jarrell considered her poetic practice a matter of defensive, withholding camouflage so that "a good deal of her poetry is specifically (and changingly) about armor, weapons, protection, places to hide."[12] His enthusiasm for Moore did not prevent him from observing how "[w]e are uncomfortable – or else too comfortable – in a world in which feeling, affection, charity, are so entirely divorced from sexuality and power, the bonds of flesh."[13] In keeping with the spirit of Jarrell's analysis rather to the letter, Moore's idiosyncratic re-definitions of female corporeality are purposely discomfiting. Along these lines, the poet's "weapons" can be defensive, but they also extend somatic limits. She acts the "perfect swordsman," as H. D. called Moore, to manipulate and mutate the poetic line as well as her figurative embodiment.

H. D., however, even emphasized Moore's ironic detachment: "if Miss Moore is laughing at us, it is laughter that catches us, that holds, fascinates, and half-paralyzes us, and light flashed from a very fine steel blade, wielded playfully, ironically, with all the fine shades of thrust and counter-thrust" ("Marianne Moore," *Gender of Modernism* 126). Yet surely these fencing metaphors implicate the flesh, for indeed, the brandishing of the sword can throw the body into a fight or flight reaction just as a blade can cut into the skin. Moore's kinesthetic devices demand "both impact and exactitude, as with surgery."[14] Fulfilling Apollinaire's notion of the artist as surgeon, she is outfitted with her various scalpels in the poem as operating theatre. At the same time, as I will later elaborate, she examines her own bodily apparatus in this theatre.

The sample of responses to Moore's work that I have surveyed exposes an ongoing "bewilderment" in the face of her seeming "excessive" intellect along with a confusion about how to situate her embodied identity. For Eliot, she is sufficiently emotional *if* the reader is intelligent enough to comprehend it; she is also convincingly "feminine." However, her so-called lack of passion was more often miscalculated as a flaw in her work, so much so that even her friend Bryher – who supported, funded, and facilitated the publication of Moore's first volume without, by the way, the poet's knowledge or consent – "could not resist offering a critique of the unnatural quality of *Poems*": "The spirit is robust, that of a man with facts and countries to discover and not that of a woman sewing at tapestries. But something has come between the free spirit and its desire – a psychological uneasiness that is expressed in these few perfect but static studies of a highly evolved intellect."[15] Is Moore then a woman who is also a man, to reiterate Alice Jardine's assessment of the oscillating figure of the hysteric, stymied in her expression of her desires?

Moore's response to Bryher's "outing" of her poems before she felt that they were ready to publish can be taken as a gloss upon the quandary over how to categorize the poet's desires. She is "touched by the beauty of all the printing details" of the Pelican Press, but she feels like a "Darwinian gosling," "a variety of pigeon that is born naked without any down whatever" (*Selected Letters* 167). After mentioning the film *The Golem* (which she thinks pales beside *Caligari*), she elaborates upon her visit to the Bronx zoo to see "the only albino in America, which [she] has been wanting to see for a month," excited by an article in *The Times* that claimed "its eyes were pink and that it was absolutely transparent, that you could see its entire mechanism when you held it to the light" (166). She rhapsodizes over "a bird of paradise from New Guinea" who she is "afraid will never get used to being caged," and as if stunned by a sudden cinematic image, she records that the "toco toucan also gave us a start." She admits: "I sound like Barnum and Bailey but must have you get an inkling of these animals since cameras were forbidden" (167). She signs the letter, "Your now naked, Dactyl." Several important elements that I will consider in this chapter surface here: Moore's unstoppable scrutiny of animals and need to represent them coalesces with her sense of film as a mediation of desire. She is both captivated by these creatures and intensely aware of their captivity. Furthermore, her extensive identification with animals is one of her main avenues for expressing her fetishist aesthetic.

The poet's baroque anatomies of animals and artifacts might well suggest that she prefers them to the human form, or even that her fixation upon them produces her most embodied acts of attention.[16] Her poems enact with a self-conscious vengeance the human habit of anthropomorphizing the non-human, as a mechanism for making familiar what persists as phenomenally unfamiliar (like the "photogénie" of "the birth of sea urchins" or a "grain of wheat sprouting").[17] Even beyond nature documentaries, cinema is a perfect conduit for conveying the "anthropomorphous physiognomy in every object."[18]

By simultaneously "objectifying" and ecstatically identifying with animals and the non-human (including objects and even geometric shapes), Moore does not seek a "triumph over bodily content." Like Pound and Eliot's "hysteric" disowning and dependence upon the bodily, Moore displaces and affirms her "being-in-the-world" through a multiplication of parts. She asserts, in the context of discussing Freud, that "the physical is as important as well as the spiritual and I don't doubt that a thousand derangements are the result of our misunderstanding of the physical" (*Selected Letters* 153). The "derangements" in her poetic forms display an ecstasy over the anomalous, for instance the wavering lines of "[t]he zebras, supreme in / their abnormality" ("The Monkeys," *CP* 40).

If Freud's revelation of "infantile sexuality" helped discombobulate a view of childhood "innocence," Darwin (who Moore read with great enthusiasm) had already solidified a suspicion that the sex-lives of plants and animals could be perhaps as complex and variegated as those of their human counterparts. Rather than assuming that Moore's poetry is devoid of sexuality or the bodily, it is more accurate to see it as refocused away from the explicitly human or genital. Human desire, once wrenched from strictly reproductive aims, adapts its environment to its own ends. In Moore's "Barnum and Bailey" mentality as much as in her role as investigative scientist, flora and fauna along with their artificial recreation provide a field for fetishist displacement, what Apter calls "an exemplary dalliance," a "foiling of civilization's righteous aim to propagate the species" (*Feminizing the Fetish* 16). As such, the "natural" in Moore's poetry is inseparable from the artificial, denaturalized, constructed as well as the cinematic.

Benjamin famously argues that the modern "technique of reproduction detaches the reproduced object from the domain of tradition" and deprives the object of its "aura" of originality and authenticity; he situates film as "the most powerful agent" for such "liquidation" ("Work of Art" 221). In cinematic experience, the spectator forges an alliance with a mechanical prosthesis: "The audience's identification with the actor is really an identification with the camera" (228). In many respects, Moore's writing participates in this mechanical liquidation. In her obsessive "construction" of phenomenon, her lens demystifies, reproduces, distorts, and refracts. Thus her poem about Mt. Rainier accumulates facts printed in the park's pamphlets, so that the "octopus / Of ice" has its "pseudopodia / made of glass that will bend – a much needed invention" ("An Octopus" 125); or in the complex ecosystem of "The Fish," an "injured fan" is one of the "crow-blue mussel-shells" alongside the "ink- / bespattered jelly-fish" (85); or "An Egyptian Pulled Glass Bottle in the Shape of a Fish" implies that artifice invigorates the "spectrum" of the "nimble animal the fish" (62).

Moore insistently blurs the distinction between the bodily and the mechanical, the natural and the artificial. This convergence is perhaps most marked, as I later suggest, in her writing about animal documentaries. I have been arguing throughout that a central paradox in modernism lies in the desire for sensate experience with the concomitant awareness that it is never entirely available. This paradox does not obliterate the bodily from the equation; it only provokes re-adjustment. The mechanical reproduction of film is an outlying medium through which each poet explores such provocation.

FETISHIST MONTAGE

In "Getting Spliced," Carolyn Burke discusses the feminist, "collage poetics" of Stein, Loy, and Moore as alternative to a masculinist tradition (100). While Pound might have praised both Loy and Moore's work, he "appears to have ignored the fact that they were women" and "failed to notice [. . .] their differently inflected awareness of how sexual difference matters" ("Getting Spliced" 100). Burke points out that collage has the slang meaning of an "illicit love affair," and she maintains that "[t]he splice that joins separate elements edge to edge (as in the splicing of film) provided Stein with the means to imag[in]e a union that was simultaneously syntactical and erotic" (101). Moore also enacts the splice, but in a "separatist version." By using the word "separatist," Burke underscores the disembodied, asexual disposition often ascribed to Moore (as well as to experimental film): "Not for Moore the splice as syntactic or social connective" (114). In this way, Burke reaffirms both Pound, who applauds Loy and Moore as "'followers of Jules LaForgue'" whose self-ironic poetry is "'the utterance of clever people in despair [. . .] a mind cry, more than a heart cry'" as well as Williams, who praises Moore because she "despised connectives" and endorsed "rapidity of movement" (114).

Yet it is the very fact that her poems are "missing nothing but the connectives" that makes them filmic and somatic.[19] As Michael Wood suggests, the famous opening montage in *Un Chien* illustrates modernism's simultaneous anti-narrative exclusion of the "reader" and demand for a visceral reading of images:

Only a range of logical leaps and suppositions converts this sequence into narrative: 'The man sharpens the razor and then cuts the woman's eye.' Film has no *and*, still less an *and then*, and in this case, no possessive apostrophe. Films replace grammar and causality by simple succession: then, then, then, then. We invent the missing syntax, supply all the connectives.[20]

Indeed, this very quality of dynamic rupture and disjunction, aligns Moore with Williams (who devised a spectator governed by visual "rents"), shifting her work from collage to a kind of hyper-montage.

Eisenstein's film theories became extremely important to Moore, who would take extensive notes on his translated essays "The Cinematographic Principle and the Ideogram" and "The Dialectic Approach to Film Form." In Moore's reading diary, she quotes a pertinent passage, descriptive of her own poetic method: "Synthesis constantly arising in the process of opposition between thesis and anti-thesis [. . .] For art is always conflict."

(This conflict is not only indicative of a Hegelian movement towards social change, but also echoes Darwin's emphasis upon the struggle inherent in natural selection.) Further indicative of her cinematic sensibility is her recording Eisenstein's insistence upon explosive form rather than plot:

> montage is not an idea composed of successive shots stuck together but an idea that DERIVES from the collision between two shots that are independent of one another (the 'dramatic' principle). ('Epic' and 'dramatic' in relation to the methodology of form and not content or plot!) As in Japanese hieroglyphics in which two independent ideographic characters ('shots') are juxtaposed and explode into a concept.[21]

What Moore excerpts from Eisenstein does not reflect direct influence, for she first reads him in the late twenties after she has written what I consider her most experimental poetry.[22] Yet these passages confirm her own methods: the juxtaposition of images that "explode" into other images as the reader/spectator pieces them together. Collisions are the frissons that her poetic "bodies" thrive upon. For instance, in "She Trimmed the Candles Like One Who Loves the Beautiful," Moore shocks us by juxtaposing a mythic beauty with a menagerie: "She / Made me think of Diana – monkeys and penguins and white // Bears and herons."[23] In "People's Surroundings," she overtly signals "collision" as a means of briskly shifting, invoking and provoking sensation: "like splashes of fire and silver on the pierced turquoise of the lattices / the acacia-like lady shivering at the touch of a hand, / lost in a small collision of the orchids – " (109). Within this tiny vortex in an extremely complicated poem, the hybrid "acacia-like lady" is scintillated, latticed by light patterns.

In his 1923 review of *Poems* and *Marriage*, Eliot describes Moore's "swift dissolving images" in "The Fish"; he also observes that "Those Various Scalpels" has a rhythm that "depends partly upon the transformation-changes from one image to another, so that the second image is super-posed before the first has quite faded" (*Gender of Modernism* 148, 147). This insight into Moore's writing anticipates Eisenstein's description of the "sensational" mechanics of montage: "each sequential element is perceived not *next* to the other, but on *top* of the other. For the idea (or sensation) of movement arises from the process of superimposing on the retained impression of the object's first position, a newly visible further position of the object" ("Dialectic Approach" 49).

Moore's poems create a "sensation of movement" dependent upon a method of fetishistic juxtaposition and splicing. If she "despised con-nectives," she also cultivates new bodily alliances based on substitution, adjacency and frottage. Grosz elaborates in another context: "To use mechanic connections a body-part forms with another, whether it be organic or inorganic, to form an intensity, an investment of libido is to see desire, sexuality as productive" rather than exclusively "reproductive."[24] In this way, Moore produces a bodily awareness outside the bounds of a strictly heterosexual narrative.

As I have intimated, Moore takes on and modifies the "perversion" most often configured as a male prerogative, fetishism – as a defining feature of her cinematic modernism. I am not referring to the depiction of fetishism per se in film, but how film itself can function as a fetish medium – with its geometries, its cuttings, its framings, its textures, its ability to zoom in upon objects and parts, its oscillation between the living and the inanimate. The word "perversion" is itself appropriate in relation to Moore – not as a pathological descriptor but in its etymological meaning of "turning away." Hers is an aesthetic of labile veering, uneven line lengths and unexpected syntactical moves.

Moore's version of the bodily is to some extent a response to cultural expectations of "normative" female identity. We have seen how the body of the hysteric can derail the subordination of the visceral to reason; the somatic ego has its own inscriptive devices where, to quote Moore, "[g]esticulation – it is half the language" ("Critics and Connoisseurs" 77). The mechanisms of the hysteric and fetishist intersect through their emphasis upon the part and partiality. But where the hysteric's topography of paralysis, anesthesia or contortion encrypts a psychic occlusion, the fetishist is more outwardly absorbed with searching for, examining, collecting, and cutting out objects, supposed substitutes for the missing phallus.

The problem in applying this "syndrome" to Moore is that it presupposes the influential psychoanalytic privileging of the phallus and the corresponding rendering of femininity as "already castrated."[25] The argument against the existence of female fetishism revolves around the fact that the phallus cannot be imperiled if it is non-existent. As the typical definition unfolds, the visual becomes the tactile in the fetishist's well-known attachment to pieces of clothing, particularly fur and shoes, such attachments apparently the arbitrary result of looking away in horror from the mother's genitals to the most immediate objects in sight. Disavowing the traumatic sight of "no-thing," the boy child casts his line of vision from the furry "Medusa," traversing from his mother's undergarments to her shoes. In this Freudian "mythology," as others have noted, women are restricted to *being* a fetish object or in a collection of such objects. Within this psychoanalytic dynamic, women shift between representing an ontological lack and the phallic-mother, who yet retains an imagined penis beneath "'misleadingly of lace'" ("An Octopus" 312).

One might argue that Moore's modernist peers make her a fetish, the exceptional woman who transcended all categories. Sandra Gilbert describes the way critics endow Moore with a "fetishized femininity" which the poet both enacted and ironized.[26] While Moore does not fully succumb to psychoanalysis (perhaps for its very alignment of women with absence), it would be safe to say that Freud, deflected through her exposure to the natural sciences, directs her toward a bodily economy of substitution, texture and tactility.

In her useful revision of Freud, Studlar clarifies that "fetishism originates as pre-oedipal"; whether or not a fetish may later stand in for a phallus, it initially resonates with the "transitional objects used to ease separation from the mother."[27] In another helpful revision, de Lauretis claims that "what the female subject of perverse desire must disavow . . . is not the perception of a missing maternal penis (actually a non-perception), toward which she could not have bodily aims and which, therefore, would have no fantasmatic value to her, but rather the absence (also a non-perception) of a female bodily image."[28] Thus, the "female bodily image" functions as an absence; for the female fetishist or "perverse subject," this image can become productive presence – or put another way, a "[v]isble, invisible, / A fluctuating charm" ("A Jelly-Fish" 342).[29]

Moore takes on and reforms several attributes of fetishist desire. In a letter to Bryher (quoted above), she points to the difficulties in delimiting psychological processes: "Freud says his object is to substitute a conscious for an unconscious – a normal for a pathogenic conflict and we must do this if we can . . . . but as Freud says, our capacity for transferring energy from one field to another is almost infinite" (*Selected Letters* 153). In the same letter, her excitement over her camera is so excessive that she "did not hold the kodak level," and she tellingly remarks that "[m]other had trouble focussing me" (153–4). Moore's transference of energy, her "anthology of transits" (Williams's phrase for her poem "Marriage") is key to how her bodily "conductors" charge and energize an "explicit sensory apparatus" ("People's Surroundings" 109). Her concerted resistance to visual coherence does not evidence lack or the search for the missing phallus but rather testifies to her newly fashioned zones of "intensity."

She appropriates as well the fetishist's double take – recognizing and disavowing absence through metonymy and "transitional" objects potentially associated with the maternal body, including fabric and hair. While her poems are highly visual, they often engage in disappearing acts, intentionally veiling and then revealing the bodies she "dis- / covers" ("Poetry," *CP* 36). If part of the allure of mechanical reproduction resides in the desire "to get hold of an object at very close range by way of its likeness" ("Work of Art" 223), then the fetishist also recognizes that close up, the "likeness" alters or evades circumscription. "A Jelly-Fish" manifests her paradigmatic "approach and withdraw" relationship to the material image: "It opens, and it / Closes and you / Reach for it – " (342). Moore's quick-paced displacement emulates the fetishist's endless search for tactile substitution.

In a departure from his general exclusion of women from the world of fetishism, Freud exclaims: "In the world of everyday experience, we can observe that half of humanity must be classed among the clothes fetishists. All women, that is, are clothes fetishists."[30] "Clothes," he declares in the same lecture, "take the place of parts of the body." Clothing as prosthesis makes particular sense for Moore, who uses the extra-corporeal to extend and stitch her bodily identity through montage. Along similar lines, the film screen as mediating, absorbent fabric resonates as "transitional object."

The performance of bodies on film accords with Moore's principle of malleable costuming. Reviewing Bryher's 1921 "coming-out" novel, *Development* (which charts "the imagination of a child joined to the freedom of a boy"), Moore perceives the book's "protest against woman's role as a wearer of skirts – in her envying a boy his freedom and his clothes" to be "somewhat curtailed" (*Complete Prose* 61).[31] Instead, she argues that "[o]ne's dress is more a matter of one's choice than appears; if there is any advantage, it is on the side of woman; woman is more nearly at liberty to assume man's dress than man is able to avail himself of the opportunities for self-expression afforded by the variations in color and fabric a woman may use" (*Complete Prose* 61). Significantly, Moore is keenly sensitive to variations in color and fabric, and to their interactions with shadow and light.

The exorbitant number of references to fashion in Moore's letters, poems, and prose underscores her sense of the constructed nature of sexuality (intimated in her review of *Development*). What for Judith Butler are "styles of flesh" are for Moore a "'menagerie of styles'" ("An Octopus" 315).[32] Costumes are also shields. For instance, in one of her more extreme examples, fashion, and "natural" defense coalesce: "(the edgehog miscalled the hedgehog) with all his edges out, / echidna and echinoderm in distressed- / pin-cushion thorn-fur coats" ("His Shield" 144). I invoke Moore's taste for "distressed" fabrics and textility – her furs, muffs, tapestries – to designate a "transitional" erotics and an overarching cinematic sense of geometric design, composition of shots, variation in chiaroscuro effects.

Moore's costume pliability emerges perhaps most notably when in the 1940s she assumes her trademark tricorn hat and cape, the result of entering a milliner's shop and boldly asking "to be fitted as Washington Crossing the Delaware."[33] Cynthia Hogue writes that fashion represents Moore's "revolutionary and performative dissociation from the masquerade of femininity (from women defined as erotic object of the male gaze)."[34] In this manner, Moore reworks her own gaze upon the feminine, her displacement and recovery of the "maternal muff," so that she even calls, for instance, a swallowtail's motion through the wind "strange as my grandmother's muff."

Moore was evidently both inventive and indulgent in her self-fashioning, seeming to possess what Joan Copjec dubs the "sartorial super-ego," the self-pleasuring "will to dress."[35] She writes from Bryn Mawr in 1909: ". . . In New York, I flourished like a bay tree. No extravagance of starch or chiffon was too much for me. I never feel at home, in fact when I'm *not* spending more than my 'income' but economy is a feat" (*Selected Letters* 57). Indeed, "New York," a fetishist cavalcade, takes place in the hotbed of haute couture. A small section of this dense poem shows a "mastery of cluttered vision":[36]

> the center of the wholesale fur trade,
> starred with tepees of ermine and peopled with foxes,
> the long guard-hairs waving two inches beyond the body of the pelt:
> the ground dotted with deer-skins – white with white spots
> "as satin needlework in a single color may carry a varied pattern"
>
>   (107)

I will need say more about Moore's method of quotation later, but suffice it to say for now that it here marks a moment of heightened absorption in the textile and tactile.

What is striking about this particular quotation is its place in a larger quotation from *The Literary Digest* (1918) that she provides in her "Notes." It details a ban upon hunting and photography of the white-tailed deer along with an incident involving the killing of a white buck, subsequently sent to a taxidermist in Detroit. The ensuing analysis of the buck's "brocaded spots" exposes the exploitation of animals for design, implicating Moore's own poetic composition. The poem thus produces recognition of the colonial

plunder upon which the metropolis is erected. At the same time, her eye
confesses to a pleasure in fashion's spoils ("the beau with the muff" or
"the picardels of beaver skin") as well as in the collisions between the
human and the animal realm ("peopled with foxes") in becoming forms of
artifice.

Fashion is a site where the animal coincides with the artificial, the organic
with the inorganic, a coincidence repeatedly noted without flagging it as
unusual, such as in her enjoyment of her mother's purchase of a coat with
"beaver fur on the collar" (*Selected Letters* 244). Moore's pleasure in such
"transitional objects" is mixed, however, with an awareness of how bodily
coverings expose the mediation of the natural; moreover, clothing signifies
the organic turned inorganic. The cribbed line on satin needlework from
Literary Digest in "New York" recalls the taxidermied body from which
it has been excised. In "Those Various Scalpels," as I will demonstrate,
clothing and ornamentation are "prosthetic appendages," and thus both
extend the somatic and emphasize what is missing.

The intersection between presence and absence, organic and inorganic, is
nowhere more evident than through hair. As Benjamin writes of fetishism:
"It is as much at home with what is dead as it is with living flesh. . . . Hair
is a frontier region lying between the two kingdoms of *sexus*."[37] Apter cites
the turn-of-the-century documentation of "scissors assaults of fetishists on
plaits of hair or patches of velvet skirts" (*Feminizing the Fetish* 16). Elizabeth
Bishop records going with Moore to the circus where she diverted the guards
while the older poet took out a big pair of scissors to cut an elephant hair to
replace one missing from an exotic bracelet.[38] On her visit to the zoo to view
a famous ablino snake, she confesses: "The Java peacock shed a tail feather
which the keeper gave me and I childishly but successfully drew myself up
a wire fence around an out-door enclosure and got myself a macaw feather
which proved to be not in the best condition" (*Selected Letters* 167). Moore
thus physically engages in a fetishistic marauding. (Two family nick-names
for Moore were suggestively "Gator" and "Fangs.")

Hair as well as feathers as fetish objects recur throughout her poem;
they situate humans and animals on a continuum as her "formula" for the
mammal in "The Pangolin" testifies: "warm blood, no gills, two pairs of
hands and a few hairs" (120). They protect: the sleeping elephant "made
safe by magic hairs!" (128) And in "New York," she observes "the long
guard-hairs waving two inches beyond the body of the pelt." As her knowledge of biology would confirm, these whiskers deploy an animal's tactile vision, its ability to detect danger; yet as the poem underlines, these
extra-sensory devices can be foiled. Further, a totemic "pelt" itself can

function like the film piece, metonym of an intermediary zone between the organic and inorganic. As I now explore, Moore's syllabic poetry and Léger's *Ballet Mécanique* operate within this zone through fetishist montage.

SYLLABICS AND *BALLET MÉCANIQUE*

During a period when free verse became the common practice of other modernists, Moore reinvented her stanzas through compulsive syllabics, a practice crystallized in 1915 when she became directly exposed to New York avant-garde circles. She later revised her syllabics, loosening them into free verse. Her syllabics are at their height in *Poems* (1921) and *Observations* (1924 and 1925), and she returned to them later in the thirties after she read Eisenstein. By defying the metrical or syntactical units that might decide line-breaks, syllabics wrench language from denotative transparency, underscoring the "body" of the text as linguistic visual substance. Moore's compulsive counting out of syllables in asymmetrical lines does not concord with an ideal lyric form but constitutes a bodily practice in and for itself.

We might remember that Eisenstein weds Japanese poetic forms with montage. He observes that "the tanka is an almost untranslatable form of lyrical epigram of severe dimension: 5, 7, 5 syllables in the first strophe (*kami-no-ku*) and 7, 7 syllables in the second (*shimo-no-ku*)."[39] Rhythm is perceptual as much as it is auditory. Moore's syllabics likewise ensure this – they are not meant for the ear so much as for the eye. This "nonsignifying," I want to pursue, is akin to the mathematic laying down of film strips in Léger's *Ballet Mécanique*.

Williams in fact links Moore's writing process to photographic development and projection of film as acts of dislocation and embodiment:

Miss Moore gets great pleasure from wiping soiled words or cutting them clean out [. . .] *taking them bodily from greasy contexts* [. . .] With [her] a word is a word most when it is separated out by science, treated with acid to remove the smudges, washed, dried and placed right side up on a clean surface. [. . .]
There must be edges. [. . .] There must be recognizable edges against the ground which cannot [. . .] be left entirely white.[40]

Words, then, are handled bodily: stripped of their referents (making the reader aware of the material, chemical process, as it were), cut, counted, and set against a white "ground" or rectangle (the page becoming a kind of film strip or screen fabric). The "effect is in the penetration of the light itself" and in "the appearance of the luminous background."[41]

Like Moore's work, Léger's *Ballet Mécanique* foregrounds its materiality and mathematical composition, joining the somatic with the mechanical.[42] The use of dis-connective edge and "cleaving" that Williams finds stimulating in Moore's poetry resonates with how Léger describes his "new realism," discovered cinematically:

Let us consider these things [various objects] for what they can contribute to the screen just as they are – in isolation – their value enhanced by every means . . .
The question of light and shade becomes of prime importance. The different degrees of mobility must be regulated by the rhythms controlling the different speeds of projection [. . .] the timing of projections must be calculated mathematically.[43]

Léger's film is known, I should add, as "the first exploration" to use "lengths of film . . . deliberately in a rhythmic beat structure."[44] Moore anticipates the merging of the mechanical as mathematical in Léger's experimental film: each of her syllabic lines can be interpreted as a measured filmic strip.

Ballet Mécanique grew out of a collaboration (in unknown proportions) with four Americans in Europe (cameraman Dudley Murphy, composer George Antheil, Man Ray as well as Pound), and as such represents a "menagerie" sampling of avant-garde aesthetics. Léger's hypnotic ballet eroticizes mechanical kinesis. Revolving train wheels, pistons, and hydraulic cylinders juxtapose with the motion of a woman on a swing, the muscular contraction of "isolated" lips into a smile, the closing and opening of an eye aperture, and the inversion of a pair of mannequin legs as they move to resemble the "hands" of a clock. Such a mechanism of "parts" – like the parts of the film itself – in their eccentric motion establish new jointures and intensities. Thus, when the camera records the "natural" rhythm of a swinging woman following the animation of Charlot's body, the viewer potentially engages in a hybridized, overlapping identification with the somatic and the apparently disembodied, the organic and the inorganic.

Léger was opposed to dissolves, iris shots, fade-in or out transitions; much like a Moore poem, he seems to have "despised connectives." He moves, for example, from a shot of oscillating eggbeaters to one of a rotating engine part. Moore's images likewise mutate and *unfold* disjunctively. She is struck, for instance, by a snake's "plastic" nature and is "compelled to look at it as at the shadows of the alps / imprisoning in their folds / like flies in amber, the rhythms of the skating rink" ("Snakes, Mongooses, Snake-Charmers, and the Like" 111).

Like Léger, Moore celebrates movement, assimilating technology into her poetics. Moved by "mechanisms, mechanics in general" as she tells Donald Hall, the "functional" aspect of objects and of animals absorbs her. Léger's admiration of Abel Gance's *The Wheel* (1922), a film made with the poet Blaise Cendrars, pivots upon how "the machine becomes the leading character, the leading actor."[45] This assessment resounds with Moore's vigilant inspection of the mechanical aspects of objects, flora, fauna and human physiognomy. Along these lines, Bishop observes: "Marianne was intensely interested in the techniques of things – how camellias are grown; how the quartz prisms work in crystal clocks; how the pangolin can close up his ear, nose and eye apertures and walk on the outside edges of his hands 'and save the claws / for digging.'"[46]

Constance Penley has noted the prominent desire to know in early avant-garde films where epistemology turns into "epistemophilia," an almost per-verse desire to investigate the mechanics of things.[47] In Moore's inves-tigations of the natural world, she often shows how the mechanic and mathematical join. Her carrot, for example, is "a tail-like, wedge-shaped engine with the / secret of expansion" ("Radical" 90); by entitling her poem "Radical," she offers a compact visual/verbal pun based upon the square root $\sqrt{}$ (from the Latin radix) that resembles a carrot.

The somatic import of mechanics crystallizes in avant-garde cinema partly because, as Thomas Elsaesser formulates it, the cinematic apparatus itself is "organized in a peculiarly contradictory way": it "is devised to func-tion so as to disguise the actual movement *of* the image (passing through the projector gate) in order to create a non-existent movement *in* the image."[48] Cinema, in these terms, becomes "a philosophical toy, a machine trans-forming the useful energy of cogs and transmission belts into a useless energy of illusionist simulation" that makes possible the "eroticizing effect of animating the inanimate."[49]

Such "useless" eroticism emerges in *Ballet*'s "looping," hypnotic repeti-tion. Figure 19 shows a series of film strips: one sequence animates a pair of mannequin legs; the repetition of cogs, each shot virtually like the one previous; and in another, an image of a washerwoman who ascends a set of stone stairs never arrives at the top because the image is successively repeated. The repeating image of the woman's bodily rhythm in Léger is eroticized insofar as it "rubs against" the preceding close-up of a pulsating machine pump moving forward and backward. In many of Moore's poems, this Sysiphysian "series production" becomes a matter of pointedly repeat-ing stylized stanza structures so that the visual aspects of her text are set against their denotative status.

19. Léger, *Ballet Mécanique.*

Along with *Ballet*'s reverie over mechanical parts and movements, the film "collects" and extracts numerous common "found objects" – kitchen funnels, gelatin molds, culinary implements, and even a horse collar – out of their original contexts, defamiliarizing them through isolating close ups. Léger admired this technique in *The Wheel* as well as in the minute arrangements that belong to the "window dresser's art." "Window dressing" finds an immediate correlative in the film's animated dance of isolated mannequin legs in a store window, followed with alternating stills of straw hat and shoe, four to six frames each.

Léger uses this device of bracketing and animating objects, in alteration with another method, apparently introduced by Murphy and Pound, of splintering or fracturing objects by filming them through an optical prism. Shattering an image to reveal its interpenetrating planes is of course familiar from modern painting, but film enhances this strategy through movement. And because early film is not stoppable for the viewer so that she might look more closely to determine the object before her, Léger simulates an experience of simultaneous seeing and not seeing in shifting between more recognizable objects to ones which intentionally splinter in multiple directions. In this way, he both tantalizes and frustrates vision. For instance, a gelatin mold filmed through a rotary prism superimposes upon the profile of the head of a live parrot. In "isolating" an object, and then letting it go after a measured rhythm, *Ballet* performs a fetishist model of compulsive attachment and substitution. The parrot's eye signals an implicit denial of vision's ultimate power to clarify in some final rationalized form.

Prismatic effects abound in Moore's poems. Thay constitute what Williams calls her "geometric principle of the intersection of loci: from all angles lines converging and crossing,"[50] or as she describes: "angle is at a variance with angle" ("Novices" 113). To offer several examples of prismatic seeing, she stares at an aquarium or "phantasmagoria of fish" and sees the Statue of Liberty ("Is Your Town Nineveh?" 59); or perspective is temporal with "round glasses spun / To flame as hemispheres of one / Great hourglass dwindling to a stem" ("Fear is Hope" 57); or sea creatures move in "submerged shafts of the // sun, / split like spun / glass" ("The Fish" 85). These "spectacular" effects, in these cases related to the splitting of light with water, are versions of her dual enactment of seeing and not seeing, as well as her extension, layering, and thickening of bodily surfaces. Think of her elephant whose skin, "– cut / into checkers by rut / upon rut of unpreventable experience –" has multiple affinities with a coconut shell, a "piece of black glass," and the "cortex really" ("Black Earth" 87).

The human body is not at the center of either Léger's or Moore's projects; rather anthropomorphic hybrids emerge as prismatic and unlikely. In Léger as with Moore, point-of-view is not tied ultimately to a single surveying gaze, but oscillates within the unpredictable collision of the natural and the artificial, the embodied and the mechanistic.

Linda Leavell dates Moore's period of most "radical experimentation" from 1915 (the year Moore visits Steiglitz's gallery) to 1919 (when Moore and her mother would install themselves in Greenwich Village).[51] During the crucial years of 1916 to 1918, the pair lived in Chatham, New Jersey and, by taking a short train ride, Moore would regularly visit New York galleries and consort with other avant-garde artists (among them Man Ray). She called this transitional time, her "Middle Pullman Period." On one such visit to New York, she saw Mina Loy perform in Kreymborg's play *Lima Beans* (*Selected Letters* 140). Burke contends that "Those Various Scalpels" might in fact have been inspired by Loy ("Getting Spliced" 120).

In a letter to H. D. in 1921, Moore recounts what she knows of Loy: "Mina Loy is English, considered very beautiful [. . .] I first met her in 1915 at the Cannell's at tea preparatory to going to the Provincetown Playhouse [. . .] She was very beautiful in the play, very rakish previous to the play owing to the necessity of wearing a mixed costume – some of the properties and also ordinary street clothing" (*Selected Letters* 140). She ends her letter quoting Robert McAlmon refuting Loy's beauty. Moore evidences a competitive attraction to Loy's motley surface. Williams, a good friend to both women, observes in 1918 that "'of all those writing poetry in America at the time she was here, Loy was the only one Moore feared'"; he also recalls that Moore "'once expressed admiration for Mina Loy [. . .] because Mina was wearing a leopard-skin coat at the time and Marianne had stood there with her mouth open looking at her'" (*KH* 112).

Whether or not Loy (or her leopard-skin coat) contributed to "Those Various Scalpels," the poem dissects the idealized nude, and transfigures the "spectacle" of the Renaissance blazon, the cataloging of the beloved's physical attributes into the flamboyantly fragmented cinematic.[52] The scalpel is raised even as the mouth might be open. The title invokes multiple tools of surgery, used for quick, precise cuts; the poem later questions: "Are they weapons or scalpels?" This question refers to the depicted figure's arsenal but also to the poem's own rebellious method.

As with avant-garde film where "[i]t is the cut, the montage principle that makes the energy in the system visible and active," cutting here invents a kinetic rhythmic structure through the varying lengths of lines along with a collision of disparate images.[53] Note the zooming in and out precipitated by her unconventional lineation in the first publication of this poem, quoted below in its entirety with the syllable count in the margin (261–2):

Those Various Scalpels

Those	(1)
Various sounds, consistently indistinct like intermingled echoes	(18)
Struck from thin glasses successively at random – the	(13)
Inflection disguised: your hair, the tails of two fighting-cocks head to	
head in stone – like sculptured scimitars re-	(15)
Peating the curve of your ears in reverse order: your eyes, flowers of ice	(26)
And	(1)
Snow sown by tearing winds on the cordage of disabled ships: your raised	
hand	(18)
An ambiguous signature: your cheeks, those rosettes	(13)
Of blood on the stone floors of French chateaux, with regard to which the	
guides are so affirmative – the regrets	(26)
Of the retoucher being even more obvious: your other hand	(17)
A	(1)
Bundle of lances all alike, partly hid by emeralds from Persia	(18)
And the fractional magnificence of Florentine	(13)
Goldwork, a miniature demonstration in opulence – a collection of half a	
dozen little objects made fine	(26)
With enamel – in gray, yellow, and dragonfly blue; a lemon, a	(17)
Pear	(1)
And three bunches of grapes, tied with silver: your dress, a magnificent	
square	(18)
Cathedral tower of unbelievably uniform	(13)
And at the same time diverse, appearance – a species of vertical vineyard	
rustling in the transverse storm	(26)
Of conventional opinion – are they weapons or scalpels? Whetted	(17)
To	(1)
Brilliance by the hard majesty of that sophistication which is su-	(18)
Perior to opportunity, these things are rich	(13)
Instruments with which to experiment. We grant you that, but why	
dissect destiny with instruments which	(26)
Are more highly specialized than the tissues of destiny itself?	(17)

The scalpels are immediately "various sounds consistently indistinct," successive sounds detached from denotative clarity. Remaking the "still-life" with its "Pear / And bunches of grapes," with its asymmetrically (if consistently) indented lines, the poem involves consciousness of eye movement as the reader moves from one image to the next, stopping according to the mathematical yet eccentric pattern of each line's counted syllables. Moore is characteristically obsessed with a tension between stasis ("disabled ships") and flux ("tearing winds"), with the tactile paradox "sown by tearing." Even as nouns and adjectives predominate over verbs as with "Cathedral tower of uniform," the frieze keeps giving up its rock-like pretense through her shuttling lines, only end-stopped in the last stanza. We traverse great distances through images of a "French chateaux" to "Florentine goldwork" to "emeralds of Persia." Rapidity accompanies the fetishist fixation upon "a collection of half a dozen little objects." In this anatomy of a costume, Moore uses superimposition to simulate the body's extravagant movement, from the horizontal "tearing winds on the cordage of disabled ships" as if impelled by "your raised hand," to the later "vertical vineyard rustling in the storm / of conventional opinion."

Motion persists even in temporary stasis, or so these lines from the first stanza suggest: "fighting-cocks head to head in stone – like / sculptured scimitars repeating the curve of your ears in reverse order." Elizabeth Joyce observes that "[t]he ostensible topic here is hair, but its real topic is disruption of the 'outline' of the image by redescribing it with increasingly elaborate comparisons to take it out of the mundaneness of its unimaginative culture."[54] Yet there seems no threat of the mundane, anywhere near this "fractional" figure with its inventive headdress. Moore composes through taunting opposition, as in another poem where she rotates before us "the mediaeval decorated hat-box, / in which there are hounds with waists diminishing like the waist of the hourglass" ("When I Buy Pictures" 101).

Like Léger's film, this poem revels in its display of geometric, idiosyncratic design. While the poem's metaphor of dissection implies probing the body's interior spaces, Moore's various scalpel techniques make us aware of edge, surface and fold. Thus she employs the seeming arbitrary line breaks of "su- / Perior" or "re- / Peating," and the nearly anagramatic optical inversion of "snow" next to "sown." The scimitars, sculptured as they are, transpose their shape. Similarly, Léger animates a pair of mannequin legs and successively inverts them, or his circles quick-change into triangles.

Moore's "converse" mathematics rhyme the one-word line "Those," after a delay of eighteen syllables, with "echoes" and later, another single word line "Pear" rhymes after another eighteen syllables with "square," resting momentarily with the image of the dress as "a magnificent square." Subsequently, the costume unveils through a string of "separating" nouns, "cathedral tower of uniform," once again at odds with the "diverse appearance" of the next line. That Moore gives articles both premiere and final positions grants a tangibility to words apart from their reference. In effect, they belong to the reader/spectator's eye movement: we dwell on texture, on the word become image. The bisecting of lines at unexpected junctures draws attention to the image cut into by the poet's rhythmic scalpel. Multiple abstract words in the last stanza ("brilliance," "opportunity," "majesty," "sophistication," "instruments," "destiny") play against with the active present-tense verb "dissect" in the poem's final question, further converting words into "little objects," like those "fractional" stones of the third stanza, part of the body's moving spectacle.

Thus, Moore seemingly eclipses the body through its excessive costume, yet as the reel unfurls with close-ups of "sapphires set with emeralds and pearls" and the exotic enameling in "dragon-fly blue," she returns us to the minimal, the "natural": "a lemon, a // Pear." She upsets divisions between the artificial and the natural just as her arbitrary, insistent syllabic counting interferes with the "useful" function of language. It is as if a unified body cannot survive the tableaux of its shifting costume or this defamiliar blazon (the cheeks become "those rosettes / Of blood on the stone floors of French chateaux"), cut into by the very "highly specialized" tools it wields. Artifice apparently does not permit static "destiny." There is no interior core implied by the poem – only the masquerade, where "womanliness," as Rivière would argue, is "the same thing."[55] Only here, Moore dissects the very concept of femininity.

As with Duchamp's "Nude Descending a Staircase," we see the figure but see its "hard majesty" shattered, and gender itself becomes an "ambiguous signature," the diction of embattlement ("fighting-cocks") coupled with amorous cataloguing ("your eyes, flowers of ice"). The instruments of surface illusion are incommensurate ("more highly specialized") yet contiguous with the bodily "tissues of destiny itself." The last stanza implicates the looker in the to-be-looked-at figure since the portrait's weapons also belong to the reader, cutting and piecing the corpus together.

While my reading of this poem cannot be here comprehensive, several pertinent questions remain. With the "retoucher," Moore crosses from the realm of the museum (the "guides" are "affirmative" presumably about the blood) into that of the photographer's studio. In this context, does the "retoucher" have "regrets" because the body is "killed" through the process of touching up the natural, or because it cannot be made to look more natural through artifice?

In Moore's alteration of the final stanza for publication in *Observations*, she writes: "these things are rich / instruments with which to experiment but surgery is / not tentative" (264). Schulze reads this line and the final question of the poem as Moore's heightened "critique of the brilliant and sophisticated woman she presents by portraying her not only as an overzealous biologist who destroys 'destiny' by dissecting it, but as a surgeon who kills her living patient" (263). If Schulze is right, this last stanza offers a double take of the blood on the chateaux floor. According to her, the blood might be the result of the "overzealous" biologist/surgeon. However, this anomalous female surgeon would have appeal for Moore, especially keeping in mind her attachment to the sciences and her earlier desire to practice medicine.

"Those Various Scalpels," in spite of its possible "critique," or what Burke calls "ironic and discreet irony," lavishes minute attention on costuming, including the surgical equipment, as an extension of the body; and to be "whetted" is after all to be stimulated. In this way, the poem could well bear a motto from "Marriage": "Eve: beautiful woman – / I have seen her / when she was so handsome / she gave me a start" (115). Moore appears to be magnetized by the dominatrix in "Those Various Scalpels" with her elaborate "cordage."

That the bloom on the cheeks becomes "blood on the stone floors" implies a body as living and as corpse. It is this very dialectic that makes the poem provocative, even erotic in the way that the pistons are when juxtaposed to the lips in Léger. After all, "the first notion of space is the mouth," a primary site of erotic cathexis (*Volatile* 45). Moore's unpredictable juxtaposition of the artificial image of "sculptured scimitars" and the natural "curve of your ears," along with the resemblance between the two, the "re- / peating" of the one in the other, constitutes a sublated erotics. The portrait of a body, true to the body in time, cannot disclose its entirety: "Human subjects are able to see or feel only parts of their bodies" (*Volatile* 42). Experimental film represents this problematic of space as it reveals the body intermittently through flicker effects, perspective and juxtaposition, creating a kind of "striptease" effect. We might think of Roland Barthes's formulation of the purpose of striptease as not "to drag into the light a hidden depth, but to signify, through the shedding of an incongruous and artificial clothing, nakedness as a natural vesture."[56] "Those Various Scalpels" draws us to a body as invested spectacle, as choreographed surface.

As if in double-exposure, Moore cuts up her poem, and by extension, presents a post-mortem of the female body; yet this body is simultaneously the surgeon at work in a figurative dissecting "theatre." Moore's experimental cutting devices suggest that this poem need not only be a response to another's dazzling prosthetics or weaponry. These devices also imply that the poet's spectral body superimposes upon the depicted figure – reversible, at once fractured and reanimated, embodied and abstract.

Moore's fixation upon animals is one of the poet's chief means of expressing an embodied identity, even as such a fixation disturbs androcentric expectations. Her enthusiasm peaks when unfolding the details of mechanics, fashion, and particularly animals as they appear on film. Thus her response to a post-card sent by Bryher seems quite typical: "This reminds me of a python we saw at a movie to which I went to see Charlie Chaplin. It was on a ledge of rock below a water-fall; it raised its head snake-charmer fashion and gradually slid over the ledge on which the fall struck to a small pool and rivulet below . . ." (November 18, 1922; *Selected Letters* 190). Isn't Moore really just stirred by nature rather than films, it might be asked. Yet she often conjoins the two, and after all, she sees the python in a film, in which Chaplin, from her eccentric perspective, only appears incidental. Her pleasure in viewing hybrid, non-human bodies is especially satisfied by the genre of the animal documentary.

The "naturalist film" is by definition oxymoronic. Like the first documentaries made by Lumière, they cross between art and science, and ultimately expose the impossibility of "objective" observation. Avant-garde cinema, here represented through Léger's film for its close affinities with Moore's fetishistic overlaying of the mechanical and the bodily, dovetails with the genre of animal documentary. Film representation – its artificial slowing down or speeding up, its dissolves and close ups – visibly distort, mutate and rearrange. Moore is highly aware of the danger of these practices in capturing wildlife on film. As we shall see with her poem "The Jerboa," she addresses art's (and implicitly film's) simultaneous killing and resuscitating the object it represents. Photographic stills, as Stewart writes, read as cadaverous; film makes the cadaver a ghost.[57] Moore's mobile fetishism oscillates between the living and the dead, the natural and the artificial.

In a review notably entitled, "Fiction or Nature?" (published in one of the final issues of *Close Up* in 1933), Moore primarily addresses animal documentaries, but frames them with cursory, yet provocative, reference to two films with homoerotic content. It opens with an endorsing sentence for Sagan's film: "*Maedchen in Uniform* shown in America last winter set our studios an example in photography and somewhat reinstated the plausibility of emotion" (*Complete Prose* 303). Even as Moore writes that *Maedchen* "is the best thing [she's] seen all winter" (*Selected Letters* 296), her omnibus article shifts abruptly away from Sagan's film to lavish microscopic attention upon travel and nature documentaries, closing with an announcement of the completed filming of Watson and Webber's *Lot in Sodom*.

Her overt intention for this side-long glance at *Maedchen* in this review, as she suggests in a letter to Bryher, is to give credit to "world-travelers [who] sometimes do things better than the studio men"; furthermore, she thinks that *Maedchen* "combines well with other content," namely with documentaries. The documentaries, she implies, optimize the effects of experimental film. Through her framing of documentaries with so-called "fiction," she questions the boundaries between the two. In fact, she anticipates a rejection of *Maedchen*'s "unnatural" proclivities through her apparent non sequitur: "No, we do not like loveing [sic] pictures. We like any kind but love'" (*Complete Prose* 303). This ironic confession exposes the cultural subordination of "love" to sexual essentialism or to species reproduction.

"Fiction or Nature?" shows Moore's displacement of bodily "intensities" along a continuum of the human, the animal and the artifact. The convergence of the natural and artificial is nowhere more apparent than in her review of *Strange Animals I have Known*. Here she showcases the fashioning of animals: for instance, "the triangular very black front of an armadillo's head" and "a royally exotic animal with its white-edged isosceles triangle from the shoulder down the foreleg, a black patch on each shin, and heavy tail of upcurving fountaining fringe" (*Complete Prose* 307). In Moore's fetishist vocabulary, the animal's exoticism is akin to the costumed body in "Those Various Scalpels."

Her raving over *Strange Animals I Have Known* further demonstrates her "composition," almost quantification, of embodied perceptions:

The wild kangaroos in flight, undulating like the rapids of a dangerous stream, as they crossed the ditches and scrub, were impressive; also a momentary but hyper-clever close-up of the flying oppossum's leg-to-leg membranes; and the above-referred-to oppossums: the gray one on hind legs in a eucalyptus tree [. . .] suspended by tail, by tail only, then up again – weaving around, back of, and through, a clump of vertical twigs, in serpent loops and eights without space to squeeze through. The platypus on land, with dry coat of furrier's beaver – was a best thing; as was the echidna disappearing in such a way as to produce no mound of accumulating earth – mere surface convulsions. (*Collected Prose* 305)

Ultimately, in such films as Wells's, "there is not a dull foot" (a triple pun for animal feet, metrical feet and film footage). They appeal to Moore's sensibility not for their realism, but rather for their rendering the artful mechanics of nature. Inversely, these documentaries defamiliarize organic processes. Similarly, the French physiologist Dr. Jean Comandon's 1909 microcinematographic film of bacteria resembles, as Standish Lawder points out, the paintings of Kandinsky.[58]

Moore often enacts a cinematic investigation of natural "facts." In "The Fish," it is as if she attaches a camera to the bodies of the "barnacles" or fish, anticipating the use of underwater cameras. This passage extends vision through fractal single words and the sweep of multiple "bodies":

> The barnacles which encrust the side
> of the wave, cannot hide
>   there for the submerged shafts of the
>
> sun,
>   split like spun
>   glass, move themselves with spotlight swiftness
>   into the crevices—
>   in and out, illuminating
>
> the
>   turquoise sea
>   of bodies.   (*CP*, 32–3)

"The Fish" uses a quirky visual rhythm to track a volatile eco-system. Conversely, "science" films (and I include Moore's poem) can present natural processes as "unfamiliar" curiosities, estranging the object of study through filming. Moore's viewing of documentaries evidences a similar consciousness of camera-work, which for her can be a means for engendering visceral "sensation" or magnifying "sumptuous effects." Of *The Haunts of the Golden Eagle*, she writes, for instance: "[t]he sensation of these five reels perhaps was the continuous very close close-up of a long-eared (i.e., rabbit) owl" (*Collected Prose* 306).

While the capture of animals on film becomes the most suitable medium (excepting perhaps her own poems) for figuring forth unique bodies in time, she is also highly aware that such representations often involve invasive practices on the filmmaker's part. Her excitement at times, however, outweighs her anxieties. In fact, she veers towards losing all restraint – thus, of the "male and female eaglet in *The Filming of the Golden Eagle*," it "is difficult not to write a bookful on work such as this" (*Collected Prose* 306). Yet in her "close close-ups" of animals, she is not concerned (as Doane might suggest) with an "over-identification with the image." Instead, she foregrounds her inevitable artificial construction of the exotic "other." "Animals on Film," an article in *Close Up*, points to the "false" representation of animals and their "moods" that results from emphasis upon human experience: "The poor frightened heroine shut in with a lion, crouching in a corner. Actually it is the lion that crouches (when the camera stops working) . . . Its fierce roar is a cry of pain."[59]

Moore is well aware of how perverse "unreason" enters into attempts to manipulate the "natural," thus her amusement at "a / mere childish attempt to make an imperfectly / ballasted animal stand up," or at the desire "to make a pup / eat his meat on a plate" ("Critics and Connoisseurs" 77). Yet she compulsively animates such anthropomorphizing acts. Perez describes the "geometric finesse" of Keaton's play with the physics of motion; Moore similarly abides by a slapstick awareness of scientific laws. Thus she can use a kind of trick photography in reproducing her sea unicorn:

> this animal of that one horn
> throwing itself upon which head foremost from a cliff,
> it walks away unharmed,
> proficient in this feat, which like Herodotus,
> I have not seen except in pictures.
> ("Sea Unicorns and Land Unicorns" 135)

She modernizes Herodotus who says of the phoenix: "'I have not seen it myself except in a picture'" (151). In the process, she replicates a moving comic strip (we recall Eliot identifies this aspect in her work). The "magical" pliable unicorn with its "unmatched device" of horn remains the elusive object of explorations, spurring the search for substitutes. Likewise, her "mechanicked" pangolin is her most cartoonishly mutable and evasive: this "armored / ant-eater" with "edged leafpoints on the tail and artichoke set leg-and-body-plates" alternately "rolls himself into a ball that has / power to defy all effort to unroll it" (*CP* 118). Even more ornately, the creature becomes a portable fetish:

> Compact like the furled fringed frill
>   on the hat-brim of Gargallo's hollow iron head of a
>   matador, he will drop and will
>   then walk away
>   unhurt

Moore's evident pleasure in these "live-action" shots counterpoint with her uneasiness over the mediation of creatures to whom she evinces such profound kinship. She seems literally compelled in a physical sense to number as a spectator, so that, for instance, when she "saw a majestic giraffe with oyster white legs. . . . Its pop eyes disaffected [her] but [she] could not look away" (*Selected Letters* 167). She notes that the equipment used to film marine creatures in *Strange Animals* operates so that "the activity of the creatures is recorded under characteristic conditions, not under the stimulus of excitement or at temperatures inimical to them"; at the same time, she also understands that film photography "like the lie detector of the criminal court, reveals agitation which the eye fails to see" (*Collected Prose* 307–8). In a sense, the film mechanism indicts itself, exposing the possible disturbance to the creature caused by intrusion into its own peculiar environment. Along these lines, she writes to Bryher that while she hasn't seen "as many movies as [she] should like to," she saw Frank Buck's *Bring 'Em Back Alive* three times, and asks tentatively: "didn't you think, in the film, that he dealt with animals rather kindly and respectfully," adding that "[a]t least I did not see him sitting on dead animals as Osa and Martin Johnson sometimes do" (*Selected Letters* 278). She thus both attempts to preserve Buck from complete approbation and aligns him with imperialist explorers. And we recognize that while she does not sit on dead animals, she wears them, perhaps even more indulgently than is the custom of the times.

In the context of her fascination with "non-fictional" cinema, it makes sense that James Sibley Watson Jr., editor of *The Dial*, encouraged and supported Moore's poetry. With a medical degree and as editor of a major modernist venue, he (like Moore) straddled scientific and artistic realms, discovering in film a medium to bridge them. He not only collaborated with the poet Melville Webber in the making of *Lot in Sodom* but also the more Expressionist *The Fall of the House of Usher*, in which the artist kills his neurasthenic, confined wife essentially by painting her image. In fact, the film's use of double exposure and superimposition make it appear as if the deranged husband's very paint strokes "retouch" and penetrate the surface of her skin. This phenomenon becomes even more visceral when the camera shifts away from the wife as compulsory sitter and positions the audience as the canvas; thus we relive the wife's epidermal evisceration.

While Moore does not directly address this particular film, *Usher* allegorizes her own investigations into the relationship between observer and observed, subject and object, explorer and animal, collector and collectible. Dr. Watson (as she addresses him in their correspondence) is himself a transitional figure for the vexed status of film within these binary positions. As Lisa Cartwright points out, Watson's "oeuvre includes a reel of cinematic animal X-ray experiments humorously called, 'Disney Animal Review' as well as his participation in a team which produced a short X-ray film of the torso of an infant in close up."[60] This "experimental" documentary of the infant's body is worth keeping in mind because of its resonance with Moore's (as well as with Léger's) fetishistic compulsion to measure and cut up rhythmic patterns of natural processes. Cartwright describes this scientific film thus:

We see the blood, made visible with the injection of a contrast medium, coursing through its system in a short sequence representing eight real-time heartbeats. Projected in a continuous loop, these eight beats were viewed over and over.[61]

This X-ray film makes a "continuous loop" of bodily rhythms, or the "real-time" flow of blood and heartbeats. In this way, it behaves, as Bryher writes of film in another context, as a preternaturally receptive "machine that records heart beats or the sensations of a leaf."[62]

Cartwright elaborates that the scientific film, like Watson's X-ray experiment, overlapped with spectacle and popular amusements. She refers as well to John Macintyre's 1897 filming of a frog's leg subjected to electrical stimulation, which served as laboratory experiment as well as dinner-party entertainment. Another of her key examples, Edison's 1903 "Electrocuting an Elephant" "documents the moment of the elephant's death," exposing the "public fascination with scientific technology and its capacity to determine the course of life and death in living beings," its ability moreover "to regulate and discipline bodies."[63]

Moore similarly evidences a tension between identifying with and objectifying or regulating animals. She places them on a potentially "spectacular" continuum with the artifacts and objects she situates in her "imaginary gardens with real toads in them." Thus "No Swan So Fine" unreels its artificial swan to denote its existence in time:

> No swan,
> with swart blind look askance
> and gondoliering legs, so fine
>   as the chintz china one with fawn-
> brown eyes and toothed gold
> collar on to show whose bird it was.
>   (*CP* 19)

In this one enjambed sentence, Moore both sets this "dead" bird in motion and halts its "gondeliering" progress by marking its status as possession. But are we to think that she prefers this swan to a so-called real one (like the one in "Critics and Connoisseurs" who "made away with what [she] gave it / to eat")? This artifact, part of the "Louis Fifteenth / candelabrum-tree of cockscomb- / tinted buttons, dahlias, / sea-urchins, and everlastings," characteristically disturbs the usual divisions between the organic and inorganic. It persists in the present ("perches on the branching foam") as a measuring-rod of the transitory. After all, the possessor has passed away as the curt last line reports: "The king is dead." From one angle, an anthropomorphic hybrid (here the candelabra) is in a sense the most enduring aspect of human time (here the King's rule), at least on a fetishist scale that values "tinted buttons, dahlias," the dazzling parts over the whole. Simultaneously, the "real" swan's motion persists as a ghost double, for its movement unveils the artifact itself as temporal.

Moore does possess what Cartwright calls the "observer's compulsion to display, reveal, and analyze bodies";[64] in fact, she broaches upon this role in "Those Various Scalpels" as poet/surgeon. Yet she also extends herself into the spectacle, into her menagerie of anthropomorphic bodies. Her bodies are never simply dispassionate depictions, for it is her "x-ray like inquisitive intensity" which allows her to see the "skeleton" beneath the physiognomy ("People's Surroundings" 110). Moreover, her bodily identity is itself revealed through this "intensity," as she states in another context, "the rhythm is the person, and the sentence but a radiograph of personality."[65]

With her x-ray powers of identification, Moore assumes, for instance, the voice of an elephant in "Black Earth," whose rutted skin reads as the "patina of circumstance," its body in "time / a substance / needful as an instance / of the indestructibility of matter." Aware of the larger cycles or "unity of life and death," this elephant defies its ultimate capture through an assertion of utter individuality, that "[t]he I of each is to / the I of each" (87–9). Yet it is the precarious suspension between the living and the dead, wildness and captivity, the skin and the skeleton, which impels Moore's fetishism.

Moore writes to her brother about taking their mother to the movies and her fascination with the animal documentary that they watch (she doesn't provide the name). She is utterly absorbed by the unfolding action, treating it as if it were a complicated drama of human action:

> In some curious way, I missed the point of the colubrid's ascending the tree after being embroiled with the leopard. The leopard sprang into the tree and the snake was pursuing it; the leopard worked higher and higher in the tree, and then out on a branch and when the twigs became fine let itself fall crashing though the leaves to the ground to escape the snake. And several other things I related out of the proper order. The tiger and crocodile fight lasted some time and the strange feature of it was the way in which they kept turning over and over, the whiteness of both showing at regular intervals, and the gator's stout, limited little legs with webbed claws at the end making slow, futile swimming motions. (*Selected Letters* 257)

In the same letter, she admits to working like "a demon to complete" her jerboa poem, taking only breaks with "these shows," such as the animal movie she so assiduously reports. She also significantly notes the "amusing" simulacra of "animals and imitation cocoa-fibre at the mouth of the theatre."

"The Jerboa" indeed records animal motion in apparent contrast to the taxidermied animals in the cinema lobby. Her poem celebrates the desert rat who can "enjoy freedom from domination and from domineering over others."[66] Moore places the jerboa in the context of Egyptian and Roman slavery where humans and animals are exploited as objects, totems, and even toys. Her creature contrasts with those in power who use "dwarfs" to add "fantasy / and a verisimilitude that were / right to those with, everywhere, / / with power over the poor." The Egyptians, not unlike the contemporary showcasing of human "oddities" in the World's Fairs,

> understood
> making colossi and
> how to use slaves, and kept crocodiles and put
> baboons on the necks of giraffes to pick
> fruit, and used serpent magic.   (*CP* 10)

The jerboa, however, is a figure at the fringes of this economy, either "[a]broad seeking food, or at home / in its burrow." Moore makes an implicit comparison between this self-sufficient jerboa and the nomadic African, who "should," like the rat, be "free-born." As Miller writes: "The Jerboa and Africans, then, trope each other, both representing an idealized nonpossessive attitude toward property and other people. Without the Africans, the poem's point would have not have been as clear; without the animal subject, Moore would have to risk much greater romantic racialism or enthnocentricism."[67] Moore offers an alternative to curating animals as objects/chattel by attending to their adaptive strengths.

Within the hierarchical system of oppression Moore depicts, there is an odd lapse of several frames, which unravel a scene of cross-dressing and potential perverse desire(s):

> Those who tended flower-
> beds and stables were like the king's cane in the
> form of a hand, or the folding bedroom
> made for his mother of whom
>
> he was fond. Princes
> clad in queens' dresses,
> calla or petunia
> white, that trembled at the edge, and queens in a
> king's underskirt of fine-twilled thread like silk-
> worm gut, as bee-man and milk-
>
> maid, kept divine cows
> and bees; limestone brows,
> and gold-foil wings.   (*CP* 12)

While the poem might be criticizing the decadent excess of the caparisoned royalty, this provocative metonymy of prosthesis ("the king's cane in the form of a hand"), gadgetry ("folding bedroom") and textured costumes registers somatic responsiveness ("trembled at the edge") and sexual pliability ("queens in a / king's underskirt"). The three enjambed stanzas above testify to an interlacing of animal, human, and object to the point where these arenas lose their distinction. To be sure, as Miller conjectures, the fact that "[t]hese people like small things" signals their meanness or spiritual paucity, yet there is also another angle to this historical allegory.

Moore herself often verges (as she does in this poem) upon reveling in a "small collection of objects" ("Those Various Scalpels"). Thus her excesses demand constant substitution as well as the quick-change of the natural into the artificial. After all, the last glimpse we have of her resourceful jerboa merges him with furniture: "pillar body erect / on a three-cornered smooth-working Chippendale / claw –" (*CP* 15). Indeed, her work confesses to a liking for "the royal totem; / and toilet boxes marked / with the contents." These Egyptian "bone boxes – the pivoting / lid incised with a duck-wing // or reverted duck-head" have their precursor in Moore's letter about writing "The Jerboa" after viewing a nature documentary and then glimpsing the "animals and imitation cocoa-fibre at the mouth of the theatre." The cinema as Egyptian "sarcophogus," as already remarked, is an important motif in the modernist imagination. Here it exposes, however off-handedly, a fusion of the organic with the inorganic.

Bazin refers to the Egyptian burial rites of embalming and the sending of tokens with the dead as enacting a faith in the continued existence of the corporeal body after death. Thinking of the cinema lobby, he notes that "near the sarcophagus, terra cotta statuettes substitute mummies to replace bodies if these were destroyed."[68] "[E]mbalming the dead might turn out to be a fundamental factor in all the plastic arts," he further assesses, revealing "that at the origin of painting and sculpture there lies a mummy complex." This is true perhaps in more ways than he suspects. Freud writes in fact that the most uncanny phenomenon is the "fear of being buried alive," which substitutes for a fear of "intra-uterine existence."[69] Castle aptly summarizes this "mummy complex": "No more unheimlich place, says Freud, than the female genitals."[70] Perhaps when Moore quotes in "Marriage" that "'[t]hese mummies / must be handled carefully,'" she is not only interrogating heterosexual union, but playfully suggesting that the mummy as phallic signifier might unravel the living/dead pre-oedipal mother.

Unlike photography, Bazin conjectures, "film is no longer content to preserve the object, enshrouded as it were in an instant, as the bodies of insects are preserved intact, out of the distant past, in amber. . . . Now, for the first time, the image of things is likewise the image of their duration, change mummified as it were."[71] The paradox of "mummified" flux points towards Moore's fetishist aesthetics. Like film, fetishism regularly requires "a perceptual denial of the difference between presence and absence"; this "denial," as Apter develops, is "not restricted to a denial of the existence of the maternal penis; it is often extended to a denial of differences of all sorts, including those between organic and inorganic material and between living and dead people" (*Feminizing the Fetish* 45). Animal movement and its vivisection in documentary film (as Moore records them) creates an intermediary zone where multiple differences meet. The king in "The Jerboa" is "fond" of his mother so he makes her a collapsible bedroom (a kind of coffin); and the "striptease" effect of "Those Various Scalpels" produces a double-take on the dead/living female body depicted.

We recall from Chapter One that Moore admired *Caligari* and its "mummy complex": "Cesare, the somnambulist on appearing – although standing with legs side by side – looks as if he had but one leg. Later, when he is roused from a trance in total darkness against the back of his cabinet, wedge-shaped lights slant down from his eyes at Lida, the heroine, the exact shape of a dagger that he uses later when intending to kill her." The scene requires "perceptual adjustment." "[W]edge-shaped lights" echo in the shape of the coffin-shaped cabinet, a potential stand-in for "intra-uterine existence." What Moore describes as a "trance in total darkness" lets her simultaneously identify with the carnival showmanship of the film's doctor with his "cabinet of curiosities."

In the same letter where she describes herself as naked gosling and praises the cubist décor in *Caligari*, Moore croons over Frank Parsons's *The Psychology of Dress*, a book that depicts the way dress exercises control over bodies through conventions of the age (*Selected Letters* 166). She relishes its outlining of idiosyncrasies in garb, for instance, a "cocoon style with small waist and two or three yards of ruffled train." Mummification meets fashion. Moore melds the moving and the static, the natural and the artificial, the male with female costume ("Princes /clad in queens' dresses" in "The Jerboa"), the animal with the totem, without I might add, transitions or connectives. She crosses moreover the maternal with the mummy, the "corps" with the corpse. This dynamic of metonymy and erotic displacement replays more explicitly in *Maedchen in Uniform* and *Lot in Sodom*.

In "The Film Gone Male," Dorothy Richardson mourns the end of the silent era as a shift away from a "feminine" mode of expression:

And the film, regarded as a medium of communication, in the day of its innocence, in its quality of being nowhere and everywhere, nowhere in the sense of having more intention than direction and more purpose than plan, everywhere by reason of its power to evoke, suggest, reflect, express from within its moving parts and in their totality of movement, something of the changeless being at the heart of all becoming, was essentially feminine.[72]

The diffuse yet omnipresent character of silent film ("being nowhere and everywhere") recreates that symbiotic quality H. D. ascribes to cinematic experience. It might also be useful in this context to think of Studlar's emphasis upon the pre-oedipal dimension to film viewing where the relationship to the screen can simulate a "pre-sleep fusion with the breast." For Richardson, sound ruins film's "innocence": by "becoming audible and particularly in becoming a medium of propaganda," it is fulfilling "a masculine destiny."

While Richardson verges on collapsing the "essentially feminine" with materiality, she identifies the heightening of suggestive somatic gesture as integral to silent film, a quality that appealed to Moore. Richardson also concedes that while sound might be used as "a weapon" of propaganda, it can make film a "council chamber" for political exchange. We recall that *Borderline* is silent, even though it could have used sound technology; notwithstanding the expense, the makers were adamant that the hieroglyphic body in a silent film could be more effective in making social and psychological criticism. *Maedchen* stands at this technological cross-roads: its anti-fascist and anti-authoritarian politics become visible, I would say, through its borrowed features from silent film as well as its strategic, minimalist use of sound.

Adjacent to Richardson's article in *Close Up*, A. Kraszna-Krausz reviews four recent German films, including *Maedchen*.[73] However, he completely misreads the film. Beneath a provocative still of the main character (Manuela) crossdressed as a male prince with another girl's hand upon her thigh and the other on her calf (fig. 20), he writes: "There is no man in this film, no real love-story, nor anything seductive."[74] What he perceives is the lack of a heterosexual story, but the film provides its

20. The cross-dressed Manuela in Leontine Sagan's *Maedchen in Uniform* (1931).

alternative "romance" along with a whole range of emotional and bodily modes of bonding between women, what Adrienne Rich describes in
another context as part of a "lesbian continuum."[75] Rather than emphasizing the oedipal model of development, Rich suggests that because of
the initial primary relation to the mother, it is more of an oddity that all

human beings are not first and foremost erotically attached to women. It is this obscured and disowned attachment which potentially leads to a form of female fetishism, redefined by de Lauretis as not the search for the missing phallus but for substitutes for the female body. In this schema, genital relations are therefore not the exclusive sphere or basis of intense attachments.

Moore appears to acknowledge this by praising *Maedchen*'s "plausible emotion," calling it a "loveing [sic] picture," the kind shunned by the mainstream. The film's expanded sense of maternal bonding operates against the grain of Hollywood productions. In spite of Moore's enthusiasm, she never develops her commentary about the film. Yet her very divergence away from treating it in detail perhaps bears significance. She glosses this kind of obliqueness in "Feeling and Precision" when she declares that "we must be as clear as our natural reticence allows us to be."[76] Perhaps the homoeroticism of *Maedchen* ruffled her "natural reticence." When she declares "omissions are not accidents" to preface *Collected Poems*, I presume Moore is both guarding her privacy and gesturing towards a quite tangible negative space. Further, a simultaneous disclosure and covering over the maternal signifier through a vocabulary of costumes, a central visual component in *Maedchen*, arguably expresses a fetishist eroticism and helps account for Moore's keen liking of the film.

Created upon the eve of Hitler's rise to power, *Maedchen* signals a world temporarily "gone male." B. Ruby Rich has explained that the film grew out of "the Berlin with dozens of gay and lesbian bars and journals, the Berlin of a social tolerance so widespread that it nearly camouflaged the underlying legal restraints which were to grow, rapidly, into massive repression."[77] The film is both a tribute to "social tolerance" as well as a rendition of fascist control. Through its "dual coming-out story," *Maedchen* specifically addresses the silencing and revelation of sexual deviance. The adolescent Manuela voices "'the love that dares not speak its name'" while Fraulein von Bernburg is "the teacher who repudiates her own role as an agent of suppression and wins her own freedom by accepting her attraction to another woman."[78]

After her mother dies, Manuela enters a boarding school devoted to producing and disciplining mothers and wives of "iron" Prussian men.[79] The establishing shots of the film pan across a set of static militaristic statues, while the school's overbearing archways and steeples set the scene for the girls in uniform marching in regiments. Hence, while there are no male actors in this film, the military patriarchy is omnipresent, finding expression in the Principal, who acts as mouthpiece for totalitarianism. Her totems are a monocle and cane, prosthetics that indicate her physical limits as well as affiliation with the repressive forms of power.

Moore's anti-war poems in *Observations*, particularly "To Military Progress" and "To Statecraft Embalmed" are, like *Maedchen*, quite prescient. In fact, written during the First World War, they reflect political criticism that would reignite in the next decade. They clarify part of the reason Moore would be receptive to Sagan's anti-militarism and her exposure of the disciplining of a person's bodily "radiograph" or rhythm. In "To Military Progress," she decapitates the body politic: its insensate torso craves to "revive again, / War" to win back the "lost / Head" (19). Supplementing this poem, "To Statecraft Embalmed" portrays the war-mongering culture as a "necromancer," an ibis-headed Thoth who must "with its bill, / Attack its own identity."

Moore is well aware of the link between sexual and social politics so that in "Marriage," she links heterosexual union with male dominance: "experience attests / that men have power / and sometimes one is made to feel it" (120). Close on the heels of this assertion, she addresses the "wearing" of power: "'Men are monopolists / of stars, garters, buttons / and other shining baubles.'" This last catalogue is relevant for the reading of the insignia of statues, objects and uniforms in *Maedchen*. "Marriage" both points towards the necromantic misuses of "curio collecting" and highlights the eroticized function of "transitional objects," the latter an important motif in the film.

The film's narrative in fact can be broken down through the clothing, a weathervane for altered emotional conditions. Clothing or "baubles" here indicate the entrapment within and attempt to decompose the strict lines imposed by the Prussian State. When Manuela first arrives at the school, she is deprived of her personal clothing as though she were entering the military or a prison; the striped school uniform operates like Moore's steam roller, who she addresses: "You crush all the particles down / into close conformity" ("To a Steam Roller" 63). Contrasting with the conformity exacted through uniforms, one silent montage sequence lingers over the girls preparing for bed; temporarily outside of strict surveillance, they cross the partitions dividing their changing rooms. In various states of undress, the girls groom each other, admire their own and each other's bodies, and indulge in fleeting tactile contact. A later scene shows the girls poised in revolt against the school and its harsh measures towards Manuela. Looking back at the camera with disgruntled inattention, the girls stand with rumpled uniforms partially off and sleeping gowns half on.

While *Maedchen* uses sound technology, it emphatically works "to evoke, suggest, reflect, express from within its moving parts and in their totality of movement" an embodied consciousness, strategically interrupting the restriction of "moving parts." The camera tracks and isolates the regimented rows of marching feet or mouths moving in unison; in opposition, it also follows the non-narrative shots of "loving love" (hair being brushed, self-washing, girls communing in shadowy alcoves).

Reinforcing the film's method of contrasts, Bernburg is the only source of affection available to the girls; in the school's highly controlled environment, she can play the "good cop," but as B. Ruby Rich argues, she thus also facilitates the maintenance of repression. All of the girls have crushes on Bernburg (one even flashes a tatooed forearm with heart and arrow, a "B" inscribed in its center), while Manuela's infatuation escalates beyond such expressions of attachment. In perhaps the most famous sequence in the film, two rows of girls in soft-focus at the edge of their beds await Bernburg's nightly kiss to their foreheads. After a build-up of erotic suspense, at her "turn" Manuela wraps her arms around the teacher and tightly embraces her. In a shockingly slow close-up, Bernburg kisses Manuela on the lips. The scene marks the deviation of their relationship from allowable forms of affection. In an ostensible attempt to maintain decorum and to pacify Manuela, Bernburg gives her a chemise, a sign both of maternal concern for the girl's lack of a "trousseau" and of erotic affection.

Like "The Jerboa," *Maedchen* underlines how bodies are disciplined and engendered, but it also demonstrates that desire is more safely mediated through totems and garments, extensions of embodied identity. If fetishism is a "form of transgressive idolatry" (as Apter puts it), Bernburg is a maternal substitute as well as Manuela's sex idol. In this context, it makes sense, as de Lauretis argues, that it is not castration that the lesbian disavows but the absence or loss of another woman's body that she must displace onto a fetishistic substitute.[80] Manuela's attachment to the "maternal muff," or rather the chemise, devolves upon the "transitional" part standing in for the whole.

In the film's turning point, Manuela cross-dresses as Don Carlos pledging love to "his" queen in the school play; at the post-performance party, she becomes tipsy (all the girls have forsaken the unusually "spiked" punch and passed it on to her). Following an extended sequence that includes a cabaret style piano performance to accompany a slow dance among paired girls, Manuela boasts of Bernburg's reciprocated passion for her, invoking the chemise as evidence. Manuela is consequently "jailed" and isolated.

After Manuela's release, she ascends the spiral staircase (its bars have cast shadows and stark lines throughout), preparing to commit suicide. The other girls, intuiting that something is amiss, rally around her as if in response to an elaborate communal system of signals. Significantly, a close-up of Bernburg's eyes, taking up the whole screen, superimposes upon Manuela's longing eyes. Significantly, this moment of superimposition testifies to their symbiotic and silent connection, heuristically adumbrating the spectator's potentially fused relation to the image. After this telepathic shot, Bernburg rushes from her classroom to Manuela's aid, in time to derail the conventional denouement of suicide for the doomed lesbian.

The aesthetic affinities Moore shares with *Maedchen* can be linked to her fetishist sensibility. Its "speechless" expressionist style, including its gestural close-ups, play with chiaroscuro, sharp lines and angles, and rapid crosscutting between scenes, would have immediate resonance for her. Moreover, these elements translate into a conflict between the totems or tatoos of "loving love" and their containment in restrictive geometries.

This tension reappears in the other "fiction" film Moore reviewed for *Close Up*. She has evident admiration for *Lot in Sodom*: it is "the best art film [she has] seen" (*Collected Prose* 310); nevertheless, once more "omissions" riddle her review. She does not indicate that the film features long sequences which choreograph bodily movement, particularly that of a number of men, mostly naked, wearing little more than "loin cloths" (there is even a brief medium shot of bare buttocks). The film shows its handsome "sodomites" engaged in elaborate dance sequences of flexing and gyrating, a ballet that even zooms in to caress the taut skin of torso upon torso, and at one point, offers a kiss between men. Of these "loving" men, Moore only hints at their divergence from the "Child's Bible," complaining that they "do not look quite so responsibly sinister as they might." In fact, the refusal to demonize homoeroticism is one of the film's greatest strengths, and it would be hard to mistake the camera's loving attention upon the "sinners" as anything but a generous reinterpretation of their fallen condition.

The film opens with an electrical charge dividing the screen (appearing like the jagged report of an electrocardiogram). This shock parts the tumultuous clouds and smoke to reveal a miniaturized Sodom. In the ensuing first sequence, the Sodomites play trumpets, elongated and phallic-shaped that revolve like spokes of a wheel. This image sequence is abstract, even mechanized like those in *Ballet Mécanique*. At the same time, it prepares for the ensuing kinesthetic "intensity" among the men.

The scenes of erotic dancing counterpoint with the "bowed, intense, darkly caparisoned, overclothed, powerful, helpless Jew" (*Complete*

Prose 310). While most of the film is silent, it sparingly uses sound sequences, and these are notably in the domain of Lot's scriptural recitations. The hooded angel who warns Lot of destruction belongs as well to this "speaking" disembodied universe.

Lot's famously unnamed wife (played by Hildegarde Watson, a close correspondent of Moore's) is the copula between the two worlds of righteous thinking and sensuous embodiment. In one scene, the "insurmountably lissom nymph" (as Moore describes the wife) is framed at a window with a female companion, the folds of her own clothing slowly moving in parallel to the curtain drapery. The "framed" women gaze longingly towards the eroticized male dancers, foreshadowing the wife's fateful turn back towards the condemned Sodom. An inter-title reads that the men beg the wife to enact the "law of kindness"; she thus mediates between the two worlds of the "law of the father" and some other "feminine" principle, identified by Richardson with the suggestive realm of silent film. Moore alludes to this aspect of the film's register, when she refers to its "illusion of quiescence of which one is scarcely conscious." The hypnotic effect, or "sensation of this kind, imparted by tested sensibility," she writes using the language of experimental psychology, "would be of interest to those who have been studying the effect of motion-pictures on the sleep of children" (*Complete Prose* 311). Hypnotic effects, including the use of slow motion, can have erotic valences.

Moore, in fact, confesses that *Lot* is "very nearly too exciting" in its use of mediating techniques. They can produce a "spinal chill," unlike the old newsreel where one on occasion "salvages from the commercial ragbag a good bisection or strange-angle shot" (*Complete Prose* 311). By contrast, she writes:

Here, the camera work, with a correlating of poetic influences – the Blake designs in the fire, the Pascin, Giotto, Doré, and Joseph Stella treatment, shows us wherein slow motion, distortion, the sliding track, can be more legitimate than the face to face stage set. Personality coalescing with a piece of stone, the obliterating cloud of doves, 'the silver cord' and other historic color, are incontrovertibly conclusive for the art of film.

Moore's metonymic sense of "[p]ersonality coalescing" with inanimate objects points towards her sublated erotics, particularly as they are achieved through experimental film devices.

One such device in *Lot* allows, for instance, two mirror-like bodies to converge and separate as they approach the viewer. Pairs of men run towards the camera and then blur together and divide. The long sequence of men dancing relies upon multiple exposure, so that we see for instance, one man's leaping and touching down broken up or "analyzed" as it would be in a Muyrbridge motion study. Moore's excitement over *Lot* perhaps stems from her ability to fetishize these otherwise abstract film studies.

In a letter to H. D. and Bryher, Moore provides a lengthy description of Anna Pavlova's costumes and physical feats in the performance of *Amarylla*. Yet she follows with a confession that she prefers "an analysis [she] saw some time ago in the movies" to "this conscious art" of ballet. In fact, it is not the precise content that signifies, but film's self-conscious manipulation of rhythmic movement. She offers an example of "the movements of football players in a match game – all the movements slowed down by the speedograph so that the players seemed to move like sea-horses or float through the air like scarfs. The ball waved when kicked instead of descending in a perfect ellipse and when the players caught it you felt as if they were catching cobwebs" (*Selected Letters*). In its own way, *Lot* (especially in its "ballet" sequences) is an homage to the lyrical motion studies Moore references as well as to the way dissected motions can displace erotic ones.

More overtly expressive but related nevertheless to the prismatic effects of abstract motion studies, *Lot* features sped-up sequences of men wrestling, embracing, jumping, twirling, kissing, crawling on a "multitude of feet" ("In the Days of Prismatic Color" 92), effectively derailing the "heterosexual imperative." Moore veers away from mention of these accumulated signs of eroticism. Yet *Lot*, and her review of it, aid us in seeing how her "scopic detailism" involves kinesthetic investments. The "high points" or "intensities" that Moore selects are visual points of cathexis: "the blur of waving candle-flame, on the undulating coarse-weave curtain; the glass-black blood quivering along a prostrate body; the glistening elaborate lily with snake-spots; the tortoise-shell spotted pallor of the snake with beady eyes" (*Complete Prose* 310). With her usual hybrid vision of décor or design, the lily has "snake-spots" while the snake has a "tortoise-shell spotted pallor."

The film deploys prismatic lighting effects and spiraling smoke to veil its homoerotic content as much as to accentuate its sensuous display. Moore herself often partakes of special effects akin to those in *Lot* to engender fetishized settings. For instance, "An Octopus" presents "an endless skein swayed by the wind" or the "cliffs the color of the clouds, of petrified white vapor –." In the post-*Lot* poem, "Frigate Pelican" proffers a semi-apocalyptic image through its acrobatic animal who "quivers about / as charred paper behaves – full / of feints" (*CP* 26). These moments, like those which Moore lists in her survey of *Lot*, act as "displacements of value" (*Feminizing the*

Fetish 20). In a sense, Moore mimics the gaze of Lot's wife, who cannot entirely disavow her somatic link to the pleasure-seekers of Sodom. Erotic scintillation after all, as Apter reinforces, lies in the "fractal, metonymic nature of the fetish" (20).

One shot dwells upon the hallucinatory image of the snake winding through a miniature house. It is followed by a metonymy of images – a flower slowly opening, fire fluttering, and water cascading. Evidently the fallen world of the Sodomites is much richer (even when doomed) than Lot's dim, one-dimensional existence. As his wife defies the interdict to look back, she turns to a block of salt, an element suggestive of the chemical conversion of elements (of which Dr. Watson must have been fond) as well as her tearful "excess" at leaving behind a landscape of bodily pleasure.

Moore does not explicitly side "against" Lot, and only grudgingly admits: "a civilization that has reached an extreme of culture, is going to have plea-sure" (*Complete Prose* 312). Nonetheless, she enjoys the film's experimental devices, geared towards heightening the kinesthetic body. With this in mind, her 1915 poem "Is Your Town Nineveh?" (written after her first long trip to New York) "compares the subject of her address, an unnamed 'you,' to a sad and angry Jonah who resists God's injunction to cry out against the sinful city of Nineveh."[81] Unlike Jonah, Lot follows the letter of the law. God punishes Jonah by having him imprisoned in the belly of a large fish; in Moore's fanciful poem, Jonah's "phantasmagoria about fishes" is a sign of bodily "freedom." In fact, her speaker is transfixed by the unexpected vision afforded by *not* protesting the "sinful city": "I myself, have stood / there by the aquarium, looking / at the Statue of Liberty" (59). By contrast, Lot refuses such eccentric shifts in perspective, implicitly dismissing the multi-faceted body, its odd angles and desires.

Moore appreciates that *Lot* "is not a talkie." The appeal of silent film has much to do with how her poetry, to use Leavell's words, "def[ies] what some consider the very essence of language itself."[82] Her poems count upon a new measuring of the line, enacting instead a "principle of control contributing to the impression obliquely" (*Complete Prose* 304). Silent film can produce, like Moore's syllabics, a fetishist montage. As such, it can disturb a foundational "logos" (as with the mostly silent *Maedchen* and *Lot*), startle through unexpected joinings (as with *Ballet Mécanique* or nature documentaries), and eroticize hybrid or unlikely bodies.

Conclusion
Modernist dissociation and all about Eve

All of the modernists explored in this study grapple with what amounts to a cultural "dissociation of sensibility," where poetry does not seem capable of conveying immediate sensation or "felt thought." In part, it is this struggle that led Stein, Williams, H. D., and Moore to adopt a cinematic style, one that redefined the polarities and connections between mind and body. The hysteric body has appeared throughout these texts as a figure theorized in psychoanalysis and experimental psychology as evidencing "somatic compliance" and fragmentation. In spite of the critical emphasis upon the "disembodiment" or abstraction of avant-garde films or in fact modernist poetry, both media make the expression of the visceral a central "crisis" and preoccupation. The modernists I have examined experiment with the shifting possibilities, ambiguities, and in-between positions for gender and sexual embodiment made legible by camerawork and montage. Likewise, modern poems are often precursors for the representation of non-codified somatic experiences within film.

Among the questions that I have considered, two have been most crucial: how did a modernist resourcefulness with the fragment both anticipate and participate in the revolutionary forms of early film? And how might this resourcefulness reflect diverse erotic economies? Stein exposes her visceral processes of clipping, repeating, and editing words together in rhythmic, even mechanical, montage. Williams replaces poetic meter with the "variable foot" and follows the line of his spectator's eye as a sign of a disjunctive body, energized by thwarted wish fulfillment. H. D. cathects to the "half-finished image" in poetry and cinema: "bits of chiffon" become "radiantly significant." In her cinematic imagination, the fragmented female body elicits both identification and desire. Finally, Moore parcels out and fetishizes her luminous details in elaborately broken syllabic structures. Like Stein, she is ready to see automatism or the mechanical body as a potential route for undermining conventional forms of female embodiment.

I will here briefly turn to Moore's "Marriage" (the poem Williams justly named "an anthology of transits" and written the same year as *The Waste Land*) as an exemplar of how modern poetic methods, assimilating those of cinema, can enact the dissociated body and offer an alternative mode of embodiment. As already mentioned, Moore's poems weave in multiple quotations from other texts, including postcards, advertisements, business documents, guidebooks, and fashion magazines.[1] In contrast to Eliot's overt citation of predominantly high culture, Moore crosses between the high and the low with seeming arbitrariness. Her sources undermine textual "authority" and genre (she includes an index and notes for her volume *Observations* as if it could be an essay). While her use of other texts is usually signaled by quote marks (they flicker across her pages), they are not always designated as such nor does she provide the source for all of her quotations. Moore calls her technique a "hybrid method of composition" in her "Note on the Notes." Referencing this method in "Marriage" as "cycloid inclusiveness," she places poetry on a par with multiple discourses, including cinema, which according to Eisenstein, "is of exactly the same order as the Doric temple, a well-executed somersault or the Brooklyn bridge."[2] Stein's love for Chaplin and distrust of literary tradition, Williams's visual embrace of moments unfolding as he drives his car, and H. D.'s cinema as temple for reconnecting body and mind each accord to some extent with Moore's receptivity to film.

Moore's allusive and inclusive method is akin to the cutting and splicing used in experimental films both to mediate an "embodied existence" and to subvert wholeness as either an artistic or kinesthetic principle. Costello aptly calls Moore a "kleptomaniac of the mind," but it is her *bodily* act of pilfering, touching, and excising that I emphasize.[3] She emphasizes the materiality of her poems, in the way Man Ray writes upon celluloid to point up its physical existence. Moore segments and interrupts her poetry through quotation, making it "impossible to quote convincingly," as Williams so justly observes. In fact, her quotations resemble the "photogramatic" stills or the individual segments composing montage. In order to achieve narrative coherence, Stewart argues, these "photograms must be *unseen*": "letters generally disappear into the words they constitute as do photograms into the motion they impel"; he concludes that it is "only under undue duress," as in modernist film and literature, that ruptures appear.[4] Moore's quotations are "photogramatic" interruptions, and in the process, implicate a larger somatic dissociation conveyed in her work, including "Marriage."

Near the beginning of "Marriage," Moore transforms the culturally maligned Eve into both an hysteric capable of multiple modes and a desired body:

> Eve: beautiful woman—
> I have seen her
> when she was so handsome
> she gave me a start,
> able to write simultaneously
> in three languages—
> English, German and French
> and talk in the meantime
>
> (*CP* 115)

This linguistic dexterity calls to mind one of the great hysterics, Anna O., who volleyed between having no speech and stitching together words from four or five different languages. However, Moore's note for the poem does not mention Breuer and Freud's case study, indicating that these tantalizing lines draw upon a quotation from an article entitled, "Multiple Consciousness or Reflex Action of Unaccustomed Range" from *Scientific American* (January 1922). I cite in full the quote she provides because of its relevance to my delineation of bodily dissociation as linked to cinematic practice:

'Miss A— will write simultaneously in three languages, English, German, and French, talking in the meantime. (She) takes advantage of her abilities in everyday life, writing her letters simultaneously with both hands; namely, the first, third, and fifth words with her left and the second, fourth, and sixth with her right hand. While generally writing outward, she is able as well to write inward with both hands.' (144)

By supplying this lengthy quotation, Moore encourages the reader to superimpose Miss A upon the poem's Eve, and thus creates a kind of split screen or double identity. The composite figure of Miss A/Eve epitomizes the "dissociation in sensibility" Eliot makes so palpable, and harkens back to many of the automaton or hysteric bodies I have catalogued throughout.

By excising and remaking a fragment from a scientific journal (albeit one framed more for the lay person), Moore both invokes and mocks the authority of experimental "science." Throughout "Marriage," one of her rare poems specifically about human relations, Moore summons the language of experiment, assuming a depersonalized tone in order to dispel an idealized vision of heterosexual union. She ties contemporary couples to that "first crystal-fine experiment," underscoring that it is "that experiment of Adam's" where Eve is the "central flaw."

It makes sense that Moore resists the body inherited through traditional representations of Eve. As discussed in relation to Stein and H. D., women poets needed to counteract cultural tropes of hyper-material or ethereal and disembodied femininity. Stein manages to remake the hysteric into a comic, forgetful body. Williams affiliates with the female body by undermining his ocular license. H. D. links the bisexual with the hysteric through reconstructing the femme fatale. By transposing Miss A with Eve, Moore "exonerates" one of the most demonized figures in literary and film history (recall the descendants of Eve, those femme fatales of German Expressionism as well as the neurasthenic women in Eliot). As a cultural body representing the breaking of the "one" into the "many," Eve is tied to the discord created through mechanical reproduction. In modernist consciousness, film often stands in for the female body – its flux, evanescence and imagined frivolous refusal of contemplation. The critique of these terms even appears in films, so that *Metropolis*, for instance, derides the notion that cinema could achieve a unitary language or Esperanto, when it recalls the creation of the Tower of Babel. An inter-title reads: "Everyone speaks the same language but no one understands it."

The content or meaning of Miss A/Eve's language(s) is unimportant; rather, it is the performance of them through physical gestures ("writing simultaneously with both hands"). In spite of her "heady" depiction of a dissociated body, Moore's character not only transgresses normal limits of physical capacity but also bridges the somatic with the mental. Miss A/Eve's writing is foremost of the porous body – simultaneously outward and inward, as the note suggestively indicates, and in this way intimates the film spectator's reversible position, simultaneously absorbing and projecting.

Through Miss A/Eve, Moore references her own "extended range," her traversing from "textbooks" to "business documents" to scientific articles. Miss A/Eve's "multiple reflex" and fragmented physical activities are not impediments but rather advantages, belonging to an extended bodily apparatus. She is a "productive" figure, pleasing herself like Moore's elephant who boasts in "Black Earth": "I do these / things which I do, which please / no one but myself" (87). Like Stein's willful automatism derived from her Radcliffe experiments and then transposed upon Chaplin's performances, Miss A/Eve "takes advantage" of her dislocated volition for her own "everyday" ends.

However, it is not only pleasing herself that distinguishes this pragmatic body, but that she also provokes desire in the spectator in a poem where beauty "tears one to pieces." In fact, the roving speaker of the poem has *seen* Miss A/Eve when she is "so handsome" that she is given a "start."

This "start" suggests a visceral frisson, combining fear and excitement. Miss A/Eve is eroticized, endowed with overtones of the "mannish lesbian." Hybrid and composed through jagged line breaks, she is not a fantasy figure cut out from romance like the woman Moore imagines in "A Carriage From Sweden": "And how beautiful, she / with the natural stoop of the / snowy egret, gray-eyed and straight-haired" (*CP* 131). Similar to Tiresias "throbbing between two lives," Miss A/Eve is "literally transsexual," for in her notebook version, Moore had originally cast this figure as male.[5]

Miss A/Eve embodies the fractal, multiple and simultaneous, those features characteristic of the hysteric body in *The Waste Land*. In fact, Moore's anomalous character can be seen as a kind of surrogate for Eliot – speaking in multiple languages as if at the same time. After all, Eliot writes in another context that "[o]ne of the reasons for learning at least one foreign language well is that we acquire a kind of supplementary personality."[6] As discussed in chapter 1, Eliot's poetry enacts its hysteric embodiment and play with sexual inversion through dissociated montage.

Of the poets I have explored, Moore appears perhaps closest to Eliot through her apparent ambivalence to the somatic. In a sense we have come full circle, like her unconsciously fastidious ant who has "returned to the point / from which it had started" ("Critics and Connoisseurs" 77–8). I have asserted that film as a corporeal medium is the very revelation of "dissociation of sensibility." Like Eliot, Moore often negotiated this dissociation by expressing and exaggerating it. By miming the "Impersonality Theory of Art," she underlines the theory's inadequacy: "one detects creative power by its capacity to conquer one's detachment" ("The Labors of Hercules" 105). Alternately, she alludes to the visual repression involved in the act of seeing (a kind of formula for not seeing the splicing of film pieces): "In these non-committal personal-impersonal expressions of appearance, the eye knows what to skip" ("People's Surroundings" 108). Such an admixture of "personal-impersonal" is in keeping for her version of the artist who finds that "'impersonal judgment in aesthetic / matters, a metaphysical impossibility'" ("To a Steam Roller" 63). She is, like her pangolin, "unemotional, and all emotion," a creature with "everlasting vigor" (*CP* 119).

"Marriage" exemplifies Moore's enjoyment of extending the body into an "uninhabitable space" (such as the one constructed by Léger) as well as into the dissecting "theatre" (such as the one found in her "analysis" of bodily movements in nature documentaries or in "Those Various Scalpels"). The phenomenology of film supplies a prosthetic relation to the image even when it calls attention to the body's fragmentation. Hence, experimental work highlights the tangible cut and pieced segments of film. The physical act of editing shows up through Moore's disjunctive quotations. To use language from "The Fish," "[a]ll / external / marks of abuse are present" and reveal the "physical features of // ac- / cident–lack / of cornice, dynamite grooves, burns, / and / hatchet strokes" (86).

Like Moore's "hybrid method of composition," my own practice has been a matter of juxtaposing otherwise unrelated domains, including psychoanalysis and experimental psychology. I use this method to reveal a paradox at the heart of modernism – the desire for bodily immediacy and the consciousness of its necessary fragmentation within both poetry and film. Considered alongside and in the context of films, poetic texts transport us beyond the exclusively referential to the gestural and embodied, beyond the auditory or solely visual to an otherwise uncharted erotics. The cubist dissection of Charlot's body repeats at the end of *Ballet mécanique* and is then followed by the image of a woman bending to smell a flower; this sequence epitomizes the ongoing tension between "logopoesis" and embodiment in cinematic modernism.

By examining poems as cinematic, both media become enlivened. We might imagine that specific modernist experiments in poetry could be revealed without resorting to analogues in film. Yet Stein, Williams, H. D., and Moore were attracted to the most cutting-edge medium of the period and necessarily saw their work in the phenomenological light of cinema. I hope that further investigation of these poets as well as others will result from my foray into the intricate crossovers between poetry and film.

Notes

INTRODUCTION: CINEMATIC MODERNISM

1 Anne Friedberg, "Approaching *Borderline*," in *H. D. Woman and Poet*, ed. Michael King (University of Maine Orono Printing Office: National Poetry Foundation, 1988).

2 H. D., "Cinema and the Classics: Beauty," *Close Up* (hereafter cited as *CU*) vol. 1 no. 1 (July 1927), p. 26. (Hereafter cited in the text as "Beauty.")

3 In an anthology of *Close Up* articles, James Donald, Anne Friedberg and Laura Marcus provide a rich contextual ground for the journal's broad historical connections with modernism. *Close Up 1927–1933: Cinema and Modernism* (Princeton: Princeton University Press, 1998). (Hereafter cited in the text as *Cinema and Modernism*.)

4 This study builds upon the work of those who have thus far probed the affinities between specific poets and film. See especially Carolyn Burke, "'Getting Spliced': Modernism and Sexual Difference," *American Quarterly* 39.1 (1987), pp. 98–121 (hereafter cited in the text as "Getting Spliced"); Susan Edmunds, *Out of Line: History, Psychoanalysis, and Montage in H. D.'s Long Poems* (Stanford: Stanford University Press, 1994); Laurence Goldstein, *The American Poet at the Movies: A Critical History* (Ann Arbor: University of Michigan Press, 1994); Mikhail Iampolski, *The Memory of Tiresias: Intertextuality and Film*, trans. Harsha Ram (Berkeley: University of California Press, 1998) (hereafter cited in the text as *Memory of Tiresias*); Charlotte Mandel, "'The Redirected Image': Cinematic Dynamics in the Style of H. D.," *Contemporary Literature*, 25.4 (1984), 411–36; Robert Richardson, *Literature and Film* (Bloomington: Indiana University Press, 1969); and P. Adams Sitney's *Modernist Montage: The Obscurity of Vision in Cinema and Literature* (New York: Columbia University Press, 1990). (hereafter cited in the text as *Modernist Montage*).

5 Gertrude Stein, "Portraits and Repetitions," in *Lectures in America* (Boston: Beacon Press, 1985), p. 177. (Hereafter cited in the text as "Portraits.")

6 *Jazz Singer* (1927) marks an historic watershed in its use of synchronized sound; by 1930, a uniform sound system was established.

7 Richard Sheppard, *Modernism – Dada – Postmodernism* (Evanston: Northwestern University Press, 2000), p. 11.

8 Miriam B. Hansen, "America, Paris, the Alps: Kracauer and Benjamin on Cinema and Modernity," in *Cinema and the Invention of Modern Life*, eds. Leo Charney and Vannessa R. Schwartz (Berkeley: University of California Press, 1995), p. 365.

9 Ibid., p. 364.

10 Michael Wood, "Modernism and Film," in *The Cambridge Companion to Modernism*, ed. Michael Levenson (Cambridge: Cambridge University Press, 1999), pp. 217–32.

11 H. D. "The *Borderline* Pamphlet"(1930), reprinted in *Cinema and Modernism* no. 75, p. 228. (Hereafter cited in the text as "Borderline Pamphlet.")

12 William Carlos Williams, "The Poem as a Field of Action," in *Selected Essays* (New York: New Directions, 1954), p. 282.

13 Marianne Moore, *Complete Poems* (New York: Penguin Books, 1994), p. 267.

14 Jean Lenauer, "The Cinema in Paris," *CU* vol. 3 no. 6 (Dec 1928), p. 16.

15 See Janet Bergstrom, ed. *Endless Night: Cinema and Psychoanalysis, Parallel Histories* (Berkeley: University of California Press, 1999).

16 Vivian Sobchack, *The Address of the Eye: A Phenomenology of Film Experience* (Princeton: Princeton University Press, 1992), p. 7. (Hereafter cited in the text as *Address of the Eye*.)

17 Quoted in Mark S. Micale, *Approaching Hysteria: Disease and Its Interpretations* (Princeton: Princeton University Press, 1995), p. 194.

18 Rita Felski, *The Gender of Modernism* (Cambridge: Harvard University Press, 1995), p. 3.

19 Sergei Eisenstein, "A Dialectic Approach to Film Form," in *Film Form: Essays in Film Theory*, ed. and trans. Jay Leyda (New York: Harcourt, Brace and Company, 1949), p. 49. (Hereafter cited in the text as "Dialectic Approach.")

20 Thomas Hardy, *Tess of the D'Urbervilles* (New York: Modern Library Edition, 1917), p. 139.

21 Ibid.

22 Arthur Rimbaud, "Letter to Paul Demeny" (1871), quoted in *The Autobiography of Surrealism*, ed. Marcel Jean (New York: Viking Press, 1980), p. 13.

23 Jonathan Crary, *Techniques of the Observer: On Vision and Modernity in the Nineteenth Century* (Cambridge, MA: MIT Press, 1993), p. 4.

24 Numerous critics have demonstrated the significant connections between poetry and painting. See especially Charles Altieri, *Painterly Abstraction in Modernist American Poetry: The Contemporaneity of Modernism* (Cambridge: Cambridge University Press, 1989); Bram Dijkstra, *Cubism, Stieglitz and the Early Poetry of William Carlos Williams* (Princeton: Princeton University Press, 1969); Albert Gelpi, *A Coherent Splendor: The American Poetic Renaissance, 1910–1950* (Cambridge: Cambridge University Press, 1987); Peter Halter, *The Revolution in the Visual Arts and the Poetry of William Carlos Williams* (Cambridge: Cambridge University Press, 1994); Linda Leavell, *Marianne Moore and Visual Arts: Prismatic Color* (Baton Rouge: Louisiana State University Press, 1995); and Wendy Steiner, *The Colors of Rhetoric: Problems in the Relation Between Literature and Painting* (Chicago: University of Chicago Press, 1982).

25 Malcolm Le Grice, *Abstract Film and Beyond* (Cambridge, MA: MIT Press, 1977), p. 7.

26 Elizabeth W. Joyce, *Cultural Critique and Abstraction: Marianne Moore and the Avant-Garde* (Lewisburg: Bucknell University Press, 1998), pp. 20–1.

27 Gilles Deleuze, *Cinema 1: The Movement-Image* (Minneapolis: University of Minnesota Press, 1986), pp. 6–7. (Hereafter cited in the text as *Movement-Image.*)

28 Maurice Merleau-Ponty, *The Primacy of Perception*, ed. James M. Edie (Evanston: Northwestern University Press, 1964), p. 5. (Hereafter cited in the text as *Primacy of Perception.*)

29 Guillaume Apollinaire, "The New Spirit and the Poets," in *Selected Writings*, trans. Roger Shattuck (New York: New Directions, 1971), pp. 227–8.

30 Vachel Lindsey, *The Art of the Moving Picture* (1915) (New York: Modern Library Reprint 2000), p. 158.

31 Jean Epstein, "Magnification" (1921), in *French Film Theory and Criticism* vol. 1, ed. Richard Abel (Princeton: Princeton University Press, 1988), p. 205.

32 Ibid., p. 235.

33 Hart Crane, *Complete Poems* (New York: Liveright, 1933), p. 11.

34 Edmund Husserl, *The Phenomenology of Internal Time Consciousness* (1905), trans. James S. Churchill (Bloomington: Indiana University Press, 1966), p. 28.

35 Tom Gunning, "The Cinema of Attractions: Early Film, Its Spectator, and the Avant-Garde"(1986), in *Early Cinema: Space Frame Narrative*, ed. Thomas Elsaesser (London: British Film Institute Publishing, 1990).

36 Siegfried Kracauer, *Theory of Film: The Redemption of Physical Reality* (Princeton: Princeton University Press, 1997), p. 158.

37 See especially Kevin Brownlow, *The Parade's Gone By . . .* (London: Knopf, 1968); Lotte H. Eisner, *The Haunted Screen: Expressionism in the German Cinema and the Influence of Max Reinhardt* (London: Thames and Hudson, 1969); Thomas Elsaesser, ed. *Early Cinema: Space Frame Narrative*; William K. Everson, *American Silent Film* (New York: Da Capo Press, 1998); Jay Leyda, *Kino: A History of the Russian and Soviet Film* (Berkeley: University of California Press, 1983); David Parkinson, *History of Film* (London: Thames and Hudson, 1995); Eric Rhode, *A History of Cinema: From its Origins to 1970* (London: Hill and Wang, 1976).

38 Laura Mulvey, "Visual Pleasure and Narrative Cinema" (1975), in *The Sexual Subject: A Screen Reader in Sexuality* (London: Routledge, 1992), p. 33. (Hereafter cited in the text as *Visual Pleasure.*)

39 Gunning, "The Cinema of Attractions: Early Film, Its Spectator, and the Avant-Garde," p. 59.

40 Williams, "The Work of Gertrude Stein," in *Selected Essays*, p. 116.

41 Louis Menand, *Discovering Modernism: T. S. Eliot and His Context* (Oxford: Oxford University Press, 1987), p. 32.

42 Henry Head uses the phrase "dissociation of sensibility" throughout *Studies in Neurology* (London: Oxford University Press, 1920).

43 Paul Virilio, *Cinema and War: The Logistics of Perception*, trans. Patrick Camiller (London: Verso, 1989), pp. 15, 16. See also *Film Problems of Soviet Russia* (Territet: Pool, 1929) where Bryher recognized that war experience was pivotal to avant-garde film: "Only a volunteer [Pudovkin] who had been through the successive phases of war hysteria and destruction could have recorded, one feels, these marvelous war sequences in *The End of St. Petersburg*. And perhaps imprisonment tends to develop concentration of the visual sense, for it is interesting to note in this connection that the greatest of the German directors, G. W. Pabst also spent several years in France as a prisoner of war" (p. 45).

44 Jacques Lacan, "The Mirror Stage," in *Écrits*, trans. Alan Sheridan (New York: W. W. Norton and Company, 1977), p. 4.

45 Christian Metz, *The Imaginary Signifier: Psychoanalysis and Cinema*, trans. Celia Britton (Bloomington: Indiana University Press, 1975), p. 4. (Hereafter cited in the text as *Imaginary Signifier.*)

46 Kaja Silverman, *The Threshold of the Visible World* (New York: Routledge, 1996), p. 17.

47 Peter Nicholls, *Modernism: A Literary Guide* (Berkeley: University of California Press, 1995), p. 4.

48 Michael North, *Reading 1922: A Return to the Scene of the Modern* (Oxford: Oxford University Press, 1999), p. 138.

49 Garrett Stewart, *Between Film and Screen: Modernism's Photo Synthesis* (Chicago: University of Chicago Press, 1999), p. 265.

50 Eliot, "Ulysses, Order and Myth" (1923), in *Selected Prose* (London: Faber and Faber, 1972), p. 177. Stephen Kern notes that Joyce "was deeply impressed with cinematic montage, and in 1909 he was instrumental in introducing the first motion picture theater in Dublin." Like this one, such facts point to the often contradictory and divergent responses to cinema among modernists. *The Culture of Time and Space: 1880–1918* (Cambridge: Harvard University Press, 1983), pp. 76–7.

51 Peter Bürger, *Theory of the Avant-Garde*, trans. Michael Shaw (Minneapolis: University of Minnesota Press, 1984), p. 49.

52 Richard Murphy, *Theorizing the Avant-Garde: Modernism, Expressionism, and the Problem of Postmodernity* (Cambridge: Cambridge University Press, 1998), p. 3.

53 The definitional debates over the imbricated terms of high modernist, modernist, avant-garde and popular culture have yet to be settled. For excellent discussions of these categories, see Art Berman, *Preface to Modernism* (Urbana: University of Illinois Press, 1994); James Bradbury and James McFarlane, eds., *Modernism: 1890–1930* (Middlesex: Penguin, 1974); Bürger, *Theory of the Avant-Garde*; Monique Chefdor, Ricardo Quinones, and Albert Wachtel, eds., *Modernism: Challenges and Perspectives* (Urbana: University of Illinois Press, 1986).

54 Robert Herring, "A New Cinema, Magic and the Avant Garde," *CU* vol. 4 no. 4 (April 1929), p. 50.

55 Andreas Huyssen, *After the Great Divide: Modernism, Mass Culture, Postmodernism* (Bloomington: Indiana University Press, 1986), p. 16.

56 Ibid., p. 49.

57 Charles Baudelaire, "The Painter of Modern Life" (1859–60), in *Modernism: An Anthology of Documents*, eds. Vassiliki Kolocotroni, Jane Goldman, and Olga Taxidou (Chicago: The University of Chicago Press, 1998), p. 105.

58 Ezra Pound, "Hugh Selwyn Mauberley" in *Selected Poems* (New York: New Directions, 1957), p. 62. (Hereafter cited in the text as Pound, *SP*.)

59 This is not to suggest that all those avant-garde writers who endorsed film were "liberated" in their gender assumptions. For instance, the Futurist Filippo Marinetti admired cinema for its "fleeting synthesis of life," yet espoused the "scorn of women" as integral to his aesthetics. "The Futurist Cinema" (1916), in *Marinetti: Selected Writings*, ed. R. W. Flint (New York: Farrar, Straus and Giroux, 1971), p. 207.

60 Linda Williams, "Film Body: An Implantation of Perversions," in *Narrative, Apparatus, Ideology: A Film Theory Reader*, ed. Philip Rosen (New York: Columbia University Press, 1986), p. 523.

61 "Cinematic delirium" is André Breton's phrase for film's capacity to simulate psychosis. Quoted in Paul Hammond, *The Shadow and Its Shadow: Surrealist Writings on the Cinema* (San Francisco: City Lights, 2000), p. 15.

62 H. D., "Joan of Arc," *CU* vol. 3 no. 1 (July 1928), p. 19. (Hereafter cited in the text as "Joan.")

63 E. Ann Kaplan, "Is the Gaze Male?" in *Feminism and Film* (Oxford: Oxford University Press, 2000), p. 122.

64 Moore, "Fiction or Nature," *CU* vol. 10 no.3 (September 1933), reprinted in *The Complete Prose of Marianne Moore* (New York: Penguin, 1967), p. 303. (Hereafter cited in the text as *Complete Prose*.)

65 Moore, "Lot in Sodom," *CU* vol. 10 no. 4 (December 1933), reprinted in *Complete Prose*, p. 311.

66 Eve Kosofsky Sedgwick, *Epistemology of the Closet* (Berkeley: University of California Press, 1990), p. 11.

1. MODERNISM, MALE HYSTERIA, AND MONTAGE

1 Lindsey, *The Art of the Moving Picture*, p. 158.

2 Walter Benjamin, "On Some Motifs in Baudelaire," in *Illuminations: Essays and Reflections*, ed. Hannah Arendt and trans. Harry Zohn (New York: Schocken Books, 1968), p. 162. (Hereafter cited in the text as "Motifs.")

3 Gertrude Stein, *Useful Knowledge* (1928) (Barrytown: Station Hill Press, 1988), p. 76.

4 William McDougall, *An Outline of Psychology* (London: Methuan and Company, 1923), p. 33.

5 Ibid., p. 33.

6 Ibid., p. 22. See Susan Bordo, "Selections from *The Flight to Objectivity*," in *Feminism and History of Philosophy*, ed. Genevieve Lloyd (Oxford:

Oxford University Press, 2002). She writes that for Descartes (unlike other philosophers such as Plato or Aristotle) "there is no ambiguity or complexity here. The body is excluded from all participation, all connection with God; the soul alone represents the godliness and the goodness of the human being" (p. 171).

7 Ibid., p. 27.

8 Remy de Gourmont, *Natural Philosophy of Love*, trans. with a postscript by Ezra Pound (New York: privately printed for Rarity Press, 1931), p. 169.

9 T. S. Eliot, "Hamlet and His Problems," in *The Sacred Wood and Major Early Essays* (New York: Dover Publications, Inc., 1998), p. 58. (Hereafter cited in the text as "Hamlet.")

10 Cassandra Laity, *H. D. and the Victorian Fin de Siècle* (Cambridge: Cambridge University Press, 1996). (Hereafter cited in the text as *Fin de Siècle*.)

11 Sandra M. Gilbert and Susan Gubar, *No Man's Land: The Place of the Woman Writer in the Twentieth Century* vol. 2 (New Haven: Yale University Press, 1989), p. 260. (Hereafter cited in the text as *No Man's Land*.)

12 Siegfried Sassoon, *Collected Poems 1908–1956* (London: Faber and Faber, 1947), p. 99.

13 Sigmund Freud, "The Interpretation of Dreams" (1900), in *The Standard Edition of the Complete Psychological Works* 4, p. 149. (Hereafter *The Standard Edition* cited in the text as *SE*.)

14 Ibid., p. 150, emphasis mine.

15 Freud, "Hysterical Phantasies" (1908), *SE* 9, p. 166.

16 Freud, "Some Psychical Consequences of the Anatomical Distinction Between the Sexes" (1925), *SE* 19, p. 250.

17 Freud, "Three Essays on the Theory of Sexuality" (1924), *SE* 7, p. 166.

18 Eisenstein, "Dickens, Griffith, and the Film Today," in *Film Form*, p. 233.

19 Eisenstein, "The Cinematographic Principle and the Ideogram," in *Film Form*, p. 38. (Hereafter cited in the text as "Cinematographic.")

20 T. S. Eliot, "Lecture I: Toward a Definition of Metaphysical Poetry," in *The Varieties of Metaphysical Poetry*, ed. Ronald Schuchard (New York: Harcourt Brace and Company, 1993), p. 227.

21 Ibid.

22 Eliot, "The Metaphysical Poets," in *The Sacred Wood*, p. 127.

23 Eliot, "Tradition and Individual Talent," in *The Sacred Wood*, p. 31. (Hereafter cited in the text as "Tradition.")

24 In Lang's *Metropolis* (1927), this dissociation is figured as the split between the "brain" (the architect of the city) and the "hands" (the slaves that built it). Rather than calling for less of a polarity, the film insists that the "heart" (i.e. the "real" feminine) is necessary to mediate between these extremes.

25 Eisenstein also subordinates the mind to the body, even as he consistently invokes the latter. He writes that shots taken in a composition are "[p]hysiological in so far as they are 'psychic' in perception, that is merely the physiological process of a *higher nervous activity*." "The Filmic Fourth Dimension," in *Film Form*, p. 67.

26 H. D., "Conrad Veidt: The Student of Prague," *CU* vol. 1 no. 3 (September 1927), p. 123.

27 Ibid.

28 Elisabeth Bronfen, *The Knotted Subject: Hysteria and Its Discontents* (Princeton: Princeton University Press, 1998), p. 176. Charcot had a number of patients from literary circles, including the poets Alphonse Daudet and Theodore de Banville. Christopher G. Goetz, Michel Bonduelle and Toby Gelfand, eds. *Charcot: Constructing Neurology* (New York: Oxford University Press, 1995), p. 250. (Hereafter cited in the text as *Charcot*.)

29 Sander L. Gilman, "The Image of the Hysteric," in *Hysteria Beyond Freud*, eds. Gilman, Helen King, Roy Porter, G. S. Rousseau, Elaine Showalter (Berkeley: University of California, 1993), p. 352.

30 Ibid., p. 355.

31 Quoted in Havelock Ellis, *Studies in the Psychology of Sex* vol. 1 (Philadelphia: F. A. Davis Company, Publishers, 1913), p. 219.

32 Christopher Bollas, *Hysteria* (London: Routledge, 2000), p. 118.

33 J. A. Omerod, "Address to Neurological Section of The Royal Society of Medicine," *Brain* vol. 33 (1910/11), p. 297. I thank Nancy Gish for directing me to this important journal.

34 Joseph Breuer and Freud, "On the Psychical Mechanism of Hysterical Phenomena" (1893), *SE* 2, p. 6.

35 Freud, "Three Essays on Sexuality" (1905), *SE* 7, p. 166.

36 Jean-Louis Baudry connects Freud's optical metaphors and "psychical apparatus" with cinema in "The Apparatus: Metapsychological Approaches the Impression of Reality in Cinema." *Narrative, Apparatus, Ideology: A Film Reader*, ed. Philip Rosen (New York: Columbia University Press, 1986), p. 691. Baudry explains how the Freudian subject's symptoms replicate the mesmerizing illusions in Plato's allegory of the cave, which "precisely describes in its mode of operation the cinematographic apparatus and the spectator's place in relation to it" (p. 693).

37 Freud, "The Interpretation of Dreams" (1900), *SE* 4, p. 150.

38 Freud, "Some Points for a Comparative Study of Organic and Hysterical Paralysis" (1863), *SE* 1, p. 164.

39 Ivan Petrovich Pavlov, *Psychopathology and Psychiatry: Selected Works*, trans. D. Myshne and S. Belsky (New York: Foreign Language Publishing House, 1927), p. 264.

40 Eliot frequently invokes scientific language in order to legitimate his theories. He turns the artist's body into a "medium"; "depersonalization" is "the action that takes place when a bit of finely filiated platinum is introduced into a chamber containing oxygen and sulpher dioxide" ("Tradition," p. 30).

41 Walter Benjamin, "Work of Art in the Age of Mechanical Reproduction," in *Illuminations*, p. 37. (Hereafter cited in the text as "Work of Art.")

42 See Stephen Heath's "Cinema and Psychoanalysis: Parallel Histories," in *Endless Night* for a discussion of Freud's specific relationship to Pabst's film. Freud framed his response in virulent terms: "'There is no avoiding film, any more

than one can avoid the fashion for hair cut in a bob; I, however, will not let my hair be cut and will personally have nothing to do with this film'" (p. 26).

43 Hanns Sachs, "Film Psychology," *CU* vol. 3, no. 5 (November 1928), p. 251.

44 Ibid., p. 253.

45 Freud, "The Interpretation of Dreams" (1900), *SE* 4, pp. 20–1.

46 S. A. K. Wilson, "Some Modern French Conceptions of Hysteria," *Brain* vol. 33 (1910/11), p. 330.

47 Apparently Sachs supplied a pamphlet entitled "Enigma of the Unconscious," distributed with the film to explain psychoanalytic principles. As Heath writes, its cover supplied a "gender-anxious, emasculating image" of "the oval of a woman's face, eyes and forehead in shadow, one long erect finger to her lips in an invitation to silence or secrecy" ("Cinema and Psychoanalysis," p. 27).

48 Breuer and Freud, "On the Psychical Mechanism of Hysterical Phenomenon" (1893), *SE* 2, p. 7.

49 Bryher, *Film Problems of Soviet Russia*, p. 47. Mina Loy's "Parturition" is said to be the first poem demystifying childbirth, but unlike *Mechanics*, does so from the point of view of the woman in labor: "I am the centre / Of a circle of pain / Exceeding its boundaries in every direction." *The Last Lunar Baedeker*, ed. Roger L. Conover (New York: Farrar, Straus and Giroux, 1996), p. 4.

50 Bryher, *Film Problems of Soviet Russia*, p. 49. Bryher also writes that Eisenstein is familiar with the reflexological school of Pavlov before 1922. She notes that he read Freud's *Concerning the Childhood Reminiscences of da Vinci* in 1916 (p. 28).

51 Plato, *The Collected Dialogues*, eds. Edith Hamilton and Huntington Cairns. Bollingen Series (Princeton: Princeton University Press, 1961), p. 50d.

52 In "An Autobiographical Study," Freud writes about aggravating the Vienna medical authorities by claiming, in agreement with Charcot, that men could be hysterics. His implication, however, is that it is much rarer.

53 See Joseph Allen Boone, *Libidinal Currents: Sexuality and the Shaping of Modernism* (Chicago: University of Chicago Press, 1998), p. 134.

54 Luce Irigaray, *Speculum of the Other Woman*, trans. Gillian C. Gill (Ithaca: Cornell University Press, 1974).

55 Alice A. Jardine, *Gynesis: Configurations of Woman and Modernity* (Ithaca: Cornell University Press, 1985), p. 160.

56 Baudelaire, "The Painter of Modern Life," p. 105.

57 The three principles articulated by Pound and F. S. Flint in their 1913 "Imagist Manifesto," demanded: "1. Direct treatment of the 'thing,' whether subjective or objective. 2. To use absolutely no word that does not contribute to the presentation. 3. As regarding rhythm: to compose in sequence of the musical phrase, not in sequence of a metronome." "Imagisme," in *The English Modernist Reader*, ed. Peter Faulkner (Iowa City: University of Iowa Press, 1986), p. 41.

58 Lindsay, *The Art of the Moving Picture*, p. 158.

59 Nicholls, *Modernism: A Literary Guide*, p. 3.

60 Charles Baudelaire, *Les Fleurs du Mal*, Trans. C. F. MacIntyre (Berkeley: University of California Press, 1947), p. 107.

61 Pound compares the volatile effects of his poetics to "driving any new idea into the great passive vulva of London." Quoted in E. Fuller Torrey, *The Roots of Treason* (Orlando: Harcourt, 1984), p. 110.

62 Marianne DeKoven, *A Different Language: Gertrude Stein's Experimental Writing* (Madison: University of Wisconsin Press, 1983), pp. 188–9. There is an etymological link between mater, matter, and metro.

63 Marjorie Perloff, *21ˢᵗ-Century Modernism: The New Poetics* (New York: Blackwell Publishers, 2002), p. 3. (Hereafter cited in the text as *21ˢᵗ-Century Modernism*.)

64 T. S. Eliot, *The Complete Poems and Plays 1909–1950* (New York: Harcourt, Brace and Company, 1958), p. 19. (Hereafter cited in the text as *CPP*.)

65 Albert Gelpi even goes so far as to write that the "complications of Eliot's relation to the feminine, and all that implied for him, comprise the crux of his poetry" (*Coherent Splendor*, p. 92).

66 Mary Ann Doane, "Film and the Masquerade: Theorizing the Female Spectator," in *Feminism and Film*, ed. E. Ann Kaplan (Oxford: Oxford University Press, 2000), p. 426. (Hereafter cited in the text as "Masquerade.")

67 Tania Modleski, *The Women Who Knew Too Much: Hitchcock and Feminist Theory* (New York: Routledge, 1988), p. 8.

68 Quoted in Laity, *Fin de Siècle*, pp. 21–2.

69 Freud, "The Aetiology of Hysteria" (1896), *SE* 3, p. 191.

70 Ibid.

71 Ibid., p. 197.

72 Ibid., p. 196. (Emphasis mine.)

73 There is no evidence that Eliot saw the 1920 German *Hamlet* with Asta Nielson cross-dressed as the male hero scintillant with desire for Ophelia; yet his elaborate annoyance with Hamlet's free-floating desires directs us to a subliminal cognizance of sexual ambiguity.

74 T. S. Eliot, *Inventions of the March Hare Poems 1909–1917*, ed. Christopher Ricks (New York: Harcourt, Brace and Company, 1996), p. 267. (Hereafter cited in the text as *Inventions*.)

75 These are Ian Fletcher's words quoted in *Inventions*, p. 267.

76 Lyndall Gordon, *T. S. Eliot: An Imperfect Life* (New York: W. W. Norton and Company, Inc., 1998), p. 53. See also James E. Miller Jr. who traces the suppression of the homoerotic elements in Eliot's work. *T. S. Eliot's Personal Waste Land: Exorcism of the Demons* (University Park: The Pennsylvania State University Press, 1977).

77 Eliot, "A Commentary," in *Criterion* 13 (April 1934), p. 452.

78 There is a general consensus that Vivienne and Eliot recognized their marriage as a sexual failure. See Carole Seymour-Jones's biography, *Painted Shadow: The Life of Vivienne Eliot, first wife of T. S. Eliot, and the long-suppressed truth about her influence on his genius* (New York: Doubleday, 2001).

79 Quoted in Miller, *T. S. Eliot's Personal Waste Land*, p. 23. Apparently, part of this treatment consisted of the Swiss psychiatrist Roger Vittoz "placing his hand on the forehead of the patient in order to feel the vibrations of the 'cerebral hemispheres'" (p. 27).

80 Wayne Kostenbaum, *Double Talk: The Erotics of Male Literary Collaboration* (New York: Routledge, 1989), p. 115.

81 *The Letters of T. S. Eliot*, vol. 1 1898–1922, ed. Valerie Eliot (London: Faber and Faber, 1988), p. 62.

82 Ibid.

83 Ibid., pp. 71–2.

84 Griffith called *Birth* an anti-war movie – as much perhaps in response to World War I as to his memory of his father, a confederate "hero." For Eliot, the Civil War had "unforseen social consequences," and he called it "certainly the greatest disaster in the whole of American history." He confessed to being convinced that "New England was ruined by the Civil War in the same way that the South had been." Quoted in Eric Sigg, *The American T. S. Eliot: A Study of the Early Writings* (Cambridge: Cambridge University Press, 1989), p. 177.

85 Everson, *American Silent Film*, p. 97. Strikingly, Anita Loos, a writer of popular fiction and screenplays, wrote the inter-titles for *Intolerance*.

86 The important stanza from Swinburne's poem reads: "Love stands upon they left hand and thy right / Yet by no sunset and by no moonrise / Shall make thee man and ease a woman's sighs, / Or make thee woman for a man's delight." As Laity writes, H. D. cites these lines as well as Swinburne's "Fragoletta," his more positive "ode to adrogyny" in *Paint it Today* (*Fin de Siècle*, p. 34).

87 Myths surrounding Tiresias mostly implicate vision. He is said to have been blinded as punishment for watching Athena bath, and apparently turns into a woman as punishment for his coming upon two mating snakes and killing the female.

88 Quoted in Helen Vendler's introduction to *The Waste Land and Other Poems* (New York: Signet Classics, 1998), p. viii.

89 Donald Spoto, *The Dark Side of Genius: The Life of Alfred Hitchcock* (New York: Ballantine Books, 1983), p. 563.

90 See Kostenbaum for his discussion of the "hysteric" collaboration between Eliot and Pound (*Double Talk*, pp. 112–39).

91 Ezra Pound, no. 181 (1921), in *The Letters 1907–41*, ed. D. D. Paige (London: Faber and Faber, 1951), p. 234.

92 Koestenbaum puts this dis-functional triad into perspective: "Confined under mysterious circumstances to an asylum in 1938, she died, still confined, in 1947. Eliot turned his hysteria into a poem that quickly and deliberately became an institution . . . It is a telling coincidence that Pound and Vivien, accomplices to Eliot's hysterical poem, each spent long years locked in asylums – Vivien at Northumberland House, Pound at St. Elizabeths" (*Double Talk*, p. 117.)

93 T. S. Eliot, *The Waste Land: A Facsimile and Transcript of the Original Drafts*, ed. Valerie Eliot (London: Faber and Faber, 1971), p. 27. (Hereafter cited in the text as *Manuscript*. In quoting from the manuscript, I include Pound's cross-outs.)

94 Huyssen links Lang's vamp to uncontrollable nature as well as to the "demonic inexplicable threat" of technology, including war machinery (*Great Divide*, p. 70).

95 Otto Weininger, *Sex and Character* (London: William Heinemann, 1906), p. 7.

96 Micale, *Approaching Hysteria*, p. 183. Baudelaire apparently "two decades before Charcot" saw hysteria as a "'physiological mystery'" which "'manifested itself in women by the sensation of a stifling ball rising in the body'" and in men "'by every kind of impotence as well as by a tendency towards every type of excess'" (quoted in Micale, p. 191).

97 T. S. Eliot, "The Beating of the Drum," *Criterion* (1923).

98 Baudelaire, "The Painter of Modern Life," p. 106.

99 H. D., "The Cinema and the Classics III: The Movietone," *CU* vol. 1 no. 5 (November 1927), p. 23. (Hereafter cited in the text as "Movietone.")

100 Gayle Studlar, *In the Realm of Pleasure: Von Sternberg, Dietrich, and the Masochistic Aesthetic* (New York: Columbia University Press, 1988), p. 184.

101 Ibid.

102 Bisexuality, of course, is itself a much disputed category. Diana Collecott offers an extensive discussion of it in her reading of H. D.'s sexuality. She refers to the widespread categorical confusion caused by bisexuality for sexologist Havelock Ellis as well as for Freud. *H. D. and Sapphic Modernism* (Cambridge University Press, 1999), see especially pp. 75–80.

103 H. D., "Loss," in *Collected Poems 1912–1944*, ed. Louis L. Martz (New York: New Directions Book, 1983), p. 22. (Hereafter cited in the text as *CP*.)

104 In her first "Continuous Performance" column, Dorothy Richardson writes about attending a Monday afternoon matinee with an audience of "almost entirely mothers," "figures of weariness at rest," and observes that film allows a necessary "forgetfulness": it is "as intimate as thought, so long as it is free from the introduction of the alien element of sound" *CU* vol. 1 no. 1 (July 1927), pp. 35–6.

105 H. D., "The Cinema and the Classics II: Restraint," *CU* vol. 1 no. 2 (August 1927), p. 33. (Hereafter cited in the text as "Restraint.")

106 Artaud, "Cinema and Reality" (1927), in *French Film Theory and Criticism*, p. 410.

107 I borrow this phrase from Paolo Cherchi Usai, *Silent Cinema: An Introduction* (London: BIF Publications, 2000).

108 Pavlov, *Psychopathology*, p. 266.

109 Freud, "Beyond the Pleasure Principle" (1920), *SE* vol. 18, p. 23.

110 Ibid., p. 27.

111 Ibid.

112 H. D., *CU* vol. 1 no. 1 (July 1927), pp. 47, 49.

113 H. D., *CU* vol. 1 no. 4 (October 1927), p. 36.

114 H. D., "Projector II," p. 43.

115 P. Adams Sitney, *Visionary Film: The American Avant-Garde 1943–78* (Oxford: Oxford University Press, 1974), p. 20.

116 Brigitte Peucker, *Incorporating Images: Film and the Rival Arts* (Princeton: Princeton University Press, 1995), p. 93.

117 Siegfried Kracauer, *From Caligari to Hitler: A Psychological History of the German Film* (Princeton: Princeton University Press, 947), p. 67.

118 Freud, "The Interpretation of Dreams," p. 31.

119 Murphy, *Theorizing the Avant-Garde*, pp. 207–8.

120 Lionel Landry, "Caligarism or the Theater's Revenge" (1922), in *French Film Theory and Criticism*, p. 268.

121 Pound, "Paris Letter," *The Dial* (February 1923), p. 273.

122 Alice Kuzniar also draws a parallel between the cabinet and the sexual "closet" which Cesare as "third sex" seems to inhabit. *The Queer German Cinema* (Stanford: Stanford University Press, 2000), p. 31.

123 It is an anxiety over such uncanny bodies that leads H. D. to dislike the idea of "talking pictures": "[t]he mask . . . seems about to be ripped off showing us human features, the doll is about to step forward as a mere example of mechanical inventiveness" ("Movietone," p. 30).

124 Jean Goudal, "Surrealism and Cinema," in *The Shadow and Its Shadow*, ed. and trans. Paul Hammond, p. 86.

125 Kracauer, *Theory of Film*, p. 60.

126 *Marianne Moore: Selected Letters*, ed. Bonnie Costello (New York: Penguin Books, 1998), p. 160. (Hereafter cited in the text as *Selected Letters*.)

127 Eisner, *The Haunted Screen*, p. 15.

128 Moore, *Selected Letters*, p. 160.

129 Virginia Woolf, "The Cinema" (1926), in *The Captain's Death-Bed* (New York: Harcourt, 1988), p. 183.

130 Eliot, "Lecture IV. The Conceit in Donne"(The Clark Lectures), in *The Varieties of Metaphysical Poetry*, p. 137.

131 Ibid., n.39.

132 Julia Kristeva, "Revolution in Poetic Language," in *The Kristeva Reader*, ed. Toril Moi (New York: Columbia University Press, 1986), p. 100.

133 These are Mina Loy's phrases for Stein's writing. "Gertrude Stein"(1924), in *The Gender of Modernism*, ed. Bonnie Kime Scott (Bloomington: Indiana University Press, 1990), p. 241.

2. "DELIGHT IN DISLOCATION": STEIN, CHAPLIN, AND MAN RAY

1 Gertrude Stein, "Mrs. Emerson" (1914) was initially written as one of her "portraits." *CU* vol. 1 no. 2 (August 1927). (Hereafter cited in the text as "Emerson.") Her portraits of "Matisse" and "Picasso" were published in Alfred Stieglitz's *Camera Work* in 1912, and were followed in 1913 by her "Portrait of Mabel Dodge." She also published "Three Sitting Here"(not otherwise published) in *CU* in vol. I no. 3 (September 1927), which continued in another installment vol. 1 no. 4 (October 1927).

2 E. H. Gombrich, *The Story of Art* (London: Phaidon, 1969), p. 281. Bürger cites cubist art as precursor to montage and calls it that "movement in modern painting which most consciously destroyed the representation system that prevailed since the Renaissance" (*Theory of the Avant-Garde*, p. 73).

3 Gertrude Stein, *How to Write* (1931) (New York: Dover, 1975), p. 13.

4 Gertrude Stein, "Composition as Explanation"(1926), in *A Stein Reader*, ed. Ulla E. Dydo (Evanston, Ill.: Northwestern University Press, 1993), p. 499 (emphasis added).

5 Maya Deren, "Cinematography: The Creative Use of Reality," in *The Avant-garde Film: A Reader of Theory and Criticism*, ed. P. Adams Sitney (New York: New York University Press, 1978), p. 64.

6 Jean Epstein, "Art of Incidence" (1927), in *French Film Theory and Criticism*, p. 412.

7 These phrases about Chaplin are from André Bazin's *What is Cinema? Volume 1*, trans. Hugh Gray (Berkeley: University of California Press, 1974), p. 151.

8 Dziga Vertov's *Man With a Movie Camera* (1929) bound the hand to the machine in its representation of Soviet labor. With its frenetic repetitions of women packaging cigarettes, operating the cords of the telephone switchboard, spinning the treadle of a sewing machine, riding exercise horses, or selecting or piecing footage on a moviola, *Movie Camera* eroticizes women's relationship to the machine.

9 Stein, *The Making of Americans* (Selections), in *A Stein Reader*, p. 61.

10 Stein, *Tender Buttons* (1914) (Los Angeles: Sun and Moon Press, 1989), p. 58.

11 Mina Loy, "Gertrude Stein," in *Gender of Modernism*, p. 241.

12 Gertrude Stein, "What is English Literature," in *Lectures in America* (Boston: Beacon Press, 1985), p. 42.

13 Gertrude Stein, "I Came and Here I Am," in *How Writing is Written* (Los Angeles: Black Sparrow Press, 1974), p. 68.

14 Gertrude Stein, *Lifting Belly* (1915–17), ed. Rebecca Mark (Tallahassee: The Naiad Press, 1989), p. 27. (Hereafter cited in the text as *Lifting*.)

15 Gertrude Stein, *Wars I Have Seen* (London: B. T. Batsford Ltd., 1945), p. 32. (Hereafter cited in the text as *Wars*.)

16 My primary focus in this book is upon the First World War, but the Second World War undoubtedly exerts an enormous pressure upon the writing of *Wars I Have Seen*.

17 Paul Fussell, *The Great War and Modern Memory* (Oxford: Oxford University Press, 1975), pp. 220–1.

18 John Keegan, *The First World War* (New York: Vintage Books, 1998), p. 166.

19 Bryher, "The War From Three Angles," *CU* vol. 1 no. 1 (July 1927), p. 17. So impressed with the film, Bryher saw it six times. The inter-titles in *The Big Parade* (such as the following) are sparse as Imagist poems:

> Dusk –
> Silence . . . Mud
> The whine of a shell . . .
> Mud . . . Silence

20 This short prefatory poem reads: "Eyes are a surprise / Prinzess a dream / Buzz is spelled with z / Fuss is spelled with s / So is business." Enacting visual similarities within linguistics, the passage reads like the spiraling puns of *Anémic Cinéma*.

21 Beinecke Manuscripts, no date.

22 Henri Bergson, *Matter and Memory* (1896), trans. Nancy Margaret Paul and W. Scott Palmer (New York: The MacMillan Company, 1950), pp. 40–1.

23 Maurice Merleau-Ponty, *Phenomenology of Perception*, trans. Colin Smith (New York: Routledge, 1999), p. 13. (Hereafter cited in the text as *Phenomenology*.)

24 Man Ray, "Emak Bakia," *CU* vol. 1 no. 2 (August 1927), p. 40. (Hereafter cited in the text as "Emak.") Man Ray's phrasing echoes William James who writes that bodily consciousness "starts from the parts, and makes of the whole a collection" (*Phenomenology*, p. 10).

25 Margaret Dickie, "Women Poets and the Emergence of Modernism," in *The Columbia History of American Poetry*, ed. Jay Parini (New York: Columbia University Press, 1993), p. 24. See also Harriet Scott Chessman, *The Public is Invited to Dance* (Stanford: Stanford University Press, 1989) for readings of how "the sensual and material aspects of language" disrupt gender hierarchies in Stein's work (p. 3).

26 Catherine Stimpson, "The Somagrams of Gertrude Stein," in *The Female Body in Western Culture*, ed. Susan Rubin Suleiman (Cambridge: Harvard University Press, 1986), p. 30. In this context, I also wonder if Marie Dressler, the famously heavy comedian who starred next to Chaplin in *Tillie's Punctured Romance* (1914), is not an equally important model for Stein's anti-romantic hysteric embodiment. One of the main features of Dressler's performance was her spasmodic movements. "Tillie's drunken dances – both alone and with tiny Charlie – are far more important to the film than the plotty attempts to swindle her out of some cash," writes Gerald Mast. *The Comic Mind: Comedy and the Movies* (Chicago: University of Chicago, 1973), p. 55.

27 Nicholls, *Modernisms: A Literary Guide*, p. 202.

28 Inez Hedges, "Constellated Visions: Robert Desnos's and Man Ray's *L'Etoile de Mer*," in *Dada and Surrealist Film*, ed. Rudolf E. Kuenzli (Cambridge: The MIT Press, 1996), p. 99.

29 North, *Reading 1922*, p. 166.

30 Neil Baldwin, *Man Ray: American Artist* (New York: Clarkson Potter, 1988), p. 134.

31 Hedges, "Constellated Visions," p. 99.

32 William James, *Principles of Psychology*, p. 445. (Hereafter cited in the text as *Principles*.)

33 The "proper name," as Rosalind Krauss suggests, is linked to "the mimetic image (or representation)." "In the Name of Picasso," in *The Originality of the Avant-Garde and Other Modernist Myths* (Cambridge, MA: The MIT Press, 1996), p. 27. Krauss assesses: "art history of the proper name can be likened to the detective story or the roman à clef, where the meaning of the tale reduces to just this question of identity" where in order to "fulfill the goal of the narrative" it is necessary to find out "'who done it'" (p. 28). Stein was herself attracted to the detective story "because the hero being dead, you begin with the corpse you do not have to take him on and so you were free to enjoy yourself." "Why I Like Detective Stories," *Harpers* (November 1937), p. 70.

34 Hedges, "Constellated Visions," p. 99.

35 Man Ray, *Self Portrait* (New York: Little, Brown and Co, 1963), 259. (Hereafter cited in the text as *Self Portrait*.)

36 Gertrude Stein, *The Autobiography of Alice B. Toklas* (New York: Vintage Books, 1990), p. 51.

37 Sabine Hake, "Chaplin Reception in Weimar Germany," *New German Critique* 51 (Fall 1990), pp. 88, 92.

38 Walter Benjamin, "Chaplin in Retrospect," in *Selected Writings*, vol. 2: 1927–34, trans. Rodney Livingstone (Cambridge, MA: Harvard University Press, 1999), pp. 222–3.

39 Robert Aaron, "Films of Revolt" (1929), in *French Film Theory and Criticism*, p. 432.

40 Jean Epstein, "Magnification" (1927), in *French Film Theory and Criticism*, p. 238.

41 Louis Aragon, "On Décor" (1918), in *French Film Theory and Criticism*, p. 167.

42 Léger based his Charlot upon a sketch from Yvan Goll's cinema-poem, *Die Chapliniade* (1920). Georges Monca's comic film *Rigadin, peintre cubiste* (1912) perhaps helped inspire Léger's remaking of Chaplin as an animated cubist construction. The main character, the artist Rigadin, after seeing a show of cubist paintings, is so obsessed with altering all his mimetic representations (along with the "mandatory" roundness of the female nude) that he reconfigures his whole household – including his own body and his housekeeper's. Cardboard cubes enclose each body part, impeding locomotion to the extent that his housekeeper has difficulty sweeping, and so moves with a mechanical jerkiness.

43 Benjamin, "Chaplin in Retrospect," p. 200.

44 Quoted in Hake, "Chaplin Reception in Weimar Germany," p. 106.

45 Elizabeth Grosz, *Volatile Bodies* (Bloomington: Indiana University Press, 1994), 128. (Hereafter cited in the text as *Volatile*.)

46 Kracauer, *Theory of Film*, p. 253.

47 Hake, "Chaplin Reception in Weimar Germany," p. 105.

48 Stein's early years in Paris brought her into the circles of prominent avant-gardists, among them Apollinaire, Max Jacob, and Picasso, and under their influence, she "moved increasingly toward the surreal." Linda Wagner-Martin, *Favored Strangers: Gertrude Stein and Her Family* (New Brunswick, NJ: Rutgers University Press, 1995), p. 112. Stein, however, never aligns herself with the "school" of surrealism and, in fact, espouses notably non-surrealist tactics, such as sobriety: "I must be sober. It is so much more exciting to be sober, to be exact and concentrated and sober" ("Portraits," p. 198).

49 Man Ray was apparently "dumbfounded when his Surrealist friends did not greet [*Emak Bakia*] with enthusiasm" (Kuenzli, *Dada and Surrealist Film*, p. 4). Man Ray writes: "I had complied with all the principles of Surrealism: irrationality, automatism, psychological and dramatic sequences without apparent logic, and complete disregard for conventional storytelling" (*Self Portrait*, p. 274).

50 Ivan Petrovich Pavlov, "A Study of Temperaments," in *Lectures on Conditioned Reflexes*, vol. 1, trans. W. Horsley Gantt (New York: International Publishers,

1928), p. 375. Pavlov's essay on animal reflex behavior, "Experimental Psychology and Psychopathology in Animals," was first published in 1903 (*Herald of the Military Medical Academy*, vol. 7, no. 2, pp. 109–21).

51 Hugo Münsterberg authored the seminal *Photoplay* (1916), a study binding the spectator's bodily experience with the mechanism of filmmaking (New York: Appleton and Company, 1916).

52 Terry Castle, *The Apparitional Lesbian: Female Sexuality and Modern Culture* (New York: Columbia University Press, 1993), p. 2.

53 Gertrude Stein, "Sitwell Edith Sitwell," in *Portraits and Prayers* (New York: Random House, 1934), p. 94.

54 In this regard, Lisa Ruddick recognizes the influence of James upon Stein: "Melanctha's pathological forgetfulness is of a piece with her mind-wandering." *Reading Gertrude Stein: Body, Text, Gnosis* (Ithaca: Cornell University Press, 1990), p. 19.

55 This is Jonathan Crary's phrase for the condition of overwhelming stimuli confronting the modern subject (*Techniques of the Observer*, p. 13).

56 Wagner-Martin, *Favored Strangers*, p. 36.

57 Stein, *The Autobiography*, p. 79.

58 Stein and Leon M. Solomons, "Motor Automatism" in *Harvard Psychological Review* (New York: The Phoenix Book Shop, 1969), p. 9. (Hereafter cited in the text as "Motor Automatism.")

59 Freud, "The Psychopathology of Everyday Life" (1901), *SE* vol. 6, p. 168.

60 Marianne Dekoven considers Stein's most "successful experimental writing" to be composed of "semi-grammatical phrases" that somewhat "fits together." *A Different Language: Gertrude Stein's Experimental Writing* (Madison: University of Wisconsin Press, 1983), p. 11.

61 William James, "Stream of Consciousness" (originally from *Psychology: Briefer Course* 1892), reprinted in *Pragmatism and Other Writings* (New York: Penguin, 2000), pp. 180–1.

62 Ibid.

63 Gertrude Stein, "Cultivated Motor Automatism," in *Harvard Psychological Review* (New York: The Phoenix Book Shop, 1969), p. 30. (Hereafter cited in the text as "Cultivated.")

64 Freud, "Some General Remarks on Hysterical Attacks" (1909), *SE* 9, p. 230.

65 In his prologue to *Improvisations: Kora in Hell* (1918) in *Imaginations*, Williams articulates this credo of "loosening" as a necessary step in modernist aesthetics: "The attention has been held too rigid on the one plane instead of following a more flexible, jagged resort" (New York: New Directions, 1970), p. 14.

66 Similarly, the very premise of Rene Clair's silent comedy, *The Italian Straw Hat* (1928), pivots upon a damaged hat (ruined by the distraction of its owner) and an endless search for a substitution. The object, propelling the momentum of the comedy, manages to derail the film's marriage plot; by the end, the hat, imbued with more significance than can be made legible, is replaced and "re-established" in a close up.

67 Stein, *Tender Buttons*, p. 11, p. 9, p. 21.

68 Münsterberg, *Photoplay*, p. 75.

69 Bronfen, *The Knotted Subject*, p. 175.

70 Ibid., p. 188.

71 Ibid., p. 180.

72 Henri Bergson, *Laughter: An Essay on the Meaning of the Comic* (1911), trans. Claudesley Brereton and Fred Rothwell (Los Angeles: Green Integer Books, 1999), p. 22. (Hereafter cited in the text as *Laughter*.)

73 Gertrude Stein, "If I Told Him: A Completed Portrait of Picasso," *Portraits and Prayers* (New York: Random House, 1934), p. 22. (Hereafter cited in the text as "Completed Portrait.")

74 Münsterberg, *Photoplay*, p. 17.

75 Stewart, *Between Film and Screen*, p. 24.

76 Ibid., p. 7.

77 Quoted in Steven Kovács, *From Enchantment to Rage: The Story of Surrealist Cinema* (Rutherford: Fairleigh Dickinson University Press, 1980), pp. 168–9.

78 Elizabeth Grosz, "Animal Sex" in *Space, Time and Perversion: Essays on the Politics of Bodies* (New York: Routledge, 1995), p. 198.

79 Rayograms are Man Ray's apparently accidental (read: automatic) process of developing images without a camera by throwing concrete objects upon photographic paper and exposing it to light. He describes this method in culinary and sensuous language: "On some strips I sprinkled salt and pepper, like a cook preparing a roast, on other strips I threw pins and thumbtacks at random; then I turned on the white light for a second or two" (*Self Portrait*, p. 260).

80 Kaja Silverman, "On Suture," in *Film Theory and Criticism*, eds. Gerald Mast, Marshall Cohen and Leo Braudy (Oxford: Oxford University Press, 1992), p. 200.

81 Stein, *Tender Buttons*, p. 27.

82 This sewing machine device was important to the invention of the means to move film forward. See also Havelock Ellis who traces the autoerotic nuances of the treadle: "The essential movement in working the sewing-machine is the flexion and extension of the ankle, but the muscles of the thighs are used to maintain the feet firmly on the treadle, the thighs are held together, and there is a considerable degree of flexion or extension of the thighs on the trunk; by a special adjustment of the body, and sometimes perhaps merely in the presence of sexual hyperanesthesia, it is thus possible to act upon the sexual organs" (*Studies in the Psychology of Sex* vol. 1, p. 177). Pervasive in the discourses of the period is the resistance to women's "grinding their own coffee" (a phrase from Lawrence's *Lady Chatterley's Lover*), a motif theorized by Freud in "Female Sexuality" (1933) where he writes that the "Oedipal crisis" for women involves the "elimination of clitoridal sexuality as a necessary precondition for the development of femininity" *SE* 22, p. 119.

83 North, *Reading 1922*, p. 171.

84 Wagner-Martin, *Favored Strangers*, p. 23.

85 Louis Aragon, "On Décor," in *French Film Theory and Criticism*, p. 165.

86 Stewart, *Between Film and Screen*, p. 24.

87 See Pavlov's *Work on the Digestive Glands* (1897) in *Psychopathology and Psychiatry* (1927), p. 559. Pavlov's study of the "psychical excitation of the gastric glands"

strangely corresponds to Stein's obsession with the gustatory as wedded to the linguistic. *Lifting Belly*, for instance, brims with "feeding" and "pleasing," with apricots, nectarines, éclairs in the face of war's deprivations. For Stein, only ink rivals butter in her cathexis to substances.

88 Stein, *How to Write*, p. 13.

89 See Louis Menand for his discussion of William James and the development of pragmatism. *Metaphysical Club: A Story of Ideas in America*. (New York: Farrar, Straus and Giroux, 2001). He explains that James "thought that certainty was moral death, and he hated to foreclose anything. His solution to this problem in his own life was to cultivate a self conscious impulsivity. He would act decisively, and then, just as decisively, change his mind" (p. 75). See also pp. 322–30 for treatment of James's argument with previous studies in attention.

90 Gertrude Stein, "Three Sitting Here," *CU* vol. 1 no. 3 (September 1927), p. 24.

91 Gertrude Stein, *Everybody's Autobiography* (New York: Vintage, 1973), p. 283.

92 Stein, "Three Sitting Here," p. 22.

93 Walter Kerr, *The Silent Clowns* (New York: De Capo Press, 1980), p. 64.

94 Micale, *Approaching Hysteria*, p. 68.

95 Gertrude Stein, "Emp Lace" (1914), in The *Yale Gertrude Stein*, ed. Richard Kostelanetz (New Haven: Yale University Press, 1980), pp. 238–9. Her "cow come out" sequence is an example (like her "rose is a rose is a rose") of Stein's "automatic" repetition of "insignia" not only within a single text but also within many of her other texts, as if she had forgotten they had already been written.

96 Freud, "Femininity" (1933), *SE* 22, p. 133.

97 William Carlos Williams, "The Work of Gertrude Stein," in *Selected Essays*, p. 117.

3. W. C. WILLIAMS AND SURREALIST FILM: "A FAVORABLE DISTORTION"

1 Webster Schott, Introduction to William Carlos Williams, *Imaginations* (1938) (New York: New Directions, 1970), p. xvi. This collection comprises work spanning between 1918 and 1932, including *Kora in Hell* (1918) and *Spring and All* (1923).

2 *The Collected Poems of William Carlos Williams volume 1: 1909–1939*, eds. A. Walton Litz and Christopher MacGowen (New York: New Directions, 1986), p. 282. (Hereafter cited in the text as *CP*.)

3 Williams, "XV. Light Becomes Darkness," *Spring and All* in *Imaginations*. (Hereafter cited in the text as *SA*.)

4 Jonathan Crary distinguishes the "observer" from the "spectator"; the former operates "within a prescribed set of possibilities, one who is embedded in a system of conventions and limitations," while the latter evokes a passive distance (*Techniques of the Observer*, pp. 5–6). I employ the word "spectator" to denote the way Williams straddles both modes.

5 Freud, "Some Psychical Consequences of the Anatomical Distinction between the Sexes," *SE* 14, p. 252.

6 Lacan, "The signification of the phallus," in *Écrits*, p. 287.

7 E. Anne Kaplan, "Is the Gaze Male?" in *Feminism and Film* (Oxford: Oxford University Press, 2000), p. 122.

8 Martin Jay, *Downcast Eyes: The Denigration of Vision in Twentieth Century French Thought* (Berkeley: University of California Press, 1993).

9 Mike Weaver elaborates upon the significance of science to Williams's art, specifically his struggle to reconcile the "percipient observer's bodily life" with mechanistic science. *William Carlos Williams: The American Background* (Cambridge: Cambridge University Press, 1971), p. 47.

10 Williams, "Lower Case Cummings," in *Selected Essays*, p. 266.

11 Sandy Flitterman-Lewis, *To Desire Differently: Feminism and French Cinema* (New York: Cornell University Press, 1996), p. 134. (Hereafter cited in the text as *To Desire Differently*.)

12 Williams, *The Autobiography* (New York: Random House, 1948), p. 3. He also writes that he does not plan to tell the reader "the particulars of the women [he has] been to bed with" in these pages but that he "is extremely sexual in [his] desires" (xi).

13 Weininger, *Sex and Character*, p. 189.

14 Bram Dijkstra, *Evil Sisters* (New York: Alfred A. Knopf, 1996), p. 135.

15 Ibid., p. 91.

16 Judith Butler, *Bodies that Matter: On the Discursive Limits of 'Sex'* (New York: Routledge, 1993), p. 40.

17 Quoted in Torrey, *The Roots of Treason: Ezra Pound and the Secrets of St. Elizabeths*, p. 110.

18 Hugh Kenner, *The Pound Era* (Berkeley: University of California Press, 1971), p. 150.

19 Quoted in Torrey, p. 109.

20 This phrase is from a 1932 story by Williams, "The Knife of the Times," quoted in Lillian Faderman's *Surpassing the Love of Men: Romantic Friendship and Love between Women from the Renaissance to the Present* (New York: William Morrow and Company, 1981), p. 339.

21 Modleski, *The Women Who Knew Too Much*, pp. 12–13.

22 André Breton, "Second Manifesto of Surrealism" (1930), in *Manifestoes of Surrealism*, trans. Richard Seaver and Helen R. Lane (Ann Arbor: University of Michigan Press, 1974), p. 123.

23 Maurice Nadeau, *The History of Surrealism*, trans. Richard Howard (Cambridge: The Belknap Press of Harvard University Press, 1989), p. 12.

24 Mary Ann Caws, *The Surrealist Look* (Cambridge: MIT Press, 1999), pp. 23, 22. (Hereafter cited in the text as *Surrealist Look*.)

25 Wallace Stevens, in fact, criticized Williams for not keeping "a fixed point of view" (*KH*, p. 15).

26 Henry M. Sayre, *The Visual Text of William Carlos Williams* (Urbana: University of Illinois Press, 1983), p. 119.

27 Apparently the reason Man Ray's surrealist friends were not as enthused about *Emak Bakia* as the creator expected was because of its "complete disregard for conventional storytelling'" (*Self Portrait*, p. 274).

28 Schott, Introduction to *Kora in Hell*, in *Imaginations*, p. 4. (Hereafter cited in the text as *KH*.)

29 Krauss, *The Originality of the Avant-Garde*, p. 103.

30 Germaine Dulac, "The Expressive Techniques of the Cinema" (1924), in *French Film Theory and Criticism*, p. 306. (Hereafter cited in the text as "Expressive Techniques.")

31 Williams, "Marianne Moore," in *Selected Essays*, p. 123.

32 Germaine Dulac writes that "pure" cinema or "cinégraphie," in opposition to narrative or realist films, creates the most dynamic emotional effects. Of the grain of wheat, she questions: "This joyful hymn of a germinating grain stretching toward the light in a slow and then a more rapid rhythm, isn't it a synthetic and total drama, exclusively cinegraphic in its conception and expression?" "Aesthetics, Obstacles, Integral Cinégraphie" (1926), in *French Film Theory and Criticism*, p. 396.

33 Artaud, "Cinema and Reality," in *French Film Theory and Criticism*, p. 411.

34 Ibid., pp. 411–12.

35 Flitterman-Lewis, "The Image and the Spark: Dulac and Artaud Reviewed," in *Dada and Surrealist Film*, p. 115.

36 Breton, "Second Manifesto of Surrealism," p. 125.

37 Luis Buñuel, *An Unspeakable Betrayal* (Berkeley: University of California Press, 1995), p. 131. (Hereafter cited in the text as *Unspeakable*.) Buñuel distinguishes montage of "material segments" from découpage, which is made, in his definition, of "ideal segments" (p. 132). The latter activity precedes the camera lens. Further, editing or the physical process of putting shots together is not "the guiding idea, the silent procession of images that are concrete, decisive, measured in time and space – in a word, the film" (p. 135).

38 Williams, "Marianne Moore," in *Selected Essays*, p. 124.

39 Williams, "The Poem as a Field of Action," in *Selected Essays*, p. 281.

40 Williams, "Cinema as an Instrument of Poetry," in *Selected Essays*, p. 114.

41 Hammond, *The Shadow and its Shadow*, p. 26.

42 Jean Goudal, "Surrealism and Cinema" (1925), in *The Shadow and its Shadow*, p. 86.

43 Quoted in J. Laplanche and J. B. Pontalis, *The Language of Psycho-Analysis*, trans. Donald Nicholson-Smith (New York: W. W. Norton and Company, 1967), p. 318.

44 Ibid.

45 Ibid.

46 Williams, "The Poem as a Field of Action," in *Selected Essays*, p. 281.

47 Kaplan, "Is the Gaze Male?" p. 121.

48 Kristeva, "Revolution in Poetic Language," p. 115.

49 Williams, *Autobiography*, p. 17.

50 Skin, as Charles Olsen suggests, is the "meeting edge of man and the world" as well as "his cutting edge." Quoted in Joseph N. Riddell, *The Inverted Bell: Modernism and the Counterpoetics of William Carlos Williams* (Baton Rouge: Louisiana State University Press, 1974), pp. 31–2.

51 Quoted in Annette Kuhn, *Women's Pictures* (London: Verso, 1982), p. 53.

52 Silverman, "On Suture," in *Film Theory and Criticism*, pp. 200, 202.

53 Kuhn, *Women's Pictures*, p. 53.

54 Marjorie Perloff, *Poetry On and Off the Page* (Evanston: Northwestern University Press, 1998), p. 131.

55 Kaja Silverman, *Male Subjectivity at the Margins* (New York: Routledge, 1992), p. 206. (Emphasis mine.)

56 Ibid., p. 206.

57 While it is true for Williams that "the priority of the subject is replaced by the priority of the object," the object is also, as Riddell describes it, both "sharply defined" and "sharply related," always situated in a field of relations (*Inverted Bell*, p. 26). This doubleness of "defined" and "related" emerges in film framing which, as Deleuze writes, "both separates and brings together" (*Movement-Image*, p. 13).

58 Linda Williams, *Figures of Desire: A Theory and Analysis of Surrealist Film* (Urbana: University of Illinois Press, 1981), p. 15. (Hereafter cited in the text as *Figures of Desire*.)

59 Stephen Heath, "Narrative Space," *Screen* 17(3) (1976), p. 60.

60 The surrealists rejected both Vertov and Eisenstein as too ideological, and in Vertov's case, using montage so that "film fragments (shots) constellate around a very specific documentary theme." Annette Michelson, ed. *Kino-Eye: The Writings of Dziga Vertov*, trans. Kevin O'Brien (Berkeley: University of California Press, 1984), p. 88. Dziga Vertov, originally Deinis Kaufman, adopted a name derived from the verb which means to spin or rotate, and "the first name . . . reproduces the repetitive sound of a camera crank turning (dziga, dziga, dziga . . .)" (p. xviii). The words spinning, revolving, rotating frequently occur in Williams to denote an attempt to "see all" and a simultaneous loss of control.

61 Dziga Vertov, "The Birth of Kino-Eye"(1924), in *Kino-Eye*, p. 41.

62 Gilberto Perez, *The Material Ghost: Films and Their Medium* (Baltimore: Johns Hopkins University Press, 1998), p. 114.

63 Barbara Low, "Mind-Growth or Mind-Mechanization? The Cinema in Education," *CU* vol. 1 no. 3 (September 1927), p. 49.

64 Quoted in Hammond, *The Shadow and Its Shadow*, p. 10.

65 Dalia Judovitz describes *Anémic Cinéma*'s rotoreliefs with alliterative puns written on them as eliciting kinesthetic experience: "the spectator is compelled to move physically." "Anemic Vision in Duchamp: Cinema as Readymade," in *Dada and Surrealist Film*, p. 51. "The Attic Which is Desire" similarly uses its visual sign to activate bodily participation.

66 Williams, "The Poem as a Field of Action," in *Selected Essays*, p. 283.

67 Grosz refers to the "melting of corporeal boundaries . . . fascinating to surrealists" that often imperil one in a way that alarms and horrifies, and at the same time, entices to the highest possible degree" ("Animal Sex," p. 202).

68 Kovàcs, *From Enchantment to Rage*, p. 185.

69 Flitterman-Lewis argues: "Too much has been made of Artaud's dissatisfaction with Dulac's cinematic execution of his scenario" (*To Desire Differently*, p. 62). She reads the riot at the screening on February 9, 1928 as due "partly out of an inability to deal with the film's revolutionary poetics" (p. 62). Yet certainly part of her "revolutionary poetics" lies in her feminism, which appears to have angered Artaud.

70 There is a "history" of ocular shock in films. Eisenstein describes creating "instantaneous action" in *Potemkin* (1925): "Woman with pince-nez. Followed immediately – without transition – by the same woman with shattered pince-nez and bleeding eye: impression of a shot hitting the eye" ("Dialectic Approach," pp. 55–6).

71 Linda Williams, *Figures of Desire*, p. 73.

72 Michael Wood, "Modernism and Film," p. 223.

73 Jay, *Downcast Eyes*, p. 260.

74 Goudal, "Surrealism and Cinema," in *The Shadow and its Shadow*, p. 93.

75 Grosz describes the preying mantis as "the femme fatale writ small" ("Animal Sex," p. 169).

76 Kaplan, "Is the Gaze Male?" p. 120.

77 Dulac, "Aesthetics, Obstacles, Integral *Cinégraphie*," in *French Film Theory and Criticism*, p. 394.

78 Ibid., p. 394.

79 Silverman, *Threshold of the Visible World*, p. 24.

80 Hélène Cixous, "Castration or Decapitation?" *Signs* 43, no. 7 (1981), p. 48.

81 H. D., *Notes on Thought and Vision* (San Francisco: City Lights Book Store, 1982), pp. 18, 19.

82 Kovàcs, *From Enchantment to Rage*, p. 210.

83 Box imagery of course is part of the lexicon inherited from *Dora*. Freud links the dream image of the jewel box with the reticule he perceives his patient suggestively fingering during therapy.

84 Kovàcs, *From Enchantment to Rage*, p. 127.

85 These are Judovitz's phrases about Duchamp's *Anémic cinéma*. The rotoreliefs in Duchamp's film alternate between concave and convex shapes, a shifting that as Judovitz suggests, is an attempt to combine the genders into a kind of third sex. "Anemic Vision in Duchamp: Cinema as Readymade," pp. 46–56.

86 Silverman explains that Freud's scenario suggests that the female spectator can make "cross-gender peregrinations." In one stage of the fantasy, "the female subject imagines herself being beaten by the father, not in propria persona but rather in the guise of a group of boys . . . The subject feels herself, but does not see herself, looking on as this event takes place; proprioceptively she stands on the margins, but visually she is fully excorporated, assimilated to the image of the male body. The masculine version of the beating fantasy has no comparable stage . . . the male subject clings to his usual terms of bodily reference. It is only the figure performing the punishment whose identity remains in a state of flux" (*Threshold of the Visible World*, p. 35).

87 This scenario is kindred to Deleuze's example of the camera's ability to offer "extraordinary points of view" in its "angle of framing"; in Lubitsch's *The Man I Killed* "a lateral mid-height travelling shot stops at a one-legged man whose missing leg provides a vista on the scene – a passing military parade" (*Movement-Image*, p. 15).

88 Luce Irigaray, *The Sex Which is Not One*, trans. Catherine Porter with Carolyn Burke (Ithaca: Cornell University Press, 1985), p. 28.

4. H. D.'S BORDERLINE BODIES

1 See Dianne Chisholm's discussion of H. D.'s obsession with the trope of the "camera obscura" or "psychic movie camera" in *The Gift* (1941–3), written during the blitz. *H. D.'s Freudian Poetics: Psychoanalysis in Translation* (Ithaca: Cornell University Press, 1992), pp. 91–101.

2 Anne Friedberg dates H. D.'s early "Imagist period" as extending from 1912 through 1920.

3 Susan Stanford Friedman, *Psyche Reborn: The Emergence of H. D.* (Bloomington: Indiana University Press, 1987), p. 17. (Hereafter cited in the text as *Psyche*.)

4 H. D., *Tribute to Freud* (New York: Pantheon Books, 1956), pp. 116–7. (Hereafter cited in the text as *Tribute*.) The centrality of psychoanalysis in H. D.'s work is greatly clarified by Friedman's edited collection of letters. *Analyzing Freud: Letters of H. D., Bryher and their Circle* (New York: New Directions, 2002).

5 Havelock Ellis was a close friend of Bryher and H. D. As Friedman writes, H. D. saw in him "the tolerant psychologist who had affirmed for the post-Victorian generation that the body and its desires were to be accepted as 'natural,' healthy and clean. Together, she and Bryher had poured over the massive volumes of his *Studies in the Psychology of Sex*" (*Analyzing Freud*, p. 3).

6 Joan Rivière, "Womanliness as a Masquerade," in *Formations of Fantasy*, ed. Victor Burgin, James Donald, and Cora Kaplan (London: Methuen, 1986), p. 35.

7 Mary Ann Doane, *The Desire to Desire* (Bloomington: Indiana University Press, 1987), p. 2. (Hereafter cited in the text as *Desire to Desire*.)

8 Josepha as stand-in for Gregg in *Paint it Today* "is suggestive of the ominous femme fatale" where romance turns "erotic thralldom" (Laity, *Fin de Siècle*, p. 131).

9 Bryher writes to H. D.: "I am just a girl by accident" (March 20, 1919, Beinecke). See also *Analyzing Freud*, pp. 3–4.

10 Diana Collecott offers an extensive discussion of H. D.'s bisexuality, detailing the widespread categorical confusion caused by bisexuality for sexologist Havelock Ellis as well as for Freud. *H. D. and Sapphic Modernism*, see especially pp. 75–80.

11 H. D., *The Gift*, ed. Jane Augustine (Gainsville: University of Florida Press, 1998), p. 50.

12 See Terry Castle's *Apparitional Lesbian* for discussion of Moberly and Jourdain, a pair of women who together saw a "vision" of Marie Antoinette at the grounds of Versailles (pp. 106–37). Such *folie à deux* mediates lesbian desire.

13 Freud, "Civilization and its Discontents," *SE* 14.

14 In *Dora*, Freud traces the "perverted phantasy of sucking at the penis" to the "innocent origin" of nursing at the breast: "It then needs very little creative power to substitute the sexual object of the moment (the penis) for the original object (the nipple)" *SE* (1905) vol. 7, p. 52.

15 Friedman, *Analyzing Freud* (March 1933), p. 142. According to object-relations theorists, most famously Nancy Chodorow, both males and females must first and foremost negotiate their relationship to the mother. *The Reproduction of Mothering* (Berkeley: University of California Press, 1978).

16 Freud, "Some Psychical Consequences of the Anatomical Distinction Between the Sexes" (1925), *SE* 19, p. 252.

17 Butler argues that the binary between soul and body is part of "the regulatory fiction of heterosexual coherence": "In other words, acts and gestures, articulated and enacted desires create the illusion of an interior and organizing gender core, an illusion discursively maintained for the purposes of the regulation of sexuality within the obligatory frame of reproductive heterosexuality." *Gender Trouble* (New York: Routledge, 1990), p. 136.

18 Teresa de Lauretis, *The Practice of Love: Lesbian Sexuality and Perverse Desire* (Bloomington: Indiana University Press, 1994), p. 25.

19 Ibid, p. 25.

20 Freud, "The Psychogenesis of a Case of Homosexuality in a Woman" (1920), *SE* 18, pp. 157–8. See also "The Ego and the Id" (1923) where Freud assesses that the oedipal crisis is "complicated" because of "its triangular character" and because "of the constitutional bisexuality of each individual" (*SE* 19, p. 31).

21 See especially H. D.'s letter to George Plank (May 1, 1934), in *Analyzing Freud*, pp. 541–2.

22 H. D., "Expiation," *CU* vol. 2 no. 5 (May 1928), p. 43. (Hereafter cited in the text as "Expiation.")

23 Castle, *Apparitional Lesbian*, p. 2.

24 H. D., *Notes on Thought and Vision*, p. 22.

25 Freud describes the transfer of erotogenic pleasure of the "actual genital zones" to other zones as a function of hysteria ("Three Essays on the Theory of Sexuality" 1905, *SE* 7); he modifies this with a footnote in 1915: "After further reflection and after taking other observations into account, I have been led to ascribe the quality of erotogenicity to all parts of the body and to all the internal organs" (n1, p. 184).

26 Freud, "The Ego and the Id" (1923), *SE* 19, p. 26.

27 Grosz is drawing upon the theories of Didier Anzieu. Lacan also writes that symptom is "imprinted on the flesh" ("The Freudian Thing," in *Ecrits*, p. 127).

28 Bryher, *Film Problems of Soviet Russia*, p. 30.

29 Ibid, p. 14.

30 Collecott, *H. D. and Sapphic Modernism 1910–1950*, p. 3.

31 Freud, *Beyond the Pleasure Principle* (1923), *SE* 19, pp. 27–8.

32 Ibid., p. 28.

33 See Leo Bersani, *The Freudian Body: Psychoanalysis and Art* (New York: Columbia University Press, 1986), p. 63.

34 H. D., "King of Kings Again," *CU* vol. 2 no. 2 (February 1928), p. 24.

35 Freud, "The Ego and the Id," *SE* 19, p. 56.

36 Freud, "Hysterical Phantasies and their Relation to Bisexuality" (1908), *SE* 9, p. 155.

37 Ibid., p. 156.

38 Freud, "Some General Remarks on Hysterical Attacks" (1909), *SE* 9, p. 230.

39 "Artemesian discourse" is Susan Stanford Friedman's phrase for the homoerotic language within H. D.'s prose novels. *Penelope's Web: Gender, Modernity, H. D.'s Fiction* (Cambridge: Cambridge University Press, 1990).

40 Bersani, *The Freudian Body*, pp. 63–4.

41 H. D., "Conrad Viedt: The Student of Prague," *CU* vol. 1 no. 3 (September 1927), p. 35.

42 Nicholls, *Modernism: A Literary Guide*, p. 165.

43 Patrice Petro, *Joyless Street: Women and Melodramatic Representation in Weimar Germany* (Princeton: Princeton University Press, 1989), p. 26.

44 Raymond Carney, *Speaking the Language of Desire: The Films of Carl Dreyer* (Cambridge: Cambridge University Press, 1989), p. 88.

45 Silverman, *Threshold of the Visible World*, p. 89.

46 Rudolf Arnheim, *Film as Art* (Berkeley: University of California Press, 1958), p. 61.

47 It is ironic that Artaud acted as one of the film's cruel judges and was therefore unable to supervise or act in *Seashell and Clergyman*. See Stephen Barber, *Antonin Artaud: Blows and Bombs* (London: Faber and Faber, 1993), p. 31.

48 In *Asphodel*, she has Hermione (H. D.) and Fayne (Gregg) look at a statue of Joan in Rouen, realizing that the Church "had caught her. Trapped her with her armour and her panache and her glory and her pride. They had trapped her, a girl who was a boy and they would always do that" (p. 9). Ed. Robert Spoo (Durham: Duke University Press, 1992).

49 Carney, *Speaking the Language of Desire*, p. 99.

50 Ibid., p. 88.

51 Mary Gordon, *Joan of Arc* (New York: A Lipper/Viking Book, 1999), p. 85.

52 Judith Mayne, *The Woman at the Keyhole: Feminism and Women's Cinema* (Bloomington: Indiana University Press, 1990), p. 225.

53 Bersani, *The Freudian Body*, p. 64.

54 Kenneth Macpherson, "As Is," *CU* vol. 2 no. 3 (March 1928), p. 8.

55 This language is reminiscent of Woolf's notion that fiction should not focus upon realistic details: "Life is not a series of gig lamps symmetrically arranged; life is a luminous halo, a semi-transparent envelope surrounding us from the beginning of consciousness to the end." "Modern Fiction," in *Modernism: An Anthology of Sources and Documents*, p. 397.

56 Eisner, *The Haunted Screen*, p. 100.

57 Janet Bergstrom, "Sexuality at a Loss: The Films of F. W. Murnau," *Poetics Today* 6 no. 1–2 (Spring 1985), p. 189.

58 H. D., "King of Kings Again," *CU* vol. 2 no. 2 (February 1928), p. 27.

59 Cixous, "Castration or Decapitation," p. 49.

60 Huyssen, *The Great Divide*, pp. 70–1.

61 Teresa de Lauretis, *Alice Doesn't: Feminism, Semiotics, Cinema* (Bloomington: Indiana University Press, 1984), p. 67.

62 See Jean Gallagher's discussion of H. D.'s "fixed stare" in *Borderline* as an enactment of static moments of "photogenie." "H. D.'s Distractions: Cinematic Stasis and Lesbian Desire," *Modernism/Modernity* vol. 9 no. 3 (September 2002), p. 417.

63 Iris Marion Young, *Throwing Like a Girl and Other Essays* (Bloomington: Indiana University Press, 1990), p. 150.

64 See Irigaray's rereading of Plato's myth of the cave: phallic vision, unable to see the female body, is trapped in its projections on the "*backcloth*": "Paralyzed, unable to turn round or return toward the origin, toward the *hystera protera*, they are condemned to look ahead at the wall opposite" so that "*hystera* is displaced, transposed, transferred, metaphorized." *Speculum of the Other Woman*, trans. Gillian C. Gill (Ithaca: Cornell University Press, 1974), p. 245.

65 Page du Bois, *Sappho is Burning* (Chicago: University of Chicago Press, 1988), p. 74.

66 Collecott, *H. D. and Sapphic Modernism 1910–1950*, p. 22.

67 Lotte Eisner, "Pabst and the Miracle of Louise Brooks," preface to G. W. Pabst *Pandora's Box* (Film Script), trans. Christopher Holme (New York: Simon and Schuster, 1971). Whiteness is also emblematic of lesbian desire in *Paint it Today* (*Fin de Siècle*, p. 79).

68 Charlotte Mandel, "Garbo/Helen: The Self-Projection of Beauty of H. D.," *Women's Studies* vol. 7 (1980), p. 130.

69 Poe's requirement that all poetry begins with a "dead woman" along with his romantic poem "Helen" haunt this poem. H. D. tells an anecdote of asking Pabst about the "still of a dead body, a very beautiful still" in *Joyless Street* but which she doesn't see upon watching it; he claimed there was no dead body on the screen, or rather he confesses: "'I did not mean you to see the body of the murdered woman on the floor.'" "An Appreciation," *CU* vol. 4 no. 3 (March 1929), pp. 66–8.

70 This is Huyssen's phrase to describe the male gaze in Lang's *Metropolis* (*The Great Divide*, p. 74–5).

71 Bergstrom, "Sexuality at a Loss: The Films of F. W. Murnau," p. 199.

72 For an in-depth treatment of *Helen of Egypt* as a montage poem, see Susan Edmunds, *Out of Line: History, Psychoanalysis and Montage in H. D.'s Long Poems*.

73 See especially B. Ruby Rich, "Maedchen in Uniform: From Repressive Tolerance to Erotic Liberation," in *Re-Vision: Essays in Feminist Film Criticism*, eds. Mary Ann Doane, Patricia Mellencamp, and Linda Williams

(Maryland: University Publications of America, 1984); Richard Dyer, "Less and More than Women and Men: Lesbian and Gay Cinema in Weimar Germany," *New German Critique* 51 (Fall 1990), pp. 5–60.

74 This is de Lauretis's phrase from *Alice Doesn't*, p. 109.

75 Nicholls, *Modernism: A Literary Guide*, p. 142.

76 According to Petro, Kracauer's narrative of Weimar film makes it a "story of male subjectivity in crisis" paradigmatic of the "crisis culminating in fascism" (*Joyless Street*, p. xviii). Such a "story," focused on the destabilization of male identity, ignores the female spectator's importance.

77 October 27, 1927; Beinecke.

78 October 29, 1927; Beinecke. Later Bryher meets Hanns Sachs at Pabst's house in 1928.

79 Ibid.

80 H. D., "An Appreciation," *CU* vol. IV no. 3 (March 1929), p. 60.

81 Ibid., p. 63.

82 Patrice Petro, *Aftershocks of the New: Feminism and Film History* (New Brunswick: Rutgers University Press, 2002), p. 99.

83 Frank Wedekind, *Foreward to The Lulu Plays and Other Sex Tragedies*, trans. Stephen Spender (London: Riverrun Press, 1972), p. 103.

84 Brooks notes that a male fan made her aware that *Pandora's Box* gave her a "lesbian" reputation and popularity in Paris; she laughed "to realise [she] had been living in cinematic perversion for thirty five years." Louise Brooks, "Pabst and Lulu," preface by Lotte Eisner to screenplay *Pandora's Box (Lulu)*, trans. Christopher Holme (New York: Simon and Schuster, 1971), p. 9.

85 A. Kraszna-Krausz, "G. W. Pabst's 'Lulu,'" *CU* vol. 4 no. 4 (April 1926), p. 26.

86 Pabst, *Pandora's Box (Lulu)*, p. 66.

87 Petro, *Aftershocks of the New*, p. 111.

88 Barbara Creed, "Lesbian Bodies: Tribades, Tomboys and Tarts," in *Sexy Bodies*, eds. Elizabeth Grosz and Elspeth Probyn (New York: Routledge, 1995), p. 100.

89 Petro, *Aftershocks of the New*, p. 138.

90 Susan Stanford Friedman, "Modernism of the 'Scattered Remnant': Race and Politics in H. D.'s Development," in *Feminist Issues in Literary Scholarship*, ed. Shari Benstock (Bloomington: Indiana University Press, 1987), p. 214.

91 Michael Rogin, *Blackface, White Noise: Jewish Immigrants in the Hollywood Melting Pot* (Berkeley: University of California Press, 1996), p. 14.

92 Macpherson, "As Is," *CU* vol. 7 no. 5 (November 1930), p. 381.

93 Martin Duberman, *Paul Robeson* (New York: The New Press, 1989), p. 131.

94 Petrine Archer-Straw, *Negrophilia: Avant-Garde Paris and Black Culture in the 1920s* (London: Thames and Husdon, 2000), p. 19.

95 Hazel Carby, *Racemen* (Cambridge, MA; Harvard University Press, 1998), p. 71.

96 Ibid., p. 67.

97 Ibid., p. 68.

98 Hitchcock's sound film *Murder* (1930) addresses a similar dynamic. The murderer turns out to be a "half caste" trapeze artist who frequently dons female costumes; in fact, he kills to preserve his racial secret. According to Hugh Castle,

the film uses dialogue as though it were an "acceleration of cutting." "Attitude and Interlude," *CU* vol. 7. no. 3 (September 1930), p. 190.

99 Silverman, *Threshold of the Visible World*, p. 19.

100 Ibid.

101 Jean Walton, "Nightmare of Uncoordinated White-Folk: Race, Psychoanalysis and *Borderline*," *Discourse* 19 no. 1 (Winter 1997), pp. 88–109.

102 Friedman discusses the importance of Ella Freeman Sharpe in H. D.'s thinking through the problem of castration. Sharpe, a British lay analyst who had been a pupil of Sachs, argued in 1930 that artistic sublimation allows for a transformation of the body into the "parental 'breast and penis.'" In the case of an analysand dancer, "'[p]erfect dancing' is her ceremonial ritual in which 'she becomes the magical phallus'" (*Analyzing Freud*, p. 122).

103 Carby, *Racemen*, p. 56.

104 Walton, "Psychoanalysis of Race," p. 407.

105 In Josef von Sternberg's *Blond Venus* (1932), Marlene Dietrich incorporates Josephine Baker's "reviled" and celebrated dance style in her nightclub performances, thus subsuming and activating a disavowed bodily identity (Petro, *Aftershocks of the New*, p. 138).

106 H. D., *Helen in Egypt* (New York: New Directions, 1961), p. 128.

107 de Lauretis, *Alice Doesn't*, p. 135.

108 Ibid., p. 110.

109 Quoted in Bollas, *Hysteria*, p. 111.

5. MARIANNE MOORE: FILM, FETISHISM, AND HER *BALLET MÉCANIQUE*

1 Charlotte Mandel, "Magical Lenses: Poet's Vision Beyond the Naked Eye," in *H. D.: Woman and Poet*, p. 302.

2 Moore uses this "data" in her poem "Elephants" as she informs us in her "Notes" in *Complete Poems*, p. 281.

3 Moore, *Complete Poems*, p. 26.

4 Robin G. Schulze, *Becoming Marianne Moore: The Early Poems, 1907–1924* (Berkeley: University of California Press, 2002), p. 72. Before Schulze's edited facsimile edition of *Observations* (1924), which has long been out of print, the tendency has been to see Moore's *Complete Poems* as the only authoritative collection, using the "elderly Moore's revisions of the texts of her own exuberant youth" (p. 7). This editorial trend has literally relegated the earlier versions to obscurity. All my citations to poems in *Observations* will be to Schulze's edition and follow her pagination, not the facsimile's; all other citations of Moore's poetry are to *Complete Poems* (*CP*).

5 Pound, "Marianne Moore and Mina Loy" (1917), in *Selected Prose: 1909–1965* (New York: New Directions, 1973), p. 424.

6 Williams, "Marianne Moore," in *Selected Essays*, p. 123.

7 Ibid.

8 See Charles Altieri's discussion of Moore's paradoxical negotiation of gender. He writes: "Moore rarely called attention to the gendered investments in her own work, probably fearing that the resulting theatrics would displace the dimensions of impersonality and transpersonality sustaining the values that her gendered position enabled her to realize" (*Painterly Abstraction*, p. 262).

9 T. S. Eliot, "Introduction to Selected Poems," quoted in *The Gender of Modernism*, p. 150. (Hereafter cited in the text as *Gender of Modernism*.)

10 An interview with Donald Hall, "The Art of Poetry: Marianne Moore," in *Marianne Moore: A Collection of Critical Essays*, ed. Charles Tomlinson (New Jersey: Prentice Hall, 1969), p. 23.

11 Emily Apter, *Feminizing the Fetish: Psychoanalysis and Narrative Obsession in Turn-of-the-Century France* (Ithaca: Cornell University Press, 1991), p. 20. (Hereafter cited in the text as *Feminizing the Fetish*.)

12 Randall Jarrell, *Poetry and the Age* (1953) (Gainesville: University of Florida, 2001), p. 199.

13 Ibid., p. 203.

14 Moore, "Feeling and Precision," in *Predilections* (New York: Viking Press, 1955), p. 4.

15 Quoted in Schulze, *Becoming Marianne Moore*, p. 26.

16 Cristanne Miller reads Moore's animal poems, not as primarily moral or accurate representations (how they are usually read), but as emphasizing the poet's own voice: "Even the poems lacking a textual 'I' reveal their author's subject position in the wild idiosyncrasy of their descriptions." *Marianne Moore: Questions of Authority* (Cambridge, MA: Harvard University Press, 1995), p. 45.

17 Germaine Dulac, "Aesthetics, Obstacles, Integral Cinégraphie"(1926) in *French Film Theory and Criticism*, p. 396. Moore might have been familiar with F. A. Talbot's *Moving Pictures* which surveyed scientific films; it has stills, for instance, of magnified microbes in movement, images that approximate those in abstract films (London, 1912). *Close Up* later exposed Moore to numerous stills from nature documentaries (many of which are lost) and to articles such as "Nature and Love" by the reviewer Oswell Blakeston (*CU* vol. 4 no. 3, March 1929). This particular piece points towards the subliminal eroticism in science films, even as Blakeston scoffs at the "censor" who "has studied his book on anatomical structure and sees sex-appeal even in the skeleton." He praises film's elastic power to reveal human "evolution": "Amoebae, glittering gold of reflected light. Groups of cells are formed, multiply, split up, reform. Perfect microscopic photography reveals more developed animalcule, showing how two bodies join together for the greater strength of the organism" (pp. 69–70).

18 Béla Balázs, *Theory of the Film: Character and Growth of a New Art* (New York: Dover, 1970), p. 92.

19 Williams, "Marianne Moore," in *Selected Essays*, p. 124.

20 Wood, "Modernism and Film," in *The Cambridge Companion to Modernism*, p. 223.

21 Moore's reading diary of Eisenstein (Rosenbach Library Archives VII: 02:02 1931; 1250). I thank Cynthia Hogue for her guidance to this archival material.

22 Elizabeth Bishop writes in "Efforts of Affection" that she frequently went to the movies with Moore in the thirties. On one occasion they went to see *Potemkin*, and Moore had "talked at length and in detail about the ingenuity of the Disney film," the short which preceded Eisenstein's film. It seems likely that she was more sympathetic to his methods (as poetic ones) than to his films in particular. *Elizabeth Bishop: The Collected Prose* (New York: Farrar, Straus and Giroux, 1984), p. 151.

23 *The Poems of Marianne Moore*, ed. Grace Schulman (New York: Viking, 2003), p. 112. Schulman's new edition collects published work along with previously uncollected and unpublished work and arranges it chronologically. "She Trimmed Candles" was never published (p. 407).

24 Elizabeth Grosz, "Refiguring Lesbian Desire," in *Space, Time, and Perversion* (New York: Routledge, 1995), p. 183.

25 Freud, "Fetishism" (1927), in *SE* 21.

26 Sandra Gilbert, "Marianne Moore as a Female Female Impersonator," in *Marianne Moore: The Art of a Modernist*, ed. Joseph Parisi (Ann Arbor: University of Michigan Press, 1990).

27 Studlar, *In the Realm of Pleasure*, p. 40.

28 De Lauretis, *The Practice of Love*, p. 263.

29 This poem was first published in *The Lantern* in 1909.

30 Freud, *Lecture to Vienna Psychoanalytic Society* (1909), quoted in Apter, *Feminizing the Fetish*, p. 80.

31 Moore praises *Development* in a letter to Bryher: "The exposition of the baffled sense one has of being outside what it is one's birthright to enjoy, is the great feature of the book"; she also "corroborates" Bryher's experience of the tedious socializing of girls, remarking that "dolls have always seemed to me, the dreariest, tawdriest things in the world" (*Selected Letters*, pp. 156–7).

32 Butler, *Gender Trouble*, p. 140. Moore takes the phrase "menagerie of styles" from an article in the *London Graphic* (1924) called "The Mystery of an Adjective and of Evening Clothes" (*CP*, p. 274).

33 Bonnie Costello, *Marianne Moore: Imaginary Possessions* (Cambridge: Harvard University Press, 1981), p. 246.

34 Cynthia Hogue, *Scheming Women: Poetry, Privilege, and the Politics of Subjectivity* (New York: State University Press, 1995), p. 77.

35 Joan Copjec, "The Sartorial Superego," *October* 50 (Fall 1988), p. 59.

36 This is Michael Gould's phrase about Josef von Sternberg's films. *Surrealism and the Cinema* (New York: A. S. Barnes and Company, 1976), p. 87.

37 Walter Benjamin, *The Arcades Project*, trans. Howard Eiland and Kevin McLaughlin (Cambridge, MA: Harvard University Press, 1999), p. 69.

38 Bishop, "Efforts of Affection," p. 125.

39 Eisenstein, "The Unexpected," in *Film Form*, p. 26.

40 Williams, "Marianne Moore," in *Selected Essays*, p. 128.

41 Ibid.

42 While it is not clear that she saw *Ballet Mécanique*, we know that it was recommended to her and that she anticipated liking it (*Selected Letters*, p. 261).

43 Quoted in Le Grice, *Abstract Film and Beyond*, p. 37.
44 Ibid.
45 Judi Freeman, "Bridging Purism and Surrealism: The Origins and Production of Fernand Léger's *Ballet Mécanique*," in *Dada and Surrealist Film*, p. 29.
46 Bishop, "Efforts of Affection," p. 149.
47 Constance Penley, *The Future of an Illusion: Film, Feminism, and Psychoanalysis* (Minneapolis: University of Minnesota, 1989).
48 Elsaesser, "Dada/Cinema?" in *Dada and Surrealist Film*, p. 23.
49 Ibid., pp. 23–4.
50 Williams, "Marianne Moore," in *Selected Essays*, p. 122.
51 Leavell, *Marianne Moore and Visual Arts*, p. 28.
52 Jeanne Heuving argues that this poem challenges the conventions of the high modernist "portrait" poem. *Gender in the Art of Marianne Moore* (Detroit: Wayne State University Press, 1992), see pp. 36–41. For Costello, "Those Various Scalpels" parodies the blazon, and its "leaps of association are a devastating weapon of wit" (*Imaginary Possessions*, p. 175).
53 Elsaesser, "Dada / Cinema?" p. 25.
54 Joyce, *Cultural Critique and Abstraction*, p. 62.
55 Rivièré, "Womanliness as Masquerade," p. 38.
56 Roland Barthes, "Striptease," in *A Barthes Reader*, ed. Susan Sontag (New York: The Noonday Press, 1991), p. 86.
57 Stewart, *Between Film and Screen*, p. 31.
58 Lawder, *The Cubist Cinema*, p. 14. See also Talbot's *Moving Pictures*, especially the chapter on "Moving Pictures of Microbes," pp. 161–81.
59 E. L. Black, "Animals on Film," *CU* vol. 1 no. 1 (July 1927), pp. 42–3.
60 Lisa Cartwright, *Screening the Body: Tracing Medicine's Visual Culture* (Minneapolis: University of Minnesota Press, 1995), p. 132.
61 Ibid.
62 Bryher, "G. W. Pabst: A Survey," *CU* vol. 1 no. 6 (1927), p. 59.
63 Cartwright, *Screening the Body*, p. 18.
64 Ibid., p. 13.
65 Moore, "Feeling and Precision," in *Predilections*, p. 3.
66 Miller, *Marianne Moore: Questions of Authority*, p. 148.
67 Ibid., p. 149.
68 Bazin, *What is Cinema?* p. 9.
69 Freud, "The Uncanny," *SE* 21, p. 244.
70 Terry Castle, *The Female Thermometer: 18th Century Culture and the Invention of the Uncanny* (New York: Oxford University Press, 1995), p. 19.
71 Bazin, *What is Cinema?* pp. 14–5.
72 Dorothy Richardson, "The Film Gone Male," *CU* vol. 9 no. 1 (March 1932), p. 37.
73 A. Kraszna-Krausz, "Four Films From Germany," *CU* vol. 9 no. 1 (March 1932), p. 40.
74 Ibid., p. 40.

75 Adrienne Rich, "Compulsory Heterosexuality and Lesbian Existence," in *Blood, Bread and Poetry* (New York: Norton, 1986), p. 23.

76 Moore, "Feeling and Precision," in *Predilections*, p. 3.

77 B. Ruby Rich, "*Maedchen in Uniform*: From Repressive Tolerance to Erotic Liberation," in *Re-Vision: Essays in Feminist Film Criticism*, p. 100.

78 Ibid., p. 102.

79 The setting of a girl's boarding school would not be unfamiliar to Moore, whose mother taught at the private girl's school the poet attended through high school (*Selected Letters*, p. 3).

80 De Lauretis, *The Practice of Love*, p. 236.

81 Schulze, *Becoming Marianne Moore*, p. 184.

82 Leavell, *Marianne Moore and Visual Arts*, p. 94.

CONCLUSION: MODERNIST DISSOCIATION AND ALL ABOUT EVE

1 A close comparison can be found between Moore and artist Joseph Cornell, with whom the poet exchanged letters. Cornell collected an assortment of materials found in New York, including images of wildlife, ballerinas, movie icons, for his boxes, collages, and for his lesser-known films. In these films, Cornell handles "found footage," pieces of home-movies and discarded film pieces, and like Moore, he delights in intersecting animal and mechanical realms. See Diane Waldman, *Joseph Cornell: Master of Dreams* (New York: Abrams Inc., 2002), especially pp. 121–4 for exploration of Cornell's life-long relationship with cinema.

2 Eisenstein, "The New Language of Cinematography," *CU* vol. 4 no. 5 (May 1929), p. 11.

3 Costello, *Marianne Moore: Imaginary Possessions*, p. 61.

4 Stewart, *Between Film and Screen*, p. 273.

5 Hogue, *Scheming Women*, p. 220, n60.

6 T. S. Eliot, "The Social Function of Poetry," in *On Poetry and Poets* (New York: Farrar, Straus, and Cudahy, 1951), p. 8.

Bibliography

Abel, Richard, ed. *French Film Theory and Criticism Vol. 1: 1909–1929*. Princeton: Princeton University Press, 1988.

Altieri, Charles. *Painterly Abstraction in Modernist American Poetry: The Contemporaneity of Modernism*. Cambridge: Cambridge University Press, 1989.

Apter, Emily. *Feminizing the Fetish: Psychoanalysis and Narrative Obsession in Turn-of-the-Century France*. Ithaca: Cornell University Press, 1991.

Apollinaire, Guillaume. *Selected Writings*. Trans. Roger Shattuck. New York: New Directions, 1971.

Archer-Straw, Petrine. *Negrophilia: Avant-Garde Paris and Black Culture in the 1920s*. London: Thames and Hudson, 2000.

Arnheim, Rudolf. *Film as Art*. Berkeley: University of California Press, 1958.

Balázs, Béla. *Theory of the Film: Character and Growth of a New Art*. New York: Dover, 1970.

Baldwin, Neil. *Man Ray: American Artist*. New York: Clarkson Potter, 1988.

Barber, Stephen. *Antonin Artaud: Blows and Bombs*. London: Faber and Faber, 1993.

Barthes, Roland. "Striptease." *A Barthes Reader*. Ed. Susan Sontag. New York: The Noonday Press, 1991.

Bazin, André. *What is Cinema? Volume 1*. Trans. Hugh Gray. Berkeley: University of California Press, 1974.

Baudelaire, Charles. *Les Fleurs du Mal*. Trans. C. F. MacIntyre. Berkeley: University of California Press, 1947.

Benjamin, Walter. *The Arcades Project*. Trans Howard Eiland and Kevin McLaughlin. Cambridge, MA: Harvard University Press, 1999.

Illuminations. Ed. Hannah Arendt and trans. Harry Zohn. New York: Shocken Books, 1968.

Selected Writings Vol. 2: 1927–1934. Trans. Rodney Livingstone. Cambridge: Harvard University Press, 1999.

Benstock, Shari, ed. *Feminist Issues in Literary Scholarship*. Bloomington: Indiana University Press, 1987.

Bergson, Henri. *Laughter: An Essay on the Meaning of the Comic*. Trans. Claudesley Brereton and Fred Rothwell (1911). Los Angeles: Green Integer Books, 1999.

Matter and Memory (1896). Trans. Nancy Margaret Paul and W. Scott Palmer. New York: The MacMillan Company, 1950.

Bergstrom, Janet, ed. *Endless Night: Cinema and Psychoanalysis, Parallel Histories*. Berkeley: University of California Press, 1999.

"Sexuality at a Loss: The Films of F. W. Murnau." *Poetics Today* 6, nos. 1–2 (Spring 1985): 185–203.

Berman, Art. *Preface to Modernism*. Urbana: University of Illinois Press, 1994.

Bersani, Leo. *The Freudian Body: Psychoanalysis and Art*. New York: Columbia University Press, 1986.

Bishop, Elizabeth. *The Collected Prose*. New York: Farrar, Straus and Giroux, 1984.

Bollas, Christopher. *Hysteria*. London: Routledge, 2000.

Boone, Joseph Allen. *Libidinal Currents: Sexuality and the Shaping of Modernism*. Chicago: University of Chicago Press, 1998.

Bordo, Susan. "Selections from *The Flight to Objectivity*." In *Feminism & History of Philosophy*. Genevieve Lloyd, ed. Oxford: Oxford University Press, 2002.

Bradbury, James and James McFarlane, eds. *Modernism: 1890–1930*. Middlesex: Penguin, 1974.

Breton, André. "Second Manifesto of Surrealism" (1930). *Manifestoes of Surrealism*. Trans. Richard Seaver and Helen R. Lane. Ann Arbor: University of Michigan Press, 1974.

Bronfen, Elisabeth. *The Knotted Subject: Hysteria and Its Discontents*. Princeton: Princeton University Press, 1998.

Brooks, Louise. "Pabst and Lulu," preface to screenplay *Pandora's Box (Lulu)*. Trans. Christopher Holme. New York: Simon and Schuster, 1971.

Brownlow, Kevin. *The Parade's Gone By . . .* London: Knopf, 1968.

Bryher. *Film Problems of Soviet Russia*. Territet: Pool, 1929.

Buñuel, Luis. *An Unspeakable Betrayal*. Berkeley: University of California Press, 1995.

Butler, Judith. *Gender Trouble*. New York: Routledge, 1990.

Bürger, Peter. *Theory of the Avant-Garde*. Trans. Michael Shaw. Minneapolis: University of Minnesota Press, 1984.

Burke, Carolyn. "'Getting Spliced': Modernism and Sexual Difference." *American Quarterly* 39.1 (1987): 98–121.

Butler, Judith. *Bodies that Matter: On the Discursive Limits of 'Sex'*. New York: Routledge, 1993.

Carby, Hazel. *Racemen*. Cambridge, MA: Harvard University Press, 1998.

Carney, Raymond. *Speaking the Language of Desire: The Films of Carl Dreyer*. Cambridge: Cambridge University Press, 1989.

Cartwright, Lisa. *Screening the Body: Tracing Medicine's Visual Culture*. Minneapolis: University of Minnesota Press, 1995.

Castle, Terry. *The Apparitional Lesbian: Female Sexuality and Modern Culture*. New York: Columbia University Press, 1993.

The Female Thermometer: 18th Century Culture and the Invention of the Uncanny. New York: Oxford University Press, 1995.

Caws, Mary Ann. *The Surrealist Look*. Cambridge: MIT Press, 1999.

Chefdor, Monique, Ricardo Quinones, and Albert Wachtel, eds. *Modernism: Challenges and Perspectives*. Urbana: University of Illinois Press, 1986.

Chessman, Harriet Scott. *The Public is Invited to Dance*. Stanford: Stanford University Press, 1989.

Chisholm, Dianne. *H. D.'s Freudian Poetics: Psychoanalysis in Translation*. Ithaca: Cornell University Press, 1992.

Chodorow, Nancy. *The Reproduction of Mothering*. Berkeley: University of California Press, 1978.

Cixous, Hélène. "Castration or Decaptiation?" *Signs* 43, no. 7 (1981): 41–55.

Copjec, Joan. "The Sartorial Superego." *October* 50 Fall 1988: 57–96.

Collecott, Diana. *H. D. and Sapphic Modernism 1910–1950*. Cambridge: Cambridge University Press, 1999.

Costello, Bonnie. *Marianne Moore: Imaginary Possessions*. Cambridge: Harvard University Press, 1981.

Crane, Hart. *Complete Poems*. New York: Liveright, 1933.

Crary, Jonathan. *Techniques of the Observer*. Cambridge: MIT Press, 1993.

Daudet, Alphonse, Theodore de Banville, Christopher G. Goetz, Michel Bonduelle and Toby Gelfand. *Charcot: Constructing Neurology*. New York: Oxford University Press, 1995.

de Gourmont, Remy. *Natural Philosophy of Love*. Trans. with a postscript by Ezra Pound. New York: Privately printed for Rarity Press, 1931.

DeKoven, Marianne. *A Different Language: Gertrude Stein's Experimental Writing*. Madison: University of Wisconsin Press, 1983.

de Lauretis, Teresa. *Alice Doesn't: Feminism, Semiotics, Cinema*. Bloomington: Indiana University Press, 1984.

The Practice of Love: Lesbian Sexuality and Perverse Desire. Bloomington: Indiana University Press, 1994.

Deleuze, Gilles. *Cinema 1. The Movement-Image*. Minneapolis: University of Minnesota Press, 1986.

Deren, Maya. "Cinematography: The Creative Use of Reality." *The Avant-garde Film: A Reader of Theory and Criticism*. Ed. P. Adams Sitney. New York: New York University Press, 1978.

Dickie, Margaret. "Women Poets and the Emergence of Modernism." *The Columbia History of American Poetry*. Ed. Jay Parini. New York: Columbia University Press, 1993.

Dijkstra, Bram. *Cubism, Stieglitz and the Early Poetry of William Carlos Williams*. Princeton: Princeton University Press, 1969.

Evil Sisters. New York: Alfred A. Knopf, 1996.

Doane, Mary Ann. "Film and the Masquerade: Theorizing the Female Spectator." *Feminism & Film*. Ed. E. Anne Kaplan. Oxford: Oxford University Press, 2000.

The Desire to Desire. Bloomington: Indiana University Press, 1987.

Donald, James, Anne Friedberg and Laura Marcus, eds. *Close Up 1927–1933: Cinema and Modernism*. Princeton: Princeton University Press, 1998.

Duberman, Martin. *Paul Robeson*. New York: The New Press, 1989.

du Bois, Page. *Sappho is Burning*. Chicago: University of Chicago Press, 1988.

Dyer, Richard. "Lesbian and Gay Cinema in Weimar Germany." *New German Critique* 51 (Fall 1990): 5–60.

Edmunds, Susan. *Out of Line: History, Psychoanalysis, & Montage in H. D.'s Long Poems*. Stanford: Stanford University Press, 1994.

Eisenstein, Sergei. *Film Form: Essays in Film Theory*. Ed. and trans. Jay Leyda. New York: Harcourt, Brace and Company, 1949.

Eisner, Lotte H. *The Haunted Screen: Expressionism in the German Cinema and the Influence of Max Reinhardt*. Trans. Roger Greaves. London: Thames and Hudson, 1969.

Eisner, Lotte. "Pabst and the Miracle of Louise Brooks." Preface to G. W. Pabst *Pandora's Box* (Film Script). Trans. Christopher Holme. New York: Simon and Schuster, 1971.

Eliot, T. S. *Inventions of the March Hare: Poems 1909–1917*. Ed. Christopher Ricks. New York: Harcourt, Brace and Company, 1996.

On Poetry and Poets. New York: Farrar, Straus and Cudahy, 1951.

"A Commentary," in *Criterion* 13 (April 1934).

The Complete Poems and Plays: 1909–1950. New York: Harcourt, Brace and Company, 1958.

The Letters of T. S. Eliot, vol. 1 1898–1922. Ed. Valerie Eliot. London: Faber and Faber, 1988.

The Sacred Wood and Major Early Essays. New York: Dover Publications, 1998.

Selected Prose. London: Faber and Faber, 1972.

The Varieties of Metaphysical Poetry. Ed. Ronald Schuchard. New York: Harcourt, Brace and Company, 1993.

The Waste Land: A Facsimile and Transcript of the Original Drafts. Ed. Valerie Eliot. London: Faber and Faber, 1971.

Ellis, Havelock. *Studies in the Psychology of Sex Vol. 1*. Philadelphia: F. A. Davis Company, Publishers, 1913.

Elsaesser, Thomas, ed. *Early Cinema: Space Frame Narrative*. London: British Film Institute Publishing, 1990.

Everson, William K. *American Silent Film*. New York: De Capo Press, 1998.

Faderman, Lillian. *Surpassing the Love of Men: Romantic Friendship and Love between Women from the Renaissance to the Present*. New York: William Morrow and Company, 1981.

Felski, Rita. *The Gender of Modernism*. Cambridge: Harvard University Press, 1995.

Flint, F. S. "Imagisme." *The English Modernist Reader*. Ed. Peter Faulkner. Iowa City: University of Iowa Press, 1986.

Flitterman-Lewis, Sandy. *To Desire Differently: Feminism and French Cinema*. New York: Cornell University Press, 1996.

Freud, Sigmund. *The Standard Edition of the Complete Psychological Works of Sigmund Freud*. Trans. and ed. James Strachey. 24 vols. London: Hogarth Press, 1953–1974.

"Approaching *Borderline*." H. D. *Woman and Poet*. Ed. Michael King. Orono: University of Maine, 1988.

Friedman, Susan Stanford. *Analyzing Freud: Letters of H. D., Bryher and their Circle.* New York: New Directions, 2002.

Penelope's Web: Gender, Modernity, H. D.'s Fiction. Cambridge: Cambridge University Press, 1990.

Psyche Reborn: The Emergence of H. D. Bloomington: Indiana University Press, 1987.

Fussell, Paul. *The Great War and Modern Memory.* Oxford: Oxford University Press, 1975.

Gallagher, Jean. "H. D.'s Distractions: Cinematic Stasis and Lesbian Desire." *Modernism/modernity* vol. 9 no. 3 (September 2002): 407–22.

Gelpi, Albert. *A Coherent Splendor: The American Poetic Renaissance, 1910–1950.* Cambridge: Cambridge University Press, 1987.

Gilbert, Sandra M. "Marianne Moore as a Female Female Impersonator" *in Marianne Moore: The Art of a Modernist.* Ed. Joseph Parisi. Ann Arbor: University of Michigan Press, 1990.

Gilbert, Sandra M. and Susan Gubar. *No Man's Land: The Place of the Woman Writer in the Twentieth Century* Volume 1 and 2. New Haven: Yale University Press, 1988, 1989.

Gilman, Sander L., Helen King, Roy Porter, G. S. Rousseau, Elaine Showalter, eds. *Hysteria Beyond Freud.* Berkeley: University of California, 1993.

Goldstein, Lawrence. *The American Poet at the Movies: A Critical History.* Ann Arbor: University of Michigan Press, 1994.

Gombrich, E. H. *The Story of Art.* London: Phaidon, 1969.

Gordon, Lyndall. *T. S. Eliot: An Imperfect Life.* New York: W. W. Norton and Company, Inc., 1998.

Gordon, Mary. *Joan of Arc.* New York: A Lipper/Viking Book, 1999.

Gould, Michael. *Surrealism and the Cinema.* New York: A. S. Barnes and Company, 1976.

Grosz, Elizabeth and Elspeth Probyn, eds. *Sexy Bodies.* New York: Routledge, 1995.

Grosz, Elizabeth. *Space, Time, and Perversion.* New York: Routledge, 1995.

Volatile Bodies. Bloomington: Indiana University Press, 1994.

Gunning, Tom. "Cinema of Attraction[s]." *Wide Angle* 8.3–4 (1986): 63–70.

H. D. *Asphodel.* Ed. Robert Spoo. Durham: Duke University Press, 1992.

Collected Poems: 1912–1944. Ed. Louis L. Martz. New York: New Directions, 1983.

The Gift. Ed. Jane Augustine. Gainsville: University of Florida Press, 1998.

Helen in Egypt. New York: New Directions, 1961.

Notes on Thought and Vision. San Francisco: City Lights Books, 1982.

Paint it Today. Ed. Cassandra Laity. New York: New York University Press, 1992.

Tribute to Freud. New York: Pantheon Books, 1956.

Hake, Sabine. "Chaplin Reception in Weimar Germany." *New German Critique* 51 (Fall 1990).

Halter, Peter. *The Revolution in the Visual Arts and the Poetry of William Carlos Williams.* Cambridge: Cambridge University Press, 1994.

Hammond, Paul, ed. *The Shadow & Its Shadow.* San Francisco: City Lights Books, 2000.

Hansen, Miriam B. "America, Paris, the Alps: Kracauer and Benjamin on Cinema and Modernity." *Cinema and the Invention of Modern Life*. Eds. Leo Charney and Vannessa R. Schwartz. Berkeley: University of California Press, 1995.

Hardy, Thomas, *Tess of the D'Urbervilles*. New York: Modern Library Edition, 1917.

Head, Henry. *Studies in Neurology*. London: Oxford University Press, 1920.

Heath, Stephen. "Narrative Space." *Screen* 17(3) (1976).

Hedges, Inez. "Constellated Visions: Robert Desnos's and Man Ray's *L'Etoile de Mer*." Ed. Rudolf E. Kuenzli. Cambridge: MIT Press, 1996.

Heuving, Jeanne. *Gender in the Art of Marianne Moore: Omissions are not Accidents*. Detroit: Wayne State University Press, 1992.

Hogue, Cynthia. *Scheming Women: Poetry, Privilege, and the Politics of Subjectivity*. New York: State University Press, 1995.

Hussel, Edmund. *The Phenomenology of Internal Time Consciousness (1905)*. Trans. James S. Churchill Bloomington: Indiana University Press, 1966.

Huyssen, Andreas. *After the Great Divide: Modernism, Mass Culture, Postmodernism*. Bloomington: Indiana University Press, 1986.

Iampolski, Mikhail. *The Memory of Tiresias: Intertextuality and Film*. Berkeley: University of California Press, 1998.

Irigaray, Luce. *The Sex Which is Not One*. Trans. Catherine Porter with Carolyn Burke Ithaca: Cornell University Press, 1985.
  Speculum of the Other Woman. Trans. Gillian C. Gill. Ithaca: Cornell University Press, 1974.

James, William. *Pragmatism and Other Writings*. New York: Penguin, 2000.
  The Principles of Psychology (1890). New York: Dover Publications, 1950.

Jardine, Alice A. *Gynesis: Configurations of Woman and Modernity*. Ithaca: Cornell University Press, 1985.

Jarrell, Randall. *Poetry and the Age* (1953). Gainesville: University of Florida, 2001.

Jay, Martin. *Downcast Eyes: The Denigration of Vision in Twentieth Century French Thought*. Berkeley: University of California Press, 1993.

Jean, Marcel, ed. *The Autobiography of Surrealism*. New York: Viking Press, 1980.

Joyce, Elizabeth W. *Cultural Critique and Abstraction: Marianne Moore and the Avant-Garde*. Lewisburg: Bucknell University Press, 1998.

Kaplan, E. Anne. "Is the Gaze Male?" *Feminism & Film*. Ed. E. Ann Kaplan. Oxford: Oxford University Press, 2000.

Keegan, John. *The First World War*. New York: Vintage Books, 1998.

Kenner, Hugh. *The Pound Era*. Berkeley: University of California Press, 1971.

Kerr, Walter. The Silent Clowns. New York: De Capo Press, 1980.

Koestenbaum, Wayne. *Double talk: The Erotics of Male Literary Collaboration*. New York: Routledge, 1989.

Kolocotroni Vassiliki, Jane Goldman, and Olga Taxidou, eds. *Modernism: An Anthology of Sources and Documents*. Chicago: The University of Chicago Press, 1998.

Kovács, Steven. *From Enchantment to Rage: The Story of Surrealist Cinema*. Rutherford: Fairleigh Dickinson University Press, 1980.

Kracauer, Siegfried. *From Caligari to Hitler: A Psychological History of German Film.* Princeton: Princeton University Press, 1947.

Theory of Film: The Redemption of Physical Reality. Princeton: Princeton University Press, 1997.

Krauss, Rosalind. *The Originality of the Avant-Garde and Other Modernist Myths.* Cambridge, MA: MIT Press, 1996.

Kristeva, Julia. *The Kristeva Reader.* Ed. Toril Moi. New York: Columbia University Press, 1986.

Kuenzli, Rudolf E., ed. *Dada and Surealist Film.* Cambridge, MA: MIT Press, 1996.

Kuhn, Annette. *Women's Pictures.* London: Verso, 1982.

Kuznier, Alice A. *The Queer German Cinema.* Stanford: Stanford University Press, 2000.

Lacan, Jacques. *Ecrits: A Selection.* Trans. Alan Sheridan. New York: W. W. Norton and Company, 1977.

Laity, Cassandra. *H. D. and the Victorian Fin de Siècle.* Cambridge: Cambridge University Press, 1996.

Laplanche, J. and J. B. Pontalis. *The Language of Psycho-analysis.* Trans. Donald Nicholson-Smith. New York: W. W. Norton and Company, 1967.

Lawder, Standish D. *The Cubist Cinema.* New York: New York University Press, 1975.

Le Grice, Malcolm. *Abstract Film and Beyond.* Cambridge: MIT Press, 1977.

Leavell, Linda. *Marianne Moore and Visual Arts: Prismatic Color.* Baton Rouge: Louisiana State University Press, 1995.

Levenson, Michael, ed. *The Cambridge Companion to Modernism.* Cambridge: Cambridge University Press, 1999.

Leyda, Jay. *Kino: A History of the Russian and Soviet Film.* Berkeley: University of California Press, 1983.

Lindsey, Vachel. *The Art of the Moving Picture* (1915). New York: Modern Library Reprint 2000.

Loy, Mina. *The Last Lunar Baedeker.* Ed. Roger L. Conover. New York: Farrar, Straus Giroux, 1996.

Macpherson, K. *Close Up.* 10 Vols. Territet: Pool, 1927–1933.

Man Ray. *Self Portrait.* New York: Little, Brown and Co, 1963.

Mandel, Charlotte. "Garbo/Helen: The Self-Projection of Beauty of H. D." *Women's Studies* Vol. 7 (1980): 127–35.

"'The Redirected Image': Cinematic Dynamics in the Style of H. D." *Contemporary Literature* 25.4 (1984): 411–36.

Marinetti, Filippo. *Selected Writings.* Ed. R. W. Flint. New York: Farrar, Straus and Giroux, 1971.

Mast, Gerald. *The Comic Mind: Comedy and the Movies.* Chicago: University of Chicago, 1973.

Mast, Gerald, Marshall Cohen and Leo Braudy, eds. *Film Theory and Criticism.* Oxford: Oxford University Press, 1992.

Mayne, Judith. *The Woman at the Keyhole: Feminism and Women's Cinema.* Bloomington: Indiana University Press, 1990.

McDougall, William. *An Outline of Psychology*. London: Methuan and Company, 1923.

Menand, Louis. *Discovering Modernism: T. S. Eliot and His Context*. Oxford: Oxford University Press, 1987.

The Metaphysical Club: A Story of Ideas in America. New York: Farrar, Straus and Giroux, 2001.

Merleau-Ponty, Maurice. *Phenomenology of Perception*. Trans. Colin Smith. New York: Routledge, 1999.

The Primacy of Perception. Ed. James M. Edie. Evanston: Northwestern University Press, 1964.

Metz, Christian. *The Imaginary Signifier: Psychoanalysis and Cinema*. Trans. Celia Britton. Bloomington: Indiana University Press, 1975.

Micale, Mark S. *Approaching Hysteria: Disease and Its Interpretations*. Princeton: Princeton University Press, 1995.

Michelson, Annette, ed. *Kino-Eye: The Writings of Dziga Vertov*. Trans. Kevin O'Brien. Berkeley: University of California Press, 1984.

Miller, Cristanne. *Marianne Moore: Questions of Authority*. Cambridge, MA: Harvard University Press, 1995.

Miller, James E., Jr. *T. S. Eliot's Personal Waste Land: Exorcism of the Demons*. University Park: The Pennsylvania State University Press, 1977.

Modleski, Tania. *The Women Who Knew Too Much: Hitchcock and Feminist Theory*. New York: Routledge, 1988.

Moore, Marianne. *Becoming Marianne Moore: The Early Poems, 1907–1924*. Ed. Robin G. Schulze. Berkeley: University of California Press, 2002.

Complete Poems. New York: Macmillian, 1994.

The Complete Prose of Marianne Moore. New York: Penguin, 1967.

The Poems of Marianne Moore. Ed. Grace Schulman. New York: Viking, 2003.

Predilections. New York: Viking Press, 1955.

Selected Letters. Ed. Bonnie Costello. New York: Penguin, 1998.

Mulvey, Laura. "Visual Pleasure and Narrative Cinema" (1975). *The Sexual Subject: A Screen Reader in Sexuality*. London: Routledge, 1992.

Münsterberg, Hugo. *Photoplay*. New York: D. Appleton and Company, 1916.

Murphy, Richard. *Theorizing the Avant-Garde: Modernism, Expressionism, and the Problem of Postmodernity*. Cambridge: Cambridge University Press, 1998.

Nadeau, Maurice. *The History of Surrealism*. Trans. Richard Howard. Cambridge: The Belknap Press of Harvard University Press, 1989.

Nicholls, Peter. *Modernism: A Literary Guide*. Berkeley: University of California Press, 1995.

North, Michael. *Reading 1922: A Return to the Scene of the Modern*. New York and Oxford: Oxford Press, 1999.

Omerod, J. A. "Address to Neurological Section of The Royal Society of Medicine." *Brain* vol. 33, 1910/11.

Parkinson, David. *History of Film*. London: Thames and Hudson, 1995.

Pavlov, Ivan Petrovich. "A Study of Temperaments." *Lectures on Conditioned Reflexes Vol. 1*. Trans. W. Horsley Gantt. New York: International Publishers, 1928.

"Experimental Psychology and Psychopathology in Animals," *Herald of the Military Medical Academy*, (1903), vol. 7, no. 2.

Psychopathology and Psychiatry: Selected Works, trans. D. Myshne and S. Belsky. New York: Foreign Language Publishing House, 1927.

Penley, Constance. *The Future of an Illusion: Film, Feminism, and Psychoanalysis.* Minneapolis: University of Minnesota, 1989.

Perez, Gilberto. *The Material Ghost: Films and Their Medium.* Baltimore: Johns Hopkins University Press, 1998.

Perloff, Marjorie. *21st-Century Modernism: The New Poetics.* New York: Blackwell Publishers, 2002.

Poetry On and Off the Page. Evanston: Northwestern University Press, 1998.

Petro, Patrice. *Joyless Street: Women and Melodramatic Representation in Weimar Germany.* Princeton: Princeton University Press, 1989.

Aftershocks of the New: Feminism and Film History. New Brunswick: Rutgers University Press, 2002.

Peucker, Brigitte. *Incorporating Images: Film and the Rival Arts.* Princeton: Princeton University Press, 1995.

Plato. *The Collected Dialogues.* Eds. Edith Hamilton and Huntington Cairns. Bollingen Series. Princeton: Princeton University Press, 1961.

Pound, Ezra. *The Letters 1907–41.* Ed. D. D. Paige. London: Faber and Faber, 1951.

Selected Poems of Ezra Pound. New York: New Directions, 1957.

Selected Prose: 1909–1965. New York: New Directions, 1973.

Rhode, Eric. *A History of Cinema: From its Origins to 1970.* London: Hill and Wang, 1976.

Rich, Adrienne. "Compulsory Heterosexuality and Lesbian Existence." *Blood, Bread and Poetry.* New York: Norton, 1986.

Rich, B. Ruby. "From Repressive Tolerance to Erotic Liberations: *Maedchen In Uniform.*" *Re-Vision: Essays in Feminist Film Criticism.* Eds. Mary Ann Doane, Patricia Mellencamp, and Linda Williams. Maryland: University Publications of America, 1984.

Riddell, Joseph N. *The Inverted Bell: Modernism and the Counterpoetics of Willliam Carlos Williams.* Baton Rouge: Louisiana State University Press, 1974.

Rivièrè, Joan. "Womanliness as a Masquerade." *Formations of Fantasy.* Eds. Victor Burgin, James Donald, and Cora Kaplan. London: Methuen, 1986.

Robert, Richardson. *Literature and Film.* Bloomington: Indiana University Press, 1969.

Rogin, Michael. *Blackface, White Noise: Jewish Immigrants in the Hollywood Melting Pot.* Berkeley: University of California Press, 1996.

Rosen, Philip ed. *Narrative, Apparatus, Ideology: A Film Theory Reader.* New York: Columbia University Press, 1986.

Ruddick, Lisa. *Reading Gertrude Stein: Body, Text, Gnosis.* Ithaca, N.Y.: Cornell University Press, 1990.

Sassoon, Siegfried. *Collected Poems 1908–1956* (London: Faber and Faber, 1947).

Sayre, Henry M. *The Visual Text of William Carlos Williams*. Urbana: University of Illinois Press, 1983.

Schulze, Robin G. *Becoming Marianne Moore: The Early Poems, 1907–1924*. Berkeley: University of California Press, 2002.

Scott, Bonnie Kime, ed. *The Gender of Modernism*. Bloomington: Indiana University Press, 1990.

Sedgwick, Eve Kosofsky. *Epistemology of the Closet*. Berkeley: University of California Press, 1990.

Seymour-Jones, Carole. *Painted Shadow: The Life of Vivienne Eliot, first wife of T. S. Eliot, and the long-suppressed truth about her influence on his genius*. New York: Doubleday, 2001.

Sheppard, Richard. *Modernism – Dada – Postmodernism*. Evanston: Northwestern University Press, 2000.

Sigg, Eric. *The American T. S. Eliot: A Study of the Early Writings*. Cambridge: Cambridge University Press, 1989.

Silverman, Kaja. *Male Subjectivity at the Margins*. New York: Routledge, 1992.

The Threshold of the Visible World. New York: Routledge, 1996.

Sitney, P. Adams. *Modernist Montage: The Obscurity of Vision in Cinema and Literature*. New York: Columbia University Press, 1990.

Visionary Film: The American Avant-Garde 1943–1978. Oxford: Oxford University Press, 1974.

Sobchack, Vivian. *The Address of the Eye: A Phenomenology of Film Experience*. Princeton: Princeton University Press, 1992.

Spoto, Donald. *The Dark Side of Genius: The Life of Alfred Hitchcock*. New York: Ballantine Books, 1983.

Stein, Gertrude. *The Autobiography of Alice B. Toklas*. New York: Vintage Books, 1990.

"Cultivated Motor Automatism: A Study of Character in its Relation to Attention." *Harvard Psychological Review*. New York: The Phoenix Book Shop, 1969.

Everybody's Autobiography. New York: Vintage, 1973.

How to Write. New York: Dover, 1975.

"I Came and Here I Am." *How Writing is Written*. Los Angeles: Black Sparrow Press, 1974.

Lectures in America. Boston: Beacon Press, 1985.

Lifting Belly (1915–17). Ed. Rebecca Mark. Tallahassee: The Naiad Press, 1989.

Portraits and Prayers. New York: Random House, 1934.

A Stein Reader. Ed. Ulla E. Dydo. Evanston, Ill.: Northwestern University Press, 1993.

Tender Buttons (1914). Los Angeles: Sun and Moon Press, 1989.

Useful Knowledge (1928). Barrytown: Station Hill Press, 1988.

Wars I Have Seen. London: B. T. Batsford Ltd., 1945.

The Yale Gertrude Stein. Ed. Richard Kostelanetz. New Haven: Yale University Press, 1980.

Stein, Gertrude and Leon M. Solomons. "Motor Automatism." *Harvard Psychological Review*. New York: The Phoenix Book Shop, 1969.

Steiner, Wendy. *The Colors of Rhetoric: Problems in the Relation Between Literature and Painting*. Chicago: University of Chicago Press, 1982.

Stewart, Garrett. *Between Film and Screen: Modernism's Photo Synthesis*. Chicago: University of Chicago Press, 1999.

Stimpson, Catherine. "The Somagrams of Gertrude Stein." *The Female Body in Western Culture*. Ed. Susan Rubin Suleiman. Cambridge: Harvard University Press, 1986.

Studlar, Gayle. *In the Realm of Pleasure: Von Sternberg, Dietrich, and the Masochistic Aesthetic*. New York: Columbia University Press, 1988.

Talbot, F. A. *Moving Pictures* (1912). London: Arno Press, 1970.

Tomlinson, Charles, ed. *Marianne Moore: A Collection of Critical Essays*. New Jersey: Prentice Hall, 1969.

Torrey, E. Fuller. *The Roots of Treason*. Orlando: Harcourt Brace Jovanovich, 1984.

Usai, Paolo Cherchi. *Silent Cinema: An Introduction*. London: BIF Publications, 2000.

Vendler, Helen. Introduction to *The Waste Land and Other Poems* by T. S. Eliot. New York: Signet Classics, 1998.

Virilio, Paul. *War and Cinema: The Logistics of Perception*. Trans. Patrick Camiller. London: Verso, 1989.

Wagner-Martin, Linda. *Favored Strangers: Gertrude Stein and Her Family*. New Brunswick, NJ: Rutgers University Press, 1995.

Waldman, Diane. *Joseph Cornell: Master of Dreams*. New York: Abrams Inc., 2002.

Walton, Jean. "Nightmare of Uncoordinated White-Folk: Race, Psychoanalysis and *Borderline*." *Discourse* 19 no. 1 (Winter 1997): 88–109.

Weaver, Mike. *William Carlos Williams: The American Background*. Cambridge: Cambridge University Press, 1971.

Wedekind, Frank. *Foreward to The Lulu Plays & Other Sex Tragedies* by Frank Wedekind. Trans. Stephen Spender. London: Riverrun Press, 1972.

Weininger, Otto. *Sex & Character*. London: William Heinemann, 1906.

Williams, Linda. *Figures of Desire: A Theory and Analysis of Surrealist Film*. Urbana: University of Illinois Press, 1981.

Williams, William Carlos. *The Autobiography*. New York: Random House, 1948.

  The Collected Poems of William Carlos Williams Volume 1: 1909–1939. Eds. A. Walton Litz and Christopher MacGowen. New York: New Directions, 1986.

  Imaginations. New York: New Directions, 1970.

  Selected Essays. New York: New Directions, 1954

Wilson, S. A. K. "Some Modern French Conceptions of Hysteria." *Brain* Vol. 33, 1910/11.

Woolf, Virginia. *The Captain's Death-Bed and Other Essays*. New York: Harcourt, 1988.

Young, Iris Marion. *Throwing Like a Girl and Other Essays*. Bloomington: Indiana University Press, 1990.

Index